THE
BEST
CONGRESS
MONEY
CAN
BUY

Also by Philip M. Stern:

The Great Treasury Raid

The Shame of a Nation (with photographs by George de Vincent)

The Oppenheimer Case: Security on Trial

The Rape of the Taxpayer

Lawyers on Trial

Oh Say Can You See: A Bifocal Tour of Washington (with Helen B. Stern)

THE
BEST
CONGRESS
MONEY
CAN
BUY

PHILIP M. STERN

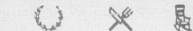

PANTHEON BOOKS

NEW YORK

LIBRARY OF CONGRESS CATALOGING-IN-PUBLICATION DATA
Stern, Philip M.
   The best Congress money can buy.

   Bibliography: p.
   Includes index.
   1. Political action committees—United States.
   2. Lobbying—United States.
   3. United States. Congress.
   I. Title.
JK1991.S73 1988   324′.4′0973   87-43116
ISBN 0-394-56628-9

Book Design by Snaphaus/Diane Stevenson
Manufactured in the United States of America

First Edition

*For Susan
with a heart filled with love and
gratitude for the happiness she
has brought into my life.*

*And for Judge J. Skelly Wright,
in appreciation of a lifetime of
having a clear-sighted vision of
justice, eloquently expressed,
and always courageously
pursued, especially when that
was the most difficult.*

CONTENTS

PREFACE   xi

1   THE CAMPAIGN-MONEY CRISIS   3

THE PACs

2   A PAC PRIMER   19

INFLUENCE-PEDDLING

3   THE BUYERS OF INFLUENCE   31

Case Studies: 1. Used-Car Dealers, 2. Dairy Farmers,
3. The Billboard Industry

4   THE SELLERS OF INFLUENCE   57

Case Studies: 1. Senator Robert J. Dole, 2. Representative
James J. Howard

THE VIEW FROM THE INSIDE

5   PRESENT AND FORMER MEMBERS OF CONGRESS SPEAK   99

Speakers: 1. Michael Barnes, 2. Toby Moffett, 3. Charles
McC. Mathias, 4. Barry Goldwater, 5. Thomas Eagleton,
6. Kent Conrad, 7. Claudine Schneider, 8. Mike Synar,
9. John C. Stennis, 10. Jim Leach, 11. Bob Edgar,
12. Lawton Chiles, 13. Tom Railsback

6   PAC MANAGERS SPEAK   123

For: 1. The Machinists' Union, 2. The Ford Motor Company,
3. The Council for a Livable World, 4. Mid-American
Dairymen

THE VIEW FROM THE OUTSIDE ─────────

7 THE TRUE COSTS OF THE PAC SYSTEM   137

The Bills: 1. The Sugar Subsidy, 2. The Dairy Subsidy, 3. Hospital-Cost Containment, 4. Domestic Content for Cars

8 CAMPAIGN CONTRIBUTION OR BRIBE? A HAIRLINE'S DIFFERENCE   146

9 HONORARIA: A LEGAL WAY OF LINING POLITICIANS' POCKETS   155

10 THE MANY WAYS OF SKIRTING THE "REFORM" LAWS   161

THE SOLUTION ─────────────

11 HOW WE CAN GET OUT OF THE MESS WE'RE IN   179

CONCLUSION   194

APPENDIX A: The Best and the Worst: The Senate   203

APPENDIX B: The Best and the Worst: The House   217

APPENDIX C: The 100 Largest PACs   277

ACKNOWLEDGMENTS   281

NOTES AND SOURCES   284

INDEX   313

PREFACE

This book—or, at any rate, my passion about the importance of money in politics—dates back to the mid-fifties. A friend called and asked me to attend a meeting to raise money for a liberal Democratic member of the Senate Commerce Committee (I don't remember his name, but it isn't important). At the time, I was research director of the Democratic National Committee, having just served as legislative assistant for Senator Paul Douglas of Illinois—and a more incorruptible man never trod the floor of the United States Senate.

At the last minute, I couldn't attend the fundraising meeting, and a few days later, I called my friend to apologize. "Oh, that's all right," he said. "X agreed to raise money from the airlines and Y said he would take care of the truckers and Z promised to cover the highway people. So I think we're all set."

I suppose I was naïve, but I couldn't believe what I was hearing. Here was a liberal senator I had considered highly principled and not, by philosophy, "pro-business," *soliciting money from the very interest groups he was supposed to be regulating!* If that was the way this liberal Democratic senator got his money, I wondered how much money more business-minded and less punctilious senators must be getting from those same interest groups. A hell of a way to run a country, I thought.

And that's how this book began.

In the ensuing years, that incident stuck in my mind, and the subject of campaign-finance reform continued to preoccupy me. In 1962, I wrote a cover article in *Harper's* magazine proposing a plan for government financing of federal election campaigns, much like the one enacted for presidential campaigns twelve years later.

In 1973, as the Watergate revelations began to unfold and congressional interest in the campaign-finance reform bubbled up, I founded the Center for Public Financing of Campaigns, a lobbying and coalition-building organization that played a significant part in the enactment of the presidential public-financing provisions of the 1974 campaign-reform law. Eleven years later, I started and directed Citizens Against PACs, a bipartisan citizens' group which published prominent advertisements in hometown newspapers setting forth the PAC record of the local representatives.

Early in 1987, I set aside my work with Citizens Against PACs to write this book. I was prompted to do so in part by this striking fact: fewer than one-third of the American people even understand what a political action committee is, much less appreciate the danger the PACs pose for representative democracy.

Some—especially members of Congress—may feel that this book's title, taken from Will Rogers, unfairly portrays the U.S. Congress. Most members, they will say, are unwilling to let campaign contributions influence their conduct, and only a few are venal. (Venal or not, it is notable that when the Center for Responsive Politics, a Washington research group, interviewed members of Congress in 1987, one-fifth acknowledged that political contributions affected their votes on legislation.) One political scientist implored me not to use this title, arguing that it would only add to the already-growing public cynicism about politicians and about Congress.

But it is the facts in this book, each one meticulously documented (see the lengthy source notes at the end) that give rise to inferences of impropriety. All too often, the public record shows that Senator X or Representative Y received a campaign contribution or honorarium from Interest Group A and then did (or had already done) as Group A desired. Or Lawmaker X or Y, a member of, say, the banking committee or a defense committee, received favors from banking interests or defense contractors. If senators and representatives resent the implications of impropriety that those facts invite, let those lawmakers change the current campaign-finance laws so as to prohibit such conflicts of interest.

This book deals only with the problems of financing congressional campaigns; the matter of paying for presidential campaigns is mentioned only tangentially, for several reasons. For one thing, Congress has already enacted public funding of presidential campaigns, although it has partially undone the benefits of that by opening up the "soft money" loophole, discussed in Chapter 10. For that reason, contributions by political action committees play a minuscule part in presidential campaigns. For example, PAC money comprised less than 1 percent of the total spent in the 1984 presidential election.

Moreover, even though presidential *primary* candidates must still raise millions of dollars of private money, the very size of their campaign budgets limits the influence that any individual gift can buy. In presidential campaigns, $1,000 contributions are so commonplace that the candidate is likely to be unaware of them. By contrast, a $1,000 contribution in a House campaign is vastly more conspicuous and therefore stands a much better chance of gaining the candidate's attention and appreciation.

So it is in the congressional arena—the subject of this book— that the need for reform is most urgent.

Many opponents of campaign-finance reform argue that there is no need for, say, a wholesale outlawing of PACs as long as the PACs have to disclose how much they are giving to whom. The best hope, say these observers, lies in bringing campaign finance out into the sunshine.

Well, obviously those who argue thus have never tried to write a book about campaign finance—for often, in the course of researching this book, I have been struck by how difficult it is to get at the truth of who gave what to whom in hopes of what.

For example, here's a simple question: How much in campaign contributions have PACs of the leading Wall Street brokerage firms given the senators on the banking committee (which regulates Wall Street) over the six years of their present terms? That *ought* to be fairly simple to discover, since the Federal Election Commission maintains all the data on PAC contributions on computers. But for a time, due to "budgetary restraints," the PAC information was available from computer only back through 1983. To get information prior to that, you had to go in person to the FEC and copy the information from microfilm records—a monumental chore at best.

Even with complete PAC data, you have rooted out only a part of the picture. For example, as described in Chapter 8, Wall Street firms have been singularly successful in mobilizing their executives to make *individual* contributions to the likes of New York Republican Senator Alfonse D'Amato, especially when he chaired the banking subcommittee most concerned with securities regulation. By law, candidates are required to report the employer or the occupation of their large donors, but all too often, that information is missing from their reports. Getting the full truth, then, requires combing through each of the thousands of names on senators' contribution lists over the six years of their term.

But you still lack an important piece of the puzzle: the honoraria that interest groups pay lawmakers as speaking fees (or merely for dropping in briefly on a Washington breakfast). Because senators and congressmen may legally pocket these speaking fees, more and more interest groups are finding the honorarium a more effective (and often a cheaper) way of getting a key lawmaker's attention. The trouble is, information about who-paid-how-much-in-honoraria-to-whom is only tardily available, and is nowhere computerized. To ascertain the data about honoraria received by U.S. senators, you have to journey to Capitol Hill and copy out the information by hand, senator by senator, year by year. (The House publishes the raw data annually in bound volumes.) Try getting *that* information on the leading Wall Street firms for all the senators on the banking committee for the past six years!

In these pages, I sometimes (as in Chapter 3) bemoan congressional victories by small interest groups such as the dairy farmers or the auto dealers over far more numerous groups such as auto buyers and dairy consumers. Lest the reader conclude that I am an absolute majoritarian, I am not. I recognize—and deplore—tyrannies of the majority (as when an inflamed majority in California brought about the internment of the Japanese-Americans at the outset of World War II). I also favor government assistance to the poor and the handicapped, even though those groups constitute minorities whose causes would be defeated on any congressional vote that followed strict one-person–one-vote lines. What I object to is the use of *money*—especially money aggregated by political action committees in a manner unworkable for inchoate groups like consumers and the poor—to magnify the political influence of small groups, thereby distorting representative democracy.

In recent years, I have become increasingly troubled about the way modern candidates allow themselves to be merchandised like laundry soap, taking their cues from marketing experts (that is, sophisticated pollsters), media consultants, and political mercenaries who, far from being homegrown, often direct the candidate's campaign strategy from behind a desk in Washington, Boston, or New York. Many who share my concern about the merchandising of candidates point the finger at the mounting piles of money available to run campaigns. Why, then, is this not a campaign-finance problem? Why, in view of my own concerns, is it not explicitly discussed in this book?

Tempted though I have often been to vent my disquiet about hi-tech politics in these pages, I have concluded that the problem of hi-tech and the problem of money are two separate topics, in the sense that even if candidates got all of their money from heaven, rather than from special-interest groups, they would still spend it on pollsters and media consultants and professional campaign managers. And they would still sell themselves primarily via television, despite all that medium's propensity for simplification and distortion.

As others have pointed out, the problem does not lie in the *amount* of money spent on politics (about as much as Americans spend on soft drinks in eight days). It lies with the *source* of the money, and the extent to which campaign money comes from people and groups with self-interested axes to grind.

In the course of conducting the interviews of current and former members of Congress that make up Chapter 5, I was struck by the contrast between two interviews that, by chance, fell on the same day.

During the morning, I talked with former Senator Thomas Eagleton of Missouri, who said that immediately after his 1980 campaign, during which he was obliged to "tin-cup it"—"begging for money literally from Maine to Hawaii"—he resolved not to subject himself to that demeaning experience again. Therefore, he observed, his final six years in the Senate were years of freedom, of not having to weigh each decision against the background of past obligations or future gain or loss. "When Mr. X came in to see me," he said, "I didn't have to put money on the scale, and say, 'How does this factor out in fundraising?' "

Just a few hours later, I spoke with Democratic Senator Kent Conrad of North Dakota. Conrad had been elected only a few months earlier. He would not face the voters again for another six years. Yet when I asked him whether he had started raising money for that 1992 campaign, he replied, "Absolutely."

What a contrast, I thought, between Senator Eagleton's six

years of freedom from the pursuit of the campaign dollar to Senator Conrad's prospective enslavement to the money chase. I do not intend any disparagement of Senator Conrad's character. On the contrary, he appears to have demonstrated unusual independence in the conduct of the public offices he held before coming to the Senate. Yet by his own acknowledgment that he has already begun his quest of reelection funds, it is clear that *the money consideration will seldom be far from his thoughts.*

That should not be. Senator Conrad deserves better. So does the country. That is why I believe so passionately in providing House and Senate candidates with an alternative of "disinterested" money, via expanding the existing public financing of presidential elections to cover congressional campaigns, as proposed in Chapter 11.

The central theme of this book is that money determines far too much in American politics today.

Far too often, money determines who shall run for office.

All too often, money determines what messages will be most forcefully conveyed.

Much too often, money is a preoccupation (or an obsession) in the minds of lawmakers.

Yet that prime determinant, money, is a poor tool of democracy, for money is indifferent to truth and to justice, since it is, essentially, unjustly distributed.

U.S. Appellate Court Judge J. Skelly Wright, who has written eloquently on the subject of campaign-finance reform, as on others, quotes Anatole France, who said in the late nineteenth century, "The law, in its majestic equality, permits the rich as well as the poor to sleep under bridges, to beg in the streets, and to steal bread." Judge Wright continues, "A latter-day Anatole France might well write, after observing American election campaigns, 'The law, in its majestic equality, allows the poor as well as the rich to form political action committees, to purchase the most sophisticated polling, media, and direct mail techniques, and to drown out each other's voices by overwhelming expenditures in political campaigns.'

"Financial inequities," concludes Judge Wright, "pose a pervasive and growing threat to the principle of 'one person, one vote' and undermine the political proposition to which this nation is dedicated—that all men are created equal."

THE
BEST
CONGRESS
MONEY
CAN
BUY

THE CAMPAIGN-MONEY CRISIS

Consider these two statements:

> We cannot turn our democracy over to an aristocracy of
> money. Yet year by year we are insidiously chopping away
> at the ability of any citizen to enter the political arena re-
> gardless of his or her economic status or ability to raise
> money.

> Unlimited campaign spending eats at the heart of the
> democratic process.
> It feeds the growth of special-interest groups created
> solely to channel money into political campaigns.
> It creates the impression that every candidate is bought
> and owned by the biggest givers.
> And it causes the elected officials to devote more time to
> raising money than to their public duties.

Neither of the speakers is the kind of person you would expect to
hear bemoaning an "aristocracy of money" or excoriating "special-
interest" groups.

The first, Senator Robert C. Byrd of West Virginia, is a centrist
Democrat; the second, former Senator Barry Goldwater of Arizona,
is the one-time standard-bearer of conservative Republicans and
one of the few who, as recently as 1985, favored a repeal of the
widely accepted law providing public funding of presidential elections.

The two represent opposing political parties and sharply differing political philosophies. But they have two things in common: Both have witnessed the impact of money on Congress and the political process from the inside. And both now see an urgent need for campaign finance reform.

Their accord on this point is one measure of the crisis in the way America pays for its congressional election campaigns.

The "special-interest groups created solely to channel money into political campaigns," to which Senator Goldwater refers, are the political action committees—the PACs.

PACs are simple in operation and clear in objective.

A fuller explanation of what PACs are and how they work is contained in Chapter 2. In brief, a political action committee is a device through which like-minded people (members of labor unions, professional or trade groups, or employees of a corporation) can elect to make political contributions, rather than giving their money directly to candidates of their choice. The PAC then pools their money and hands it out to federal candidates in large amounts ($1,000, $2,000, up to a ceiling of $5,000 per election) to tens, or even hundreds, of House and Senate candidates—a feat far beyond the reach of any individual contributor save, say, a Rockefeller.

But federal election laws now place an annual $25,000 ceiling on the gifts individual Rockefellers may make to all federal candidates in any election. By contrast, *there is no legal limit on the total amount a PAC can give.* In the 1986 congressional elections, sixteen PACs each handed out more than $1 million to candidates for the U.S. House and Senate, and three PACs—the National Association of Realtors, the American Medical Association, and the National Education Association—each dispensed over $2 million.

Most PACs have a simple objective: to gain influence with—or, at the least, favored access to—congressmen and senators.

That influence-buying motive is often surprisingly (some would say shockingly) transparent. For example, the PACs have shoveled money at New York Democratic Representative Charles Rangel even though in recent elections he has won, on the average, 96 percent of the vote in his Harlem district. Apparently he doesn't need to collect or spend a dime to be reelected. Yet his PAC receipts tripled in four years (1980–84). But even that trebling was not enough for the PACs. In the ensuing two years, their contributions to this unbeatable congressman increased by half again, so that in 1986, Congressman Rangel received a third of a million dollars from

PACs. They appeared indifferent that their gifts helped the congressman emerge from his 1986 campaign with a cash surplus of over a quarter of a million dollars, *which he can legally take with him when he leaves Congress.*★

The average citizen, with limited funds to give politicians and expecting nothing special in return, would not dream of contributing so much as a dollar to a sure-shot winner like Charles Rangel. Why, then, did the PACs continue to boost their contributions to him?

Simple. Number 1: Congressman Rangel is the fourth-ranking Democrat on the House Ways and Means Committee, which writes all the tax laws. Number 2: In 1985, the Reagan Administration had proposed the most sweeping tax reform in recent history. For industry after industry, multi-billion-dollar tax loopholes seemed in jeopardy. Thus, favored access to Congressman Rangel's ear might come to be worth many times the third of a million dollars the PACs gave him for his 1986 "campaign."

The political action committees expose the nakedness of their influence-buying in another way: the manner in which they lopsidedly favor incumbent congressmen and senators and spurn challengers. If you were to give a sum of money to each of a hundred randomly chosen citizens and ask that they use it to contribute to candidates in fifty congressional races, you might expect them to divide their gifts fairly evenly between challengers and incumbents —no more than, say, 60–40 either way—if only because the country is fairly evenly divided as to political party preference. You would expect such an even split, that is, with one crucial proviso: that those hundred citizens had no selfish axes to grind, that they expected nothing for themselves in return for their contributions.

But the PACs *do* have axes to grind. They *do* expect something in return for the support they give candidates—namely, influence, or at least preferred access to ears of the powerful. Hence, in 1986, in House races where the sitting congressmen sought reelection, the PACs did not split their contributions 50–50 or 60–40. *They gave more than 88 percent of their contributions to incumbents, less than 12 to challengers.* Can virtually all incumbents be that worthy, and the challengers so universally unmeritorious? Did the PACs give more—20 percent, on average—to House committee chairmen

---

★ This and other significant facts are documented in the Notes and Sources, at the end of the book.

than to the average representative because those chairmen are one-fifth more intelligent and worthy than the others?

There is another malign consequence of PAC favoritism for incumbents. Suppose Abraham Lincoln were alive today and aspired to a seat in the U.S. House, but had the misfortune to reside in a congressional district represented by a powerful committee chairman. Chances are that, whatever his personal merits or the qualities of his ideas, most PACs would greet candidate Lincoln with, at best, polite snickers and send him away empty-handed. Since Lincoln's committee-chairman opponent could raise almost infinite funds from special-interest groups, Lincoln's candidacy would be snuffed out—sheerly for want of *money*. What a price to pay! What a way to ration candidacies!

The giving tactics of PACs as a whole leave little doubt that their prime motive is to buy influence or access. As shown in Chapter 3, they give to candidates who have no opponent and have no need for the money. They give to candidates who, like Congressman Rangel, are shoo-ins for reelection. They contribute to both candidates in some contests (as illogical as giving to both Reagan *and* Mondale in 1984). They contribute to candidates whose philosophies they don't share. And *after* the election, when they find they have backed a loser, some PACs unabashedly switch and give to the new winner, the candidate they had previously tried to defeat. Doubtless, many of those who gave to the PAC would neither engage in or condone such opportunistic tactics. Too late: they have surrendered control over their money to less fastidious PAC managers.

PAC defenders publicly minimize how much political action committees influence Congress. But the PACs are, in Wall Street parlance, very much a "growth industry." Since 1974, their campaign contributions to congressional candidates have grown, on average, at the exceptional average rate of 50 percent every *election* (not adjusted for inflation). Evidently, the PACs have no doubt they're getting their money's worth.

In the congressional influence-peddling game there are, of course, two sides, and on occasion the sellers are as brazen as the buyers. For example, in January 1987, when the Democrats regained control of the Senate, Texas Senator Lloyd Bentsen ascended to the chairmanship of the Senate Finance Committee, which, like House Ways and Means, handles tax legislation. Bentsen lost little time in inviting lobbyists to a series of intimate breakfast meetings with him. The price of a seat at the Bentsen breakfast table: a $10,000 campaign contribution. Even at that price, lobbyists eagerly subscribed to the breakfast series. Then the story of Bentsen's naked influence-peddling broke in the *Washington Post*. The report provoked editorial indignation on the part of those unaware that Bentsen's predecessor as chairman of Senate Finance, Oregon Republican Bob Packwood, had held similar breakfast meetings at $5,000 a ticket. The editorial outcry prompted Bentsen to cancel his breakfast series, refund the money already given him, and admit he had made a "doozy" of a mistake.

Most PACs make no bones that their aim is to further *their own group's* special interests. The director of the American Trucking Association's PAC put it bluntly: "We'll buy a ticket to anyone's fundraising event, *as long as he didn't vote the wrong way on trucking issues*" (emphasis added).

That "me-first" attitude is also reflected in the way interest groups balkanize Congress, carefully cultivating their special provinces. The nation's top defense contractors, whose PAC contributions tripled between 1980 and 1986, focused their contributions on members of the defense-related committees of Congress (the Armed Services and Defense Appropriations panels). Although those congressmen and senators comprised only 18 percent of the entire Congress, they received 47 percent of the top ten defense companies' 1906 PAC gifts as well as three-fourths of the 1985 honoraria, or speaking fees, those firms paid to members of Congress.

Today, it seems as if every organized group has a PAC: from the Concerned Romanians for a Strong America to the Oral and Maxillofacial Surgeons. The dairy farmers and realtors have large PACs; so do most major labor unions, as do defense contractors, the beer wholesalers (who at one time nicknamed theirs SIXPAC), peace groups, and of late, a growing number of pro-Israel organizations.

Neither factions nor special-interest money is new to American politics. In *Federalist Paper No. 10*, James Madison warned of the dangers of factionalism. From William McKinley's 1896 election, financed largely by special assessments on corporations, to Richard Nixon's 1972 campaign, to which corporations made illegal contributions, business interests have sought to use their financial might to sway elections. Beginning in the 1930s, organized labor began efforts to offset the influence of business.

But suddenly, in the last two decades, three new developments have converged on the American political scene:

First, *new legal limits on rich givers* ($1,000 per candidate, $25,000 per year to all federal candidates combined), which means that office-seekers can no longer rely on "fat cats" to finance their campaigns, but must look elsewhere to raise their money.

Second, *the advent of hi-tech political campaigns*, with their expensive polls, high-paid consultants, costly direct-mail solicitations—and, above all, television, the indispensable political communicator and a maw that devours all the dollars politicians will feed it.

Campaign costs have shot up. For example, in 1978, the major-party candidates for the U.S. Senate in South Dakota spent a total of $602,000. Just eight years later, the figure was up more than elevenfold to $6,777,000. Between 1974 and 1986, the cost of an average House campaign rose nearly fivefold, the average Senate campaign over sixfold (see Chapter 2).

As a result, politicians are increasingly obsessed with money. Their preoccupation was compounded in 1976, when the Supreme Court banned compulsory ceilings on campaign spending. Thus, even "safe" candidates, ever fearful of being outspent, are never free of the money-raising fixation.

With politicians desperate for more and more money, enter the third new force: *the political action committees*. PACs have the perfect answer for satisfying candidates' hunger: the capacity to *aggregate* money and to offer that money, often unsolicited, in amounts, and to numbers of candidates, in a manner beyond the reach of individual citizens.

This power to pool political money makes the PACs peculiarly enticing to politicians in frantic search of shortcuts. The PACs, proffering gifts of $5,000 (and even $10,000, to candidates who have both a primary and a general-election contest), offer tempting paths of least resistance.

The PACs' allure is the prime cause of a disturbing trend: congressmen and senators are becoming more and more indebted to outside special-interest PACs. Thus, those lawmakers obligate themselves, morally at least, to accord favored treatment to those PACs' lobbyists, even though those lobbyists are not permitted to vote in their elections. In 1986, for 185 representatives—nearly half the U.S. House—more than 50 percent of their campaign funds came from outside political action committees rather than from their own constituents. Many congressmen got 60 or 80 percent— and in two cases, more than 90 percent—of their money from out- side PACs.

The U.S. Constitution calls them "representatives." But when congressmen are obligated to outsiders for 60 percent or 80 percent of their campaign funds, whom do they *really* represent? When, over an eight-year period, a congressman like Banking Committee Chairman Fernand St Germain, the Rhode Island Democrat, takes nearly a third of a million dollars from banks and other financial institutions, is he the representative of his Rhode Island congres- sional district? Or is he the representative of the banking industry?

The capacity to aggregate money, the crucial *new* element the PACs have introduced, endows interest groups with two new and important powers:

First, it permits them to magnify their group's political influence without relationship to the numbers of their members or the merits of their arguments.

Second, it allows the group to impose huge costs on the rest of the population. For example, most consumers and taxpayers are probably not aware of it, but every time they buy milk or butter at the supermarket, they are the victims of just such a cost that results from a single measure approved by Congress. In September 1985, the U.S. House of Representatives voted on an issue—the dairy subsidy—that squarely pitted the interests of tens of millions of dairy *consumers* against those of, at most, 200,000 *farmers*. On a strict one-person–one-vote reckoning—that is, if each person counted equally in each representative's political calculation—the tens of millions of consumer-taxpayers should have decisively de- feated those 200,000 farmers in that House vote. But that was not the result. Instead, the farmers prevailed, by a margin of 78 votes.

Something, apparently, had thwarted one-person–one-vote de- mocracy. The raw evidence suggests that at least a *part* of that something was money—$12 million collected by three huge dairy cooperatives and distributed, over eight years, to hundreds of rep- resentatives—not just rural congressmen, but big-city representa- tives, as well. Of those who received $30,000 or more, all voted with the dairy lobby in 1985; of those who received $2,500 to $10,000, 60 percent did; of those receiving nothing, only 23 percent did (see table on page 47).

Consider the line-up of forces as the House of Representatives prepared to vote that September afternoon. On one side stood the dairy farmers, comparatively few in number, but each with a significant stake in the outcome of that vote, well organized through their cooperatives, and with a highly effective means of collecting, pooling, and distributing political money (described in detail in Chapter 3).

On the other side were tens of millions of consumers and taxpayers, large in number but each with a comparatively tiny stake in the dairy subsidy and with no means of communicating with one another or for collecting and pooling money to give to politicians.

Senator Robert Dole summed up the unevenness of such congressional battles: "You might get a different result if there were a 'Poor PAC' " on Capitol Hill.

But there *is* no Poor PAC. There is no Consumer PAC.

Nor is there a PAC representing the interests of the Average Taxpayer. Most large corporations and other special-interest organizations have a Washington lobbyist or a PAC or both. But other more inchoate groups, such as dairy consumers, the poor, or average taxpayers, have no PAC to plead for, say, tax fairness on their behalf.

Consider, for example, this anomaly: the U.S. tax law obliges tens of millions of average taxpayers to pay 10 to 30 percent of their incomes to the Internal Revenue Service every April. By contrast, 130 large corporations contrived, in one or more of the years 1982 through 1985, through adroit use of tax loopholes enacted by Congress, to escape without paying a penny of tax on their billions of dollars of profits.

Illinois Democratic Senator Paul Simon summed up this irony when he declared, "The astonishing result is that the janitor at General Electric pays more taxes than GE"—one of the zero-tax companies.

But the plight of the GE janitor, who has no PAC, is lost sight of in the Washington influence-peddling game, which is increasingly winked at and laughed about by influence-buyers and -sellers alike.

The GE janitor did not loom large, for example, in the minds of the several hundred people—mainly lobbyists—who each paid $500 in June 1985 to pay tribute to Illinois's Dan Rostenkowski, the Democratic chairman of the committee that handles all tax legislation, House Ways and Means.

The main speaker was *the* Speaker, Tip O'Neill. He beamed over the audience. "Danny," he said, "this is really marvelous. All this for just a little piece of legislation—which might or might not get to the [House] floor."

The crowd roared with laughter.

Why were they laughing? They knew that this fundraising party was not about "just a little piece of legislation." It was about the most sweeping tax-loophole-closing measure in memory—the Reagan tax reform program, unveiled only months earlier. Tens of billions of dollars were at stake.

The lobbyists in the audience also knew that Dan Rostenkowski needs campaign money about as much as the Sultan of Brunei needs scholarship money for his children's schooling. Rostenkowski is a political fixture in his north Chicago congressional district, typically winning by a four-to-one margin.

So everyone—the Speaker, Rostenkowski, those in the audience—everyone knew what this fundraiser was *really* about. It was about buying insurance, to be sure to stay on the good side of the King. In blunter terms, it was buying access to a crucial ear for that critical few seconds in the legislative process when that access might mean success or failure for a lobbyist.

Those in the audience might have suspected that Congressman Rostenkowski, being both a prodigious fundraiser and a sure-fire winner who need spend very little on his campaigns, had built up an immense campaign surplus which he, like Congressman Rangel, *can transfer to his own bank account when he leaves Congress*—to act, in effect, as his personal pension fund. At the time of that 1985 fundraising party, Rostenkowski had ended his previous campaign with $593,000 left over in his campaign treasury, the fourth highest in the U.S. House. These campaign-surpluses-cum-retirement-funds are a fast-growing phenomenon, as shown in Appendix B.

Moreover, in 1985, Rostenkowski was by far the House's leading recipient of honoraria, or speaking fees, which can be an even more effective device for winning a lawmaker's appreciation than a campaign contribution. Unlike campaign gifts, honoraria can be pocketed by the lawmakers themselves. Thus, such fees are a perfectly legal, and sometimes even a tax-deductible, way of lining a representative's or senator's pocket—although House rules permit members to keep honoraria equivalent to only 30 percent of their congressional salary; amounts over that must be given to charity. (Senators may keep up to 40 percent.) Even so, in 1985, Congressman Rostenkowski permitted corporations and other interest groups to ingratiate themselves to him to the tune of $137,500. The second-ranking congressman, Speaker O'Neill, received only $88,000 in speaking fees. (The subject of honoraria is discussed more fully in Chapter 9.)

Despite the patent conflicts of interest involved—in accepting campaign contributions from groups with a huge stake in his official decisions, in Rostenkowski's amassing of an immense surplus that he can transfer to his own bank account when he leaves Congress, in his formation of a personal PAC to expand his own powers in Congress, in his acceptance of nearly $140,000 in speaking fees, much of it from special-interest groups—all of it is entirely legal.

At the time of the O'Neill-Rostenkowski money-raising event, there was some grumbling among the lobbyists about how, even in this nonelection year, the "going rate" for Ways and Means fund-raisers had doubled or even quadrupled since the Reagan Treasury Department unveiled its sweeping reform proposals.

Yet, with all the grumbling, the *Wall Street Journal*'s Brooks Jackson reported that "lobbyists say privately that with billions of dollars at stake . . . they can't afford" to turn down a member's request for a contribution.

So the money poured in to Ways and Means members: from insurance companies, from military contractors, from drug companies, and even from horse breeders, each group eager to protect its own pet tax loophole.

Compared with two years earlier, when there was no tax-reform proposal before the committee, the Reagan program had spurred striking increases in PAC giving, even to the most safely ensconced members of Ways and Means. For example, PAC money flowing to Florida Congressman Sam Gibbons, a consistent three-to-one winner in his Tampa district, jumped two-hundred-fold—from $750 in the first half of 1983 to over $156,000 in the same period in 1985.

PAC statistics of that kind shrink from the dramatic to mere common sense in light of the immense amounts at stake. Viewed in that manner, PAC contributions can be looked upon as the cheapest investment most interest groups could make.

For example, because of the tax loopholes enacted by Congress over the years, a single company (AT&T) was able to earn nearly $25 billion in profits from 1982 through 1985 without paying one penny of taxes—in fact, the government actually paid AT&T $635 million in tax rebates. The company's tax savings totaled more than $12 billion.

AT&T has had a number of PACs. From 1979 through 1986, those PACs contributed nearly $1.4 million to congressional candidates, mainly incumbents. So an officer or director of AT&T might calculate that on the $12.1 billion tax savings alone, the nearly $1.4 million given by the company PAC netted a return of 867,145 percent.

Using similar reasoning, directors of General Electric (another lightly taxed company) might conclude that their company's PAC was producing a 673,759 percent rate of return, Sears Roebuck's directors might gloat over the firm's 510,581 percent return, and so forth.

Obviously there is not a direct cause-and-effect relationship between these companies' PAC contributions and their tax savings, and those rate-of-return calculations are far from rigorous. The point is that with stakes so immense and PAC contributions relatively so tiny, it requires only a grain of success to make the PAC gifts pay off. To turn the coin over, most PACs can afford to expand their total contributions almost indefinitely before they hit the point of diminishing returns. (Other examples of legislative battles in which minute PAC outlays brought towering returns to their sponsoring groups—often at great expense to American taxpayers and consumers—are set forth in Chapters 3 and 7.)

Combine the soaring costs of campaigns with politicians' constant anxieties about being outspent, and mix in the almost infinite capacity of the interest groups to feed the politicians' appetites for money, and you have the perfect recipe for a Congress beset by money fever and prey to corrupt influence. Increasingly, lawmakers are obsessed with the quest for money, money, money. Virtually all Senate candidates echo former Congressman Mike Barnes's statement (see Chapter 5) that 80 to 90 percent of their time and attention is spent in raising money rather than meeting with voters. It's the rare Washington evening that passes with fewer than three congressional fundraisers; often there are six or more. The U.S. Senate even suspends roll-call voting during the cocktail hour, the favored time for money-raising, so that senators are free to forage for money without fear of missing a vote. PAC managers and lobbyists drift from one lawmaker's party to another, making their appearance, making sure they're seen and given credit, then moving on to the next event, having achieved their objective: to be sure they are recognized as having paid the requisite dues when the favor-seekers are lined up ten deep in the corridors and lawmakers have only so many precious minutes to parcel out.

We would all be shocked, of course, if those lobbyists-in-the-corridors behaved like a patron in a chic, in-demand restaurant seeking favored treatment from the maître d'—shaking the hand of the maître d' while pressing an appropriately large amount of cash into his palm. In Congress, though, the system is more sophisticated: the money has changed hands well in advance, through a campaign contribution at one of those six-an-evening fundraisers.

Increasingly, lobbyists privately tell tales of extortion tactics by members of Congress, as lawmakers have come to *expect* campaign contributions in return for a favor, or even for an appointment to see them. In recent years, one Washington law firm after another has been obliged to form a PAC of its own, to kick into the campaigns of lawmakers important to its clients. As recounted in Chapter 4, sometimes the extortion is brazen. More often, though, it is far more subtle, almost taken for granted by both sides. As Jerald terHorst of the Ford Motor Company's Washington office put it, "If a congressman or senator comes to you as a loyal supporter, and says, 'I'd like to have your support again this year,' what do you say? 'Get lost'?"

More and more, the current campaign-finance system runs counter to our sense of fairness and our concepts of representative democracy. If we imagine the entrances to congressional offices as turnstiles, most of us would like to believe that all citizens have *roughly* equal access through those turnstiles. Being practical, we know that absolute equality is not achievable. For one thing, the turnstile isn't open twenty-four hours a day.

The question, then, is: Who gets to go through the turnstiles? More important: *How does that question get decided?*

The central theme of this book is that under the present system, *that question is decided altogether too much on the basis of money.* That is why the PACs are so unfair. With their capacity to pool money, they almost certainly have the power to proffer a higher price of admission than ordinary, unorganized citizens. It is the rare voter who could contribute $250, much less $1,000, to a politician's campaign. But for most PACs, $250 is routine (and typically given to *many* candidates); $1,000 is frequent; and a $5,000 contribution to *the* strategically positioned senator or representative entirely feasible.

As noted earlier, lawmakers are indebted to outside interest groups for their campaign money to a growing—and alarming—degree. Thus, the PACs and their lobbyists are often able to push their way in through the turnstile ahead of a lawmaker's own constituents, even though they do not live, vote, or pay taxes in the lawmaker's state or district. To the extent this is so, the influence of local voters is diluted—a setback for the gains in voter influence achieved by the civil-rights movement in the sixties.

This book is about how money affects congressional decision-making: money as campaign contributions, money in the form of honoraria, of posh trips, of contributions to lawmakers' own PACs and to their charitable foundations.

This book is about how the aggregation of money through the PACs is distorting representative government in America.

It is about how the PACs and their money have enabled numerically small groups—the auto dealers, the dairy farmers, and the billboard industry, for example—to prevail in Congress and to impose huge costs on the majority of the population.

It is about how outside PACs lavish money on politically secure but powerful congressmen while shunning challengers.

It is about how, as a result, the PACs help entrench sitting congressmen and senators and deprive the public of new personalities and new ideas.

It is about how even the most idealistic congressmen quickly get caught up by money fever.

It is about how PACs help institutionalize the practice of congressional foxes guarding the chicken coops, as lawmakers routinely accept large campaign contributions, honoraria, and other favors from interest groups with an immense stake in their official actions.

It is about how congressmen shape their choice of committee assignments by seeking out the "PAC heavens"—committees that deal with large-stake legislative controversies and hence are magnets for PAC contributions.

It is about how the line between a campaign contribution and a bribe is only, as one senator put it, "a hair's breadth"—and how the PACs make it difficult for even the most upstanding lawmakers to be sure what side of the line they're on.

It is about how honoraria, or speaking fees, are a perfectly legal way for special-interest groups to line politicians' pockets, and to win their favor in the process.

It is about how the present system of financing American political campaigns costs consumers and taxpayers tens of billions of dollars every year.

It is about how loopholes in the election laws still permit interest groups and well-heeled individuals to give unlimited political gifts, often in secret, despite the legal limits and the disclosure requirements of the seventies that most people believe were cures to the worst abuses.

And it is about some ways America can extricate itself from the mess the campaign-finance laws and the PACs have produced.

The crisis in the way we now finance our congressional election campaigns can be summarized in two concise facts:

First: Campaigns have become so expensive that, to wage a winning campaign, the average United States senator must raise nearly $10,000 a week *every week during his or her entire six-year Senate term.*

Second: Under the current system, even the most idealistic senator has no alternative for achieving that task other than to rely on special-interest groups.

The result is this: In the first six months of 1987, thirteen U.S. senators raised over $3 million in campaign funds. More than half of that money came from outside special-interest PACs—far above the normal proportion for senators. Well over half of that came from PACs who were now switching horses and contributing to senators they had previously tried to defeat.

These thirteen are not a random sampling of senators. *All of them had just been elected in November of 1986.*

Their next election is not until 1992.

THE PACs

A PAC PRIMER

2

What, precisely, *is* a political action committee, or PAC? How did PACs come about? How do they work? How were political campaigns paid for before there were PACs?

Basically, PACs are entities to which like-minded people—employees of a corporation, or members of a labor union or a trade association such as the American Medical Association, or dairy farmers who sell their milk through a cooperative—make voluntary political contributions. The PAC then pools the money and parcels it out to federal candidates in amounts vastly larger, and more attention-getting (and to greater numbers of candidates) than would be possible for any individual.

It is this capacity to pool individual contributions that makes the PACs new in American politics.

PACs fall into five major categories. There are those formed by labor unions; by corporations; by trade associations and professions, such as the automobile dealers or the doctors; and by cooperatives, such as the dairy co-ops mentioned above. The fifth group consists of the "ideological" PACs—such as those pursuing peace, environmental, or across-the-board liberal or conservative agendas.*

By and large, PACs may, by law, solicit only their group's members, employees, and shareholders, which the PACs typically do once a year. Occasionally, PACs employ a most efficient collection

---

* A sixth, tiny group consists of the so-called "leadership" PACs, formed by potential presidential candidates (such as Senator Robert Dole of Kansas) or by congressional leaders (such as House Speaker Jim Wright of Texas or Democratic Whip Tony Coelho of California).

mechanism—the checkoff. Under that system, contributions are automatically and regularly subtracted from members' paychecks or, in the case of the dairy cooperatives, from farmers' monthly milk checks. The $3,309,000 amassed by the three large dairy co-ops from their 47,500 members in the 1984 elections attests to the efficacy of this collection device.

A random-sample study conducted by University of Virginia Professor Larry J. Sabato in 1981 and 1982 found that typically one-quarter to one-third of the eligible contributors actually gave to their PAC. The overall average contribution for the two-year election cycle was $100, ranging from an average gift of $160 for corporate PACs and $81 for trade-association PACs down to $14 for labor PACs.

PACs almost always decide which candidate gets how much in a more or less undemocratic manner. The who-gets-how-much question is almost never submitted to a plebiscite of all the contributors, if only for the practical reason that during an election year, time and the rapidly changing circumstances do not permit such contributor participation. Whatever the reasons, those who give their money through PACs essentially turn over control of their money to a very few. Professor Sabato found that in three-quarters of the PACs he surveyed, the decision was made by a small board or committee.

The PACs' lack of consultation with their contributors forms, in a sense, a rebuttal of one of the most frequently heard defenses of the political action committees—namely, that they serve to increase citizen participation in the political process. For one thing, there is a paucity of hard statistical data to support that contention. For another, as University of Minnesota political scientist Frank Sorauf has observed, a citizen's contribution to a PAC is "one of the least active forms of political activity"; it "requires little time or immediate involvement; in a sense, it buys political mercenaries [and] frees the contributor from the need to be personally active in the campaign."

The criteria for selecting the favored candidates vary somewhat, but basically all the PACs follow the same bottom-line reasoning: what will best advance the interests of their group and its members? Given that line of reasoning, it is only natural that PACs usually concentrate their gifts on members of the congressional committees that most affect them. In 1986, for example, the PACs of banks and other financial institutions favored members of the House and Senate banking committees with campaign contributions totaling more than $3.4 million.

More and more, over the years, PACs have come to give the bulk of their money to incumbent members of Congress and to spurn challengers. The PACs' unbalanced kindness to incumbents has increased steadily since the PAC explosion began in 1974. But between 1982 and 1986, the share PACs gave to incumbents leapt a full nine percentage points, far more than it had in any previous four-year period. In 1986, in House races where the incumbent sought reelection, PACs as a whole gave more than 88 percent of their money to sitting members of Congress. Less than 12 percent went to challengers. That imbalance, in turn, helped House incumbents outspend challengers more than three to one, and may well have played a part in the remarkable 1986 statistic that 98 percent of House incumbents who sought reelection won—a postwar high.

The respective categories of PACs differ in the degree of their pro-incumbent favoritism, especially in contests for the House. In those 1986 House races where incumbents sought reelection, the business-minded PACs—those formed by corporations and trade associations—gave roughly 90 percent of their funds to incumbents, and only 10 percent to challengers. Corporations' PACs led the pro-incumbent pack in 1986, giving 96 percent of their gifts to present officeholders. Labor and "ideological" PACs also preferred to give to incumbents, but significantly less than corporate and trade PACs. In 1986, in House contests where incumbents were running, labor PACs gave 77 percent to incumbents, "ideological" PACs about 72 percent.

This pro-incumbent proclivity on the PACs' part is easily explainable by their acknowledged reason for existing: to promote the interests of their members. With that objective in mind, favoring the incumbents makes logical sense. After all, those are the people who occupy the positions of power and are in a position to help or hurt the sponsoring group and its members. What's more, the incumbents are, increasingly, odds-on favorites to retain their seats, especially in the U.S. House—consider the 98 percent victory rate among House members who sought reelection. As former Senator Eagleton put it, "A PAC contribution is an investment. Find me anyone on Wall Street who will give you a 98 percent chance your investment is going to pay off."

———

The modern political action committee, a relatively recent phenomenon in American politics, was introduced by organized labor. That fact is ironic, since in recent years, contributions by business-minded PACs (those formed by corporations, trade associations, and professional groups) have far outstripped those of labor PACs. By 1986, the business-labor ratio of contributions to congressional candidates had grown to nearly three to one.

The first modern PAC, organized to collect and pool *voluntary* political contributions, was established in 1943 by the Congress of Industrial Organizations, the CIO, and in the 1944 election, the CIO-PAC raised more than $1.2 million.

It was not until the early sixties that business-minded groups began to adopt the idea. In 1962, the American Medical Association formed AMPAC, followed, a year later, by the National Association of Manufacturers' Business-Industry Political Action Committee (BIPAC).

Before the days of PACs, campaigns for the House were inexpensive and could be largely financed by contributions from political parties and by fundraising barbecues and chicken dinners and somewhat larger contributions from businessmen. House Ways and Means Chairman Dan Rostenkowski recalls paying for his first House campaign, in 1958, largely out of his own pocket. Back then, though, the price tag was only $25,000, one-tenth of the average cost of a modern House campaign.

Presidential campaigns, involving a different magnitude of money, were financed in considerable part by business. In the 1896 presidential campaign, for example, assessments against corporations imposed by Republican National Chairman Mark Hanna filled William McKinley's campaign coffers. The revelation that McKinley's successor, Theodore Roosevelt, had received a secret $50,000 contribution from a New York life-insurance company in the 1904 election ignited national headlines, and prompted Congress, in 1907, to prohibit direct corporate contributions to federal campaigns.

But neither the 1907 law nor a subsequent law passed in 1925 materially changed business's methods of steering money to federal candidates—either by "laundering" the funds through petty cash funds, professional fees, or by "bonuses" to compensate executives for their political contributions, or simply through that least traceable means: cash. Russell Hemenway, who now directs a liberal PAC, the National Committee for an Effective Congress, remembers Oklahoma's Democratic Senator Robert Kerr distributing the largess of the oil industry to congressmen "in plain envelopes, always in cash." Lloyd Hackler, a former Lyndon Johnson aide, once said that "Under the old system, I bagged a lot of money; everybody did."

In 1971, amid widespread uneasiness about such under-the-table tactics, Congress enacted new election laws containing three important new features. The first tightened the loophole-ridden reporting-and-disclosure requirements for political gifts. The second laid the basis for government financing of presidential election campaigns by permitting taxpayers, in filling out their income-tax forms, to earmark a dollar (two dollars for a married couple) for that purpose. The third, and the most important for the formation and growth of political action committees, explicitly permitted both corporations and labor unions to tap their respective treasuries to pay the expenses of soliciting PAC contributions and administering PACs. That feature proved to be the critical springboard for PAC growth, because it opened up the enormous corporate and union treasuries to finance the PACs' often-considerable administrative costs. PAC expert and political scientist Herbert Alexander estimated that in the 1984 election, certain PACs spent $75 million, or roughly one-fourth of their expenditures, on administrative expenses.

In view of the way business PACs have outdistanced those of labor, it is ironic that the unions, in 1971, pushed Congress to approve the tapping of union and corporate treasuries to run political action committees. At the time, labor leaders were convinced that the formation of business PACs would be limited by the prohibition against political involvement by those with government contracts. Union leaders believed that obstacle would surely bar most large corporations from starting PACs. Three years later, though, in 1974, Congress removed even that barrier to corporate PAC development—again, paradoxically, with labor's assent. By then, unions had secured federal job-training contracts, which they felt would be endangered as long as the prohibition against mixing politics with government contracts remained in force.* David Cohen, then a lobbyist for Common Cause, the group most actively oppos-

---

* That same 1974 law contained other important reform features essentially unrelated to PAC growth, principally ceilings on political contributions by individuals. That had the indirect effect of increasing candidates' reliance on PACs.

ing the PAC legislation, recalls with an ironic smile that labor lobbyists roamed Capitol Hill, pressing for an end to that prohibition —unaware, he says, that their business counterparts were secretly pursuing the same goal.

Cohen says he foresaw the superior capacity of corporations to raise PAC money and warned labor leaders of the dangers that lay ahead for them. His admonition has surely been borne out. By 1978 (the earliest year for which comparative figures are available), business-related PACs gave congressional candidates twice as much money as labor PACs. By 1986, the margin had grown to nearly three to one.

The 1974 law set off a PAC explosion. In the next twelve years, the number of PACs was to grow from 608 to more than 4,200 (although a significant number of those are currently inactive), and PAC contributions to congressional candidates rose from $12.5 million to over $132 million.*

YEAR	NUMBER OF PACs	TOTAL PAC GIFTS TO CONGRESSIONAL CANDIDATES
1974	608	$ 12.5 MILLION
1978	1,653	$ 34.1 MILLION
1982	3,371	$ 83.6 MILLION
1986	4,157	$132.2 MILLION

As television became the undisputed number-one way of selling candidates, campaign costs rose meteorically. Barbecues and chicken dinners mixed with gifts from a few wealthy donors became hopelessly inadequate means of financing House and Senate campaigns. Candidates, especially incumbent congressmen and senators, found that the PACs—able and, at times, only too eager to make large contributions—were by far the easiest source of money. At the same time, a study by Richard P. Conlon, the able director of the Democratic Study Group in Congress, found that between 1974 and 1984 there was a marked decline in small contributions in

---

* As with all campaign-finance dollar figures in this book, these are unadjusted for inflation, since it is difficult to make such an adjustment precisely and fairly. The consumer price index, the traditional inflation adjustor, which rose 122 percent from 1974 to 1986, the period this book is most concerned with, is of limited value because campaign costs are made up of narrow and specialized components, such as TV rates, polling costs, consultants' fees, and the like, which often bear no relation to normal consumer costs such as food, housing, and entertainment.

congressional campaigns. The under-$100 gifts fell from 38 to 23 percent of receipts in Senate campaigns and from 46 to only 15 percent of receipts in House campaigns. So lawmakers, especially members of the House, became more and more dependent on PACs. Between 1974 and 1986, the percentage of House members dependent on special-interest PACs for roughly a third of their money grew from 28 percent to over 80 percent (see the lower table on page 73).

A sharply growing number of congressmen began to receive more than *half* their funds from political action committees: 63 in 1978, and 185 in 1986 (see the upper table on page 73). Still more disturbing, by 1986, nearly one-fourth of the representatives got 60 percent of their campaign money from PACs headquartered outside their districts.

Most disturbing, though, was the rise in campaign costs:

YEAR	AVERAGE COST OF A WINNING CAMPAIGN FOR: U.S. HOUSE	U.S. SENATE
1976	$ 87,200	$ 609,100
1978	$126,900	$1,208,600
1982	$263,000	$2,066,308
1986	$355,000	$3,099,554

Many considered those figures to be the most troublesome, for these escalating campaign costs are the root cause of candidates' appetite—indeed, desperation—to raise more and more money. That, in turn, makes them more and more prey to those paths of least resistance: the political action committees.

Despite these trends, efforts to reform the financing of congressional elections since Watergate have met with little success. In large part, this is due to the historic near-solid Republican opposition to reform, especially to any form of government financing of election campaigns. Only the Watergate revelations persuaded enough Republicans to join the Democrats to enact the 1974 law providing public financing of presidential campaigns. In 1973 and 1974, Congress even came close to expanding the public-financing plan to cover its own elections—a fact unknown, or forgotten, by those who now despair of Congress ever enacting such a plan.

But after public interest in the Watergate scandals subsided, the notion of taxpayer financing of House and Senate contests quickly sank into the category of the politically impossible. In the thirteen years after Watergate, the most that leading congressional reformers dared espouse was a limitation on the total amount of PAC money a House or Senate candidate could receive in one election, and there were few roll-call votes on reform measures in either House.

In 1986, Oklahoma Democratic Senator David Boren stubbornly forced the Senate to vote on a similar per-candidate-PAC-ceiling amendment he tacked on to a bill on another subject. The Boren amendment passed, 69 to 30. Many attributed this top-heavy margin partly to the success of Common Cause and other groups in portraying the Boren amendment as a "clean-government" measure that few dared openly oppose. A more important factor was the widespread belief among senators that the measure was almost surely headed for ultimate death, if only by dint of a Reagan veto. Thus, even those unenthusiastic about reform could go on record as favoring a housecleaning without risk that the job would actually be done. The Boren measure never went further.

When the 100th Congress convened in January 1987, an apparent sea change had taken place in Senate sentiment about campaign-finance reform. Control of the Senate had shifted to the Democrats. Eleven new Democratic senators had been elected the previous November, many of them seared by the tribulation of having to raise millions of dollars. Most important, the campaign-finance reform banner was now seized by the Senate Democratic leader, West Virginia Democratic Senator Robert C. Byrd, who felt passionately about the need for change. Byrd believed that the root of the problem lay in spiraling campaign costs, the cause of candidates' incessant preoccupation with raising funds. But he was also aware that the Supreme Court had interposed an obstacle to a legislated ceiling on candidates' campaign spending. In 1976, the court ruled that any such mandatory ceiling violated candidates' free-speech rights under the First Amendment. On the other hand, the court had approved a spending limit for candidates who accept federal assistance for their campaigns, on the ground that since candidates are not obliged to accept the aid, the ceiling is voluntary, not required.

Accordingly, as a means of capping candidate spending, the new reform measure that Senators Byrd and Boren introduced on the second day of the new Congress included a provision for taxpayer financing of Senate elections—the first time since 1974 this concept was put forward by anyone in a leadership position. To the surprise of most, one of the earliest sponsors of the bill was conservative Democratic Senator John Stennis of Mississippi, an index of the change in the reform climate. Soon fifty-three senators had joined in sponsoring the bill.

But Senate Republicans were having none of it, and when the bill came to the Senate floor, they mounted a filibuster. After seven unavailing efforts to break the filibuster, Senator Byrd shelved the reform effort for the balance of 1987.

No comparable reform wave swept over the House in 1987. The appropriate committee held a few hearings. A Democratic "task force" sought to work out a consensus measure. But the prospect of a near-sure Reagan veto of any significant reform bill made the task seem more futile than urgent.

Meanwhile, the problems of the campaign-finance system recounted in this book continue to mount.

INFLUENCE-PEDDLING

★　★　★　★　★　★　★

THE BUYERS
OF INFLUENCE

3

If you unexpectedly inherited some money from a distant aunt and decided to contribute your windfall to candidates for the U.S. House and Senate—

- Would you contribute to a candidate who had no opponent?
- Would you contribute to a candidate who disagreed with you on the issues you consider most important?
- Would you consider contributing to both opposing candidates in a given election?
- Would you consider contributing to one candidate *during* the campaign and then, if your candidate lost, switching and giving to the winner *after* the election?

If your answer to those questions is "No," you reason differently from most political action committees. At any rate, your logic would be different from General Electric PAC's when it handed out money to 1986 House and Senate candidates.

For example, you would not consider giving to an unopposed or a sure-to-win candidate. But in the 1986 election, the GE PAC gave money to thirty-four House candidates who faced *no* opponent, and to another thirty-four who had won by at least three-to-one margins in their most recent elections, and hence could be predicted to coast to easy victories. Those sixty-eight candidates hardly needed GE's money to win reelection.*

---

* The research on the General Electric PAC's giving pattern was conducted in connection with a shareholder's suit against GE, in which the author of this book is plaintiff.

Moreover, just as candidates' political philosophies count heavily with most contributors, you would expect a candidate's pro- or anti-business attitude to be of paramount concern to General Electric, America's sixth largest industrial corporation. Surprise. In 1986, GE's PAC managers appeared singularly indifferent to candidates' attitudes toward business, as measured by the approval rating given lawmakers' congressional voting records by the U.S. Chamber of Commerce. For example, in the 1986 California U.S. Senate race, the GE PAC gave the nod to Democrat Alan Cranston (average Chamber of Commerce approval rating: 12.8 percent) in preference to the Republican challenger, Congressman Edward Zschau, whose voting record in the House had received an 81 percent Chamber approval rating in 1984, and 100 percent the year before.

As to betting on both horses in a single election or making a postelection switch, in 1986, GE's PAC managers had no scruples about contributing to opposing candidates in nine Senate elections, and in two instances, one in the Senate and one in the House, when their preelection "horse" lost, the General Electric PAC directors found some extra money, after the votes had been counted, to give to the candidate they had previously tried to defeat.

The GE PAC is a microcosm of the 4,000-plus PACs extant in 1986. For example, in 1986 PACs as a whole gave slightly over $8.5 million to House candidates who had no major-party opponent, and an added $14.8 million to House candidates who had won their previous four elections by margins of at least three to one—that is, nearly $23 million to predictably sure winners.

Moreover, two studies by Common Cause unearthed at least 494 instances in which PACs gave to both opposing candidates in 1986 Senate elections, and 150 postelection switches. Thirty-nine of these occurred in the state of North Dakota, where Democrat Kent Conrad upset the Republican incumbent, Senator Mark Andrews. Example: after the election, the American Bankers Association, which had made the maximum contribution of $10,000 to Andrews before the election, turned around and gave the same amount to Senator-elect Conrad.

Likewise, the Marine Engineers Union, displaying a mystifying interest in the entirely landlocked state of North Dakota, at first bestowed $6,500 on Andrews and then, after he lost, gave a $5,000 gift to his victorious opponent.

The General Electric PAC, which had spent $2,000 trying to defeat Conrad, now came to his aid with a $1,000 contribution.

The title of the Common Cause study sums it up: "If at First You Don't Succeed, Give, Give Again."

Surveying the facts about 1986 contributions leads to this conclusion:

If the PACs had deliberately set out to convince the public that they are unabashed and unprincipled purchasers of influence, they could not have done a better job than to leave behind them the damning trail of evidence—the contributions to unopposed candidates; the betting on both horses; the postelection switch-giving when their horse lost.

But it is in their overwhelming favoritism for incumbents that the PACs have furnished the most persuasive evidence of influence-buying motives.

Consider again the example of the General Electric PAC. In 1986, out of 214 House contests in which the incumbent sought reelection, GE backed the incumbent in 211 (including 34 in which the incumbent had no opponent). That is, GE selected the incumbent *98.6 percent of the time.* Aside from a single instance where GE backed both the incumbent and the challenger, in only 3 of 214 contests—1.4 percent—did the GE PAC managers find the challenger preferable to the incumbent. It was as if someone from On High had issued instructions: "Never mind candidates' party affiliation, their attitudes toward big business, or their need for campaign funds. Whatever you do, *support the incumbent.*"

That apparent edict certainly applied to GE PAC giving in the 1986 Senate contests. Not once in twenty-seven Senate races in which the GE PAC gave and the incumbent sought reelection did the PAC forsake the incumbent—although in five contests, it gave to both incumbent *and* challenger.

GE's penchant for supporting incumbents is characteristic of PACs as a whole—particularly in races for the U.S. House. A 1987 Common Cause analysis revealed that one-third of all PACs gave at least 80 percent of their money to incumbents in the 1986 elections. Moreover, in contests where incumbents were seeking reelection in 1986, *PACs overall gave more than 88 percent of their money to them and only 12 percent to challengers.* PACs formed by corporations like incumbents the best. In 1986, corporate PACs as a whole gave 96 percent of their money to those already in office.

In considerable part as a result of that PAC imbalance, 1986 House incumbents outspent challengers more than three to one. And in considerable part as a consequence of *that*, of incumbents seeking reelection in 1986, fully 98 percent won—a postwar high. Only 2 percent of challengers managed to upset sitting congressmen.

Clearly, PACs' pattern of political giving differs sharply from that of the ordinary citizen. To the average $5 or $10 contributor, the PACs' giving habits must seem illogical and thoroughly unprincipled.

The main difference between average citizens and PACs lies in their motives for contributing. Most small donors contribute to candidates not because they expect anything for themselves in return for their money, but because they want to help them win. That is, private citizens, especially small givers, typically make political contributions because they want to influence the outcome of the election.★

Most PACs also care about influence, but it's *post*election influence they want. That is, they give because they want to maximize their chances of access to the ear of an officeholder who has the power to help them, and to have that access at the moment they need help.

Usually, when they make a contribution, most PACs don't know precisely what they want or when they may want it. But they assume that they will want a lawmaker's attention on some future occasion. When that moment arrives, they want to be as sure as possible of being able to make their case directly to the pivotal representatives and senators *themselves*, and not to some junior assistant. Moreover, when the legislative machinery shifts into high gear, especially in the hours before Congress adjourns for the year, the time to see the lawmaker is *now*. Tomorrow—or even three

---

★ As will be pointed out in the discussions of the billboard industry's contributions to Congressman James J. Howard of New Jersey, chairman of the House Public Works and Transportation Committee (Chapters 3 and 4), many who contribute over $200 give in hope of a financial return. That is, they are connected with a company or industry with a financial interest in the lawmaker-beneficiary's official conduct.

hours from now—won't do. By then the vote will be over, and it will be too late.

So when it comes to making political contributions, the difference between the typical citizen-contributor and a PAC can be summed up this way:

The average citizen is mainly interested in influencing the outcome of an election.

A PAC is less interested in the influence it has on an election outcome than in the influence it buys with the winner after the ballots have been counted.

That summing-up explains the PACs' apparently irrational behavior toward Republican Congressman John J. Duncan, of Tennessee.

Few ordinary citizens would give a dime to Duncan no matter how much they might agree with his conservative voting record. Why? Because he doesn't need the money to win. Duncan is a solid fixture in his Knoxville district; in his last five elections he has been, on average, a four-to-one winner. Yet, although he didn't need to spend a dollar to win reelection in 1986, that didn't discourage the PACs from heaping $401,000 on his campaign—more than twice what they had given him two years earlier.

How does one explain this illogical PAC behavior?

If you're in tune with PACs' reasoning, the explanation is perfectly obvious.* Number one, Congressman Duncan is the highest-ranking Republican on the House Ways and Means Committee, which handles tax legislation. Number two, while the PACs were doubling their gifts to Duncan, the Reagan administration had proposed, and Duncan's committee had before it, a sweeping tax-reform program. Multi-billion-dollar loopholes were threatened. Throwing a few thousand dollars Duncan's way—enough so he would be hard pressed to refuse an audience to a PAC's lobbyist—could be cheap at twice the price.

Ever since the PAC movement began in earnest in 1974, PACs have consistently given the lion's share of their money to incumbents—particularly in House races. But, as noted above, from 1982 to 1986, pro-incumbent partiality took a marked leap. In 1982 House

---

* It also parallels the logic behind PAC giving to Congressman Charles Rangel, described in Chapter 1.

elections in which the incumbent sought reelection, the PACs gave just under four-fifths of their money to incumbents. In 1986, the figure rose from 79 to nearly 88 percent.

That increase coincided with an equally marked rise in the percentage of incumbents who were successful at the polls. In 1986, incumbents who sought reelection had a 98 percent success rate, a jump of more than seven percentage points over 1982.

YEAR	PERCENT OF PAC MONEY GOING TO HOUSE INCUMBENTS SEEKING REELECTION	PERCENT OF HOUSE INCUMBENTS REELECTED
1974	n.a.	87.7%
1978	71.8%	93.7%
1982	78.9%	90.6%
1986	87.9%	98.0%

It would unduly oversimplify matters to claim that the PACs are solely responsible for incumbent success. A multitude of other factors come into play: the inherent advantages of incumbency, and pro-incumbent redistricting, to mention just two. Nonetheless, the "bottom line" fact bears repeating (and reflection):

> *In 1986, only 2 percent of the challengers for the U.S. House of Representatives were successful; 98 percent of the incumbents emerged unscathed.*

Brooks Jackson of the *Wall Street Journal* has suggested that we are witnessing a phenomenon—or is it an institution?—that the Founding Fathers never envisaged: the *Congressman-for-Life*.

Given that most PACs' preeminent desire is to buy influence or access, their pro-incumbent bias is perfectly natural.

Natural, perhaps. But good for the country and its political system? I believe not. The PAC favoritism of incumbents has three malign consequences:

First, it tends to freeze out congressional candidates of experience, ability, and idealism—solely for one reason: money.

Consider this snapshot of the electoral picture in contests for the U.S. House of Representatives as of June 30, 1986, four months before the 1986 elections. The incumbents' treasuries had an average balance of $132,000. The *challengers'* campaign bank balances, by contrast, averaged less than $11,000. The incumbents' PAC advantage was a large factor.

Is it really good for the country to ration candidacies on the basis of how much money candidates possess or can raise—particularly when the incumbents have the unique advantage of being able to collect massive amounts of money from outside special-interest groups?

Suppose that a modern Andrew Jackson lived in Congressman Duncan's congressional district or a new Martin Luther King in Congressman Charles Rangel's Harlem district (see Chapter 2). What chance would such historic figures have of successfully competing with Rangel or Duncan and their campaign war chests?

Former Senator Barry Goldwater put it this way:

> What are we doing? Are we saying that . . . only the people who have influential friends who have money can be in the Senate? We're excluding a lot of young people that I think would make damn good additions to this body by not giving them access to money. . . .

Second, to the extent that the PACs' pro-incumbent favoritism reduces challenge, it narrows the spectrum of public discourse, and offers the voters less choice.

Worst of all, as the 98 percent success rate for House incumbents in 1986 demonstrates, the PACs' preference for incumbents helps lock the sitting officeholders into office. It protects them from serious challenge even though their conduct in office may be seriously defective. Incumbency carries enough other inherent advantages, even without the political action committees. PAC favoritism compounds the imbalance.

The political action committees have introduced a new meaning to the word "constituent"—one that the Founding Fathers doubtless did not foresee.

Most of the PACs—at least those representing business interests—belong to one interest group or another: banking, or oil, or chemicals, or the defense industry. Usually, a given industry's activities are supervised by one or two special congressional committees: banking legislation is dealt with by the banking committees in the House and Senate, whose members take on special importance to banks. The energy committees and their members hold special powers over the oil, gas, and chemical industries; members of the telecommunications subcommittees are of special interest to the broadcasters. Each industry, therefore, has its own lawmaker "constituents"—those select few congressmen and senators pivotal to its future.

United Technologies Corporation's PAC actually used the word "constituent" in soliciting new PAC contributions. "We *have* strengthened our relationships with our 'constituent' senators and congressmen. One or more of us on the PAC Steering Committee have developed a personal relationship with each incumbent to whom we have given campaign contributions" (emphasis theirs).

Perhaps United Technologies did not intend any connotation of proprietorship over its "constituent" congressmen. Yet it is undeniable, given the financial power of many companies and industries, that they have the capacity to heap money and other favors in memorable amounts on those lawmakers most important to them.

Chapter 1 has already noted the behavior of the top ten defense-industry contractors, who concentrated 41 percent of their 1986 contributions and three-quarters of their 1985 honoraria on the 18 percent of lawmakers who make up the defense-related committees of Congress. Narrowing the lens to the top defense contractor, General Dynamics, you find that the firm's PAC carefully gave to every single member of the House Defense Appropriations Subcommittee (the committee that actually votes the money), and to forty-one of the forty-seven members of the House Armed Services Committee.

Naturally, as a "constituent" committee member rises in seniority and power, the pocketbooks of defense contractors open up correspondingly. As observed in Chapter 4, since 1979, for example, Alabama Representative William Dickinson, the ranking Republican on the House Armed Services Committee, received more than $268,000 in campaign contributions from the leading defense contractors. In that same period, leading defense firms have lavished more than $343,000 on Florida Democratic Congressman Bill Chappell, who presides over the House Defense Appropriations Subcommittee.

Congressmen Dickinson and Chappell are the public's representatives in dealing with these colossal defense firms, supposedly dealing with them fairly but toughly to protect against excessive profits or cost overruns. But with hundreds of thousands of dollars from defense firms going into the campaign coffers of these two, how can the taxpayers be sure they are fulfilling their duties dispassionately?

Another example of a lawmaker carefully cosseted by those he regulated: the 1985–86 contributions by executives of sundry Wall Street firms to Republican Senator Alfonse D'Amato of New York. In the years 1981 through 1986, while the Republicans controlled the Senate, Senator D'Amato exercised critical control over many of these firms in his capacity as chairman of the Senate Securities Subcommittee. During those years—D'Amato's freshman term in the Senate—the PACs of twelve Wall Street firms gave Senator D'Amato a total of $78,200. But during that same period, *executives* of seventeen Wall Street firms gave the senator a grand total of $360,780—nearly five times the amount given him by PACs. As we see in Chapter 8, Senator D'Amato was a *very* good friend to the securities industry.

Paul Houston of the *Los Angeles Times* graphically summed up the new meaning of interest-group "constituents" this way: "In a city where money is the grade-A milk of political nutrition, the PACs and other large contributors have become political milkmen, each with a route of Congressional customers who are accustomed to timely deliveries of cash for their campaigns or personal use. And the lobbyists in turn are close at hand when the time comes for important legislative decisions to be made."

Political action committees, then, are the principal but not the only means by which interest groups give to politicians. As we have seen, money from companies' and industries' PACs is on occasion outweighed by personal contributions by their executives and employees.

For example, the reports submitted to the Federal Elections Commission by Senate Republican Leader Robert Dole for 1985–86 show a $1,000 campaign contribution to Dole's Senate reelection committee by Dow Chemical's PAC. Since contributions from PACs and contributions from individuals appear on separate FEC forms, Dole's PAC reports do not disclose $16,000 in personal contributions by Dow executives *all on the same day*. Nor do those PAC records show that twenty-six executives of USX (formerly U.S. Steel) had such regard for Senator Dole that they contributed a total of $8,750 to the senator just five days before Christmas, 1985.★

Wealthy individuals and families strew campaign gifts among

★ As recounted below, the billboard industry supplemented the contributions from its tiny PACs with much larger gifts from individuals connected with the industry.

congressmen and senators, occasionally in search of special favors. The political generosity of Ernest and Julio Gallo, the winemakers who bottle one-fourth of the wine sold in the United States, seems to have played a role in the approval by the House Ways and Means Committee of a special tax provision that came to be called "the Gallo Amendment." According to the *Wall Street Journal*, over an eight-year period, the Gallos contributed a grand total of $325,000 to parties and candidates, divided about equally between Democrats and Republicans.

The Gallo Amendment would have permitted the Gallo brothers to pass roughly $80 million on to their grandchildren without paying a 33 percent estate tax. That would make the amendment worth nearly $27 million in tax savings to the Gallo brothers or their heirs.★

Among the political contributions that helped the Gallo brothers' special tax provision along the legislative track were $13,000 in campaign contributions to their own representative, California Democrat Tony Coelho, plus $31,750 to the Democratic Congressional Campaign Committee, which Coelho chaired at the time. The *Wall Street Journal* reported that Coelho, a powerful member of the House Democratic leadership, said he "checked with Congressman Edgar Jenkins [of Georgia, the amendment's sponsor] several times on the progress of the amendment." For a congressman as busy as Coelho, that was an extraordinary display of energy and interest. (Federal records show no Gallo contributions to Representative Jenkins.)

In order to clear all the congressional hurdles, the "Gallo amendment" would have to pass through the Senate Finance Committee, of which Senator Robert Dole was ranking Republican member. In 1986, the two Gallo brothers and their wives made the maximum legal contribution to Dole's PAC. If Dole had not formed his own PAC, that maximum would have been $1,000 apiece, or a total of $4,000 for the brothers and their spouses. But Dole *had* established his own PAC, to which individuals can legally contribute $5,000, rather than $1,000. Accordingly, the Gallo brothers and their wives could quintuple their expression of regard for Senator Dole; each gave $5,000, for a more conspicuous total of $20,000.

★ The provision would also have applied to other wealthy persons with lots of grandchildren, but they are few in number. The Gallos appear to have been the instigators of "the Gallo amendment."

As recently as 1980, the Washington law firm of Verner, Lipfert, Bernard, McPherson & Hand did not have a PAC. Nor did the huge Omaha-based legal colossus, Kutak, Rock & Campbell. Today, both have PACs, which give significant amounts of money to the election campaigns of congressmen and senators. So do many other law firms, as the table shows.

LAW FIRM	HOME BASE	PAC DONATIONS	
		1980	1986
AKIN, GUMP, STRAUSS, HAUER & FELD	DALLAS	$47,025	$129,521
VINSON, ELKINS, SEARLS, CONNALLY & SMITH	HOUSTON	$56,175	$126,275
JONES, DAY, REAVIS & POGUE	CLEVELAND	$ 2,000	$ 84,525
VERNER, LIPFERT, BERNARD, MCPHERSON & HAND	WASHINGTON	—	$ 76,852
DICKSTEIN, SHAPIRO & MORIN	WASHINGTON	$15,825	$ 57,575
BAKER & BOTTS	HOUSTON	$44,000	$ 52,230
KUTAK, ROCK & CAMPBELL	OMAHA	—	$ 49,882
FULBRIGHT & JAWORSKI	HOUSTON	—	$ 43,000
PILLSBURY, MADISON & SUTRO	SAN FRANCISCO	—	$ 41,845
MANATT, PHELPS, ROTHENBERG & TUNNEY	LOS ANGELES	—	$ 40,425

All of these firms have one thing in common: they all have Washington offices and clients whose problems call for special attention from Congress or the executive branch. Among the most important services those law firms can offer such clients is entree to just the right senator or representative.

Increasingly, as observed in Chapter 4, a campaign contribution is the most effective—and, on occasion, the necessary—means of gaining that entree. Many law firms argue that forming a PAC is the fairest way of apportioning that distasteful access-buying burden among the firm's partners. It's unfair, they maintain, for the entire cost of buying tickets to the incessant fundraisers to be borne solely by those members of the firm who "work the Hill."

The PAC has another advantage: it is the cheapest way of gaining entree for *all* members of the firm. A former junior associate in the Washington "legislative department" of the Texas-based firm of Akin, Gump, Strauss, Hauer & Feld, which includes former Democratic National Chairman Robert Strauss, describes how that works:

Sometimes it fell to me to make the rounds of all those three- or four-an-evening fundraisers that are held every damned night, it seems, on Capitol Hill. I'd go with an Akin Gump check in my pocket representing the firm. At the door, I'd present the check and make damned sure it was properly noted. Then I'd make sure to introduce myself to the guest of honor, pronouncing the words "Akin Gump" loud and clear, to make sure it registered that the firm was here and had done its bit.

Then I'd go around the room carefully searching out all the staff members, and do the same thing: "Hi, I'm from Akin Gump." It was the firm *name* that would register, not my face. That way, whenever *anyone* from the firm would call the congressman or senator or anyone from the staff and say "Akin Gump," it would register. "Oh, yeah. I remember Akin Gump was at the fundraiser."

After that, I'd slip out the back, and go on to the next party and do the same thing—maybe three or four times in an evening. It worked like a charm.

This attorney emphasizes that Akin Gump was by no means unique. On the contrary, he says, his own party-going pattern was standard operating procedure for law firms in the PAC business— so much so that he could expect to bump into the same lawyer-lobbyists at party after party on the same evening.

As congressional expectations of contributions from lobbyists grow, a keeping-up-with-the-Joneses syndrome is developing among law firms with Washington branches. One by one, they are falling into line with the PAC strategy. In 1987, one of the most prestigious of Washington law firms, Arnold & Porter, formed a PAC. Observers wondered how long the starchiest and most traditional Washington law firm, Covington & Burling, can hold out.

The net effect of the mounting torrents of political money—from the PACs, from rich individuals and families, from the executives and employees of companies and industries and, finally, from growing numbers of law firms affordable only by the most wealthy—is to further widen the power gap between the monied and the unmonied, between the organized and the unorganized, between sellers and consumers.

The interest groups' amalgamation of political money has another effect: to enable small but highly organized groups to use money to win the day in Congress, *and to impose huge costs on the rest of the population.* In the civics-class picture of American democracy, that is supposedly impossible, or nearly so. The reality, as we shall see, is otherwise: it is more than possible, almost easy.

The three groups that carried the day in Congress in the following case studies do not boast millions or even hundreds of thousands of members like, say, the AFL-CIO, the Moral Majority, or a nationwide environmental or peace organization. One group, the used-car dealers, numbers about 27,000. The dairy farmers add up to 200,000 at most. The third—the billboard industry—is made up of only a few hundred companies, dominated by fewer than a dozen firms.

At the ballot box, then, all three groups combined account for a minuscule number of votes.

Moreover, none of the three enjoys the widespread public appeal of organizations like the Red Cross or the Boy Scouts. Indeed, with many consumers, used-car dealers rank in popularity on a par with bill collectors. And it is the rare family that has sallied forth on a Saturday afternoon in search of the best buy in a billboard.

Nonetheless, these three groups succeeded in getting their way with Congress. The used-car dealers even carried the day by margins of two-to-one.

Whatever they lacked in people-power, all three groups more than compensated in their adroit use of money-power.

★
1. THE USED-CAR DEALERS AND THE "LEMON LAW"

The used-car dealers' problem can be simply stated: in the late 1970s, the Federal Trade Commission began to formulate an administrative ruling, nicknamed the "lemon law," to require used-car dealers to reveal to their customers *any* defects they *know* of in the cars they offer for sale.

Such a rule set up the following political equation: on one side of the equation, millions of used-car buyers, many of whom had been stung by buying lemons, stood to benefit enormously. On the other side, a comparative handful of dealers feared two consequences of the rule: the possible expense entailed with disclosure and repairs of defects, but, more, the potential loss of sales. So the dealers strenuously opposed the lemon law.

Millions of buyers versus thousands of dealers. On a strictly one-person–one-vote basis—that is, with lawmakers making a simple ballot-box calculation—the dealers would seem to face an impossible task in trying to win a majority of Congress to their side.

Nonetheless, when in 1980 Congress passed a law permitting a congressional veto of FTC rules like the lemon law, the used-car dealers went to work.

Their principal instrument was the political action committee that had been formed in 1972 by the National Automobile Dealers Association, or NADA. After a slow start, the NADA PAC grew explosively. In 1972, it dispensed a paltry $9,950. By 1976, though, its collections had swelled to over $368,000, which it distributed in gifts of memorable size among 270 candidates—half the entire Congress.

Four years later, after Congress acquired the veto power over FTC rules, the auto dealers really stepped on the gas. NADA PAC's 1980 contributions virtually tripled from 1976, breaking the million-dollar mark. Throughout 1981 and 1982, as Congress readied itself to vote on the lemon-rule veto, the NADA PAC continued to pour forth further campaign contributions.

Here is a typical sequence of events, involving Republican Congressman Mickey Edwards of Oklahoma City:

- *August 19, 1981:* Congressman Edwards receives a $2,500 campaign contribution from the NADA PAC, even though it's not an election year.
- *Sept. 22, 1981:* Congressman Edwards signs up as cosponsor of the resolution killing the FTC used-car lemon law, in keeping with NADA's strong wishes.
- *Oct. 19, 1981:* Congressman Edwards receives an additional $200 campaign contribution from the NADA PAC.
- *May 26, 1982:* Congressman Edwards votes for resolution killing the FTC used-car rule.
- *Sept. 30, 1982:* Congressman Edwards receives an added $2,000 contribution from NADA PAC—bringing the total he had received from that PAC since 1979 to $8,100.

Did those contributions buy Representative Edwards's vote? He insists that with his generally conservative antigovernment philosophy, he would have voted that way with or without the campaign gifts.

Perhaps so. But to focus on Congressman Edwards alone is to miss the central question: Did the NADA PAC contributions influence the vote of the House as a whole? There is statistical evidence that it did:

OF THOSE RECEIVING THIS AMOUNT FROM THE NADA PAC IN 1979 THROUGH 1982 . . .	. . . THIS PERCENT VOTED AGAINST THE LEMON LAW IN 1982
MORE THAN $4,000	90.2%
$1,000 TO $3,000	88.3%
$1 TO $1,000	68.0%
ZERO	34.2%

University of Virginia Professor Larry J. Sabato, a leading student of political action committees, concluded that the NADA contributions substantially affected and attracted the votes of congressmen "who were decidedly more liberal or conservative than NADA."

A few thousand car *dealers* prevailed over millions of car *buyers* in both houses by greater than two-to-one margins—first in the Senate, 69–27, and then in the House, 286–133. Apparently something had gotten in the way of strict one-person–one-vote democracy. The figures above suggest that at least part of that something was money, in the form of auto-dealer campaign contributions.

In the succeeding Congressional elections of 1982, NADA continued to reward its friends. Of the 251 House members who voted with the auto dealers on the lemon-law veto and who ran for reelection, 89 percent received NADA campaign contributions averaging $2,300. By contrast, only 22 percent of the congressmen who voted against the dealers got NADA money, with contributions averaging less than half as great.

Journalist Elizabeth Drew asked one congressman why the House had voted as it did on the lemon law. His answer: "Of course it was money. Why else would they vote for used-car dealers?"

★ ─────────────────────────────────

2. THE DAIRY FARMERS AND THE DAIRY SUBSIDY PROGRAM.

On September 26, 1985, in the U.S. House of Representatives, a face-off took place between 200,000 dairy farmers on the one hand

and tens of millions of dairy consumers on the other. The issue: whether to continue a government program of dairy-price supports at a high level that would oblige consumers to pay an extra 60 cents a gallon more for milk by 1990, *plus* their share of $2.7 billion more in taxes over the next five years to pay for the higher subsidy program.

On a strict one-person–one-vote reckoning—that is, if each person counted equally in each congressman's political calculation—the millions of dairy consumers should have won decisively that September afternoon. But the consumers did not win. On the contrary, they were defeated by a seventy-eight-vote margin.

As with the vote pitting used-car consumers vs. dealers on the lemon law, something had apparently derailed one-person–one-vote democracy. And, as with the lemon-law vote, a part of that something seems to have been money strewn throughout the Congress in the form of campaign contributions. In this case, the money was collected by three large dairy cooperatives, through which individual farmers sell their milk, using a highly efficient mechanism: the PAC contributions were withheld from the monthly milk checks sent to the farmers. Once a farmer assents to this perfectly legal arrangement, the comparatively tiny monthly PAC dues are automatically—and painlessly—subtracted.

This collection system enabled the three major dairy co-ops, in the 1984 elections, to amass three separate kitties totaling $3.3 million—ample to disseminate sizable campaign contributions among 327 House candidates, including those running in big cities.

Dallas's Democratic Representative Martin Frost offers an illustrative case study of the dairy PACs' generosity to such an urban representative. His largely big-city district contains, at most, three dairy farmers—and some 527,000 dairy consumers. Many of the latter have incomes below the official government poverty line and can ill afford to pay the higher dairy prices the government subsidy program almost surely causes.

Therefore, in voting for the higher subsidy level, Congressman Frost sided with the three dairy farmers in his district against the interests of the hundreds of thousands of consumers. Why?

A relevant factor to consider while pondering that question is the $45,050 the dairy lobby had lavished on this big-city congressman in the eight years 1979 through 1986. That made him the fifteenth-highest recipient of dairy money among the 435 members of the House, rural or urban.

Representative Frost is not the only urban representative favored with dairy-lobby campaign contributions. Over the same eight-year period, $18,500 went to Kansas City's Alan Wheat, $15,000 to Birmingham's Ben Erdreich, and $12,000 to Peter Rodino of Newark, New Jersey. All are Democrats.

This is not to suggest that the dairy-lobby campaign contributions affected the way these particular representatives voted. But the current *system* of financing congressional campaigns permits that inference—one of the system's unhappy consequences. The statistical evidence, though, does show a perceptible correlation between dairy money and the voting behavior of the House taken as a whole:

OF THOSE RECEIVING THIS AMOUNT FROM THE DAIRY LOBBY IN 1979 THROUGH 1986 . . .	. . . THIS PERCENT VOTED FOR DAIRY SUBSIDIES IN 1985
MORE THAN $30,000	100%
$20,000 TO $30,000	97%
$10,000 TO $20,00	81%
$2,500 TO $10,000	60%
$1 TO $2,500	33%
ZERO	23%

★ ━━━━━━━━━━━━━━━━━━━━━━━━━━━━━━━━━━━━━

3. THE BILLBOARD INDUSTRY AND REGULATION OF BILLBOARDS ON FEDERAL HIGHWAYS

Compared with the car dealers and the dairy farmers, the billboard industry had an infinitely smaller chance of winning the U.S. Congress—at least in theory. After all, the car dealers do number 27,000; there are at least a few of them in every congressional district; and they do sell a product that a great many people need and want. So do the 200,000 dairy farmers, some of whom are to be found in each of the fifty states.

Not so the billboard industry. It consists of several hundred companies, ten of which dominate the industry. What's more, although a certain number of small businesses, especially hotels and restaurants in rural areas, feel they need outdoor signs to direct travelers to them, billboards are hardly a popular consumer item.

Yet, while the billboard industry's problem was seemingly more difficult, the industry succeeded far more than the car dealers and, in a way, more than even the dairy lobby in working its will with the U.S. Congress.

The billboard industry's need to deal with the U.S. Congress began in 1965, when the new Highway Beautification Act set out to limit billboards along federally funded highways.

At the time, the new law was widely acclaimed. It seemed to offer real hope for controlling billboard blight. Two decades later, though, the results hardly measure up to the hope. The taxpayers had laid out nearly a quarter of a billion dollars for the removal of some billboards; yet far more had sprung up in their place. The precise number is not known (no one regularly collects the nation-wide figures), but in 1983, when data *was* gathered, the taxpayers had paid for the removal of 2,235 signs, but 13,522 new signs had been erected.

Moreover, under industry pressure, the limits on the signs' size and height were relaxed. The twin result: billboard-company income swelled enormously in two decades; and the new and larger roadside signs became even worse polluters of the landscape.

By 1982, so completely had the industry turned the Highway Beautification Act to its benefit that Vermont's Senator Robert Stafford, one of the most tenacious of the billboard reformers, bitterly observed the law would be more aptly labeled the Billboard Compensation and Protection Act, and sought to repeal the 1965 law. Ironically, only the billboard industry sought to keep the law regulating signs on and near federal highways.

Many believe that the industry's thwarting of the Beautification Act began with the original law itself. It now appears that in 1965, the industry hoodwinked Congress into writing a law that relaxed rather than tightened billboard regulation and made the process vastly more costly than before.

The background is this: prior to 1965, billboard regulation had been largely a municipal affair. When cities used local ordinances to order billboards removed, signs could be removed without any expenditure of taxpayers' funds. The courts had consistently approved compensating the owners by allowing the signs to remain up during a grace period, with the revenues earned during the grace period serving as proper compensation. After all, the courts reasoned, the signs derived their value solely because of the traffic on the public roads, which had been built at taxpayer expense.

Enter, now, First Lady Lady Bird Johnson, pressing, in 1965, for *federal* billboard control. Everyone expected the industry to dig in its heels and fight. But much to the surprise and delight of the bill's sponsors, the industry agreed that "billboards have no place in the scenic areas of our highways."

But when the dust had cleared, it turned out that, while publicly pledging support, industry lobbyists had persuaded Congress to toss aside five decades of court decisions approving the grace-period formula, and to require that signs removed pursuant to the new federal law be compensated exclusively in cash—the cash to come out of the taxpayers' pockets.

What's more, in selecting which signs were to be removed and paid for, the government often had to choose from lists volunteered by the billboard owners. In practice, the owners typically offered their least desirable signs, often obsolete signs that they had scheduled for demolition anyway. Most galling of all, billboard owners could—and did—use the taxpayers' cash to build new and bigger signs, *often on a nearby stretch of that same road.*

Apparently, even that wasn't enough for the industry. In 1978, the billboard lobby persuaded Congress to make the law twice as sweet for the sign owners—and twice as expensive for the taxpayers. The new law stripped states and cities of much of their power to use the grace-period formula for removing signs under *local* ordinances. Henceforth, if a city wanted to order the removal of *any sign visible from a federal highway*, it would have to compensate the owner in cash, even if the removal was strictly pursuant to a local ordinance and had nothing to do with federal law.

In that single stroke, the billboard industry added about 38,000 signs to the number eligible for cash compensation, estimated at a third of a billion dollars. This was in addition to the $427 million already due to the industry for billboards covered under the 1965 law. With federal expenditures on billboard removal reduced to an annual rate of $2 million a year (in 1984), that new sum added to $427 million already due the industry meant that the last billboard wouldn't be torn down until at least the year 2367.

Perhaps most offensive, from the beginning, the industry exploited gaping loopholes in the 1965 law, later made more serious by state regulations. The most flagrant: the "unzoned commercial zone" loophole. Under that provision, a stretch of country road previously barred to billboards could be transformed into an approved billboard zone simply by painting the pretext of a sign,

MIKE'S WELDING SHOP, on an empty shack overgrown with weeds, or terming a single long-unused gasoline pump a filling station. (These are *actual* examples. The U.S. Department of Transportation issued a report replete with photographs of those and other similar examples.) In 1985, the General Accounting Office found that in the year ending in mid-1983, just such pretenses made possible the erection of 4,712 billboards. That was twice as many signs as the government paid to tear down that same year.

Compared with the auto dealers, the billboard industry is a midget. The industry's sales are but one-twentieth as great, and its 1986 PAC contributions to congressional candidates amounted to a puny $110,000, compared with over $1,059,000 from the car dealers' PAC.

How, then, has this bantam industry managed to work its magic on Congress over the years?

Answer: by aiming its favors like a rifle, rather than scattering them, shotgun style, over the entire Congress, as the car dealers could afford to do.

The billboard industry was able to adopt this narrow-target strategy, because billboard legislation is consistently embedded as a tiny part of immense and complex highway bills handled by the transportation committees. Moreover, billboard questions seldom come to name-by-name roll-call votes, especially in the House. On billboard matters, therefore, most lawmakers are content to follow the lead of their respective public-works committees that oversee highway and billboard legislation.

Thus, unlike the auto dealers and dairy farmers, the billboard industry did not have to woo all 535 lawmakers. In general, all it took was to win and maintain influence with the chairmen and a few pivotal members of the public-works committees—and, not incidentally, key committee staff members.

It is therefore instructive to focus a microscope on the variety of favors the industry has lavished upon one James J. Howard, a Representative from the state of New Jersey and the chairman of the House Public Works and Transportation Committee.

First, there are industry PAC contributions to Congressman Howard's compaigns. In the past five elections, those totaled $15,250—enough to get any congressman's attention, if not win his sympathies.

But the industry's PACs are tiny, and their contributions to

Congressman Howard were supplemented—indeed, far over-shadowed—by gifts from *individuals* connected with the industry, principally company executives and employees and, on occasion, their wives.

The billboard industry, being small and unusually close-knit, is peculiarly well positioned to orchestrate contributions from company executives. Acting as a role model for others has been Vernon Clark, now a consulting lobbyist but for years the president of the Outdoor Advertising Association of America (OAAA), the umbrella trade association for most billboard concerns, and the industry's chief lobbyist in Washington. Clark and his wife Elaine are extraordinarily generous political givers. In the 1986 congressional elections, they contributed a total of $45,800 to candidates for Congress.

The couple was particularly openhanded with Chairman Howard. In the three previous elections, they had given him a total of $6,150; now, toward his 1986 reelection campaign, they gave him $3,500 more.

Overall, individuals affiliated with the industry supplemented the Clarks' largess with 1985–86 campaign contributions totaling $40,075*—more than six times what industry PACs gave.

In addition to swelling Congressman Howard's campaign coffers, the billboard industry has enlarged his personal bank account with speaking fees, and has treated Howard and his wife to all-expenses-paid, fun-in-the-sun vacations. For openers, the industry regularly pays Howard's (and often his wife's) way to the yearly Outdoor Advertising Association conventions. These meetings take place in sunny Palm Springs, California, each January, when the weather in Washington, D.C., is at its most frigid. According to Sheila Kaplan, writing in *Common Cause Magazine*, billboard interests picked up the tab for four years running for Congressman and Mrs. Howard to attend the OAAA festivities. In 1985, the Howards were OAAA's guests for six nights. In that time, Congressman Howard was able not only to soak up a California tan, but to pick up $4,000 in speaking fees—$2,000 from individual billboard com-

---

* This figure is conservative in that it represents contributions only from those individuals I have been able to identify as definitely associated with the billboard industry. That leaves out (a) some individuals who failed to list their occupation or affiliation and (b) some whose connection with the industry was not self-evident (e.g., lawyers who represented billboard companies).

panies, and $2,000 from the Tobacco Institute, which always meshes its annual meetings with those of the OAAA. (The tobacco industry, of course, is a leading user of billboards.)

These visits had two-way benefits: for the Howards, they meant several days in the California sunshine. For the billboard industry, they afforded several days for billboard executives to make their names and faces known to the chairman and to share with him the problems of the outdoor-sign industry in a relaxed and friendly atmosphere impossible to duplicate in Washington.

The industry was also adroit enough to extend its Palm Springs hospitality to key congressional staff aides, who often play a pivotal role in shaping not only legislation but their bosses' views as well. According to the *National Journal*, at least fifteen Senate and House aides participated in the OAAA Palm Springs festivities in January 1986. The *Journal* reported that "the aides were offered an honorarium—in some cases $1,000—air travel and a hotel room for several nights; the association paid the air fare for at least one participant's wife." Among the staff members attending the OAAA convention: Kevin Gottlieb, then executive assistant to Michigan Senator Donald W. Riegle (Gottlieb now heads the Washington lobbying office of the OAAA); Roy F. Greenaway, administrative assistant to California's Alan Cranston; and David M. Strauss, administrative assistant to North Dakota Senator Quentin Burdick. All three senators are Democrats. A year later, when the roll was called in the Senate on a billboard-reform proposal, all three of those senators, who are ordinarily environmentally minded, sided with the industry and against the strongly expressed views of the most activist environmental groups.

The *National Journal* adds that these invitations to congressional staffers to conferences at vacation spots is a regular practice of the billboard industry. The *Journal* quoted one Senate aide who has attended other conferences held by the outdoor advertisers "in locales such as Orlando and Lake Tahoe, Nevada. 'It happens all the time to get invitations for events like this,' [the aide] said. 'That's the way the system works.' "

For the OAAA, the system works extraordinarily well, judging from the group's remarkable success, in 1982, in getting Chairman Howard to propose, and the entire Public Works Committee of the U.S. House of Representatives to approve, a sweeping change in the billboard law. The OAAA's case could hardly have been harmed by the $20,500 in honoraria to members of the committee during the prior four years.

The committee's action was exceptional in that the wording in the billboard provision adopted by voice vote and without debate was virtually identical to that proposed by the industry, even down to the definition of "free coffee" in a provision exempting signs offering "free coffee" to travelers by nonprofit groups.

While the provision did not survive, *Washington Post* reporter Howard Kurtz termed the phenomenon of "a bill passing through the Congressional maze almost exactly as it was written by an industry group" a "lobbyist's dream."

In 1986, for one fleeting moment, the billboard lobby's grip on Congress appeared in jeopardy. Under the leadership of Vermont Republican Senator Robert T. Stafford, a veteran in the billboard-reform fight, the Senate Public Works Committee passed a reform proposal by a surprising 11–4 margin. But the highway bill, of which the billboard reform was a part, never passed the full Congress.

When Congress returned to the subject in January 1987, the Senate had shifted to Democratic control. Stafford's chairmanship of Senate Public Works had been assumed by North Dakota's Quentin Burdick, a long-time ally of the billboard industry. But the committee had three newly elected Democratic senators who all had sufficiently good records on environmental issues to receive the endorsements, in their 1986 Senate races, of both the Sierra Club and the League of Conservation Voters, an environmental activist group with its own PAC. The three were Robert Graham, former governor of Florida, and former Democratic Representatives Harry Reid of Nevada and Barbara Mikulski of Maryland.

Billboard reformers had hopes of their support when the reform measure came up again. But when the committee roll was called on January 21, all three sided with the billboard lobby. The 11–4 vote of 1986 had evaporated. The new reform proposal lost—by an 8–8 tie vote. If any of the three had voted for the reform, it would have cleared the committee.

Senator Graham's staff members are said to be at a loss to explain why their boss voted with the billboard industry that day. Thirteen days later, after his vote stirred up an angry tempest in his home state of Florida, he reversed his stance in the full Senate.

The other two new committee members, Senators Mikulski and Reid, were beneficiaries of another technique by which the tiny billboard industry magnifies its influence: underwriting fundraising parties for candidates. That technique assures that, in the mind of the beneficiary, the industry gets credit for the entire amount raised at the industry-hosted party, rather than for a mere thousand dollars or two.

For example, on February 10, 1986, the OAAA PAC paid $1,545 to B&B Caterers to cater a Washington fundraising party for Maryland senatorial candidate Barbara Mikulski. While Mikulski's campaign reports don't show precisely how much that particular function raised and her office declines to discuss the matter, fundraising experts guess that the take was in the thousands of dollars.

In the case of Nevada's new Senator Reid, on October 2, 1986, the OAAA laid out $552.94 to the Pisces Club in Washington's fashionable Georgetown, as an "in-kind contribution" to Reid's senatorial campaign—presumably to pay part of the expenses of a fundraising party for Reid.

On February 3, 1987, during debate on the highway bill, Senator Stafford brought up his reform proposal for a vote by the full Senate. While the reform's fate was uncertain, there was one person whose vote the Stafford forces felt sure they could count on: Brock Adams, the newly elected Democratic senator from Washington State. There were three reasons to believe Adams would vote with Senator Stafford: his is an environmentally conscious state; his predecessor, Slade Gorton, had been a reform leader; and, most of all, in 1978, as Secretary of Transportation in the Carter administration, Adams had, in writing, vigorously supported the core of the Stafford proposal.

But in 1987, when his name was called, Adams cast his vote against the Stafford reform.

Federal Election Commission records show that in Adams's 1986 senatorial campaign, the billboard industry favored him with $12,200 in contributions, principally from billboard executives, owners, and other persons connected with the outdoor-sign industry.

For its size, the billboard industry undoubtedly lavishes more money on members of Congress in the way of speaking fees and honoraria than any other industry group. In 1985, for example, the total honoraria paid to members of Congress by this comparative runt of an industry ranked third, surpassed by only two others: the defense contractors (annual sales to the government alone: $163 billion) and the tobacco industry (annual sales: nearly $34 billion)—compared with the $1.2 billion for the billboard industry.

A 1979 fundraising appeal by Roadside Business Association, a trade association of highway advertisers, explains why. The RBA entreated its members to contribute to a special fund to pay speaking fees because, said the letter, the honorarium "approach" is more effective than a campaign contribution in bringing "the member [of Congress] closer and more personal [*sic*] to all RBA members." The appeal concluded, "This is the end of the pitch! You all know how the game is played in Washington. Need I say more?"

Edward McMahon, a former Georgetown University law professor and now director of the newly formed Coalition for Scenic Beauty, is not surprised by the success of the billboard industry in manipulating Congress and thwarting federal regulation. These achievements, McMahon says, grow out of decades of practice in fighting billboard controls at the municipal level. McMahon feels the industry's skill has a simple explanation. He regards billboards as polluters of the scenic environment. But, he says, the billboard industry is different from other polluters, such as chemicals or steel. In those industries, McMahon observes, the pollution is the *by-product* of making something society wants or needs (chemicals, say, or steel). But in the case of billboards, the pollution *is* the product, and to regulate it is, in the industry's view, to threaten the very lifeblood of the industry.

Therefore, he concludes, the industry trains its personnel to think of thwarting (McMahon calls it "subverting") public regulatory efforts as an *integral* part of their jobs.

To illustrate his point, McMahon displays the syllabus for a "Corporate Development Seminar" conducted in June 1982 by the Naegele Outdoor Advertising Company, the nation's sixth-largest billboard company. "Ordinarily," McMahon says, "you'd expect a 'corporate development' seminar to be devoted to sales and marketing. But almost none of this agenda has to do with that. Almost the entire program is devoted to 'strategy' in blocking local billboard ordinances."

Look at these items in the "Job Description—Corporate Development Department": "1. Amending Ordinances . . . Political Contributions . . . know Local Politicians."

And here is an entire section on offering "public-service" billboads to promote the mayor's favorite charity. See how it carefully notes that "The Mayor (being a politician) will recognize the value of being able to get credit for favors to various civic-minded persons, [who are] generally the same persons that vote and that are active at election time."

As an example of the selective use of these "public-service" billboards, McMahon cites a giant sign placed in West Des Moines by the Naegele company while it was locked in a court fight with the city over a billboard ordinance. The sign carried the legend, "A Shriner never stands so tall as when he stoops to help a crippled child." The city's attorney, in a letter to the City Council, questioned whether it was "accidental" that the judge deciding the Naegele billboard case "is both a Shriner and a resident of West Des Moines."

THE SELLERS OF INFLUENCE

4

On May 11, 1976, a disciplinary action was brought against Justice Frank Vaccaro of the New York Supreme Court for alleged acts of judicial misconduct committed when Vaccaro was a lower-court judge—namely:

- *staying, with his wife, at a hotel for a weekend as the guest of a friend's law firm.*
- *presiding in a handful of cases (out of thousands he heard) involving a law partner of his own law clerk.*
- *presiding over a small-claims case in which his long-time friend was defendant. The amount at issue: $106.81.*

Other than the value of that hotel room, no one had given the judge so much as a dollar. Moreover, the judges ruling on his case were at pains to point out that there was no evidence that any injustice had occurred or that he had given anyone preferred treatment.

Nonetheless, they said, Justice Vaccaro's behavior did technically *violate the canons of judicial ethics and did "convey the* impression *of impropriety" (emphasis added). Their sentence:* Six months suspension, without pay.

As the Vaccaro case makes clear, because the public expects judges' decisions to be based as much as possible on merit, it is unthinkable for a judge to accept money (or the slightest of favors) from a defendant or a plaintiff—or *anyone* with a stake in that judge's decisions.

It is *not* unthinkable, though, for senators and representatives to do just that. They routinely accept campaign contributions and other favors from interest groups that have hundreds of millions of dollars—sometimes even *billions*—riding on their decisions.

And no one blinks an eye.

William L. Dickinson and Fernand St Germain sit, in effect, as judges. Indeed, they possess powers far greater than any judge— the power to impose immense burdens on, or grant colossal favors to, parties who appear before them.

St Germain, a Democratic representative from Rhode Island, is chairman (in effect, chief judge) of the House Banking Committee. That committee wields enormous powers over commercial banks, savings banks, credit unions, and other financial institutions.

The public has a right to expect Congressman St Germain's decisions, like Judge Vaccaro's, to be based as much as possible on merit—in any event untainted by considerations of money or gifts. Yet from 1979 through 1986, St Germain took $316,540 in campaign contributions from financial institutions subject to his committee's jurisdiction.

Alabama's Dickinson is the highest-ranking Republican on the House Armed Services Committee—a principal judge, in effect, over matters of multi-billion-dollar importance to the nation's defense contractors.

Since 1979, Representative Dickinson has accepted $268,100 in campaign contributions from defense contractors with enormous stakes in his decisions as a chief judge over their fates.

Both St Germain and Dickinson not only vote on matters critically affecting their benefactors, but, as senior members of their respective panels, play leading roles in shaping their committees' decisions.

Neither St Germain nor Dickinson has ever been suspended— not even for one day.

Dickinson and St Germain are typical. All but a handful of congressmen gratefully accept campaign money from groups over whom they sit, in effect, as judges.

For the few representatives who come from closely contested districts and win or lose by narrow margins, accepting campaign contributions from parties affected by their congressional votes is at least understandable. For them, eking out every last dollar can be a matter of political life or death.

But most representatives are safely ensconced in their congressional seats. An example is Ronnie G. Flippo, a Democrat from Florence, Alabama, who represents the state's Fifth Congressional District.

Representative Flippo has become a PAC favorite. Between 1978 and 1986, his PAC receipts rose nearly ninefold, from $33,000 to $287,000.

This dramatic rise was not prompted by his need for campaign money. On the contrary: in the last five elections, Congressman Flippo has not faced serious opposition in any primary contest, and has received, on average, nearly 90 percent of the vote in the general elections.

Why would the PACs heap money on such an invincible congressman? Was it out of interest in the welfare of the people of the Fifth District of Alabama? No; the PACs' generosity was, more probably, wholly unrelated to Alabama, but very much related to Congressman Flippo's powerful seat on House Ways and Means, and, in particular, to the fact that the committee would consider, in 1985 and 1986, a sweeping tax-loophole-closing program proposed by the Reagan administration.

Since Congressman Flippo constantly wins reelection without having to spend much money, the question arises: What happens to all the money the PACs contribute? Answer: It builds up into a huge surplus. Here is the way Congressman Flippo's campaign-fund bank balance has grown at the end of each successive election since 1978:

1978	$ 35,315
1980	$126,279
1982	$139,348
1984	$338,016
1986	$603,947

Representative Flippo has several options for that $604,000. One is *to transfer the entire amount to his own bank account when he leaves Congress.* Flippo enjoys that remarkable privilege because that's how the law was originally written. Only in 1979 was it amended to prohibit the lawmakers from enriching themselves from their campaign chests—but the amendment governed only those members of the House who came to office after January 8, 1980. Happily for himself, Congressman Flippo was first elected in 1976, and thus qualifies for the privilege.

Thus, when an interest group makes a politically unnecessary campaign contribution to a lawmaker like Congressman Flippo, the money serves two purposes. It buys the legislator's sympathetic attention and, potentially at least, it serves as the congressman's personal pension fund.

While no retiring representatives have thus far helped themselves to the whole amount of their campaign surplus, several have transferred substantial sums. According to a Common Cause study, fifteen representatives transferred a total of more than $360,000 to their own bank accounts when they retired in 1981 and 1983. Topping the list: South Carolina Democrat Ken Holland, who conveyed nearly $75,000 to his personal use.*

These large cash balances are an explosively growing phenomenon in the House. At the end of the 1986 elections, congressional campaign surpluses totaled $59 million, a 33 percent rise in just two years. In 1976, only three representatives had leftover funds greater than $100,000. A decade later, 40 percent did. The election-by-election figures are as follows:

ELECTION CYCLE ENDING	NUMBER OF REPRESENTATIVES WITH CAMPAIGN SURPLUSES OVER $100,000
1976	3
1978	6
1980	24
1982	59
1984	120
1986	174

In addition to serving as a retirement fund for lawmakers, campaign surpluses can fulfill a second appealing purpose: the cash balances can scare off would-be challengers.

---

* Some congressmen tap their campaign coffers for private purposes while still in office. Louisiana Democratic Congressman Jerry Huckaby's campaign treasury spent $2,150 to buy the congressman a shotgun. Veteran Pennsylvania Republican Congressman Joseph McDade used $1,155 of campaign funds to pay his country-club dues.

In tapping their campaign treasuries, congressmen find House rules elastic in separating the "political" from the private. California Democrat Robert Matsui, for example, charged his campaign $2,007 for a "campaign-related reception," even though it was held in Hawaii, three thousand miles from his Sacramento district. And when Ohio Democrat Louis Stokes tapped his campaign funds for $10,000 to pay his lawyer for defending him against a drunk-driving charge, the House chief counsel approved the expenditure on the ground "you can argue that the congressman's ability to exonerate himself through the legal process is going to be important . . . in his ability to get re-elected."

A few are candid about this use of leftover funds. For example, in 1984, Republican Congressman Henson Moore of Louisiana was challenged about $467,000 he had left over in his campaign treasury. In response, he complained that this amount was not too high, but too low—too low, that is, to discourage opposition. It is well known, he said, that a contested House campaign costs $600,000.*

Incumbent senators, too, sometimes end their campaigns with mammoth surpluses, especially when, having exploited their incumbency to raise huge sums, they coast through to victory against a weak opponent. For example, Republican Senator Bob Dole of Kansas ended his 1986 senatorial campaign with $2,166,732 in his campaign treasury, tops among senators elected that year. Second highest was Democrat John Glenn of Ohio, with $818,910. Both won easily over feeble opposition.

These vast sums earn interest, of course, so that even if Senator Dole doesn't raise another dime during his newest six-year Senate term, in 1992, when he faces reelection (if his presidential ambitions are frustrated), his $2,166,000 will have grown to about $3,200,000, assuming a 7 percent return compounded semiannually. Few prospective opponents will relish taking on an incumbent senator with $3 million in the bank. But the sum is bound to be larger than that. In 1987, five years before his next Senate election, the farsighted Dole set up a 1992 Senate reelection fund.

Even when senators don't end their campaigns with large surpluses, they can exploit the power of their incumbency over the course of their six-year term to build up a forbidding campaign treasury.

A dramatic example is freshman New York Republican Senator Alfonse D'Amato. D'Amato never stopped shaking the money tree. By the end of 1981, the very first year after his surprise election to the Senate, his campaign bank balance approached a quarter of a million dollars. With unceasing fundraising effort, the coffers grew

---

* Ironically, Congressman Moore may have been hoist with his own petard. In 1984, he is said to have been dissuaded from making a U.S. Senate race against the incumbent, Democratic Senator Bennett Johnston, in part because of the early war chest Johnston had amassed.

Two years later, though, Moore demonstrated another prime utility of a campaign surplus accumulated primarily by virtue of his incumbency. He used the $726,000 in his House campaign treasury at the end of 1984 as a springboard for his own unsuccessful Senate campaign to fill the seat left vacant by the retirement of Senator Russell B. Long.

steadily. At each year's end, his campaign bank balances stood as follows:

1982	$ 430,574
1983	$1,383,418
1984	$2,037,486
1985	$4,190,268

On January 1 of an election year, many senators—and virtually all challengers—have not even begun to raise serious money. But here was Alfonse D'Amato, entering *his* election year sitting on a balance of more than $4 million!

"Without his pockets" (as used to be said about J. P. Morgan), D'Amato was not a formidable candidate—judging by the conventional political racing forms, at least. He was a first-term Republican senator in a nominally Democratic state (registered Democrats outnumber Republicans by three to two). In 1980, he had won a slender victory only because of a freak three-way race.

But with $4 million-plus in his campaign treasury, Alfonse D'Amato appeared formidable. As 1986 rolled on, two prominent Democratic candidates stepped up to the hurdle of a Senate race, only to balk at the last minute. The logical candidate was former Congresswoman Elizabeth Holtzman, who had come within 81,000 votes of defeating D'Amato six years earlier. She, too, backed away, citing D'Amato's large war chest as a major reason.

Finally, late in the game, two relatively unknown Democrats entered the race. There was John Dyson, a multimillionaire who spent $6 million—most of it his own money—in his primary race. He was opposed—and narrowly defeated—by former Nader-raider activist Mark Green. Green was the only Senate candidate in the United States to forswear PAC gifts. Hence he had to run both his primary and general-election campaigns on a shoestring and was outspent heavily in both contests. D'Amato won handily in November.

Alfonse D'Amato vividly illustrates a growing phenomenon that has lobbyists and interest-group givers grumbling: incumbents' use of their power to demand (some say extort) contributions from those who want their help.

For example, from 1981 to 1986, while the Republicans controlled the Senate, D'Amato occupied a strategic position as chairman of the Senate Banking Subcommittee on Securities. As such, he was the key player shaping legislation of vital concern to the stocks-and-bonds industry. During his first five and a half years in office, at his encouragement, PACs and executives of seventeen Wall Street firms contributed half a million dollars to his reelection campaign. The *Wall Street Journal* reported that Senator D'Amato was not "bashful about asking for donations." According to the *Journal,* the forcefulness of the D'Amato fundraising tactics in the securities industry produced grumblings on Wall Street. "Nothing is enough," said one top Wall Street lobbyist. "It's continuous pressure. If you don't contribute, they don't return your calls."

That is a complaint heard with increasing frequency in the Washington lobbying community. One of the leading champions of the PACs, Richard Armstrong, who heads the Public Affairs Council (a group of Washington corporate public-affairs officers), has publicly charged lawmakers with "extortion." Congressmen and senators, he says, "are very heavy-handed."

Heavy-handed is a precise way of describing the tactics employed by South Dakota's Republican Senator James Abdnor in hitting up Washington lobbyists and PAC managers to buy $1,500 tickets to a fundraising dinner at which President Reagan was to be the star attraction. Abdnor sent the invitation around by messenger, with a reply card giving the invitee three choices: to make a $5,000 PAC contribution; to buy one or more tickets; or to say "No, our PAC does not wish to support the Salute to Jim Abdnor featuring President Reagan." What angered many PAC managers was Abdnor's instruction to the messenger not to leave the invitee's office without a response of some kind.

One lobbyist (who asked not to be identified) tells of a congressman chastising him and his confreres for failing to come through with campaign contributions when he had done them "a favor" earlier. He told the group that this time, they would have to produce the support *in advance* if they expected his help on a key vote coming up.

Another lobbyist (who also requested anonymity) reports requesting an appointment with a U.S. senator from one of the senator's junior aides. The lobbyist was referred upward to the senator's administrative assistant, who consulted a list of campaign contributors. "We've only got you down for $500," he said. "That's not enough."

Yet another lawyer-lobbyist recounts that when he and his part-

ners declined an invitation to an "expensive" fundraiser for a senator to whom they had already contributed generously, the lobbyist
was soon favored with a personal call from the senator himself,
reminding the lobbyist how his door had always been open to the
lobbyist, and how receptive he had always been to the lobbyist's
requests. "The terrible thing," this lobbyist told me, "was that even
though my partners and I had given as much as we thought we
should, we still gave more. After a 'hint' like that senator gave us,
what could we do?"

Sometimes a member of Congress openly acknowledges the
price tag for obtaining a personal audience. One such is Wisconsin
Democratic Congressman Les Aspin, the controversial Democrat
who in 1985 leaped over several seniority hurdles to be elevated
unexpectedly to the chairmanship of the potent House Armed Services Committee. Aspin told a newspaper in his district that the
defense contractors know they must contribute "if they want to talk
to the chairman." Not surprisingly, after Aspin ascended to the
chairmanship, the campaign contributions he received from the
PACs of defense contractors in the first ten *months* were nearly 50
percent above the total for the previous six *years*.

On occasion, the influence-buying game is played without a
word being spoken or an arm twisted. It is just understood that
everyone wants to be on the good side of those who occupy the seats
of the mighty.

In November 1985, for example, after Speaker Tip O'Neill had
announced his intention to retire and Texas Congressman Jim
Wright announced his candidacy to succeed him, Wright held what
he called a "Cowtown Jamboree" in his hometown of Fort Worth.
No serious candidate had yet emerged to oppose Wright for the
speakership, and the turnout at the jamboree was enormous.
Wright said later that the "overwhelming bulk" of the $1.3 million
he raised that year, nearly half of it from PACs, was raised at that
single event.

On its face, the success of the jamboree had one curious aspect.
Congressman Wright had, only a year earlier, won reelection without opposition.

Why, then, did he need the million dollars? Answer: He planned
to put part of it into a PAC of his own, from which he would dispense financial aid to the reelection campaigns of Democratic colleagues who would choose the next speaker. In the 1986 elections,

Wright's PAC handed out $392,000 to 141 Democratic members. Let would-be challengers for the speakership trump *that* card.

Thus, in part, does Congress choose the person two heartbeats away from the presidency.

At a lesser level, some representatives have found it helpful to form and use their own personal PACs in order to win a subcommittee chairmanship.

Case in point: a PAC bearing the intriguing name of the "24th Congressional District of California PAC." What in the world is *that* PAC? Who are its beneficiaries—and on what basis does it select them?

As the *Almanac of Federal PACs* gently puts it, the 24th District PAC makes its gifts "in consultation with" Representative Henry Waxman, a Democrat who represents California's 24th District in the U.S. House. Since Congressman Waxman consistently wins reelection by two-to-one margins, he can afford to devote his fundraising powers to the cause of his PAC. He then donates the proceeds to the campaigns of certain select colleagues. The *PAC Almanac* notes that some $24,000 of Waxman's PAC money was channeled to Democratic members of the House Energy Committee (on which Congressman Waxman sits), whose votes determine the chairmanship of the committee and its subcommittees. And that, the *Almanac* continues, "may have played a role in Waxman's 1979 [upset] election as chairman of the committee's Health and Environment Subcommittee . . . over a more senior panel member," former Democratic Congressman Richardson Preyer of North Carolina.

Even the most reform-minded lawmakers succumb to the temptation to form a so-called "leadership" PAC of their own as a means of expanding their power within the Congress.

Consider the example of Illinois Democrat Paul Simon, elected to the Senate in November 1984, after a campaign that required raising $4.6 million. Although he detests the PAC system, he felt he had no choice but to accept $908,000 from special-interest PACs. Moreover, although his trademark as a congressman had been in-person communication with his constituents, as a Senate candidate he had found himself obliged to take precious days from campaigning in Illinois and spend them on fundraising forays to New York, California, and Texas in search of contributions from the rich. After the campaign, he said of the crushing and incessant fundraising burden he had just felt obliged to bear: "I hated every minute of it!"

Obliged to bear. In the context of a multi-million-dollar Senate campaign (Simon's opponent, Republican Senator Charles Percy, spent $5.3 million), that word seems appropriate. Simon's acceptance of $908,000 from special-interest political action committees can be looked upon as an involuntary act, and once in office, he lost no time in introducing legislation to provide full public funding of Senate general elections, as a means of offering candidates such as himself an alternative to the experience he had so hated.

But with another six years before his next senatorial race, one would think he would welcome a respite from the constant preoccupation with money.

Yet in early 1985, just a few months after his expensive election campaign, Paul Simon formed his own PAC, the Democracy Fund. He did it, he said, "to have a liberal influence in upcoming House and Senate elections—to be a player." Yet the formation of his own PAC would keep Paul Simon on the fundraising treadmill.

And that was a *voluntary* act on his part.★

At the opposite end of the political-security spectrum from the Wrights and the Waxmans are those first-term congressmen and senators who have personally loaned their campaigns large sums and mortgaged their families' futures to finance their costly campaigns. Those lawmakers are peculiarly vulnerable to offers of interest-group contributions that will reduce their personal debt.

For example, in his successful 1982 campaign to unseat Republican Senator Harrison Schmitt in New Mexico, the Democratic challenger—Jeff Bingaman, an attractive young liberal with independent means—personally loaned over $790,000 to his campaign.

During the election campaign, the American Medical Association's PAC (AMPAC) contributed $7,500 to Senator Schmitt. But Bingaman defeated Schmitt, and on December 29, 1982—after the votes had been counted and it was too late to affect the outcome of the election—AMPAC made a $10,000 contribution to Bingaman, the very man it had tried to defeat.

★ On December 31, 1986, after the Democrats regained control of the Senate, Simon's PAC ceased raising and dispensing money because, a spokesman said, "The PAC had served its purpose."

Later, when Citizens Against PACs, a citizens' group cochaired by the author of this book, questioned Bingaman's acceptance of the AMA's post-election switch-gift, Bingaman was stung. He insisted that the AMA's gift would not sway his votes in Congress, which would be dictated by the best interests of all the people of his state.

The citizens' group suggested that there was a convincing way of dispelling all questions on that score: to return the AMA's contribution.

Senator Bingaman's reply: *"I can't afford to."*

According to figures reported to the Federal Election Commission, in the 1986 elections, North Carolina's new Democratic senator, Terry Sanford, loaned his campaign just over a million dollars. Alabama's Richard Shelby and Washington State's Brock Adams, both Democrats, made personal loans to their campaigns of $210,000 and $100,000 respectively.

In addition, at least nine newcomers to the House loaned their campaigns more than $100,000. These included:

- Democrat James A. Hayes, Louisiana: $464,126.
- Democrat Joseph P. Kennedy II, Massachusetts: $250,000
- Democrat Elizabeth Patterson, South Carolina: $237,753
- Republican Ernest Konnyu, California: $170,000
- Republican Fred Grandy, Iowa: $166,970

To list these new senators and representatives is not to disparage them. If anything, it is to question an electoral system that can put so heavy a price tag on candidacy and election, thus making even the most high-minded of candidates prey to offers of campaign contributions from special-interest groups.

Political-science courses traditionally teach that members of Congress choose their committee assignments according to what committees will best serve their constituents (e.g., a farm-state senator will opt for an agriculture committee) or will win them prestigious headlines or speaking engagements (foreign affairs or armed services).

The advent of the PACs has introduced an important new factor: the likelihood of attracting campaign contributions from affected interest groups. Today, lawmakers are likely to clamor for membership on committees that are magnets for PAC dollars, even though that choice promises no headlines and is wholly unrelated to their constituents' needs.

Veteran Democratic Congressman Robert Kastenmeier of Wisconsin, for example, remembers a time when representatives had to be virtually dragooned into serving on the Civil Liberties, Courts, and Administration of Justice Subcommittee of House Judiciary. Then one year, Kastenmeier noted a curious change: members were inexplicably eager to serve on that subcommittee. Had there been a sudden, renewed interest in civil liberties? he wondered. On reflection, he noted a much more practical reason for the change. The subcommittee had jurisdiction over so-called intellectual property —patents and copyrights and the like—and suddenly two lucrative battles had cropped up in that area of the law. One was the desire of the pharmaceutical industry to prolong drug patent protection, supposedly to make up for the lengthy Food and Drug Administration trial-and-approval period for new drugs. The second was a fierce, high-stakes battle between the motion-picture and video-recorder industries about the right to record movies on home television sets. On both issues the stakes were high and the parties well financed and politically sophisticated—the perfect recipe for producing PAC money.

So conscious are lawmakers of the money factor that some committees have come to be known as "PAC heavens"—such as the banking and energy committees, which supervise well-heeled and savvy banking, oil, and chemicals industries. But the committees that write the tax laws (House Ways and Means and Senate Finance) stand indisputably at the apex of the PAC heavens. California Democrat Robert Matsui has observed that being on Ways and Means (as he is) means the difference between taking in $70,000 and a mere $25,000 at a Washington fundraiser.

The sudden PAC popularity of a new member of Ways and Means can be truly dramatic. Former Democratic Representative Kent Hance of Texas quadrupled his PAC intake (from $32,000 to $142,000) in the election after he joined the committee. Similarly, PAC gifts to Arkansas Democratic Congressman Beryl Anthony jumped from $28,000 to $165,000 after he won a prized Ways and Means seat.

Such is the power of a seat on Ways and Means that it enabled an obscure New Jersey Democratic congressman named Frank J.

Guarini to conduct what might be termed a poor-man's Lloyd Bentsen breakfast series. As we saw, Senate Finance Committee Chairman Bentsen charged lobbyists $10,000 a ticket—before embarrassing headlines caused him to cancel his breakfast meetings. Guarini was only able to command a mere $1,000.

Congressman Guarini is not among Congress's Hundred Neediest Cases, either in campaign funds or in votes. In 1982, for example, he raised and spent about $170,000 and won three to one. Nonetheless, he apparently felt he wasn't raising enough money. In particular, he wasn't raising enough from PACs. In 1984, the figure went up to $237,000.

So, according to an account by the enterprising *Los Angeles Times* reporter Paul Houston, Mr. Guarini decided to initiate a series of small, quiet breakfasts, to which he would invite select groups' lobbyists, one industry at a time. His reasoning: the intimate settings would appeal to lobbyists because "you can discuss in depth the issues pertinent to a particular industry instead of mixing ten different issues" at a larger meeting. For example, at one breakfast, twenty-seven lobbyists from the insurance industry paid $1,000 each to eat scrambled eggs, sausages, and kiwi fruit with Congressman Guarini. Presumably the $1,000 not only gained them admission to the breakfast, but improved their chances of getting Congressman Guarini's attention should the need arise in the future. If that breakfast served to increase even in the smallest degree Congressman Guarini's sympathy for the multi-billion-dollar tax preferences the insurance industry enjoys, the $1,000 price of admission was cheap indeed.

As noted earlier, another member of House Ways and Means, Congressman Flippo from Alabama, has needed no breakfasts to attract PAC funds.

It is difficult to see how many of the PAC contributions to Congressman Flippo's campaigns were prompted by an interest in the welfare of his Alabama district. The twenty-six closely printed pages listing the PAC contributions to Congressman Flippo's 1986 campaign raise question after question.

- How many members does the National Venture Capital Association of Washington, D.C., have in Congressman Flippo's district? And, if the answer is none or almost none, what would lead that association to give $6,000 to Flippo's 1986 election?

- Why would five giant New York banks (Citicorp, Chemical, Chase Manhattan, Manufacturers Hanover, and Morgan) give a total of $5,500 to a small-town congressman from Alabama whose reelection is a foregone conclusion? Why, for that matter, should the American Bankers Association and other financial groups and institutions around the country contribute nearly $20,000?

  To that question there is a plausible answer. On October 15, 1985, Congressman Flippo proposed that the Ways and Means Committee vote to enlarge a long-standing tax loophole that the Reagan administration had suggested closing entirely. The Flippo amendment, which passed that day by a vote of 17 to 14 but was later killed, would have meant $7.6 *billion* in tax benefits to the banking industry. If Representative Flippo had had his way, that would have meant $7.6 billion that the rest of the taxpayers—including those in his district—would have had to make up for in one way or another.

- What connection do the Chicago Board of Trade and the Chicago Mercantile Exchange have with Alabama's Fifth District that would prompt each of those groups to contribute $1,000 to Representative Flippo's 1986 campaign? (Coincidentally, traders on both those Chicago commodity exchanges had tax problems that would give them a natural interest in a member of the Ways and Means Committee; see Chapter 8.)

- Why, although not a granule of beet or cane sugar is grown in Flippo's district, would two national sugar associations each contribute $1,500 to his campaign? Was it to ensure his continued support of a sugar subsidy that obliges American consumers— including the 151,000 families in his district—to pay more for sugar than if that price were governed by the free market? (For more on the operation of this sugar subsidy, see Chapter 7.)

- The following national groups made sizable 1986 contributions: the American Medical Association ($10,000), the American Dental Association ($4,000), the American Academy of Ophthalmology ($1,000), and the American Podiatry Association ($500). What, if anything, did they expect from Congressman Flippo? Is the legislation they favor in the best interests of the people of the Fifth District of Alabama? (As recounted in Chapter 7, the defeat of a hospital cost-containment bill proposed by President Carter cost American consumers approximately $10 billion a year.)

• Others that contributed were: the American Yarn Spinners Association of Gastonia, North Carolina, and the American Horse Council's Committee on Legislation and Taxation of Washington, D.C. (which calls itself COLT, and was interested in preserving the tax preferences long enjoyed by horse owners). Then there were the following law firms, each of which maintains a Washington office, with registered lobbyists: Dow, Lohnes & Albertson, of Washington ($3,000); Vinson & Elkins, of Houston ($1,500); Akin, Gump, Strauss, Hauer & Feld, of Dallas ($1,000); and Jones, Day, Reavis & Pogue, of Cleveland ($500). And let's not overlook the National Beer Wholesalers Association ($2,000) and the National Wine and Spirit Wholesalers ($2,000).

The voters of the Fifth District of Alabama have good reason to ask: From whom does their representative get his campaign money? To whom is he indebted? Whom does he really represent? The people of his district—or outsiders?

For Ronnie Flippo, the answers, for the 1986 election, are:

• Nearly two-thirds (65.5 percent) of his money came from outside special-interest PACs.
• An added 10.4 percent came from individual contributors who reside outside his district. Over half of that money came from people who do not even live in Alabama.

Thus, in 1986, more than three-fourths of Congressman Flippo's campaign funds came from groups or people who don't live, vote, or pay taxes in his district—people who are not even *permitted* to vote for him.

Some observers do not find that fact unduly disturbing because, they contend, Congress is a *national* legislature. Representatives and senators have a broader responsibility than representing their constituents, these observers argue, and if lawmakers base their votes in Congress solely on the parochial interests of their own districts or states, the national interest suffers.

Congress is, indisputably, a national legislature. But is that fact relevant to the PAC money on which lawmakers are increasingly dependent? Are most political action committees really concerned with the *national* interest, or with the interests of their particular group? The bankers' and trial lawyers' PACs exist first and foremost to promote the interests of bankers and trial lawyers. That's why their members contribute to the PAC. So to the extent that that is true, lawmakers' dependence on PAC money detracts from, rather than adds to, Congress's role as a truly national legislature.

In that same vein, many members of Congress object strenuously to characterizing PACs as "outside" special-interest groups. They argue that the PAC of a company that has a local plant, or of a union with members in their district, cannot fairly be called an outside group.

I contend that with the two exceptions given below, all PACs headquartered outside a given candidate's district—even those with some connection inside the district—can and should be characterized as "outside" interest groups. In fairly separating outside from local, the important questions are: Who decides which candidates get how much of a PAC's money? *Where* is that decision made? And on what basis?

To illustrate: the American Bankers Association and the Association of Trial Lawyers each gave about $5,000 to Congressman Flippo's campaign. Of course there are some bankers and trial lawyers in Mr. Flippo's district. Members of each group within his district may well have contributed to their respective PACs. But the bankers' and the trial lawyers' PACs are headquartered in Washington, D.C. It was the respective PAC managers *there*, and not in Alabama, who allocated $5,000 to Congressman Flippo. What's more, they did so on the basis of their groups' *national* agendas, not with the problems of the Fifth District of Alabama primarily in mind.

Given those circumstances, I believe it is fair to call those PACs' contributions outside money, rather than local.

For purposes of a PAC contribution to a representative's campaign, I would accept the characterization of a PAC as local, rather than outside, under two circumstances: (1) if the PAC's headquarters are located within the district and the PAC has no substantial interests in other districts, so that the decision as to how much to give the local representative is made primarily or exclusively on the basis of what's good for that district alone; or (2) if the PAC's contribution to the local congressman comes exclusively from PAC members who reside or work in that district, and who have earmarked their contributions to go to that representative. But PACs with those characteristics are the rare exceptions among the more than four thousand extant today.

———

High as was the proportion of Congressman Flippo's 1986 funds coming from outside PACs (65.5 percent), it was far from the highest in the House. Surpassing Flippo by far was California Democrat Augustus Hawkins, who received 92 percent of his funds from PACs. Pennsylvania Democrat William Coyne ranked second, with 91 percent.

In the past decade, more and more members of the House have been falling into deep dependency on outside special-interest PACs. As mentioned in Chapter 2, there were 185 representatives who got at least half their 1986 campaign funds from PACs, and 95 —nearly one-fourth of the House—got at least 60 percent.

YEAR	NUMBER OF HOUSE WINNERS TAKING AT LEAST HALF OF THEIR CAMPAIGN FUNDS FROM PACs
1978	63
1980	85
1982	94
1984	164
1986	185

Moreover, of the fifty representatives who got the highest percentage of their 1986 money from PACs, forty are in "safe" seats— that is, in none of their past five elections have those forty received less than 55 percent of the vote, the customary definition for a "contested" seat.

That raises questions unflattering to both receivers and givers: Why did the PACs give to those unbeatable congressmen? And why did those representatives who are shoo-ins for reelection rely on outside special-interest PACs for such a high proportion of their campaign funds?

The increase in the number of congressmen who depend on PACs for 30 percent or more of their campaign money is even more alarming.

YEAR	PERCENTAGE OF HOUSE WINNERS TAKING MORE THAN 30 PERCENT OF THEIR FUNDS FROM PACs
1974	28%
1978	55%
1982	69%
1986	82%

To me, those statistics say this:

Four-fifths of U.S. representatives are "hooked" on special-interest PAC money—in the sense that they depend on PACs for a third of their campaign funds, and therefore feel they can't survive, politically, without the PACs.

That is, once they come to rely on PACs too much, they, like alcoholics, cannot "take it or leave it"—they've got to have it.

Perhaps most distressing is the universality with which the influence-peddling practices described here—especially the conflicts of interest—have come to be accepted by lawmakers.

For example, Paul Houston reported in the *Los Angeles Times* that, as of August 1984, members of the House Banking Committee had received (and accepted) a total of $57,750 from the American Bankers Association's PAC. In 1983 alone, they had also accepted a total of $18,000 for speaking fees from the ABA, as well as travel and lodging to such vacation spots as Hawaii, site of the ABA's 1983 annual convention. Houston observed, "A decade ago . . . revelations of such payments might have mortified the [banking committee] legislators. Today, the committee's embarrassment of riches seems to embarrass virtually no one."

Appallingly, the "PAC habit" is quickly adopted—by even the most idealistic lawmakers. Take, for example, Bruce Morrison, a liberal Democratic congressman from New Haven. Elected in 1982 by a scant 1,700 votes, the thirty-eight-year-old Morrison came to Washington with the reputation of a reformer. As director of the New Haven Legal Services office, he was motivated to run for Congress in 1981 by President Reagan's effort to halt the entire Legal Services program. According to the political almanac *Politics in America*, the professional "pols" looked on Morrison as an idealistic political novice, and reacted skeptically to his candidacy. But he assembled a devoted organization of social-service workers, community activists, and union members, and won the Democratic nomination over the local Democratic organization's choice. Then, even more surprising, he went on to defeat the popular Republican congressman, Lawrence DeNardis.

As challenger to a sitting Republican congressman, Morrison had certainly not been the darling of the PACs. Business PACs, in particular, did not provide a dollar of his 1982 campaign money.

Despite his idealistic beginnings, once in Washington, Morrison quickly adopted the fundraising tactics of the most traditional of congressmen. He won a seat on the House Banking Committee. Suddenly, his prowess at raising compaign contributions from business interests soared. In July 1984, he voted for a measure to erect a legal fence to separate the activities of banks and their nonbank rivals. The *Los Angeles Times* reported that only days later, he was on the phone to some of the bill's beneficiaries (Merrill Lynch and J.C. Penney, for example), urging them to buy a ticket to a New York fundraising party. Some of the invitees considered Morrison's tactics heavy-handed and "gauche," but the phone calls worked. By mid-1984, he had taken in $7,000 from PACs interested in banking bills. By the time of the 1984 election, Morrison's receipts from bank PACs had risen to nearly $21,000.

Didn't the new congressman see anything amiss in his raising campaign funds from groups that had a clear interest in his conduct as a Banking Committee member? His answer—after less than two years in the House: That's "standard practice."

As a result of being an incumbent rather than a challenger and of his willingness to adopt the "standard practice" of fundraising, Morrison's PAC contributions quintupled—from $70,000 (as a 1982 *challenger*) to over $361,000 (as a 1984 *incumbent*). In addition, he raised half a million dollars of non-PAC money.

And so, in a repeat of the 1982 battle, spending more than $900,000, he defeated former Congressman DeNardis by 14,000 votes, and went on, two years later, to win again with 70 percent of the vote.

Whatever else might be said about Morrison's "standard practice," it worked.

Before finding fault with Bruce Morrison rather than with the current system of paying for congressional campaigns, put yourself in Morrison's shoes. With the help of a lot of idealistic people's hard work, you've clawed your way to a seat in Congress. You think it likely that ex-Congressman DeNardis is going to try to win back his seat. You also assume that he will be well bankrolled—from PACs in general and business PACs in particular. (DeNardis did, in fact, spend half a million dollars on his 1984 campaign.)

All around you, you see your colleagues in Congress using the power of their incumbency to rake in money.

Given those realities, what do you do? You have two choices:

either play the game, or tie your hands by rejecting interest-group money.

The seond choice amounts to unilateral disarmament.

There's another part to your mental calculation. Picture yourself receiving a PAC check for, say, $5,000. There's a fair chance the contribution came in without your asking for it. You sit there, looking at the check, and thinking, "Now how much would it take to raise this amount of money in small gifts? Let's see . . . This check is for $5,000—that's the equivalent of two hundred $25 gifts. Think of the trouble, the work—and the expense—involved in getting two hundred people to give $25! Getting it door-to-door would require ten canvassers five evenings each—and if you had to pay the canvassers $5 an hour, that would double the time it would take to net $5,000. And getting that much from direct-mail solicitations would involve enormous printing and mailing expenses . . .

"Here, on the other hand, is this PAC check for $5,000. It's unsolicited: I didn't have to lift a finger to get it."

The more you look at that check, and the more you think about the alternatives, the sweeter that PAC money looks to you.

Bruce Morrison is by no means unique. There are many members of Congress just like Morrison—champions of the "public interest" movement, who came to Congress through the efforts of environmentalists or peace activists—who become inured to "the system," the "standard practice" of taking PAC money, and lots of it. Either they don't perceive conflicts of interest or the conflicts don't seem to inhibit them much.

Two such are Republican Congresswoman Claudine Schneider of Rhode Island and Democratic Congresswoman Barbara Boxer from Marin County, California. They have virtually identical election histories: each won narrowly the first time she was elected to the House, and since then, has won by increasingly lopsided margins. In 1984, for example, each received 68 percent of the vote—helped along by substantial amounts of PAC money. Two years later, however, despite their two-to-one victories, each accepted large PAC gifts—about $165,000—and each piled up even larger victory margins (72 and 74 percent, respectively), outspending their opponents five to one and twenty-seven to one, respectively.

Why does Barbara Boxer, a lifelong reformer, do that? "I play the game by the rules. I don't have any problem taking PAC money if it's legal. I want a hefty war chest to be ready for a serious challenge." Congresswoman Boxer, who sits on the Armed Services Committee, accepts money from defense contractors, although she refuses money from the top ten firms.

Claudine Schneider actively seeks out the interest groups that are affected by the committees she sits on. For example, she spends time with her fundraising staff thinking of high-tech companies that might be interested in the work she has been doing as a member of the Science and Technology Committee.

And why not? As Bruce Morrison said, it's all "standard practice."

The present system of financing congressional campaigns poses two core problems for idealistic representatives like Bruce Morrison and Claudine Schneider and Barbara Boxer. First, campaigns are expensive and getting more so (and there are no limits on what an opponent can spend). Second, and more important, until and unless Congress enacts public funding of congressional elections (comparable to the presidential system already in the law), public-spirited congressional candidates will have no alternatives for raising the enormous sums required—other than to accept money from special-interest groups.

★ ━━━━━━━━━━━━━━━━━━━━━━━━━━━━━━━
CASE STUDY 1: ROBERT J. DOLE

Senator Robert J. Dole of Kansas has no illusions about what political action committees expect from a candidate when they contribute. He has said it himself: "When these political action committees give money, they expect something in return other than good government."

Yet Dole is undisputed champion in the Senate at raising money from PACs. According to Federal Election Commission statistics, from 1972 to the end of 1986, he received $3,366,305 from special-interest PACs. That was more, by a margin of $760,000, than any other senator.★

The PACs contributed over $1 million toward Dole's 1986 reelec-

---

★ Democratic Senator Alan Cranston of California, second highest, has received $2,606,585 since 1972.

tion campaign. He didn't need the money. Long in advance, that contest was expected to be a charade, since no important challengers came forward.★ In fact, Senator Dole raised so much and spent so little that he emerged with over $2 million left over in his campaign treasury—nearly *three times* as much as any other senator facing reelection that year.

So why, if he didn't need the money, and if he knew that the PACs expected something in return for their money, did Senator Dole raise and accept the PACs' million dollars?

Even more intriguing: in light of what he himself has said about political action committees, why did Dole start a PAC of his own, thereby providing yet another channel for PACs and other influence-seekers to contribute money and expect something from him "other than good government"?

Finally, why did Dole open the door to inferences of improper influence-seeking by establishing a charitable foundation to which large corporations and wealthy people could (and did) make enormous, attention-getting gifts?

This is the story of the multiple channels that Robert J. Dole made available to those doing business with the U.S. government— channels that at the very least created the opportunity for those groups to attract Dole's sympathetic attention. It is also the story of the special favors that Senator Dole reportedly did for some of them.

Robert Dole's money-raising success is entirely expectable. There are many good reasons why people doing business with, or receiving favors from, the U.S. government should want to be on the good side of this particular senator.

For openers, as a senior Republican member of the Agriculture Committee, he can be helpful to farmers and large agribusiness interests.

Second, as *the* senior Republican on the Finance Committee, he can offer crucial assistance to anyone desiring (or hoping to protect) a tax loophole worth hundreds of millions or even billions of dollars.

Most important, since 1985, Dole has been the Republicans'

★ Dole's Democratic senatorial opponent in 1986 was Guy MacDonald, a political unknown who didn't believe in raising or spending large amounts of campaign money (he apparently raised less than $5,000, for he failed to file a report with the Federal Election Commission).

Senate floor leader, and therefore influential across the legislative spectrum.

And then . . . in 1985 and 1986 (the period this chapter examines) there was a real possibility that Robert J. Dole just might be the next president of the United States.

And so it's not surprising that, even though Dole didn't need the money for his reelection campaign, the following interest groups across the economic spectrum gave at least $5,000 toward the election of this shoo-in senator: the American Medical Association, the Associated General Contractors of America, the National Association of Homebuilders, the American Bankers Association, E. F. Hutton, Chrysler, auto dealers selling imported cars—and six PACs from the sugar and sweetener industry, to which, as will be recounted shortly, Senator Dole gave special help. In all, the PACs gave $1 million toward Dole's reelection. But even that was surpassed by gifts from *individuals,* which totaled $1.3 million.

Another way to get Senator Dole's attention is by making contributions to Campaign America, a personal PAC established in 1978 partly to help the campaigns of other Republican candidates for Congress, but more to finance the springboard for Dole's own presidential aspirations. Campaign America had a shaky start, but after Dole became Senate Republican leader, it blossomed. In 1985 and 1986 alone, PACs contributed $500,000 while well-heeled individuals kicked in gifts totaling $2.5 million.

Once again, individual gifts to Campaign America outstripped PAC contributions. Take the commodity industry, for example. In 1983–84, PACs from that industry gave Campaign America $21,000. But individuals connected with the industry contributed $49,500. Their generosity may or may not be related to the fact that in 1984, Senator Dole, in a complete reversal of his previous position, was instrumental in conferring a multi-million-dollar tax blessing on 333 commodity traders. More about that later in this chapter and in Chapter 8.

Some of these individual givers seemed happy to take advantage of the higher ceiling on personal gifts to PACs—$5,000, rather than the $1,000-per-donor-per-election limit on contributions directly to candidates. Among those were Ernest and Julio Gallo, the celebrated California winemakers, whose generosity we have encountered in Chapter 3. Apparently their enthusiasm for Senator Dole was shared by their wives, for, as previously noted, each of the four contributed $5,000 to Campaign America, for a tidy and conspicuous total of $20,000.

From many donors' viewpoint, however, a more advantageous way of attracting Robert Dole's attention has been by contributing to the Dole Foundation, a charitable foundation dedicated primarily to helping the handicapped.

Giving to a foundation like Dole's is preferable to a political gift in a number of respects. For one thing, corporations, barred since 1907 from contributing to federal campaigns, may give freely to charitable foundations such as Dole's. AT&T, for example, made memorable gifts totaling $100,000 to the Dole Foundation. Atlantic Richfield, IBM, and the R. J. Reynolds Tobacco Company each contributed $25,000.

Second, gifts to a charitable foundation such as the Dole Foundation are tax deductible. Since deductible gifts reduce the taxes of the donor—for example, AT&T's $100,000 gift saved that company $46,000 in taxes—part of the burden is shifted to other helpless taxpayers.

Third, gifts to foundations are not limited in size, as are political contributions.

Finally, unlike political gifts, contributions to foundations may be made in secret, even though they are connected with political figures. For example, as of June 1986, New York Republican Representative Jack Kemp repeatedly refused to disclose the list of donors to the Fund for an American Renaissance, the charitable foundation he founded and controlled (finally, in late summer 1986, he released the data). The Dole Foundation does not pursue such a policy of secrecy; on the contrary, it willingly released its full list of contributors. In doing so, the foundation's president, Jackie Strange, emphasized the nonpolitical nature of the foundation, that there is "absolutely no interference with the foundation's operation." Moreover, while Congressman Kemp's foundation paid to publish Kemp's speeches and other writings as well as paying the travel expenses of Kemp and his aides on a fact-finding trip, the Dole Foundation's outlays have been confined to grants to conventional charities unrelated to the senator's political activities.

Nonetheless, the Dole Foundation is undeniably a means by which donors can attract the sympathetic attention of the Senate Republican leader. In the year ending June 30, 1986, major companies and four individuals donated slightly over $1 million. Various industries and interest groups, many of which are regulated by the government or receive federal subsidies, are prominent on the list of contributors. For example, life-insurance companies and oil firms, both of which enjoy major tax preferences, gave a total of $136,000; pharmaceutical companies, subject to strict federal regulation, gave $45,000; tobacco firms (beneficiaries of federal subsidies, and the objects of Senator Dole's special help) gave $40,000.

In his financial disclosure reports to the Senate, Dole lists himself as chairman of the Dole Foundation. Presumably, then, he is aware of all these acts of generosity. Presumably, too, he has a warm place in his heart for those who have furthered his charitable enthusiasm for helping the handicapped.

Beyond contributing to Dole's Senate and presidential campaigns and to his foundation, interest groups and companies may favor Senator Dole with speaking fees, embellished, perhaps, with a comfortable ride on a company jet—as when an R. J. Reynolds jet flew Dole to Winston-Salem, where he picked up a $2,000 honorarium (which he gave to charity), and then carried the senator on to Fort Lauderdale.

For Dole—the top honoraria recipient in the Senate for five of the last six years—speaking fees for 1978 through 1986 brought in $825,266. According to the *Kansas City Star* and Senate financial-disclosure reports, he kept $395,967 of this and gave the balance to charity, as required by Senate rules.

Even with these charitable gifts, however, the fact remains that through 1986, Senator Dole accepted honoraria from seventy-eight groups whose PACs also contributed to the Dole political entities, the Dole Foundation, or both.

The Dole-for-Senate Committee. Campaign America. The Dole Foundation. Honoraria. Corporate jet trips.

Surveying that array of possibilities of gaining the attention of the Senate Republican leader (and possible future president), an interest group may ask itself, "Why choose just one?" In fact, many have found it just too hard to choose. In the period 1985 through mid-1987, several pursued more than one avenue provided by Dole. And in many cases, employees of the donating group made further individual donations, just to make sure the senator noticed.

In pursuing multiple channels to Robert Dole's attention, gratitude, and friendship, none has been more resourceful than the

FUNDS GIVEN TO SENATOR DOLE FROM 1985 TO MID-1987				
BY	**THROUGH**			
	Dole for Senate	**Campaign America**	**Dole Foundation**	**Honoraria**
MASS. MUT. LIFE INS. CO.	$ 5,500	$ 5,000	$10,500	$ 5,000
MERRILL LYNCH	$ 2,000	$ 1,000	$ 5,000	$ 2,000
MERRILL LYNCH EMPLOYEES	$ 4,000			
FORD MOTOR CO.	$ 1,000		$20,000	
FORD EMPLOYEES	$12,000			
MARRIOTT CO.	$ 2,000		$20,000	$ 2,000
MARRIOTT EMPLOYEES		$ 4,000		
5 TOBACCO COMPANIES	$13,400		$40,000	$ 2,000
TOBACCO EMPLOYEES	$ 1,000	$ 5,000		
INSURANCE INDUSTRY	$86,000	$ 3,500	$30,500	$15,000
INSURANCE EMPLOYEES	$ 1,000	$26,148		
8 SUGAR & SWEETENER PACs	$40,000	$ 7,000	$25,000	
SUGAR-INDUSTRY EMPLOYEES	$ 5,000			

multi-billion-dollar food-processing firm of Archer-Daniels-Midland (ADM) and its charismatic principal stockholder, Dwayne Andreas.

ADM and the Andreas family have been extraordinarily generous to the Dole conglomerate. The ADM PAC provided $15,500 to the Dole for Senate campaign and to Campaign America from 1978 through mid-1985. The ADM Foundation gave $25,000 to the Dole Foundation. Over a seven-and-a-half-year period, Andreas himself donated $5,000 and Andreas family members have contributed a total of $16,500 to Dole political committees. Dole received $4,000 as fees for two speeches ($2,000 from ADM and $2,000 from ADM's foundation), which Dole gave to charity. And Dole's Senate disclosure report for 1983 reveals three Dole trips on ADM corporate planes.

Moreover, in 1982 the Doles bought a three-room apartment in an oceanfront cooperative building in Bal Harbour, Florida—of which Dwayne Andreas is chairman, secretary, treasurer, and major stockholder. According to a *New York Times Magazine* article in November 1987, the Doles received, at the least, "preferential treatment from Mr. Andreas" in having access to the shares and, arguably, a price break on the apartment; a similar apartment in a less desirable location in the same building sold for $190,000 three months before the Doles bought theirs for $150,000.

Finally, since 1984, ADM has, with Mobil Oil, sponsored "Face-Off," a three-minute daily radio debate carried on 160 Mutual Broadcasting Network stations featuring Dole and Senator Edward M. Kennedy. Michael Fumento, a Legal Services lawyer who wrote a major investigative article on ADM's political activities for the conservative *National Review*, calculates that ADM has, through "Face-Off," provided Dole—as well as Kennedy—$195,000 of free radio exposure through 1986.

Altogether, then, one could say that Robert Dole is indebted to ADM and the Andreas family for a total of $261,000.

One could also say that he owes a debt of gratitude—

- to political action committees for the $3,366,000 they have given his senatorial campaigns since 1972.
- to wealthy donors, many of them affiliated with companies or industries vitally affected by U.S. government actions, for the $1,300,000 they gave his senatorial committee and the $2,500,000 they gave to his own PAC, Campaign America, during 1985 and 1986.
- to the companies and industries that have given him over $800,000 in speaking fees, even though he passed slightly more than half of that sum on to charity.
- to the companies and rich people who gave over $1 million to the Dole Foundation in the twelve months ending mid-1986.

With so much money from so many interest groups on Robert Dole's political debit books, it is only natural that reports surface, from time to time about actions that he has taken to further the interests of one or another group that has helped him. Here are a few:

————— **Reportedly aiding passage of a high sugar subsidy—an indirect help to ADM and other producers of corn sweeteners** In 1981, and again in 1985, Congress enacted a program to support the price of domestically produced sugar far above the world market (see Chapter 7). That opened the way for sugar to be undercut by sellers of a lower-priced corn sweetener, produced by ADM at great profit (21.5 percent, compared with 6 percent for flour milling). The higher the price of domestic sugar, the greater the price at which a corn sweetener could undercut sugar and the greater ADM's sweetener profits.

One way to keep sugar prices artificially high is to choke off imports of foreign sugar. That trade restriction worried free-trade advocates such as Republican Congressmen Philip Crane of Illinois and Bill Frenzel of Minnesota, who were members of the House-Senate conference committee on the 1985 farm bill. Crane and Frenzel proposed, and understood they had agreement on, a provision supported by the Reagan administration that had the effect of easing the sugar-trade restrictions.

But, according to an article by Sheila Kaplan in the May/June 1986 *Common Cause Magazine*, when the sugar portions of the farm bill had been printed by the Government Printing Office and returned to Congress to be voted on by the House and Senate, the Frenzel-Crane provision was missing. Crane and Frenzel, incredulous and incensed, demanded to know what had happened. Reporter Kaplan quotes Harris Jordan, a Crane aide, as saying the deletion of the provision had been ordered by "a very senior Senator from Kansas." (According to Kaplan a Dole spokesman denied that "the senator went anywhere near the printing office," but did acknowledge that "Dole's staff read the substitute [Frenzel-Crane] provision and rejected it.") Crane aide Jordan recalls congressional staff members and sugar lobbyists who were following the bill at the time telling him that the excision of the Frenzel-Crane provision was known among them to be "ADM's deal."

──────── **Promoting a tobacco subsidy** Although only minuscule amounts of tobacco are grown in Senator Dole's home state, David Corn reported in the *Nation* that in the fall of 1985, Senator Dole pushed hard in the Senate Finance Committee to rescue a tobacco-subsidy program that Republican Senator Jesse Helms, from the tobacco state of North Carolina, had failed to get approved by the Agriculture Committee, which Helms chaired. Dole attempted the rescue operation by tying the subsidy to a cigarette-tax measure under consideration by Finance. Reporter Corn says the tobacco cause was so important to Dole that committee chair Packwood delayed taking up the cigarette tax until Dole could be present.

The Helms-Dole plan called in part for selling government-owned tobacco to cigarette manufacturers at up to a 90 percent discount, a move opposed by the Reagan administration. Budget Director James Miller estimated that that aspect of the plan would cost the taxpayers over $1 billion.

Why would a Kansas senator expend so much energy on behalf of a crop almost nonexistent in his state? A spokesman explained that Dole supported farm commodities whether or not produced in Kansas. Reporter Corn lists other possible reasons, among them his appreciation for Senator Helms's support in Dole's 1984 election as Senate Republican leader, and Dole's desire to help tobacco-state Republican senators in the 1986 elections. But there is an additional factor to be considered: the generosity of the tobacco industry in contributing to various parts of the Dole political conglomerate. Federal Election Commission records show that in 1985 and 1986, the Big Five tobacco companies contributed a total of $13,400 to Senator Dole's reelection campaign. Three of them (Philip Morris, R. J. Reynolds, and U.S. Tobacco) contributed a total of $40,000 to the Dole Foundation, and tobacco firms in the past four years have given the senator $6,000 in honoraria.

In addition, one tobacco firm, U.S. Tobacco, also furnished Dole its plush executive jet for a 1987 weekend campaign trip to Iowa. U.S. Tobacco only charged the Dole campaign $7,272, less than 40 percent of the $19,000 required to charter an equivalent jet. Said a U.S. Tobacco spokesman: "When a congressman or senator asks for this kind of help, it gives us the opportunity to help them in a unique way. We've known Senator Dole for many years and have admired his work."

—————— Tax help for 333 Chicago commodity traders

In 1984, Senator Dole, in a 180-degree about-face, came to the rescue of 333 wealthy Chicago commodity traders who were embroiled in a controversy with the Internal Revenue Service over their questionable use of a special tax loophole (see Chapter 8). Two years earlier, Dole had chided Senate Democrats for helping these very commodity traders, who had been politically generous to the Democrats. Moreover, as reported in *Common Cause Magazine*, Dole had gone to the trouble of writing the IRS, taking the opposite stance from the one he now adopted. Nonetheless, during a late-night House-Senate conference-committee session on the 1984 tax bill, Dole abruptly reversed himself and approved a proposal that would let the traders off the hook with the IRS. Dole's reversal was worth at least $300 million for the traders, an average of $866,000 apiece.

Federal Election Commission records show that in the preceding two years, individuals and PACs in the commodity industry contributed $70,500 to Campaign America—six times what they had given two years earlier.

_____ **Promoting subsidies and tariffs on gasohol, of which ADM is a major producer**   ADM is the nation's largest producer of the grain alcohol that goes into "gasohol," a nine-to-one mixture of gasoline and alcohol. Gasohol came into vogue during the oil shortages of the late seventies. It has always received enormous federal subsidies, estimated by the Federal Highway Administration at nearly half a billion dollars in 1986 alone.

According to Michael Fumento's article in *National Review*, Senator Dole sponsored a major tax concession for gasohol in 1978, and has sponsored at least twenty-three other bills to promote gasohol.

In 1980, despite the government subsidies, American gasohol was undersold by Brazil, and Dwayne Andreas pushed for a tariff against Brazilian gasohol. Late that year, Robert Dole introduced such a tariff as an amendment to a complicated revenue bill and, according to Fumento, "rammed [it] through the Senate Finance Committee and the full Senate without debate."

Four years later, Dole was part of a successful effort to persuade the U.S. Customs Service to tighten up on imports of Brazilian gasohol, an effort in which he was joined by several other senators, the Corn Growers Association, the secretary of agriculture—and Archer-Daniels-Midland.

Both in 1980 and 1984, Dole responded to criticisms about his help to a large campaign contributor such as Andreas by saying no one needed to bribe him to support farmers and to protect them against a "flood" of imported Brazilian alcohol. In response to questions from *Washington Post* reporter Michael Isikoff, Dole said, "Our primary goal was not to help any one company. I'm a farm-state senator, and our interest was in finding an outlet for some farm commodities." But Fumento points out that while the "nobody-here-but-just-this-farm-senator" argument is plausible, it has its weaknesses. For example, a given increase in demand for corn to produce gasohol may raise *corn* prices two to four cents a bushel. But Fumento says that the resulting by-products cut *soybean* prices twelve to thirteen cents per hundredweight. In total cash value, the two crops are almost equal in Kansas. Moreover, energetically pushing an increase in tariffs against Brazil is a tricky business for a Kansas senator, given that Kansas's biggest crop is wheat and that Brazil is the world's fifth largest importer of wheat. Not only does an anti-Brazil tariff invite retaliation; it also deprives Brazil of the dollars it needs to buy American wheat.

Item: Manifold generosity to Dole by the Archer-Daniels-Midland Company and its principal stockholder, Dwayne Andreas, followed by special Dole favors for ADM.

Item: Generous contributions by the tobacco industry to Dole causes, after Dole had energetically pushed a tobacco subsidy, even though virtually no tobacco is grown in his home state.

Item: Increased campaign contributions to Dole political causes by Chicago commodity traders, followed by a Dole flip-flop on a tax problem many traders were having with the IRS, resulting in a multi-million-dollar tax benefit to the traders.

Was Senator Dole prompted to take any of those actions because of the contributions of his benefactors? The public cannot be sure. That's not good for the public or fair to Senator Dole. But the inferences are there.

To the extent that implications of impropriety exist, Senator Dole can only blame the campaign finance *system* under which he and all other lawmakers must now function. The inferences are built into the election laws under which senators and congressmen routinely and legally accept large amounts of money from strangers (or even friends) who have immense amounts at stake in those lawmakers' conduct. Senator Dole has created opportunities for the offering and receiving of such conflict-of-interest contributions as imaginatively as any member of Congress. And he continues to do so. In early 1987, he formed a new Dole-for-Senate committee, and began accepting contributions for his next Senate race, in 1992, six years hence.

If Senator Dole objects to the implications of impropriety, he has two alternatives:

First, let him cease actively seeking (indeed, let him decline to accept) money tainted with conflicts of interest; or

Second, let him use his position of national power to change the system so as to give candidates and lawmakers an alternative to accepting money and other favors that inevitably give rise to inferences of impropriety.

In the latter respect, Senator Dole has been inconsistent. After insisting in 1985 that the campaign-finance "system cries for reform," in August 1986 he voted *against* a bipartisan PAC limitation cosponsored by Senators David Boren and Barry Goldwater, which nonetheless passed the Senate, 69–30. Moreover, in January 1987, when Senators Boren and Byrd introduced a new and more comprehensive reform bill, Senator Dole said, "I do not believe there will be any effort to stall any such legislation." Yet Dole voted seven successive times *against* breaking a filibuster that was delaying a Senate vote on the Byrd-Boren reform bill.

So if Senator Dole wishes to avoid criticism of his campaign-finance activities, he would do well to bring his actions more in line with his cries for reform.

★ ▬▬▬▬▬▬▬▬▬▬▬▬▬▬▬▬▬▬▬▬▬▬
CASE STUDY 2: JAMES J. HOWARD

Robert J. Dole is a nationally known figure. But who is James J. Howard?

Here are a few clues:

- Representative Howard is known in Corvallis, Oregon, where the PAC of the CH2M Hill Company thought well enough of him to contribute $500 toward his 1986 reelection campaign.
- Congressman Howard is also known in Grand Rapids, Michigan. The American Seating Company's PAC there sent him a $1,500 campaign contribution in 1986.
- He's known, too, in Baton Rouge, Louisiana, where the Lamar Corporation PAC contributed $2,500 to his 1986 campaign.

It would be difficult to guess, from those scattered clues, that James J. Howard is a congressman from New Jersey. His district includes once-grand seaside resorts like Long Branch and Asbury Park. But why is New Jersey's James Howard known, and apparently highly regarded, by companies in Oregon, Michigan, and Louisiana? Why do firms so far away care who represents the Third District of New Jersey?

Here are some further clues to Congressman Howard's identity:

- In 1986 he received campaign contributions totaling $10,000 from American, Eastern, TWA, Delta, and five other airlines.
- He also received a $1,000 contribution from Greyhound Bus,

$2,250 from Trailways—and $10,000 from the American Bus Association.

- He got $8,500 in campaign contributions from the American Trucking Association, a $5,500 contribution from Yellow Freight System, Inc., a trucking firm located in Shawnee Mission, Kansas, plus a total of $8,650 from seven other trucking firms.
- He also received $10,000 from the Teamsters Union.

No more clues. Democratic Congressman James J. Howard is Chairman of the House Public Works and Transportation Committee.

Its jurisdiction spans a number of multi-million-dollar economic activities, including:

- The building and maintenance of federal highways and bridges.
- The construction of all federal buildings.
- The dredging of rivers and harbors and inland waterways.
- The regulation of bus, airline, and inland-waterway transportation.
- The regulation of billboards on federal highways.

The committee's decisions on those subjects can vitally affect the prosperity of companies or even whole industries. And, by congressional custom, the most powerful single individual in shaping a committee's decisions is its chairman.

In short, James J. Howard is an extraordinarily powerful member of Congress.

That may explain why contributions to his 1986 reelection campaign came from an engineering firm in Corvallis, Oregon, from a Grand Rapids company that, among other things, makes bus seats, and from the Lamar Corporation of Baton Rouge, a major billboard company. But the average citizen reading the report on Congressman Howard's campaign finances would have difficulty perceiving those connections.

As with Robert Dole, there are several ways to gain the favorable attention of Representative James Howard.

There is, however, one important difference. Dole, as the Senate Republican leader, is a potent force across the spectrum of legislative issues. His sympathetic attention is equally important to virtually every industry, be it broadcasting, banking, oil, or insurance.

Howard, by contrast, has no special sway over, say, broadcasting or banking legislation, so broadcasters' and bankers' PACs have no particular interest in contributing to his campaigns. But on legislation involving highways, trucking, air transport, billboard regulation, the construction of federal buildings, or the dredging of inland ports and waterways, James J. Howard, as chairman of the House Public Works and Transportation Committee, is *the* most important member of the House. So when it comes to soliciting or accepting attention-getting favors, those interest groups—the truckers, the airlines, the billboard industry, and the rest—they, not the half-million residents of New Jersey's Third District, are Congressman Howard's "constituents."

Congressman Howard is conspicuously receptive to campaign contributions and other favors from those "constituent" interest groups. As a consequence, Howard is remarkably indebted for his campaign money to groups and people *outside* his congressional district. Five out of every six dollars of his 1986 campaign funds came from people who do not even live in his district.

For starters, $340,000—more than half his 1986 campaign money—came from special-interest political action committees which, being headquartered outside his district, may properly be regarded as outsiders.★

Did he really need to accept the $340,000 from special-interest PACs?

The best answer is: He had no way of knowing. Unlike most committee chairmen, who represent politically lopsided districts and usually win by overwhelming margins, Howard has never been secure in his. In twelve elections, his victory margins have bobbed up and down with the national trends, often dipping below the 55 percent mark that represents a safe seat. In 1980, the year Ronald Reagan first won the presidency, Howard had a real scare: he won by only 2,000 votes. That year, his opponent nearly equaled him in campaign spending. Since then, he has overwhelmed his opponents in overall spending and, especially, in the money he has raised from PACs. In 1986, he outspent his Republican challenger three to one,

---

★ Many congressmen object to a blanket categorization of *all* PAC money as "outside" money. My reasons for doing so are set forth on page 72.

and raised thirty-four times as much money from PACs as his opponent!

Whatever the reasons, in 1986 James Howard accepted more than a third of a million dollars from special-interest PACs—twenty-fourth highest in the entire U.S. House. Roughly $155,000 of that came from the PACs of groups with a stake—sometimes an immense stake—in actions of the committee Howard chairs.

In 1986, Congressman Howard's campaign contributions from PACs and interested individuals included the following:

- $34,600 from airline companies, unions, and trade associations.
- $38,150 from trucking interests.
- $27,250 from bus companies and unions.
- $31,350 from construction firms, unions, and trade associations, who have an interest in the public works projects and federal buildings.
- $88,500 from individual donors who could be identified, from Federal Election Commission records, as associated with companies having a stake in the Public Works Committee's decisions.★

As noted earlier, it would be unthinkable for a judge to accept so much as a dollar from a defendant or a plaintiff, or *anyone* with an interest in a case before that judge. The acceptance of such a gift would lead to uncertainty about the fairness of that judge's decision. But the election laws permitted James Howard to accept over $241,000 in campaign contributions from individuals and groups with immense stakes in his official decisions.

Campaign contributions are but one way interested parties can confer favors on the likes of James J. Howard.

For example, judging from the evidence in public records, Howard has a fondness for traveling to warm climes when the weather in New Jersey and Washington turns frigid—especially, it would seem, if his way is paid by his interest-group constituents.

The American Busing Association, for example, has a direct

★ The $88,500 does not include gifts from individual contributors whose occupations are not listed on the reports Congressman Howard submits to the FEC. Presumably some are associated with firms with an interest in his committee's actions.

interest in the decisions of Howard and his committee on two
scores: the level of federal highway building and maintenance, and
federal regulation of bus safety. Over the years, the ABA has been
strikingly openhanded with Howard. In addition to the $21,500 the
ABA's PAC has contributed to Howard's campaigns in the last
three elections, it has hosted him (at least once with his wife) on
three all-expenses-paid trips to Puerto Rico during its annual conventions. These jaunts, which lasted as long as five days, usually
occurred in December, a chilly month in New Jersey. Apparently,
too, the American Bus Association never tires of hearing Howard
speak, for since 1980, they have paid him honoraria, which he could
personally pocket, totaling $9,500. In addition, Howard was the
ABA's guest on a visit to Palm Springs, California, in mid-February
1985.

That was his second trip there that year—only four weeks earlier, he and his wife had spent seven days in Palm Springs at the
annual meeting of the billboard industry's trade association, the
Outdoor Advertising Association of America. The OAAA customarily chooses the month of January and the sunny climate of Palm
Springs for its convention, and Congressman Howard attends reli-
giously. Various billboard companies take turns paying for the Howards' transportation and hotel bills, plus the $18,000 in honoraria by
which the congressman has been personally enriched. Coinciden-
tally, Howard's committee can greatly affect the prosperity of the
billboard industry, depending on the leniency or severity of the
legislation it enacts regulating billboards on federal highways. Inter-
estingly, Howard himself has treated the industry with extraordinary kindness, as detailed in Chapter 3.

Since cigarettes are (like liquor) a mainstay of the billboard industry, the Tobacco Institute also customarily holds its convention
in Palm Springs on the same days as the OAAA. Legislators receiving speaking fees from the billboard convention customarily stop by
and pick up more from the Tobacco Institute; in three successive
years, 1984 through 1986, Howard received a total of $6,000 in
honoraria from that source.

Other interest-group "constituents" that have been particularly
generous to Howard since early 1981 are shown in the table on the
next page.

If these interest-group favors merely amounted to a few days in
the sun for Congressman Howard and his wife, that would be disturbing enough. From the public's viewpoint, more troubling still is

NAME	TOTAL PAC CONTRIBUTIONS	TOTAL HONORARIA	SPECIAL TRIPS
AMERICAN TRUCKING ASSOCIATION	$19,000	$4,000	DENVER, COLO. KEY LARGO, FLA.
AMERICAN ROAD AND TRANSPORTATION BUILDERS	$ 6,500	$9,000	HOUSTON, TEX. TAMPA, FLA. PHOENIX, ARIZ. KISSIMEE, FLA. HERSHEY, PA.
ASSOCIATED GENERAL CONTRACTORS OF AMERICA	$11,250	$4,000	SAN FRANCISCO, CAL. HONOLULU, HAWAII

Howard's regular attendance at the annual meetings of the very groups over which he has regulatory responsibilities.

In theory, Congressman Howard and his committee colleagues are supposed to be the public's watchdogs over the various industries their committee regulates. Citizens are entitled to feel that Howard and the committee are free of special-interest influence in dealing with bus and airline safety and protecting against undue visual pollution of the countryside by billboards. Even if Howard had been scrupulous about paying his own expenses and had turned aside all honoraria, he has, over the years, turned up at the billboard industry's annual meetings as faithfully as if he were a member (probably more regularly than many members). Every year he has spent many days and evenings eating, drinking, and relaxing with billboard-company owners and industry lobbyists, presumably forming first-name friendships. How, after attending all these conventions, can "old Jim" Howard consider laws dealing with the livelihoods of his old drinking buddies Steve and George and Hank as objectively as if those laws had to do with the Mr. Jones and Mr. Smith with whom Congressman Howard deals at arm's length?

Even with the new disclosure laws and the computerized reports of the Federal Election Commission, to identify all the interested contributors to a congressman such as James Howard is a task worthy of a Sherlock Holmes.

Take, for example, the FEC's computer printout of Congressman Howard's 1986 PAC contributions—covering twenty closely printed pages. That printout lists $2,500 contributions from the PACs of the Lamar Corporation and of the Ralph M. Parsons Company. What do those firms make or sell? Where are they located? The FEC reports contain no clue that Lamar is a billboard company in Baton Rouge, Louisiana, and Parsons an engineering firm that consults on highways and bridges—information obtained for this book by telephone calls to the firms themselves.

Identifying *individual* givers is even trickier. In the 1986 election, Congressman Howard received nearly $44,000 in contributions from individuals connected with the billboard industry. Either they are lawyers representing billboard interests, or employees of billboard companies or trade associations *or, in some cases, their spouses.* The detective work comes into play in those frequent instances when James Howard, and many of his fellow candidates, do not report the occupation or profession of all the over-$200 contributors. Who, other than someone who follows the billboard industry full time,★ would ever guess that Eric Rubin—listed only as an "attorney"—is the lawyer for the OAAA, the billboard industry's trade association? Or that Barbara White of Crown Point, Indiana —a $1,000 contributor listed in FEC reports as "homemaker"—is the wife of Dean White, executive of a billboard company, Whiteco Metrocom?

Neither Barbara White nor her husband Dean (who gave $575 to Representative Howard's 1986 campaign) can cast a ballot for Howard on election day, because they don't live in his district. The same is true of attorney Eric Rubin. In fact, those who gave 90 percent of the money that Howard received in over-$200 contributions reside outside his district.

Some representatives, such as Colorado's Pat Schroeder or Wisconsin's Les Aspin, are sufficiently known nationally as to be natural drawing cards for out-of-state contributors. But James Howard of New Jersey has no such national renown. Therefore, the people of the Third District of New Jersey (and, indeed, the people of the United States) are entitled to wonder:

- Why do $200-and-over contributors from Florida give nearly twice as much and those from Massachusetts two-and-a-half times as much to Congressman Howard as people who live in his own district?
- Why do comparable contributors who live in and around Wash-

---

★ Such as Edward McMahon, executive director of the Coalition for Scenic Beauty, who spotted these donors' connections with the billboard industry. But McMahon was able to do so only because of his close familiarity with the industry.

ington, D.C.—who, of course, include lawyers and lobbyists doing business with the House Public Works and Transportation Committee—contribute three times as much to Congressman Howard as do his own constituents?

- Why, for that matter, do large donors in California contribute more than Congressman Howard's own constituents? Do people 3,000 miles from the Atlantic Ocean really have the interests of the Third District of New Jersey—or even the nation's interest —in mind when they make their $200-plus gifts?

Adding the contributions from out-of-district *individual* donors to the 57 percent of Howard's 1986 campaign funds he took from outside special-interest PACs reveals this disturbing fact:

> *Only one dollar out of every six of Representative Howard's 1986 campaign money came from his own constituents. The other five came from individuals or groups not qualified to vote in his district on election day.*

When a congressman like Howard is indebted for five-sixths of his campaign money to people and groups outside his district, whom does he *really* represent? His constituents? Or those outsiders? Is this the kind of representative democracy the Founding Fathers had in mind?

THE VIEW
FROM THE
INSIDE

★ ★ ★ ★ ★

5

PRESENT AND FORMER MEMBERS OF CONGRESS SPEAK

What is the effect on members of Congress of the skyrocketing need for campaign funds and the resulting never-ending scramble for money? What is its impact on the legislative process? How has campaigning been affected?

To find out, I interviewed several current and former members of Congress.

Here is what they told me:

★
1. FORMER CONGRESSMAN MICHAEL BARNES OF MARYLAND

Mike Barnes came to national attention when, as the beneficiary of a liberal revolt on the House Foreign Affairs Committee, he became the chairman of the Western Hemisphere Subcommittee and a principal spokesman against the Reagan administration's policies in Central America.

Barnes represented a Maryland bedroom suburb of Washington, D.C., from 1978 to 1986, when he ran unsuccessfully for the U.S. Senate. He has a mild-mannered bespectacled mien ("I'm criticized by my friends for not being more flamboyant," he once said). But he displays great passion when speaking about the urgent need for campaign-finance reform. His convictions on this subject were solidified by his 1986 experience as a senatorial candidate, during which money-raising was a constant preoccupation ("There was never a waking moment that I was not either raising money or feeling guilty that I was not").

Barnes now practices law in Washington.

As I spoke to political consultants, they all said I should not even consider running for the Senate if I weren't prepared to spend 80 or 90 percent of my time raising money. It turned out that they were absolutely correct. That's an absolute outrage, because the candidates should be talking about the issues and meeting with constituents and voters and working on policy questions.

As a congressman, I had plenty of phone calls from political directors of PACs, in which the conversation went something like this:

"Mike, we're getting ready to make our next round of checks out, and just want to let you know that you're right up there at the top. We really think we can help you with a nice contribution."

"Gee, that's great. Really appreciate it. Grateful to have your help."

"Oh, by the way, Mike, have you been following that bill in Ways and Means that's going to be coming to the floor next week? It's got an item in there we're concerned about—the amendment by Congressman Schwartz. You know, we'll be supporting that and we hope you'll be with us on that one. Hope you'll take a good look at it, and if you need any information about it, we'll send that up to you."

That conversation is perfectly legal under the current laws of the United States, and it probably takes place daily in Washington, D.C. It is an absolute outrage!

You know, if that conversation took place with someone in the executive branch, someone would go to jail.

I regard it as really demeaning to both people—the guy who gets the phone call and the guy that has to make it. It's just a terrible, terrible blight on our political process.

I remember standing on the floor of the House one night when we were voting on the issue of regulations affecting the funeral industry that were, in my view, eminently reasonable. The funeral industry was opposed to this regulation. I remember the evening it was voted on, a rumor swept across the floor of the House that anybody who voted against the regulation would get $5,000 from the industry PAC for his or her upcoming campaign. I don't know if that rumor was true or not, but it flew around the place. Everybody was sort of laughing about this. There's not a doubt in my mind that that rumor had an effect on votes. I was standing next to a guy who, as he put his card in the machine [that registers representatives' votes in the House], said, "You know, I was going to vote against the industry on this thing, but what the hell, I can use the $5,000."

During the months preceding an election, I would say that more than half the conversations between congressmen relate to fundraising. "How are you doing with your fundraising? Will you stop by my fundraiser? God, I'm having a tough time getting money out of X—do you know anybody over there that could help? Do you have access to a rock group or a movie star that could help me with my fundraising?"

More often than not the question is not "Who's your opponent?" or "What are the issues in your race?" It's "How much money have you raised?" Money permeates the whole place.

You have to make a choice. Who are you going to let in the door first? You get back from lunch. You've got fourteen phone messages on your desk. Thirteen of them are from constituents you've never heard of, and one of them is from a guy who just came to your fundraiser two weeks earlier and gave you $2,000. Which phone call are you going to return first?

Money just warps the democratic process in ways that are very sad for the country. You have otherwise responsible, dedicated public servants grubbing for money and having to spend inordinate amounts of their time raising money rather than addressing the issues that they come to Washington to deal with. And you have people trying to present their cases on the merits, feeling they have no choice but to buy access to the people who will make the decisions. It demeans both sides in ways that are very sad. You've got good people on both sides, a lot of dedicated lobbyists in Washington who are trying in a responsible way to present their points of view and get forced into becoming fundraisers and contributors in a way that's really outrageous.

★
2. FORMER CONGRESSMAN TOBY MOFFETT OF CONNECTICUT

Toby Moffett was thirty years old when, as a former Na-derite (he was the first director of the Connecticut Citizen Action Group, one of Ralph Nader's early grass-roots orga-nizations), he was elected to Congress as a member of the post-Watergate class of 1974.

He soon won a seat on the House Energy and Commerce Committee, one of the PAC hot-spots, handling legislation regulating the oil, chemical, broadcasting, and health in-dustries.

An unalloyed liberal (he might prefer the term "progres-sive") with prodigious energy, he initially chafed at the need, in Congress, for compromise and accommodation. As a new congressman, he observed, "After you stay in the House for a while, all the square edges get rounded off, and you get to look like all the other congressmen." Later, though, he took pleasure in the legislative skills he developed in "working the system."

In 1982, he made an unsuccessful run for the U.S. Senate against incumbent Republican Lowell Weicker. In 1984, he ran for the Connecticut governorship. He is now a TV an-chorman in Hartford.

There was always pressure to raise more and spend more, and build up your margin. If you win by 58 percent, it's one heck of a big difference from winning by 52 percent—in terms of what you have to face next time. So the goal is always to try and get yourself up over 60 or 62 and then 64 percent, and then, in many states, if you get up over 70 or 75, maybe you'll be unopposed. That's the dream, to be unopposed. So as a result, you go to where you have to go to get the money to build up that margin.

I remember during the Carter years, right in the middle of the hospital-cost-control vote*—the hospitals and the AMA were just

---

* See Chapter 7.

throwing money at the [House Commerce] Committee [which was handling the bill] as fast as they could. It was coming in wheelbarrows.

Our committee was a prime target, because the Commerce Committee had clean-air legislation, we had all the health bills, we had all the energy stuff—you know, natural gas, pricing, and that sort of stuff. We had all the communications stuff. So there was a lot of PAC money aimed at neutralizing the committee. The PACs took those ten or fifteen [swing] votes, and they really went to work on 'em. It was just no secret. Everybody in the room knew it.

You're sitting next to a guy on the committee and you're trying to get his vote on a clean-air amendment, and you suddenly realize that the night before he had a fundraiser, and all the people who were lobbying against the bill were at the fundraiser. Ways and Means members used to boast about the timing of their fundraisers. What kind of system is that?

In my 1982 Senate race, we had some fundraising people, the kinds of people that you bring on when you've got to raise a lot of money—I mean, very cold-blooded. You know, never mind the issues, let's get the money in. And I remember very, very well their telling me in, maybe, September, that we had to come up with $25,000 immediately for a down payment on a television buy. And I remember sitting down with a member of the House from the farm states, and he said, "How's it going?" I said, "Horrible, I've got to come up with $25,000." He said, "How about some dairy money?" And I said, "Oh, no! I can't do that." Remember, in the seventies, dairy money had a pretty bad name.★

He said, "Well, I can get you ten or fifteen thousand." I said, "Really?" He said, "Yeah. You know, your record has been pretty good on those issues. I think I can do it." Well, I went back to him the next day and said, "Let's do it."

By the time I got to the last month of the campaign, I was telling my wife and my close friends that here I was, somebody who took less PAC money, I think, than anybody running that year, but I felt strongly that I wasn't going to be the kind of senator that I had planned on being when I started out. I felt like they were taking a

---

★ Because of the dairy lobby's offer of $2 million to the 1972 Nixon campaign in exchange for a higher government dairy subsidy.

piece out of me and a piece out of my propensity to be progressive and aggressive on issues. I felt like, little by little, the process was eating away at me. One day it was insurance money, the next day it was dairy money.

★ ━━

3. FORMER SENATOR CHARLES McC. MATHIAS OF MARYLAND

To say that "Mac" Mathias was not a mainstream Republican is the height of understatement. An illustration: in the Senate "club," where the ordinary rule is politeness and accommodation, Mathias's fellow Republicans prodded South Carolina's Strom Thurmond to give up his senior position on the Armed Services Committee solely to elbow Mathias out of the spot of ranking Republican on the Judiciary Committee. Later, when the Republicans won control of the Senate, Thurmond abolished the important Antitrust Subcommittee, which Mathias was in line to head, and instead gave Mathias the unglamorous Subcommittee on Patents.

Mathias was almost as unwelcome among conservative Republican party officials in his home state. In 1984, he barely eked out a place on the Maryland delegation to the 1984 Republican National Convention. Asked why he fared so badly, one Baltimore Central Committee member answered, "Because he's a liberal swine."

On the other hand, his moderate stances made him popular among Maryland Democrats, and helped him win three successive Senate terms, beginning in 1968.

Mathias's seniority made him the chairman of the Senate Rules Committee, which handles campaign-finance reform legislation. So it was significant that in 1985 he was the prime sponsor of a bill providing government financing of Senate general elections. At the time, public financing was widely considered an impossible dream. But in the following Congress, his basic ideas were adopted by Senate Majority Leader Robert Byrd of West Virginia, and made the prime campaign-finance reform bill on the Senate's agenda.

In 1986, Mathias chose not to seek reelection. A factor in that decision was what he called the "daunting" prospect of having to raise millions in campaign funds.

In all honesty, money was not the crucial factor in my decision not to run again. But the thought of going out to raise $4 million, or anything like $4 million, was too much. In 1980 my campaign cost $1 million, which was a substantial effort. The thought of doubling that, let alone quadrupling, was a daunting prospect.

The need to raise money has now gotten so serious that the practice has grown up in the last several years of providing "windows" in the Senate schedule. A window is a period of time in which it is understood that there will be no roll-call votes. Senators are assured that they won't be embarrassed by being absent for a recorded vote. Windows usually occur between six and eight in the evening, which is the normal time for holding fundraising cocktail parties. The Senate Majority Leader says, "There will be a window between six and eight"—or between seven and nine, or whatever. That is a euphemism for saying that's the period in which you can go out and raise money while the Senate's in session. You're giving senators time off to raise the money. It seems to me the public should be shocked into action.

I think the Supreme Court was wrong in the Valeo case [a 1976 ruling that in politics, money is a form of speech protected by the First Amendment]. Instead of *protecting* freedom of expression, I think they have provided a means of *suppressing* freedom of expression. As it is, the big contributor can just drown out the little contributor by creating these enormous disparities. If I'm only able to give $100 to the candidate of my choice and someone else can give thousands, that's just going to submerge my voice completely.

I did one of those TV debates for the U.S. Chamber of Commerce. I was shocked because one of the Chamber's people, in the course of this discussion, said, "You can't do away with campaign contributions because no public official would do anything for you. How would you ever get anything done?" In some circles that is really the naked truth—that is, this is an outright lever that you can *buy* to get governmental action. And this person said so right on the air.

I don't think that the majority of the members of Congress are venal. But there are degrees of temptation. If someone came in and said, "I contributed $1,000, or am about to contribute $1,000, to your campaign and I expect you to vote No," I think most members would, if not kick 'em out of the office, at least make an outraged statement. But, a contributor calls you up on a busy day when your inclination is not to take any calls, and if that person says, "I must speak to you urgently," the chances are you will take that call when you wouldn't have taken any other calls. So to that extent I think money does have impact.

★
4. FORMER SENATOR BARRY GOLDWATER OF ARIZONA

First elected to the Senate in 1952 from a seat on the Phoenix city council, Barry Goldwater quickly rose to be his party's presidential standard-bearer, and the champion of the conservatives within the GOP, in 1964.

To do that, he had to give up his seat in the Senate, but returned four years later, and remained (despite one narrow escape at the polls in 1980) until his retirement in 1986.

In 1985, disturbed by the effects of the ever-mounting costs of campaigns and the demands this placed on candidates, he joined Democratic Senator David Boren of Oklahoma in leading the fight for campaign-finance reform. The Boren-Goldwater measure to limit the amount of PAC money a congressional candidate could receive passed the Senate by a top-heavy 69–30 margin in 1986 (see page 88), but went no further before Goldwater's retirement at the end of that term.

My first election in 1952 cost $45,000. We used to have $50 dinners, $25 dinners. I don't think I saw a $100 dinner until maybe 1955, '56, along there. If I had run again last year, I would have had to raise at least $3 million. When I ran the first time, the state [population] was about 800,000 and now it's about, coming up 3 million. So say two and a half times. So theoretically, if I lived on the same dollar basis, I would have spent $100,000. But that's not the way it's going. Up, up, up, up.

Today, the congressmen are more interested in being reelected than in their country. The day after they're elected, literally, they want to have a fundraising dinner for the next campaign. I don't know how many letters I've had from sitting senators and sitting congressmen wanting me to either raise money, come to dinner, or put my name as the chairman of a fundraising committee. I don't like the attitude that I have to be reelected and that's the prime thing I'm going to work on in the coming two or six years.

There's many subtle things they [interest groups] can do. They can take your wife and you on a trip to Florida, or California, or Honolulu, or the Bahamas. A very social event. Not just the two of you, but your entire—you go as a group. And you can travel on the company airplane. So it doesn't cost you a cent.

There's no question that the Senate has changed in its performance. The Senates of today can't compare with the Senates of thirty, thirty-five, forty years ago. Those great men that we had never worried about money, they just ran on their record. And they weren't faced with the initial job of raising millions of dollars. When I first came to the Senate, nobody that I knew was immediately thinking of next time. I didn't begin worrying about my reelection until about two years before. But, as I say, today, it's the next day! Will you raise some money for me?

★
5. FORMER SENATOR THOMAS EAGLETON OF MISSOURI

By the time Tom Eagleton vaulted into the national spotlight as George McGovern's 1972 running mate, Missourians had long known him as a liberal boy wonder. Elected city attorney in St. Louis three years out of law school, Eagleton celebrated his thirty-fifth birthday in 1964 by winning a two-to-one victory as lieutenant governor. He moved on to the U.S. Senate four years later.

Eagleton consistently opposed U.S. involvement in Vietnam, and in general had a solid liberal-labor voting record. But he was no rubber-stamp liberal. For example, he favored a ten-word constitutional amendment reversing the Supreme Court ruling that sanctioned abortion.

A chain-smoker, he also crusaded against the tobacco subsidy and favored a cigarette label, "WARNING! Cigarette smoking causes CANCER, EMPHYSEMA, HEART DISEASE, may complicate PREGNANCY, and is ADDIC-

TIVE." He was persuaded to drop the words "and may cause
DEATH" only on the ground it was redundant.

 Shortly after his reelection in 1980, Eagleton and his wife
decided he would not seek another term in 1986, largely
because he was disaffected by what he called "tin-cupping"
to raise campaign funds. But the Eagletons kept the decision
to themselves for two years.

 Senator Eagleton now practices law and teaches in St.
Louis.

There were about three compelling reasons not to seek reelection, and the money-raising factor was very high on the list. I just did not want to go through what I called the tin-cup routine—that is, begging for money, literally, from Maine to Hawaii. Psychologically, I didn't want to do it. It was just making me view the whole process of seeking reelection in a very negative way. My wife and I knew in '80 that that was the last one I was going to go through that. After raising $1.3 million, I said, "I'm just not going to do the tin-cupping again."

So the question of where the money was going to come from wasn't a problem for me for the final six years. When Mr. X came in to see me on behalf of, or opposed to, a certain amendment, I didn't have to put money on the scale and say, "How does this factor out in fundraising?"—as might be the case if I were running for reelection. If I'd been thinking of running again, I'd have said, "That's a good potential fundraising source. Those people are some big bucks."

When I ran for the Senate in 1968, I had a hotly contested primary. I think I spent about half a million dollars. In the general election, I think we spent about $300,000. In 1974, I think I spent, total, about $600,000. In 1980, my final Senate race, I spent $1.4 million, my opponent $1.2 million. Now get this. In 1986, the Democratic nominee for my seat, Harriett Woods, spent $4.3 million. And the winner, Christopher Bond, spent about $5.4 million. So from '80 to '86, the cost of a Senate race in Missouri on the Democratic side went up three and a half times. Thus, for the last two years, a senator is personally spending 60 or 70 percent of his time either thinking about, planning, or implementing fundraising strategy. And the other 30 percent, he is spending being a senator.

There's really not the need to spend all that money, except your opponent may be spending huge sums, and thus, psychologically, you don't want to be outspent three and four to one. You don't want to see your opponent every time you turn on the television in prime time. You do it to keep up with the Joneses.

An enforceable legal ceiling on the amount candidates could spend would be hallelujah. It would be a benefit to the candidates. It would be a benefit to the public. Part of the reason we have low voter turnout, in my opinion, is political oversaturation: people, between September and November, buffeted with never-ending blasts of political ads. One of the ways they protest about it is by not voting at all.

It just stands to common-sense reason that if the backbone of political financing is the $5,000 PACs and the $1,000 individuals, then a candidate, wittingly or *un*wittingly, tends to be more predisposed to those contributors. I read the other day that over 40 percent of the funds of House members who sought reelection came from PACs. Used to be 26 percent. That means that for that candidate, those House winners, those PACs get priority attention and access into his office, his staff, him personally, and to what I call his witting or unwitting predisposition.

We would get some calls from Missouri from Joe Citizen—just worried about an issue. Some of them had a beef because of a vote —but it's a Missouri call, OK? I don't know him, but he's a guy out there in St. Louis. I never took one of those calls. Some staffer took all of them. That's just the way, from a pragmatic view, that it was. I didn't have enough time in the day to answer them all. If I got a letter from J. P. Morgan and he was a big contributor, I would answer it personally. "Dear J.P., good to hear from you." But what about answering Joe Citizen? Well, staffer, send Joe Citizen a nice answer. You know, what did Jimmy Carter say? Life ain't fair.

Every PAC has its special interest or special interests. If I take X thousands of dollars from a dairy PAC, I know what it is the dairy boys are interested in. If I take X thousands of dollars from a tobacco or a trucking PAC, I know what it is those fellows are interested in, because I've been around 'em. So the minute you accept their money, you are tacitly acknowledging that you are part of their philosophical orientation.

I had any number of senators come up to me and say, "Someday I guess I'll make the decision to retire. I know how you feel about the money-raising thing. God, I feel the same as you do . . . except I just want to serve one more term." You could talk privately to a hundred members of the Senate—ninety of them would deplore the present fundraising system. But not all ninety of them would vote to change it.

PAC people are investors. It's like going to Wall Street or going to Merrill Lynch and saying, "Find me a stock that's going to go up." The same with a PAC. A PAC wants the best investment. The record shows the best investment is incumbency. In the House, 98 percent of incumbents were reelected in '86. Tell me an investment that you can get that's 98 percent successful on Wall Street.

★ ————————————————————————————————

6. SENATOR KENT CONRAD OF NORTH DAKOTA

The narrow election of Kent Conrad to the U.S. Senate in 1986 resulted from a grass-roots farm revolt among farmers and residents of small towns hurt by a steadily declining farm economy.

As state tax commissioner since 1981, Conrad had won popularity by closely auditing out-of-state corporations and criticizing the Burlington Northern railroad for its abandonment of North Dakota rail lines used by farmers.

The 1986 senatorial campaign in North Dakota was extraordinarily expensive for that state (total spending was about six times what it had been six years earlier). Both Conrad and his opponent, Republican incumbent Mark Andrews, relied to an unusual extent on PACs (each got half his money from PACs, far above the average in a senatorial contest). And both traveled to distant states in search of contributions from wealthy individuals.

Yet in the end, Conrad's election, as well as other 1986 senatorial contests, demonstrated that financial superiority has diminishing returns, for Conrad won despite being outspent two to one—$1 million for Conrad versus $2 million for Republican Andrews.

You ask if I've already started raising money for the next time. The answer is absolutely.

Those who want to represent the broad public interest find themselves in a terrible dilemma. If you're going to run successfully in the country today, you have to have sufficient funds to do so. Take my own state. I spent about $900,000 in my campaign, my opponent probably three times as much. There's no way you can raise that kind of money in a state like North Dakota. So you're going to California to raise money for a race in North Dakota. You're going to New York to raise money for a race in North Dakota. It just doesn't make any sense. It's in the national interest to put a cap on spending.

I had tremendous trouble raising PAC money as a challenger. I even had trouble getting phone calls to PACs returned. This current system puts such weight on incumbency. It is very difficult for a challenger to win. Very difficult for them to mount a respectable campaign.

★
7. CONGRESSWOMAN CLAUDINE SCHNEIDER OF RHODE ISLAND

Congresswoman Claudine Schneider, a person who ex-udes electric energy, is a political anomaly: a Republican officeholder—and an apparently invincible one—in the sol-idly Democratic state of Rhode Island.

When she first ran for Congress in 1978, the conventional wisdom did not hold out a prayer for her. That year, she raised a total of $56,000—almost all through bake sales, art auctions, and the like. PACs that year gave her a grand total of $1,700. Yet even spending just $54,000, she received 48 percent of the vote.

So when she ran again in 1980, her cause was no longer regarded as hopeless and the PACs came through with nearly $105,000. She won comfortably that year, with 55 percent of the vote. In ensuing years, her popularity has increased (she has won, successively, 56 percent, 68 percent, and, in 1986, 72 percent of the vote).

And as her popularity with the voters has increased, so has the money she has received from PACs. In 1986, even though she does not sit on any of the lucrative "PAC heaven" committees (she sits on the Merchant Marine Committee and *the Science and Technology Committee) she received $163,000 from PACs, nearly half her total campaign receipts.*

When I went to the PACs for money in 1978, they said, "You've got to be kidding. Rhode Island is a hard-core Democratic state. They haven't had a Republican since 1938. Not a chance." Secondly, the comments were, "Wait a minute, that's a very ethnic state." We have a lot of Italians in my district, and I had many older Italian men and women say to me, "You know, you ought to be home making spaghetti and having babies." And that was very frustrating. And the PACs basically anticipated that: "The likelihood of them selecting a woman is pretty slim. So I'm afraid we can't help you on two counts." So it was [my being] both a woman and a Republican that were the deterrents to many to make contributions.

I don't spend much time raising PAC money at all, now. It didn't require a whole lot of effort to go and raise that $163,000 of PAC money I got in 1986. The fact is that it was coming in; I wasn't about to say, "Hold off, boys." My feeling is whenever I can raise money, even though I got 68 percent of the vote, or whatever, is that what I raise today, I won't have to raise tomorrow. I spend more time strategizing and trying to figure out who I would like to get money from that I haven't yet. I'm on the Science and Technology Committee. So what am I doing that would be of interest to, for example, the high-tech community?

I don't feel a conflict of interest being on the Merchant Marine Committee and getting contributions from interested maritime PACs. I think a more direct way to put that question is, "Do I feel like I am compromising my decision-making by soliciting funds from those groups? Am I encouraging them to buy my vote?" And my answer there is no. When I first ran, people were taking a chance on me, PACs were taking a chance on how I would vote. I was an unknown entity. Then once I started voting, and they saw my philosophy, which direction I might be going, a number of PACs pulled out and don't support me anymore. Other PACs joined on the bandwagon. Those contributions are usually made after I have performed something, not because they have come to me and said, we want you to do X, Y, and Z.

I think that one of the unfortunate situations is the return of so many incumbents. And I think that a lot of that has to do with contributions made to people who are in very powerful positions. Obviously, someone who is on the Ways and Means Committee raises infinitely more money than someone on Merchant Marine and Fisheries. And a challenger who is attempting to unseat an incumbent on one of those more powerful committees has a very tough time trying to get elected.

★
8. CONGRESSMAN MIKE SYNAR OF OKLAHOMA

Since he came to the U.S. House in 1978 at age twenty-eight, Mike Synar has been anything but a typical congressman. He thinks in national terms.

He set himself apart in a New York Times *profile, early in his career, when he said, "I want to be a U.S. congressman from Oklahoma, not an Oklahoma congressman."*

That determination found expression in 1985 when Mike Synar voted against the Gramm-Rudman-Hollings deficit-reduction act, at a time when most legislators, even many liberals, rushed to embrace it. Synar also filed a lawsuit challenging the constitutionality of a pivotal section of the law (calling for automatic budget cuts to meet deficit targets). Synar said that "If members [of Congress] can't make hard choices, they ought to seek other employment." Synar's lawsuit prevailed in the Supreme Court, 7–2.

Synar is one of the few members of Congress who refuse to accept campaign contributions from PACs. He says he raises all he needs from two mammoth barbecues a year— one in his home district and one in Washington. Those are unusually successful events, for in the 1984 and 1986 elections, he took in $335,000 and $271,000, respectively.

Synar is a passionate advocate of campaign-finance reform in general and government aid to election campaigns in particular.

In 1978 when I ran for office, a winning person spent about $52,000 to get elected. Today that number is over $400,000. What that means is that someone like Mike Synar, if he was sitting in Muskogee, Oklahoma, today, could not run for the United States Congress.

The second problem is the amount of time that a member of Congress has to spend raising money. When you figure that an average race costs $400,000 to win, and you figure that there's only twenty-four months in a campaign cycle, and you divide those out, you're talking about having to raise somewhere in the neighborhood of $20,000 a month. Think of the amount of time that you have to focus to do that. That is time taken away from the duties of your office, which is representing people.

With more and more demands on elected officials' time, they try to seek the path of least resistance, and the path of least resistance is large globs of money from political action committees. So PACs have a disproportionate role in the process. Individual contributors aren't competitive with PACs.

How bad is it? Well, I'll tell you how bad it is. If you're a Republican from Oklahoma and you want to run against Mike Synar today, you could fly here to Washington, D.C., and based upon my liberal voting record, walk around this town for two days and raise $250,000 and become a legitimate candidate for my office without ever having raised a penny in my home district. I think there's something wrong when you can become a legitimate candidate without showing any sense of support financially or organizationally within your own district.

There's only two things in politics now—money and media. The day of the grass-roots organization is a thing of the past. In Oklahoma, in 1986, we had a Senate campaign and a governor's campaign where the last thing you would see is the candidates out in the rural areas campaigning. It's a waste of their time. All they really did was raise money and go on TV. The hands-on type of approach is a thing of the past. It's all money and media.

★
9. SENATOR JOHN C. STENNIS OF MISSISSIPPI

When it comes to matters of senatorial honor and ethics, few members of the U.S. Senate are more highly respected than the most senior member of that body, John Stennis of Mississippi.

Elected to the Senate in 1947 after serving ten years as a judge, Stennis was a member of the committee inquiring into the conduct of Wisconsin Senator Joseph R. McCarthy. In 1954, Stennis was the first to publicly denounce McCarthy as pouring "slush and slime" on the Senate. To condone McCarthy's conduct, he said, would mean that "something big and fine has gone out of this chamber. . . . "

A decade later, he was the unanimous choice to head the Senate Select Committee on Standards and Conduct (even though he had opposed the committee's establishment). The work of that committee paved the way for the Senate's first code of ethics.

In 1973, President Nixon took advantage of Stennis's reputation to fend off efforts by the Senate Watergate Committee and the courts to obtain the tapes of conversations in the White House. He offered to have Stennis listen to the tapes and authenticate the written transcripts, provided federal prosecutors would cease their efforts to obtain the tapes. Some senators agreed, but Special Prosecutor Archibald Cox would not. The outcome was the celebrated Saturday Night Massacre, in which President Nixon dismissed Cox.

Stennis, immensely popular in his home state, was accustomed to coasting through to uncontested victories until 1982, when the Republicans mounted a serious campaign against him. For the first time, Stennis found himself obliged to raise substantial campaign funds. He raised over $1 million—a sharp contrast to the $20,000 he spent in his first special election in 1947.

Because of his reputation as a conservative, senators were surprised when Stennis became one of the earliest co-sponsors of a measure to provide government funds for Senate election campaigns. And because Stennis speaks only rarely on the Senate floor, his colleagues were even more impressed when, during the ensuing debate on the measure, he felt strongly enough about the need for reform to speak not once, but on three occasions.

In the fall of 1987, Stennis announced his intention to retire from the Senate at the conclusion of his current term in 1988.

I remember when the average person didn't have anything to do with electing his United States senators. But in 1913, a constitutional amendment made them elected by the people.

I remember one campaign for the United States Senate soon after that. I was just a boy. They emphasized to the people that this is the first time in your life you've been called to directly select your two United States senators. That would appeal to a fellow, you know. I was just a little boy, standing there, but I caught the point. Joe Doakes, this fellow, this voter that lived there in the community was on his way to the top.

The current method of campaign financing is putting local decisions in the hands not of people who live in the area, but it is putting elections in the hands of money from far away. It comes from people who live perhaps thousands of miles from that voting precinct.

We cannot continue to operate that way and maintain the integrity of our local elections.

★
10. CONGRESSMAN JIM LEACH OF IOWA

Congressman Leach is one of a handful of House members who refuse to take campaign money from PACs, and is at the forefront of the campaign-reform movement in the House. In 1985 and 1986, he joined with Democratic Representative Mike Synar of Oklahoma in sponsoring a bill to limit the amount of PAC money any House candidate could receive in an election.

Although a Republican, Jim Leach sides with the Democrats in the House on issues such as arms control, the cessation of chemical-warfare weapons production, sanctions against South Africa, and denying funds for the Contra forces in Central America.

I argue that what you have in a campaign contribution is an implicit contract with the person that gave. If you listen carefully to that group's concerns, and abide by them, there is an implicit promise of another contribution for the next election.

What you've done is turn upside-down the American premise of government, which is the idea that people are elected to represent people. Officeholders should be indebted to the individuals that cast the ballots. Today candidates are becoming increasingly indebted to the people that *influence* the people who cast the ballots. It's a one-step removal. And so we're having an indirect, secondary kind of democracy—one that is increasingly group-oriented and financially influenced.

If I had my way, I would eliminate all group giving to campaigns. Prohibit group giving, period. I'd make all contributions individual. I would also prohibit giving from outside the state. That is, why allow an Iowan to influence a Nebraskan or a New Yorker to influence a Californian? That's why in my own campaigns I don't accept PAC money and I also don't accept out-of-state gifts.

We have $10 or $20 receptions throughout the district. We have hog roasts, we have barbecues in which we seek small contributions. But it's very time-consuming and difficult as contrasted with the people around Washington. Every night of the week, here, there's a reception at the Capitol Hill Club for candidates, and they can raise $10,000 to $15,000. That takes me three weeks. Twenty events. But on the other hand, my way gets more people involved in the process. And I think it makes them feel a little bit more part of it. For example, how much a part of a campaign is someone going to feel if they give $10 to a candidate who just got $10,000 from ten different unions? Or ten different businesses?

There's always an argument that PACs get more people involved. I've never seen it. I think it's exactly the reverse. Not having PACs forces candidates to go to the voters. I don't raise near as much as other candidates. But I raise over $100,000 and sometimes $150,000. That should be adequate to run a campaign in a state like Iowa. The fact that others in our state spend two to four to five times as much is an indication of how sick the system has become. In part, one side raises all that money because the other side does. It amounts to an arms race. What you need is a domestic SALT agreement.

★
11. FORMER CONGRESSMAN BOB EDGAR OF PENNSYLVANIA

Bob Edgar, a Methodist minister with a serious, almost prim, aspect, was elected in a lopsidedly Republican congressional district in the Philadelphia suburbs in the post-Watergate year, 1974. Thereafter, for six successive elections, the Republicans resolved to unseat this Democrat with a solidly liberal-labor voting record. Six times they failed—but never by much. Not once did Edgar win by more than 55 percent of the vote.

A member of the House Public Works and Transportation Committee, where mutually congenial back-scratching on water and other public-works projects is the order of the day, Edgar was an unpopular loner, opposing what he considered pork-barrel enterprises dear to his colleagues. But his stance only served to win him Republican votes in his home district.

As chairman of the Northeast-Midwest Coalition, a group of congressmen defending their regions against the Sunbelt, Edgar, far from a loner, proved to be a legislator of such skill that before he left Congress, a Sunbelt coalition had sprung up in response.

When first elected, Edgar announced he would serve six terms in the House and no more. True to his word, in 1986 he left the House and made an unsuccessful run for the U.S. Senate.

After leaving Congress, Edgar stayed close to politics, becoming finance chairman for the presidential campaign of his former House colleague, Illinois Senator Paul Simon.

A hundred days before the November 1986 election for the Senate, I realized that I had to raise $2.5 million. That's $25,000 a day, every day, from that hundredth day down to zero. Anyone who has ever raised money knows that if you're a really good fundraiser, you can probably raise $25,000 in one event. Think about raising that today and waking up tomorrow morning knowing you had to raise it tomorrow, the next day, the following day, to raise enough money to continue to keep your message on the air.

Eighty percent of my time, 80 percent of my staff's time, 80 percent of my events and meetings were fundraisers.

It has a terrible impact on you, when you start making choices in your schedule. Rather than going to a senior center, I would go to a party where I could raise $3,000 or $4,000. I started to go to fundraising events—three, four, five a day. That whole fundraising fever has a dramatic impact on a campaign that wants to talk peace-and-justice issues, women's rights, senior-citizen rights, environmental issues. It really gets you warped at the way in which you make those choices.

In the 1986 election in Pennsylvania, the major candidates for governor and the U.S. Senate spent a total of about $21 million, $18 million of which was spent on television. You know, it's just an obscenity to have that kind of an investment in time, energy, and resources flow into a media message where the candidate who gets the cleverest commercial or the nastiest commercial can shape his image and his message, and prevail over the candidate who might be the most thoughtful, the most insightful in terms of the future problems that we face.

So, in addition to some form of public-private financing of campaigns, I'm very much for opening up the airwaves so that people can get access to their candidates without the candidates having to spend a bundle. They're public airways.

I don't think that we ought to assume that lobbyists and lobbying are bad. If you have an eight-hundred-page health-care bill and three paragraphs deal with the dentists, it is very helpful to have a dental lobby in Washington and in the district teaching their people the impact of those three paragraphs on dentists. If you have a technical amendment on electroplating in an environmental bill, it's very helpful to hear from the electroplaters who are going to be impacted by that. It's where they get involved in hosting a fundraising event and get twenty-five of their friends in twenty-five different businesses to give a $5,000 contribution that you begin to see the buying of influence.

★ ━━━

12. SENATOR LAWTON CHILES OF FLORIDA

In 1970, an unknown state senator running for the U.S. Senate pulled on a pair of khaki trousers and hiking boots and spent ninety-two days hiking across Florida. His thousand-mile trek transformed his long-shot candidacy into a seat in the U.S. Senate.

One of his trademarks in the Senate became "sunshine government"—conducting the processes of government out in the open rather than behind closed doors, and subjecting officeholders' personal financial statements and the activities of lobbyists to public-disclosure requirements.

In his next campaign, in 1976, Senator Chiles limited contributions to $10 and refused to accept contributions from out-of-state donors. In 1982, when the Republican Party promised to underwrite his opponent heavily, he apologetically raised the donor ceiling to $100, but added a new restriction: he would not accept contributions from political action committees. Much to the frustration of his fundraisers, he retained all of those limits for his would-be 1988 reelection campaign.

However, in late 1987, Chiles announced he would not seek a fourth Senate term in 1988.

Today, PACs are running in packs, where segments of industry or segments of labor, or segments of this group, get together with multiple PACs and decide how they are going to contribute. Sometimes you're talking about $250,000 for a campaign. Overall I think they're distorting the electoral system and what I sense is, very strong, that your John Q. Public is saying, "I don't count any more. My vote doesn't count, I can't contribute enough money to count. No one is going to listen to me."

I'm looking at congressmen 50 percent of which, I don't know exactly, but around half that get half of their money or more by PACs. They don't even have to come home. Their money is raised at cocktail parties.

At the same time, when I sit down with my fellow senators, they say, "The bane of our existence is fundraising. We're having to do it over six years and we're having to go to Chicago, Los Angeles, New York, Florida. A lot of us spend a lot of time there. But that's what I have to do at night. That's what I have to do on weekends. And, of course, for these big, big PACs, I have to be pretty careful about what my voting record is going to be."

I think if out-of-state contributions were prohibited, you'd have a better chance of those people in your state making the decision based on the merit of the candidate. I think if one candidate, who usually would be an incumbent, can go raise all kinds of out-of-state money, I think he can [distort] his record very much.

A lot of people seem to think that somebody gives you a PAC contribution, then they come in and say, "I expect you to vote for this." It never happens that way. All that person wants you to do is to take and take and take, and then when he comes in, he never says, "I expect." It's always on the basis of, "This is a big one for me, and maybe my job's on the line." He doesn't need to say anything more than that because the hook is already in you, and if you've taken it, you know it, and you *know* you know it.

★ ────────────────────────────────
13. FORMER CONGRESSMAN TOM RAILSBACK OF ILLINOIS

Television viewers over thirty will remember Tom Rails-back from the televised impeachment proceedings against President Nixon before the House Judiciary Committee in early 1974. Railsback was considered a "swing" vote among the Republicans as he wrestled with the question of whether to vote to impeach a president of his own party. Railsback's public agonizing remains vividly in the minds of many who followed those hearings. Ultimately, he voted for impeachment on two of the counts presented.

In the House, where he represented a southeastern Illinois district from 1966 to 1982, Railsback's name was prominently associated with the cause of campaign-finance reform. Along with his Democratic colleague, David Obey of Wisconsin, he authored the Obey-Railsback bill, to limit the amount of money any congressional candidate could receive from PACs.

In 1982, Railsback was defeated in the primary by a conservative Republican. He now practices law in Washington, D.C.

I'm inclined to think that campaign-finance reform may have been influenced by the PACs. In other words, I think a lot of people wanted to vote for reforms of the campaign-financing laws and the political action committees, but they backed off when they saw it was going to affect their ability to raise money from PACs.

———

I favor trying to even the playing field and give challengers a better opportunity to present their views. I say that as a Republican. That was my argument during the seventies and I could never persuade my Republican brethren why they would stand to benefit if there was a more even playing field. I kept pointing out that labor PACs were giving 95 percent of their money to Democrats and the business PACs were giving anywhere from 55 to 60 percent to Republicans. Incumbents were getting a lot more money and Republicans were in the minority in the House. But I think we were able to get only 24 percent of the Republicans in the House to vote for the original campaign-finance reform bill.

THE PAC
MANAGERS SPEAK

6

How do the people who manage the political action committees view what they do? How do they see the role of their PACs in the political process? How do they decide how to distribute their PACs' largess? Do they think their money buys influence—or if not outright influence, do they believe their dollars gain them access to lawmakers' ears?

Here are the answers to those questions offered by four PAC managers, representing four of the major categories of PACs (labor, corporate, ideological, and cooperative): Bill Holayter, legislative and political director of the Machinists' Union; William Brown, director of national governmental affairs in the Ford Motor Company's Washington office; John Isaacs, legislative director of the Council for a Livable World, a major national peace organization; and Frank Vacca, vice-president for governmental relations of Mid-America Dairymen, one of the three major dairy cooperatives.

★ ───
1. BILL HOLAYTER OF THE MACHINISTS' UNION

Ebullient Bill Holayter of the International Association of Machinists and Aerospace Workers is a long-time union man with a pungent tongue and a full, graying beard. He is a man much to be cultivated by congressional candidates, for he is the person most responsible for dispensing the $1,364,000 the Machinists' PAC handed out in the 1986 elections. That sum made his the tenth-largest PAC. Holayter hopes that in 1988, the figure will top $2 million.

The Machinists' PAC collects its money in annual gifts of $10 or more from roughly seventeen thousand of its members nationwide. According to Holayter, a "standard" contribution is about a dollar a month. Payroll deduction plans, provided in some union contracts, yield the PAC $400,000 a year.

Operating out of a Machinist-owned building in Washington, Holayter divides his time between directing the union's political activities and its lobbying (assisted by a full-time lobbyist). Thus, he stays in touch with senators' and representatives' voting records and gathers political intelligence on upcoming House and Senate contests from union officials in the various states.

The final who-gets-what decisions are made by a committee of three top union officers. But they act largely on the basis of Holayter's recommendations.

The decision-making process of the Machinists' PAC contains one democratic element unusual to political action committees: no candidate receives a dollar without the endorsement of the local or state branch of the union. But there is a limit to the say the PAC contributors have about where their money goes. Earmarking of contributions to a particular candidate, for example, is strictly forbidden; Holayter declares, "We don't want anybody telling us what to do with the money they send us. Once you start earmarking, you'll get back to the situation of too much money going to the wrong people. A person that gives to the union PAC has to put some trust in the judgment of the leadership."

The Machinists' selection criteria differ in one critical respect from those of other PACs, whose decision-making begins with one question: Which congressmen and senators can help or hurt our group the most? PACs starting with that question tend, in their giving, to favor incumbents—especially members of the committees that handle legislation most vital to the group—whether or not the incumbents face tight contests and need the PAC's help.

By contrast, Holayter says that in selecting candidates to receive Machinist money, his PAC's analysis starts with a deliberate survey of the probable "marginal" House and Senate contests in the forthcoming election—the contests that are up for grabs, where a contribution could affect the outcome. To identify the marginal contests, Holayter collects political intelligence from Machinist leaders in the various states and from other union political operatives in Washington. Half the Machinists' PAC money goes into those marginal races.

On occasion, the Machinists' PAC does stray from the marginal-district criterion and, like the PACs of Ford, Mid-America, and the others, it gives to candidates sure of easy reelection—for example, 1985 and 1986 gifts totaling $5,000 to Michigan Democrat John Conyers, even though he typically wins 94 percent of the vote in his Detroit district. Why give even a dollar of union members' money to a sure-fire winner like Conyers? "Because," Holayter says, "he still has to run a campaign, or feels he does." But Holayter insists that you'll never see the Machinists giving $10,000—the legal maximum—to an easy winner, nor a contribution to a candidate who doesn't agree with the Machinists' viewpoint. "You can't compare the bankers with us. You'll find the American Bankers Association giving all over the place, whether a person's a friend or not."

Holayter draws a sharp distinction between "people PACs" such as his, and "PACs that represent money interests," such as General Electric's or the American Bankers Association PAC. Those are "special-interest PACs"; they "don't represent people."

But how does Holayter distinguish between his PAC and those others? After all, the Machinists' PAC is looking out for the machinists just as the bankers' PAC is looking out for the bankers.

"Because we're not parochial like they are. We're broad-based. Where most of your corporate PACs—take General Dynamics: all they give a shit about is what happens on the Armed Services Committee and where the Pentagon contracts go. We're interested in a hell of a lot more than that. Safety laws, consumer laws—you can go on and on about the interests we have, because we figure what's good for a Machinists' Union member is good for the whole population, and vice versa."

How does that differ from what GM president Charlie Wilson said in the fifties—"What's good for General Motors is good for the country"?

"Because the Machinists' Union member is no different than any other person that's a worker in this country. They just happen to be a machinist."

Holayter entertains no doubt that his PAC magnifies the political power of individual Machinists' Union members. "If you walk up to a candidate and give them ten dollars—which is about all some of our members can afford—it doesn't mean a goddamn thing. But if we as an organization walk up to a candidate and give him or her $10,000, it means a whole lot more. Also, our union is big and strong in some places and we have hardly any members in others. By pooling the money, we can put New York members' money into Wyoming or New Hampshire, where a senator's vote is just as important to us."

Holayter declares emphatically that his PAC *never* gives to opposing candidates in an election contest, as many PACs do. In one instance when the union local wanted to contribute to both candidates in a primary election in California, "I said, 'Bullshit. You've got to pick one or the other, or nobody's going to get money.' "

Does the PAC money get Holayter greater access to lawmakers' ears?

"Oh, I don't think there's any question that it makes it easy for me to pick up the phone and get a call back. I'm not just 'Bill Holayter, *who*?' I'm Bill Holayter of the Machinists, the people who gave you a good chunk of dough. We don't get a vote from 'em all the time, but we sure have the access."

What does Holayter expect from the lawmakers who get Machinist money? "We expect them to vote right, by our standards."

Isn't that me-first politics?

"Of course it is. That's what we're in business for. Even if you didn't have a PAC, you'd be in business for that. A PAC is just incidental. It's just a money-flowing vehicle."

Bill Holayter stands apart from most of his fellow PAC managers in his distaste for the whole PAC system. "I would like to get out of the business of going around begging for money from our members, because we spend an awful lot of time doing that."

Holayter's view is consistent with that of his union, which, as far back as 1972, plumped for government financing of congressional campaigns. That remains the union's position today.

★ ▬▬▬▬▬▬▬▬▬▬▬▬▬▬▬▬▬▬▬▬▬▬▬▬▬▬▬▬▬▬▬
2. BILL BROWN OF THE FORD MOTOR COMPANY

In appearance, Bill Brown, director of national government relations in the Ford Motor Company's Washington office, strikes a sharp contrast with Bill Holayter. He is very tall and lean, and, in his speech, smooth, quiet, and deliberate. An engineer by training, he first came to Washington in 1971 to help the auto company deal with government regulations on such subjects as safety and emission standards, then rose to head the company's seven-person lobbying staff. In his shirtsleeves in the Ford suite in a downtown

Washington office building, he answers questions about his company's PAC. He is joined by the company's director of national public affairs, Jerald terHorst, a former Washington bureau chief of the *Detroit News* who became Gerald Ford's presidential press secretary, but soon resigned in protest when Ford pardoned Richard Nixon.

The Ford Motor Company was among the early corporations to form a political action committee. Ford began its PAC in 1976 in order, Brown says, to "become better known" on Capitol Hill. Since then, the PAC's giving has risen to $145,000. Brown considers that an "embarrassingly small" figure, considering the company's size —and says it's the result of Ford's soft-sell appeal to the managerial employees from whom the election law permits the company to solicit PAC contributions. The company declines to reveal how many Ford employees give to its PAC, or the size of the average gift. Unlike the machinists' union, Ford does permit its employees to earmark their contributions to specified candidates, but Brown says few do so.

Ford's candidate selection system is markedly different from that of the Machinists' PAC. Rather than putting its money into "marginal" political races, Brown says that Ford concentrates its contributions on members of the committees "that regulate our industry, where we have most of the legislation going through." Therefore the suggestions for Ford PAC donations originate with Brown and his Washington staff, who sift the requests from congressmen and senators that "inundate" Ford's Washington office. Brown then sends the distillation of the Washington group's views to company headquarters in Detroit. There, a committee of five makes the final decisions, choosing, Brown says, candidates "who we think favor positions that would be in the national interest and in the interest of the Ford Motor Company."

Do challengers have as good a crack at getting Ford PAC money as incumbents? "That's a little difficult to respond to," Brown answers. "If there is a congressman who pretty much votes our way, the challenger, frankly, has got a hell of a tough time. I mean, that's what it's all about."

What about a person who challenges a consistent opponent of Ford's desires?

"We're likely to put some money on the guy if he's got any chance at all. But you've got to weigh that. We're not going to throw money away."

An analysis of Ford's official disclosure reports shows that in 1986 House races where the incumbent sought reelection and Ford contributed money, the Ford PAC supported the incumbent 95 percent of the time. Furthermore, it gave to twenty-five House candidates who historically have won by at least four-to-one margins. When told that, both Brown and terHorst expressed great surprise.

Why did Ford give a part of its "embarrassingly small" resources to those shoo-in candidates who don't need the company's help?

"Well," responds Bill Brown, "you're never certain what the situation is going to be this time. If an incumbent comes to you in the campaign and says, 'I've got some polling data that indicates I'm in a little bit of trouble,' then yeah, we support him."

Jerald terHorst adds, "The question, though, is not, 'Does he need your money?' The question is that if a congressman or senator comes to you as a loyal supporter, and says, 'I'd like to have your support again this year,' what do you say? 'Get lost'? The guy may be chairman of a committee. He may be an important leader of Congress."

Do Ford PAC contributions gain the company influence with the donees?

"I don't know," Brown replies. "What's influence? Does it help us? Yeah, it helps us versus not giving. If we didn't support an incumbent whose views are consistent with ours and meets the guidelines of our PAC, I think we would probably be missed. But does it buy influence? No. I can't think of a single occasion where I've ever felt, gee, because we gave a guy $250 or $300 that he voted with us."

Well, do the people you help answer your phone calls quicker?

TerHorst fields that question: "I would hope so. I live in Virginia, and I've given a couple hundred dollars to candidates for governor and state legislature and I would hope they would remember that when I call them up with a problem. So I hope candidates would respond to corporations the same way they respond to individuals."

What role does Brown feel his PAC plays in the political process?

"PACs have become a way of helping guys get elected. Candidates look to PACs to collect a piece of their money. Personally, I feel PACs are definitely a net plus for the republic, because when I put my money into the Ford kitty, I feel that I stand a little better chance of being heard, that I'm part of a bigger action. I think the people who work for Ford are much more likely to respond to a call from company leaders they respect than they are to a politician, when they have no sense of whether or not the guy's being responsive to them."

TerHorst adds, "Besides, what would you do otherwise? If you didn't have a PAC, you would then have your corporate VPs quietly and secretly funding people who the employees would never hear about. That's what happened before there were PACs."

What do Brown and the Ford PAC expect from the candidates to whom they give money?

"Good government. That they'll be good members of Congress who will represent their districts—you know, their piece of the government."

★ 3. JOHN ISAACS OF THE COUNCIL FOR A LIVABLE WORLD

John Isaacs, a small, intense, bearded man, runs one of the "ideological" PACs: that of the Council for a Livable World, one of the nation's major peace organizations.

The Council, which concentrates on arms-control issues, is one of the nation's oldest nonlabor PACs. It dates back to 1962, the year the American Medical Association's PAC was formed.

But the Council's PAC operates differently from conventional PACs. In his cluttered Capitol Hill office, Isaacs explains the distinction: "Most PACs want to maintain control over the money that's sent to them. They want to decide who gets the money and who doesn't. They are the ones who play God. But we let our supporters make that decision."

The Council achieves that by mailing letters to its supporters on behalf of one or another specific candidate the Council's board of directors endorses. The letter asks those who wish to contribute to that particular candidate to send their checks directly to the Council in Washington, pledging that the entire amount of the contribution will go to the candidate and that none will go to support the Council.

Isaacs says that has been an extraordinarily effective fundraising mechanism. In the 1986 election, the Council raised, and gave to congressional candidates, about $1.3 million.

The difference between the Council's PAC and others goes beyond the sheer logistics of soliciting and collecting the money. It steers clear of candidates headed for easy victories, concentrating instead on marginal races. It also diverges sharply from most PACs in the proportion of its help that goes to challengers versus incumbents. In contrast to the Ford PAC, 95 percent of whose 1986 beneficiaries were incumbents, Isaacs says that in Senate races "the overwhelming majority of the money we raise is for challengers. In the House, it is probably a little less. It might be more half and half." Isaacs acknowledges that "we will stay with an incumbent who is a friend as opposed to a challenger who may promise to have a good voting record, and we stay with our friends if they are running for reelection. [Republican] Senator Mark Hatfield in Oregon had a very good opponent the last time he ran. But Hatfield had been an important leader in arms control, and we weren't going to abandon him for some challenger.

"We prefer small states where our money can make a difference. We'd rather get involved in South Dakota and Nevada than California or New York, because the money goes further."

Unlike most conventional PACs, the council does not concentrate on the members of any particular committee. "Our preference is for leaders, not committees," Isaacs says. Democratic Senator Dale Bumpers of Arkansas, for example, "is an important leader in arms control. He's not on Armed Services or Foreign Relations. But he's a leader in this arms-control field, and someone we'd help."

Like the Machinists' Bill Holayter, John Isaacs himself detests the current PAC system and strongly favors abolishing all PACs, including his own. "I think the current campaign-finance system is a disgrace. I think the amount of time people have to spend raising funds is terribly destructive to our whole democratic system.

"But," he quickly continues, "as long as the system's there that way, we'll continue to try to operate with that system, even if we'd like to see it changed."

So despite the things that set Isaacs' PAC apart from all the rest, a basic similarity connects his with the others: what he wants from the candidates he and his PAC help.

"We hope, in general, that they'll vote in the direction we'd like to see. And if they're not sure of the position we hold, at least we hope that they'll give us a hearing. Clearly the money helps us to get that hearing."

★
4. FRANK VACCA OF MID-AMERICA DAIRYMEN

Frank Vacca's dairy PAC has it made. It has the perfect mechanism for collecting money from the dairy farmers of the marketing cooperative, Mid-America Dairymen, it represents: the co-op deducts farmers' PAC contributions from their monthly milk checks. That is, once a farmer signs up for that plan, the monthly deductions become automatic and relatively painless.

In the early seventies, the dairy PACs suggested to their members making monthly PAC contributions of $8.25—a total of $99 a year. That figure barely squeaked under the new disclosure law, which required gifts of $100 or more to be separately listed. Later, when the disclosure threshold was raised to cover gifts greater than $200, the dairy groups doubled the recommended monthly contribution to slide under the new disclosure requirement—"for their privacy," Frank Vacca explains.

Vacca, Mid-America's strikingly handsome vice-president for government relations, sits in the Capitol Hill townhouse that doubles for his office and home, relating with pride how, since he went to work for "Mid-Am" in 1976, the proportion of the Mid-America farmer-members contributing to the PAC has risen from 28 percent to 46 percent. (Mid-Am membership has declined from 12,000 to 11,000.) Result, with roughly 5,000 farmers contributing an average of $65 to $70 a year, the Mid-Am PAC amassed $467,000 to toss into the 1986 congressional elections, enough to put it in forty-seventh place among the more than four thousand PACs.

For Mid-America and the other two giant dairy co-ops, the system of deducting PAC contributions from the monthly milk checks has become a money machine, generating huge sums to throw into the campaigns of friendly representatives and senators. Dairymen, Inc., with a remarkable 74 percent participation among its 6,400 dairy farmers in the Southeast, gave away $232,000 in 1986. Associated Milk Producers, Inc., or AMPI, the giant of the three, dispensed $887,000, making it the twenty-second-largest PAC. The three dairy PACs thus were able to contribute over $1,500,000 to 1986 House and Senate candidates.

With such immense PAC treasuries, all three can easily afford to—and do—spread their largess across the congressional spectrum, including contributions to big-city congressmen in whose districts nary a dairy cow roams, as we saw in Chapter 3. In 1986, the three dairy PACs contributed, on average, to 250 House and Senate candidates, most of them incumbents.

Before the dairy PACs were formed, Vacca explains, the National Milk Producers Federation had "been around for seventy-five years as a lobby—not political, not involved in campaigns. Just up here on Capitol Hill." Then dairy leaders "realized that a way to be more involved in the political process was to establish a PAC" as another step in becoming "better known to the elected officials."

The three dairy co-ops formed their PACs unusually early—in the late sixties, long before the 1974 law laid the framework for the PAC explosion. The biggest co-op—AMPI—got a black eye when it was revealed that its pledge of $2 million to Richard Nixon's 1972 reelection campaign was a quid pro quo for Nixon's raising the federal dairy price-support level.

Frank Vacca, a veteran of sundry Democratic congressional and presidential campaigns (including that of Robert Kennedy in 1968), is Mid-Am's sole operative on Capitol Hill. He says he also spends a great deal of his time extolling Mid-Am's PAC to the organizations' hundred field workers, who in turn sell it to the farmer-members.

Vacca freely acknowledges the need for his PAC to sell a majority of the Congress on the problems of the declining number of dairy farmers, who are concentrated in a few congressional districts. How many dairy farmers *are* there nationwide? "Less than 200,000," Vacca says. "Probably about 180,000. Twenty years ago, there were over a million of them. It's a dying breed. They're projecting that by, oh, 1995, there will be probably around 135,000, somewhere around there.

"You've got to look at it this way," Vacca says. "Today, there are about fifty congressional districts that produce over half the milk. There are about 138 districts that don't produce one ounce of milk. So in the other roughly 250 districts, the congressmen don't look at the dairy farmers' issues unless someone brings it to their attention. So these PACs were started, not to buy votes—that wasn't their intention at all—but as just another way to get the ear of the congressman so the dairy farmers could present their story."

That reasoning underlies the shift in Mid-Am's giving pattern since Vacca took over its political relations in 1976. Before Vacca's arrival, Mid-Am's political action committee followed the traditional pattern of concentrating its contributions in the committees that most affected dairy farmers, primarily the agriculture committees. But after surviving the various committee hurdles, farm legislation must finally come before the full 435-member House of Representatives. "Then the magic number is 218," Vacca explains. "What are you going to do concentrating on the 17 or so on the Agriculture Committee? You've got to get 218 votes. You need a shotgun approach—spread it out all over the place.

"You know, there's some guys from the urban-suburban areas that know nothing about dairy. But they've got to vote on the dairy issue. They should know something about it. Who the hell is going to educate them?"

Mid-America occasionally does contribute to coast-in candidates, even congressmen who have no opponent. In the 1986 election, Mid-America gave to 38 incumbents who had won by an average of at least four to one in the previous four elections; 29 recipients were unopposed. ("Every candidate needs a little maintenance money to carry on. I mean, a candidate has to get his name before the public, even if he's unopposed.") And Vacca has "no problem" with a postelection switch, with Mid-Am giving to the winner after backing the other candidate before the votes were counted. In some such cases, lawmakers "hold it against you" for having backed their opponent. "When you visit their offices, it'll take you an hour or two before you get in to see them. Things like that. That's happened." Others, though, "are broad-minded and they understand it's a professional thing. Not personal."

How does Vacca view the role of PACs in the political system?

"With congressmen and congresswomen representing half a million people, they cannot run around on a horse and bag of oats like they could when the country was rural and they represented about 35,000 people. And with the disappearance of the parties and the city clubs and the ward parties, there is still a need for the candidates to get their message across. The PACs act as another vehicle—to do what ward clubs and city clubs used to do. I see nothing wrong with that at all."

Do Mid-Am's PAC contributions win influence with lawmakers?

"I'd be a fool to say no. But what is influence?" Vacca goes on to explain that some Mid-Am beneficiaries "say, 'Thank you very much,' and go right on their way." Others pay more attention.

Does Mid-Am money gain Vacca favored access to congressmen and senators?

"It can. It should. That's what we said it would. Sure. Because you're a friend. You've helped them out at a time when they needed it."

Does Vacca ever feel extorted by lawmakers' requests for money? Are those requests more heavy-handed than they used to be?

"It's not heavy-handed. It's getting to the point where the candidates feel that the PACs are a natural source of contributions"— especially the PACs that have Washington representatives like Vacca, who "are somewhat easier to get to. It's becoming more onerous for us PAC contributors."

Vacca makes a mental calculation. "There are about 100 days a year for congressmen to hold Washington fundraisers. Now you take those 100 nights and divide it into 435, you're going to come up with four or five a night. Some nights I'll go to ten or twelve. How can we handle that? And that doesn't include the fundraising steering committees that congressmen ask me to serve on.

"Really," says Frank Vacca, "it's getting out of hand."

THE VIEW
FROM THE
OUTSIDE

★ ★ ★ ★ ★

THE TRUE COSTS
OF THE PAC
SYSTEM

One major alternative to having PACs and private individuals pay for congressional election campaigns is for those campaigns to be publicly financed by the federal government, just as presidential campaigns have been paid for since 1976.

But mention that idea to that proverbial man or woman on the street and you're liable to be greeted with a protesting roar. "What —*me* pay for the campaigns of all those lousy politicians?"

The truth is that the average man or woman on the street—in fact *all* the men and women on the street—are paying for those politicians' campaigns *right now*. For instance, they pay every time they buy a quart of milk or a pound of sugar at the supermarket. And they pay every April 15, when they write their checks to the Internal Revenue Service.

That doubtless comes as a surprise to many citizens, who may have assumed that because the present system of financing congressional campaigns involves no direct government outlays it entails no cost. Not so. The present system is immensely costly to all citizens, both as consumers and as taxpayers.

The dairy subsidy offers the ideal illustration. As noted in earlier chapters, year after year, in the face of mounting government stockpiles of cheese and butter, Congress persists in enacting a high dairy price-support program that obliges every American family to pay more for dairy products at the supermarket—and higher taxes to pay for the subsidy program. The manner in which Congress clings to that subsidy flies in the face of a strict one-person–one-vote political calculation, for the subsidy pits the interests of 200,000 dairy farmers, concentrated in a few states and congressional districts, against the interests of tens of millions of consumers and taxpayers throughout the country. So for the dairy farmers to prevail, they must win the support of big-city representatives who don't have a cow in their districts.

There are, of course, two sides to the dairy-subsidy debate. But it is a matter of record that that debate takes place against the backdrop of millions of dollars of campaign contributions the dairy lobby has strewn throughout the Congress, benefiting big-city as well as rural congressmen. Chapter 3 laid out the evidence that those contributions affected the outcome of the dairy vote in the House. So to whatever extent political money affected the vote on the dairy subsidy, part of the cost of that subsidy may fairly be attributed to the current system of financing congressional campaigns.

Similar statistics, presented in this chapter, suggest with equal force that the American Medical Association's multi-million-dollar generosity to hundreds of lawmakers played a part in Congress's defeat of President Carter's plan to curb the incessant rise in hospital costs. Thus, some portion of the billions that plan could have saved hospital billpayers is also part of the price tag attached to the existing campaign-finance system.

To indicate the magnitude of that price tag, this chapter presents four recent congressional actions in which there is evidence of influence by campaign contributions, and therefore a discernible cost to the citizens of the United States.

★ ────────────────────────────────
1. THE SUGAR SUBSIDY

On September 26, 1985, the House of Representatives cast a vote that departed from strict one-person–one-vote politics in a manner even more mystifying than the dairy-subsidy vote.

On the sugar vote, the House was deciding whether to continue a federal sugar subsidy that annually pays the 12,000 American sugar growers an average of a quarter of a million dollars *each*. As against those 12,000 growers, the potential losers numbered in the tens of millions—namely, every American family, forced to pay among the highest sugar prices in the world. A quantity of sugar that costs 85 cents in Washington, D.C., costs just half as much a few hundred miles away, in Ottawa, Canada, and only 31 cents in Mexico.

For growers, the subsidy is enormously lucrative: sugar beets in

Minnesota are nearly four times as profitable as corn; in Louisiana, cane sugar yields $458 per acre, compared with just $69 for soybeans.

Sugar is grown in only 16 of the 50 states and roughly 50 of the 435 congressional districts. Why would the congressmen and senators in the other 385 districts and 34 states vote to give massive help to people who can't cast a vote for them, while injuring every family in their own constituencies? To find the answer, let's look at the sugar subsidy through two ends of a telescope: the consumers' end and the growers' end.

The sugar subsidy makes an estimated $3 billion difference. From the consumers' end of the telescope, that $3 billion costs the average household $41 a year, or about 80 cents a week. Consumers have no way of making common cause to protest high prices. And they certainly lack the means of organizing a political action committee.

From the growers' viewpoint, however, that $3 billion looks quite different. If all those 12,000 growers were equal, the $3 billion would come out to $250,000 each. But of course all growers are *not* equal. In Hawaii, for example, 95 percent of the sugar is grown by five companies. In Florida, three companies produce half the crop. There, to take but one example, the American sugar subsidy has made the four Fanjul brothers rich. The Fanjuls fled Cuba when Castro came to power, and now operate seven sugar companies, own 120,000 acres of sugar land in Florida, have branched into real estate and Caribbean resorts, and, for $200 million, bought from Gulf & Western three resort hotels and 240,000 acres of prime sugar land in the Dominican Republic.

The propped-up price of American sugar has, as noted in Chapter 4, paved the way for a boom in corn sweeteners, a sugar substitute whose manufacturers can make extraordinarily high profits merely by undercutting the price of sugar by a few cents and selling their product to, say, the soft-drink makers. In 1984, just three corn-sweetener firms—Cargill, Staley, and Archer-Daniels-Midland—had total sales of nearly $40 billion.

Moreover, they and the sugar growers are generous political givers. Because they are few in number and highly concentrated, the sugar growers and their allies have successfully formed political action committees. In just four years (1980 to 1984), the major sugar PACs alone expanded in number from ten to seventeen, and their contributions to congressional candidates doubled.

In the 1980s the corn-sweetener industry joined forces with the sugar forces, and by 1984, they had built up an impressive pool of money to throw into congressional campaigns. According to *Common Cause Magazine*, the sugar PACs put about $640,000 into 1984 campaigns. The three largest corn companies sweetened the pot with an added $260,000, bringing the total to $900,000. On top of that, a single individual—Dwayne Andreas, largest stockholder in Archer-Daniels-Midland—and his family contrived to contribute a grand total of $152,100 to congressional candidates, notwithstanding the $1,000 ceiling on individual gifts in the election laws.

Grand total: over $1 million—enough to shower money on a very large number of congressmen and senators. In fact, in the 1984 elections, the sugar–corn-sweetener alliance contributed to the campaigns of more than 450 congressional candidates.

Come 1985—a nonelection year but an important one for the sugar lobby, for Congress was scheduled to cast its quadrennial votes on farm legislation. Over half a million dollars of sugar money flowed to members of Congress in that year alone.

That's the prelude to the September 1985 vote in the House of Representatives. As the House prepared to vote, the forces lined up this way: *For* retaining the sugar subsidy at a high level: the sugar growers' associations; the corn-sweetener companies; and other agricultural commodity groups that receive generous subsidies. Arrayed against them, in favor of a mild cutback of the subsidy: a variety of consumer, labor, and sugar-using industries (candy, ice cream, bakeries, etc.)—plus the Reagan administration.

The outcome: the consumer-labor-administration forces lost, 142 to 263.

Here is the evidence that sugar-lobby campaign contributions had an effect on that vote.

OF THOSE RECEIVING THIS AMOUNT FROM THE SUGAR LOBBY IN 1983 THROUGH 1986 . . .	. . . THIS PERCENT VOTED FOR SUGAR SUBSIDIES IN 1985
MORE THAN $5,000	100%
$2,500 TO $5,000	97%
$1,000 TO $2,500	68%
$1 TO $1,000	45%
ZERO	20%

As a result of that vote, and a correspondingly lopsided vote in the Senate, hundreds of millions of sugar consumers will have to go on paying an added $3 billion a year *through 1991*. That's the next time Congress will have an opportunity to vote on the $3 billion sugar subsidy.

★ ━━━
2. THE DAIRY SUBSIDY

On the same afternoon as the vote on the sugar subsidy, the House was called on to choose between two alternative programs for subsidizing the nation's dairy industry. The choice was between continuing to increase dairy price supports while paying farmers to take cows out of production, as proposed by the House Agriculture Committee, and a gradual lowering of the dairy supports, as proposed by Democratic Congressman Jim Olin of Virginia and the House Republican Leader, Bob Michel of Illinois.

The Department of Agriculture and the Congressional Budget Office estimated that, over the years 1985–90, the Agriculture Committee bill would cost taxpayers $2.77 billion more than the Olin-Michel bill in direct supports. In addition, the Milk Industry Foundation estimated that the higher subsidy would, over those same years, cost consumers an added $11.52 billion in higher prices for dairy products at the checkout counters.

That September day, the higher subsidy contained in the committee bill and favored by the three giant dairy PACs prevailed in the House by a vote of 244 to 166. And campaign contributions by those dairy PACs had an impact on the 1985 House vote (see the table on page 47): the more money a representative got, the more likely he or she was to vote with the dairy lobby.

★ ━━━
3. THE HOSPITAL-COST CONTAINMENT BILL

In 1977, President Carter proposed to Congress a bill to curb soaring hospital costs, which had quintupled in the preceding decade. His program was aimed at holding the future rise of hospital costs to 9 percent a year. The Department of Health, Education, and Welfare estimated that this could save consumers about $27 billion through 1982.

The Carter program was strenuously opposed by the American Medical Association because, the AMA said, it would be a regulatory nightmare; it would unfairly single out the hospital industry for price controls; and it was unnecessary because the industry's Voluntary Effort campaign was already bringing down the rate of hospital-cost inflation. The AMA's PAC is one of the largest (in 1986, second-highest in contributions to congressional candidates) and most active in the United States.

On July 18, 1978, the House Commerce Committee defeated the Carter proposal by a single vote, 21–22, and the bill went no farther that year. When President Carter submitted a new plan to Congress in 1979, he estimated that savings to consumers and to federal, state, and local governments would amount to $53 billion over the ensuing five years—about $10 billion a year.

On November 15, 1979, the new measure was defeated by a vote of 166 to 234 in the House of Representatives. Did AMA campaign contributions affect that vote? Again, the figures suggest that they did.

OF THOSE RECEIVING THIS AMOUNT FROM THE AMERICAN MEDICAL ASSOCIATION IN 1977 THROUGH 1980 . . .	. . . THIS PERCENT VOTED AGAINST CONTAINING HOSPITAL COSTS IN 1979
MORE THAN $15,000	100%
$10,000 TO $15,000	95%
$5,000 TO $10,000	82%
$2,500 TO $5,000	80%
$1 TO $2,500	38%
ZERO	37%

★ ─────────────────────────────
4. THE DOMESTIC-CONTENT BILL ON CARS SOLD IN THE UNITED STATES

In 1982, the American automobile industry faced a crisis. Sales of domestic cars plunged while foreign cars flooded the U.S. market.

Arguing that foreign automakers—especially in Japan—received government subsidies and were engaging in unfair trade practices, the United Auto Workers union in 1982 began pressing Congress to enact a "domestic-content" bill, requiring all cars sold in the United States to contain a certain percentage of U.S.-made parts and components.

Critics contended that the domestic-content measure would

cause car prices in the United States to rise; that it would result in a net loss of U.S. jobs; and that it would invite retaliatory trade measures by foreign countries. The Congressional Budget Office estimated that the measure would raise car prices $500, on the average. If the domestic-content measure had applied to the 7.9 million cars sold in the United States in 1982, it would have cost American consumers approximately $3.9 billion that year.

The UAW has long operated one of the foremost PACs; in 1986, it was the fourth largest, dispensing over $1.6 million to 344 congressional candidates. The domestic-content bill passed the House in 1982, by a vote of 215 to 188, and again in 1983, by 219 to 199. (In neither year did it pass the Senate.) Again, campaign contributions correlate strongly with the 1982 House vote.

OF THOSE RECEIVING THIS AMOUNT FROM THE AUTO WORKERS' PAC IN 1979 THROUGH 1982 . . .	. . . THIS PERCENT VOTED FOR THE DOMESTIC-CONTENT AUTO BILL IN 1982
MORE THAN $20,000	100%
$10,000 TO $20,000	91%
$2,500 TO $10,000	82%
$1 TO $2,500	62%
ZERO	17%

★ THE TOTAL COSTS

Let us recap the estimated annual cost to consumers and taxpayers of the four votes described above:

THE VOTES ON THESE MEASURES . . .	. . . WOULD COST THE PUBLIC ABOUT THIS MUCH EVERY YEAR
SUGAR SUBSIDY	$ 3 BILLION
DAIRY SUBSIDY	$ 3 BILLION
HOSPITAL COSTS	$10 BILLION
DOMESTIC CONTENT ON AUTOS	$ 4 BILLION
TOTAL	$20 BILLION

Calculating how much of that $20 billion may be fairly attributed to the existing campaign-finance system is a tricky and imprecise business. For example, how much of the $10 billion annual cost of the defeat of the Carter hospital cost-containment plan may fairly be assigned to campaign contributions by the AMA's PAC? All of it? Surely that would be a hard claim to support, for that would require proving that a Congress uninfluenced by AMA money would have passed the Carter plan wholly unchanged. Such an event is too rare, with or without special-interest money, to be credible.

On the other hand, to argue that *none* of the $10 billion is due to the millions contributed by the AMA is to say all those campaign contributions had no impact whatever—an equally implausible proposition.

So the answer as to how much of the cost to attribute to the current campaign finance system lies somewhere between zero and 100 percent. Those who put little credence in this whole line of reasoning might put it at 10 percent, which would be a $2 billion annual cost for the four legislative measures covered in this chapter. Others might prefer to place 50 percent of the blame on the PAC system, for an annual cost of $10 billion.

The point is that whichever one chooses, the cost of the way we now finance congressional campaigns—even the low-end $2 billion figure—is prodigious, and almost surely far exceeds the cost of any foreseeable program of public financing for congressional campaigns.

For example, $2 billion a year is nearly *fifteen times* the cost of one plan for government financing of congressional general elections introduced in 1984.* That plan would provide $200,000 to every Democratic and Republican nominee for the U.S. House in all 435 congressional districts. It would also provide varying public grants to senate major-party nominees, depending on the voting population of the state, ranging from $500,000 for the smallest state to $5.7 million for California.

That public-financing scheme would cost $87 million a year for the House and $49 million for the Senate, a total of $136 million a year.

Partial public financing of primary elections for the House and Senate—with the government matching small contributions, as in

---

* That plan was provided in S. 1787, co-sponsored by Republican Senator Charles McC. Mathias and Democratic Senator Paul Simon of Illinois, and in H.R. 3806, of which Democratic Congressman Anthony Beilenson of California was the leading sponsor.

the presidential primaries now—would doubtless cost considerably more. But there is slim likelihood such a plan would equal the $2 billion a year—the conservatively-reckoned cost of the present system for just four bills. And if the program became undesirably costly, Congress could cut it back.

The point is: it is difficult to conceive a plan for government financing of congressional campaigns that would be more costly to taxpayers and consumers than the current special-interest-dominated system of paying for those elections—if we face up to the *true* costs of the present system.

CAMPAIGN CONTRIBUTION OR BRIBE? "A HAIRLINE'S DIFFERENCE"

8

The distinction between a large campaign contribution and a bribe is almost a hairline's difference.
—Senator Russell B. Long

The distinction between a campaign contribution and a bribe can indeed be thin—so thin, in fact, that the U.S. Court of Appeals ordered a new trial in the 1972 bribery conviction of Maryland Senator Daniel B. Brewster because the trial judge had failed to make that distinction clear to the jury.

Presented below are the facts about the official behavior of certain U.S. senators and representatives either shortly before or shortly after they received campaign contributions from various interest groups. Considering all the facts, were those campaign contributions? Or were they bribes?

In posing that question, I am not asking readers to sit as jurors and render a court-of-law verdict on whether these legislators should be sent to jail. Nor am I suggesting official laxity in the failure to prosecute these cases. On the contrary, so sophisticated is the minuet performed by givers and receivers that evidence of an explicit *quid pro quo* is extremely difficult to come by. Indeed, such are the subtleties that not even the lawmakers themselves may know for certain which side of the line they are on.

My point is to illustrate the difficulty of distinguishing between campaign contribution and bribe, and to demonstrate that our election laws tolerate official behavior that comes far closer to bribery than most of us would feel comfortable with.

As background, here are the critical phrases of the bribery statute, which subjects to criminal prosecution any—

public official [who],
directly or indirectly,
corruptly demands, seeks, receives, accepts, or agrees to
    receive or accept
anything of value personally or for any other person or entity
in return for
being influenced in the performance of any official act. . . .

Against that backdrop, here are the facts concerning eight recent congressional actions:

Very late one June night in 1984, members of the Senate and
House strove to reconcile the differences between their respective
versions of a tax bill.

Suddenly, and without warning, Illinois Democratic Congressman Dan Rostenkowski, leader of the House negotiators, brought
up a proposal to solve a pressing tax problem faced by some 333
wealthy commodity traders (whom we met in Chapter 4), most of
them from Rostenkowski's home city of Chicago.

According to an account of the incident in *Common Cause Magazine*, Kansas Senator Robert Dole, who was heading the Senate
negotiating team, quickly agreed to Rostenkowski's proposal.
Within a matter of minutes, the commodity traders had secured a
provision potentially worth at least $300 million—an average of
$866,000 per trader.

Senator Dole had not always been so sympathetic to the traders'
tax problem. Indeed, three years earlier, he had been instrumental
in blocking a proposal to single out the traders for preferred treatment involving the same provision of the tax law. The 1981 plan that
Dole blocked had been spearheaded by Democrats to whom the
traders had been politically generous, and on the Senate floor, Dole
had chided the Democrats. The commodity traders, he said, are
"nice fellows . . . and they are great contributors. They haven't
missed a fundraiser. If you do not pay any taxes, you can afford to
go to all the fundraisers."

But Dole's efforts to thwart the traders' tax avoidance had gone
beyond a mere Senate floor speech. When the traders claimed that
the compromise provision enacted in 1981 gave them amnesty for
their past tax avoidance maneuvers, *Common Cause Magazine* reports that Dole took the trouble to write the Internal Revenue Service saying the IRS was free to go after traders who in earlier years
had unlawfully abused the tax law. The IRS did just that, and soon

several thousand cases were pending in the Tax Court, involving several hundred million dollars in disputed taxes.

Enter now Representative Rostenkowski and Senator Dole with their late-night rescue—a provision one senator claimed would "virtually preclude" the IRS from pursuing tax cases.

During the period when Dole was reversing field, the commodity industry and individual traders had been most generous about contributing to Dole's own PAC, Campaign America. Through Campaign America, Dole had spent $300,000 helping the campaigns of forty-seven of fifty-three Republican senators—surely no hindrance in his election in 1984 as Senate Republican leader.

A *Common Cause Magazine* scrutiny of official records disclosed that—

- in 1983–84, individuals and PACs from the commodity industry gave Campaign America $70,500—six times what they had given in 1981–82.
- in the three months prior to Senator Dole's approval of the late-night amnesty provision, they had given $10,500 to Campaign America.
- just three *weeks* before the Dole-Rostenkowski rescue, individual traders had contributed $3,600 to a fundraiser cohosted by Campaign America.

Political contributions? Or bribes?

As recounted in Chapter 3, on February 3, 1987, the Senate voted on a provision to vastly reduce the cost to the taxpayers of removing billboards that violate the Highway Beautification Act.

The provision, offered by Vermont's Republican Senator Robert T. Stafford, would have revived the procedure the states and localities had historically used to compensate billboard owners for signs torn down pursuant to local laws. That traditional method, as we have seen, granted billboard owners a grace period before having to remove a sign, with the revenues the owners collected during that interval considered proper compensation. But in the sixties and seventies, Congress required that billboard owners be paid in cash for signs they were obliged to take down.

Among the senators voting against reviving the grace-period method of compensation was Brock Adams, the newly elected Democratic senator from the state of Washington. He told his colleagues in the Senate that while "the government may have the right to take property, it also has an obligation to provide direct compensation for it."

That had not always been Adams's position. Nine years earlier, as secretary of transportation in the Carter administration, Adams had vigorously protested the very cash-only compensation formula he now defended. On August 17, 1978, Secretary Adams had written to Pennsylvania's Democratic Representative Peter H. Kostmayer that to require cash payments and strip localities of their historic ability to use the grace-period method of compensation "would represent an unprecedented intrusion by the federal government into the prerogatives of localities to control land uses within their jurisdiction."

But in 1987, what had been for *Secretary* Adams a government "intrusion" had, for *Senator* Adams, been transformed into a government "obligation." (Senator Adams explained to the *Washington Post* that he had assumed his 1978 stance to conform with the policies of the Carter administration.)

In the intervening period, Brock Adams had conducted a successful senatorial campaign, in the course of which he had received campaign contributions totaling $12,200 from the billboard industry and from individuals connected with it. Many of the latter resided outside the state of Washington.

Had those contributions played *any* part in Senator Adams's change of heart between 1978 and 1987?

The fast-rising millions the leading defense contractors are pouring into lawmakers' pockets (via honoraria) and their reelection campaigns (via contributions) inevitably raise questions about the crossing of the slender bribery line. Three illustrations:

────────── **Illustration No. 1:** In late 1985, Congress enacted a measure aimed at reducing the price of military equipment by obliging Pentagon contractors to report on how well they control their labor costs.

The *Wall Street Journal* reported that a few months later, a group of Pentagon lobbyists met to decide what could be done to repair the damage. The result: a concerted congressional effort to repeal the 1985 provision outright. According to the *Journal*, leading the Senate repeal effort was Indiana Republican Senator Dan Quayle, the chairman of the military procurement subcommittee that had cleared the labor cost-control measure only a few months earlier. Senator Quayle faced reelection in November 1986. According to the *Journal*, between January 1983 and June 1986, he received $92,000 in campaign contributions from defense contractors' PACs, 5 percent of all the campaign money he had raised in that time. In addition, in 1984 and 1985, defense firms gave the senator $7,500 in honoraria, which he could legally put in his pocket.

Quayle's office said it was "outrageous" to infer a connection between those $92,000 of defense contractor campaign contributions and the senator's flip-flop on the cost-reporting measure. Other repeal proponents pointed out that the cost-reporting law had been passed in 1985 without any hearings and was poorly written. The heavily taxed public might wonder why the solution to those problems didn't lie in holding hearings and perfecting the 1985 law, rather than repealing it. (Ultimately, a compromise version was passed.)

_____ **Illustration No. 2:** In 1983, the Dravo Corporation of Pittsburgh was low bidder to build a $103 million steam plant for the Navy in Portsmouth, Virginia. Later, though, Dravo found that it had to redesign the plant, and faced a $25 million cost overrun on the project. According to *Time* magazine, rather than "waste time trying to persuade unsympathetic Navy brass to renegotiate," in September 1986, Dravo lobbyist Martin Hamberger went to Pennsylvania Republican Senator Arlen Specter, to whose 1986 reelection campaign the Dravo PAC had already contributed $4,000. Hamberger presented to Specter a draft of what Dravo wanted inserted in the defense appropriation bill: a provision instructing the Navy to reimburse Dravo for its cost overrun. Without telling the Navy what he was doing, Specter inserted the brief provision within the ninety-seven-page bill. After Hamberger's September visit, the Dravo PAC gave Specter an added contribution of $2,500.

Senator Specter declined to comment on the matter, but a member of his staff said he "did nothing for Dravo that he doesn't do regularly for Pennsylvania companies, many of whom are not contributors." But Republican Congressman Robert Badham of California saw the Dravo incident as far more than a constituent-service matter. "It was an extremely dangerous precedent," said Badham. "It gives a whole new dimension to bidding and contracting: If all else fails, go to the Congress."

Did Dravo's $6,500 campaign contributions have any connection

with Senator Specter's asssistance to Dravo that set that "dangerous precedent"? The public cannot be sure. But both are fixed on
the public record: the Dravo contributions and the Specter rescue.

——————— **Illustration No. 3:** In December 1982, Congressman Joseph Addabbo, a Democrat from Queens and chairman of
the House Appropriations Subcommittee on the Defense Department, was reported to be a "prime mover" in an action to end the
monopoly theretofore enjoyed by the Avco Corporation in making
engines for the Army's M-1 tank. Addabbo and his colleagues had
ample reason to urge competitive bidding on the engine contract:
Avco's engines cost more than targeted, were delivered later than
promised, were often defective, and consumed five gallons per mile
(not five miles per gallon; five gallons *per mile*).

But on July 20 of the following year, Congressman Addabbo
reversed himself, and voted to continue the Avco monopoly, even
though in the meantime the Army had received a bid from a competing firm that could have saved the taxpayers $300 million.

In the interval, Representative Addabbo (now deceased) received two $2,500 campaign contributions from Avco, one on April
13 and one on May 10.

Those facts are all contained in easily available public documents. When the facts were published in the *Wall Street Journal* in
October 1983, no one in an official position apparently thought to
inquire whether Avco's gifts crossed the line between bribe and
legal political contribution.

In 1975, Texas billionaire H. Ross Perot faced a peculiar tax
problem. On November 4 of that year, by a 20–14 vote, the House
Ways and Means Committee approved an amendment carefully tailored to solve Perot's problem. The amendment stood to save Perot
$15 million in taxes.

An examination of federal campaign reports later disclosed that
in the 1974 elections, Perot had favored various congressional candidates with twenty-six campaign contributions totaling $75,900. All
but two of the gifts were made *after* the election.

Twelve members of the Ways and Means Committee received
Perot gifts. Of the twelve, ten supported the specially tailored provision to confer a $15 million tax saving on their Texas benefactor.

Two Ways and Means members, Democrats Joe Waggoner of
Louisiana and Omar Burleson of Texas, each received $5,000 from

Perot just after the election. Perot made the campaign gifts, and Waggoner and Burleson accepted them, even though both congressmen had been unopposed in the 1974 primary and general elections. Both supported the "Perot amendment" in committee.

Later, after the exposure of the Perot campaign gifts in the *Wall Street Journal* set off a storm of controversy, the special Perot provision was overwhelmingly defeated on the House floor, by a vote of 379–27. Waggoner and Burleson cast two of the 27 pro-Perot votes.

In May 1985, at Chasen's restaurant in Beverly Hills, California, New York Senator Alfonse D'Amato was beneficiary of a $1,000-a-plate fundraising dinner for his reelection campaign. The dinner was arranged by the investment banking firm Drexel Burnham Lambert, Inc. Drexel was the nation's leading (and pioneering) underwriter of so-called "junk bonds"—high-risk bonds typically used to finance corporate mergers and takeovers.

Senator D'Amato was chairman of the Senate Subcommittee on Securities, and during the week following the Chasen's dinner, the subcommittee was scheduled to hold a hearing on legislation to regulate the sale of junk bonds. D'Amato's subcommittee had two proposals before it: one, to curb the use of junk bonds in corporate takeovers, and the other to limit the purchase of those bonds by federally insured savings banks. Either proposal would have put a major crimp in Drexel Burnham's business.

Of the $33,000 raised at the dinner, $23,000 came from the twenty-three Drexel Burnham executives who each contributed $1,000 to Senator D'Amato's campaign. Another $4,000 came from two executives of Columbia Savings & Loan Association, a prime customer of the Drexel firm. At the time, Columbia already owned far more junk bonds than would be permitted under legislation to be considered at the D'Amato hearing.

According to a story by Brooks Jackson in the *Wall Street Journal,* when D'Amato finally introduced his bill regulating corporate takeovers later that year, "the provision [regulating junk bonds] so dreaded by Drexel was missing."

Five days after the D'Amato shoe dropped, Jackson reported, Drexel's chief executive officer and thirty-five other Drexel executives from New York donated $500 each to Senator D'Amato's campaign. D'Amato called the timing "absolutely coincidental."

———

In 1974, the U.S. Senate passed a bill mandating a system of "no-fault" auto accident insurance for the entire United States. Under no-fault, accident victims are paid their medical expenses and wage losses regardless of who (if anyone) was at fault. One of the aims of no-fault is to reduce the expensive and time-consuming lawsuits on auto accidents. No-fault proponents say such a change would save billions of dollars that now go to pay lawyers' fees and put them into the pockets of accident victims. Twenty-four states now have some form of no-fault auto insurance.

No-fault auto insurance was and is fiercely opposed by the Association of Trial Lawyers, which had one of the country's fastest-growing PACs.

The House failed to act on the no-fault bill the Senate passed in 1974, and in 1976, the measure came up for a new Senate vote. This time, nine senators who had supported no-fault two years earlier switched, and voted against the new bill. Now it lost by four votes, 45–49.

The nine vote-switches included five senators up for reelection in 1976. All five received generous campaign contributions from the trial lawyers' PAC following their anti-no-fault vote. Four of the senators got contributions of $5,000 each, the fifth received $2,500.

Had all five senators undergone a 180-degree philosophical turn-about on the no-fault issue? Was there *any* connection between the money and the votes? If so, did those campaign contributions bear any of the earmarks of a bribe?

At least one of the five—Ohio Republican Senator Robert A. Taft—seems to have felt so uncomfortable about the trial lawyers' contribution that he later returned the money.

In the no-fault example, or any of the others, did anyone step over the narrow line between contribution and bribe?

Perhaps, perhaps not. We don't know for certain. We aren't privy to what was said by giver or receiver.

But, even if we had been, we might not be certain whether the line had been crossed. Recall what former Democratic Congress-man Mike Barnes reported hearing frequently from PAC managers during his eight years in the House (see Chapter 5): "Mike, we're getting ready to make our next round of checks out. . . . We really think we can help you. . . . By the way, Mike, have you been fol-lowing that bill in Ways and Means . . . ? It's got an item we're concerned about . . . and we hope you'll be with us on that one."

Even if a representative on the receiving end of such a call believes there is a bribe embedded in that interchange, there's no way to be sure. And should one affront an ally (not to mention a potential large contributor) by accusing him or her of so grave an act?

Most disturbing of all, not only will the public remain unsure whether the bribery line has been crossed—*the recipient of the contribution may also be unsure.* That is, once the knowledge of a large contributor's interest in the amendment is planted in an office-holder's mind, can even the most honest of lawmakers wholly banish that thought when considering the measure—especially when caught up in a hard-fought and expensive campaign for political survival? If not, can the lawmakers themselves be positive they have not violated the bribery statute by accepting something of value "in return for being influenced in the performance of any official act"?

As the U.S. Court of Appeals said in sending the bribery conviction of Senator Brewster back for retrial:

> No politician who knows the identity and business interests
> of his campaign contributors is ever completely devoid of
> knowledge as to the inspiration behind the donation.

In 1986, the House Agriculture Committee considered a proposal by the Reagan administration to levy a fee on commodity traders to finance the federal agency overseeing that trading. When Agriculture Committee members were showered with campaign contributions from traders opposing the fee, the *New York Times* said, "[It all] sounds very much like legal bribery." Was the *Times* far wrong?

HONORARIA: A LEGAL WAY OF LINING POLITICIANS' POCKETS

9

If you tend to blanch a bit when reading that big-time lawyers charge $500 an hour, how do you react upon learning that many representatives and senators get paid $1,000 or even $2,000 an hour —and by the very interest groups that lobby before them every day?

More and more, such heady fees to lawmakers are becoming routine. Here's a concrete illustration of how those enormous hourly "fees" are possible:

The American Trucking Association owns a townhouse on Capitol Hill, a short walk from the Capitol itself. Congressman X or Senator Y is invited for breakfast. Jerald Halvorsen, the association's chief lobbyist, has described for the *Wall Street Journal* what takes place at a typical session. "The congressman comes over at eight. We have twenty to twenty-five staff. The congressman answers questions and leaves." It's usually over in an hour, and the representative picks up a check for $1,000—usually $2,000 if it's a senator.

These honoraria, or speaking fees, can be a more effective way of gaining a legislator's attention and favor than a campaign contribution. For while campaign contributions may warm lawmakers' hearts, they do not swell their personal bank accounts. Honoraria, on the other hand, are paid directly into the hands of the senator or representative. Thus, these fees provide a means of lining lawmakers' pockets in a manner that is entirely legal and therefore, in a technical sense, carries no taint of bribery.

Increasingly, interest groups—especially the less weighty

among them that cannot match the heavy-hitting PACs*—are coming to view speaking fees as the poor folks' alternative to PAC contributions as a way of winning congressional friends. A few interest groups come right out and say so. Fred Meister, chief executive of the Distilled Spirits Council, says, "We have a virtually nonexistent political action committee. . . . We're not out there giving huge political contributions; what we do is to give very modest $1,500 and $2,000 honorariums. . . . We're not buying any votes, or trying to. We have to use the few legitimate ways we have to get our views across." To get its views across about the dangers of raising liquor taxes, the council stepped up its breakfast invitations to key legislators. In 1985, the distillers handed out $55,701 in honoraria, three-fourths of which went to members of the tax-writing committees.

Formerly, lawmakers were expected, so to speak, to sing for their supper—that is, to at least deliver a speech in return for their "speaking" fees. Not these days. The *Wall Street Journal* reported that members of the tax committees can pick up a $2,000 fee just for dropping by the monthly meeting of the beermakers' coalition to listen to plans it is brewing.

The rules about congressional honoraria stand in sharp and ironic contrast to those governing other favors in official Washington. For example, members of the cabinet and other employees of the executive branch are forbidden to accept so much as a dime for giving a speech, even if no conflict of interest is involved. Moreover, congressional rules forbid members of Congress to accept other kinds of favors exceeding $100.

By contrast, Congress has placed honoraria paid to its members beyond legal challenge, regardless of the flagrancy of the conflict of interest involved. A member of, say, a House or Senate transportation committee is free to accept—*and pocket*—a $2,000-an-hour fee for breakfasting with the Trucking Association without transgressing the law or any congressional rules. Members of the congressional banking committees were similarly beyond legal challenge when they took $140,000 from the banking industry in 1983, despite the manifest conflict of interest.

The law for executive-branch employees dates back to 1917, and

---

* Even the American Pork Congress is among the groups that "figure prominently" in paying honoraria, according to the *Washington Post*.

it even forbids business concerns paying travel expenses. In 1922, Attorney General Harry M. Daugherty, explaining his ruling to that effect, said the purpose of the 1917 law was to assure "that no Government official or employee should serve two masters to the prejudice of his unbiased devotion to the interests of the United States."

But senators and representatives take a more relaxed attitude about the masters they serve. For example, members of the defense committees of Congress (Armed Services and Defense Appropriations) apparently saw nothing wrong in accepting over $182,000 from the leading defense contractors in 1985. Lawmakers are often paid their fees just for touring a defense plant and chatting with company officers. Evidently, defense firms find honoraria an effective way to gain congressional friends, for between 1981 and 1985, the top ten defense companies increased their honoraria to members of Congress from $26,100 to $236,163.

Members of Congress are limited in the annual honoraria they may keep ($25,880 for the House, $34,990 for the Senate—30 and 40 percent, respectively, of their salaries). Lawmakers must give any excess amounts to charity, although on the average, they keep over three-fourths of their fees.

Honoraria to lawmakers are also limited to $2,000 per occasion. Legislators may, however, receive more than one fee in a day. In a single day's trip to Chicago, a legislator can pick up one fee for touring the Chicago Mercantile Exchange and another for a similar visit to the Chicago Board of Trade (two groups that are ordinarily at each other's throats).

On occasion, the maximum $2,000 fee can be "earned" under highly agreeable circumstances. In mid-1986, for example, Virginia Democratic Representative Frederick Boucher wrote to several of his colleagues, inviting them to spend an afternoon as the guest of the United Coal Company. The group would fly from Washington to Bristol, Virginia (company headquarters), on the company's private Boeing 727; tour the company's mines; dine with coal-company executives; then jet back to Washington that same evening—each $2,000 richer than when they left Washington, thanks to a fee paid by United Coal.

Congressman Boucher's invitation letter made it clear that the trip would not take place under hardship conditions. United Coal's 727 jet, he wrote, is "a truly outstanding custom designed aircraft which I think you will enjoy." To leave no doubt on that score, he enclosed a color brochure picturing the aircraft's "Statesman's Salon/Dining Area," wet bar, and executive stateroom.

To *Washington Post* reporter Sandra Sugawara, who unearthed the story, Congressman Boucher defended the $2,000 honorarium, explaining that "members of Congress, taking the time to do something like this *expect to get some compensation for it*" (emphasis added).

In selecting the representatives to invite, Congressman Boucher didn't choose randomly. Many of the fourteen who made the trip sat on the Energy and Commerce Committee, which deals with many issues of interest to mining companies; one was a member of the House Appropriations Committee, which controls the future of a $400 million coal-research program, including a grant to United Coal; and one was a member of the tax-writing Ways and Means Committee, which had before it a Reagan administration proposal to repeal tax preferences long enjoyed by the coal industry.

There appears to be an abundance of interest-group money eagerly waiting to be placed in the pockets of lawmakers who are in a position to be of special help. For example, in the wake of a *Wall Street Journal* story depicting the difficulties New Orleans Republican Congressman Bob Livingston was having making ends meet, the congressman was inundated with speaking invitations. Most came from defense contractors, who had a special interest in cultivating Livingston as a member of the House Defense Appropriations Subcommittee. Within one year, Livingston's honoraria earnings more than doubled.

The amounts of speaking-fee money that can be marshaled by a given industry can be massive. A 1984 study by Congress Watch, Ralph Nader's lobbying group, found that over a five-year period, the three hundred companies that had formed a coalition favoring legislation to protect industry from product-liability lawsuits had paid a total of $687,300 in speaking fees to seventy-eight U.S. senators. Average: $7,900 per senator. These honoraria supplemented nearly $5 million in campaign contributions made by PACs of the same firms in the same period.

Interest groups large and small (especially small) find that dispensing honoraria to lawmakers carries ancillary benefits—mainly the rare opportunity to have a legislator's focused attention. Russell Campbell, chief Washington lobbyist for General Telephone and Electronics, finds that his company's breakfast series provides the "full time and attention" of legislators such as Representative Al

Swift, the Washington State Democrat who ranks second on the House Telecommunications Subcommittee and is hence a *very* important person for GTE. Swift received a $1,000 honorarium from GTE in 1986.

The tiny Electronic Funds Transfer Association, too small to have an important PAC, was having trouble getting appointments to see key representatives handling banking legislation. So the association offered a $1,000 fee to Georgia Congressman Doug Barnard, a member of a key subcommittee, to speak at a Washington conference. The congressman accepted. The occasion offers a classic illustration of the "captive-audience" advantage of which GTE's Campbell spoke. James Callan, the association's chief Washington lobbyist, picked up Congressman Barnard outside his Capitol Hill office building in a rented limousine, which afforded Callan the congressman's undivided attention on the drive across town. That trip was followed by a half-hour visit with association president Dale Reistad prior to Barnard's forty-minute speech.

Occasionally, interest groups wrap their honoraria invitations in bright fancy packages, such as all-expenses-paid trips (often including spouse or family) to one of the group's "business meetings"—sometimes at exotic resorts far from Washington. Example: in November 1986, the American Council of Highway Advertisers held its 50th annual meeting on Barbados, one of the more distant Caribbean islands (round-trip coach airfare from Washington, D.C.: $777). Among members of Congress who found several free days in their schedule to accept the council's invitation: Senator Larry Pressler of South Dakota (and Mrs. Pressler), who spent four days on the island, courtesy of the council, and picked up a $2,000 honorarium. Among the House members who made the journey: Representative Wayne Dowdy of Mississippi (and Mrs. Dowdy), who stayed three days and received $1,000, and Pennsylvania Democrat Robert Borski, who got a $1,000 honorarium.

Sophisticated interest groups carefully include congressional staff members (who shape the tiny but vital details of legislation) on these expense-paid resort junkets. We have already seen them as guests of the Outdoor Advertising Association of America at Palm Springs (see Chapter 3).

Many members of Congress apparently feel such personal financial pressure that they not only take but actively seek speaking fees. An example: Representative Pat Williams, a liberal Democrat from

Montana. Williams is an ex-schoolteacher without any savings. He is obliged to carry two home mortgages (one in Washington, and one in Montana). He has one child already in college and two daughters soon to go. Williams says he has no choice but to "hustle" speaking fees, and to do it "a little more as college gets closer."

Whether or not under pressures like Williams, nearly everybody in Congress now plays the honorarium game. All but fifty-six representatives and eleven senators took honoraria in 1985. Twenty representatives and two senators accepted honoraria but gave all of the money to charity.

More disturbing, most lawmakers appear to feel it is natural and wholly acceptable that they should have their pockets lined by perfect strangers—often strangers who have enormous amounts to lose or gain by the recipients' official actions.

For example, in the case of the jet visit to coal country described earlier in this chapter, Virginia Congressman Boucher said he saw nothing wrong in inviting members of the committee overseeing the coal industry to be the guests of a coal company. Nor did he see anything amiss in those members "expecting" a $2,000 fee from the company for picking up information about the mining industry that they should receive anyway in the conduct of their public duties.

Indeed, Boucher said, the trip was entirely proper because House members "cast votes on legislation that affects the coal industry, yet most have no firsthand knowledge of the coal industry *or have never talked to coal executives*" (emphasis added).

Nor did others in the congressional delegation that day see anything improper about either the trip or the fee. Democratic Congressman Ron Wyden of Oregon explained that "we spoke about the issues all day *with company people*. It's a question of someone getting their point across" (emphasis added).

Doubtless the congressmen did return to Washington richer not only financially but in their knowledge of the views of company people and coal executives. But were they also exposed, on that trip, to the viewpoint of the widows of miners killed in unsafe mines, or of taxpayers who for years have borne higher tax burdens because of the $100 million in annual tax favors to the coal industry? What about the inability of such widows and ordinary taxpayers to treat congressmen to a luxury jet ride (complete with wet bar) for an in-person visit, much less to pay them $2,000 for listening?

THE MANY WAYS OF SKIRTING THE "REFORM" LAWS

10

The Watergate investigation laid bare a host of under-the-table abuses in political giving in 1971 and 1972:

- The International Telephone & Telegraph Corporation had pledged $400,000 to the Republican National Committee, and had received a favorable antitrust ruling from the Justice Department.
- The milk producers pledged $2 million to the reelection of President Richard Nixon; soon thereafter, Nixon raised dairy price supports, overriding the initial recommendations of key cabinet members.
- Illegal contributions from Gulf Oil, American Airlines, and other corporations, some "laundered" through foreign countries, found their way, in cash, into the Nixon campaign.

At the same time, super-rich individuals made enormous personal contributions to presidential candidates in both parties. Herbert Kalmbach, Nixon's later-indicted-and-convicted personal "bag man," scouted the country picking up, among others, personal pledges totaling $3 million from Chicago insurance magnate W. Clement Stone and John Mulcahy, president of a firebrick subsidiary of the Pfizer pharmaceutical firm. Richard Mellon Scaife, the Pittsburgh banker, pledged $1 million.

On the Democratic side, Stewart Mott, a General Motors heir, contributed about $400,000 to the McGovern cause.

Most of this high political finance was hidden from the public's view.

Then in the early seventies, Congress enacted two reform laws. In 1972, disclosure requirements came into effect—to eliminate, or at least reduce, the secrecy. And in 1974, as noted in Chapter 2, stringent ceilings were imposed on personal contributions. Now a W. Clement Stone could only give $1,000 per election to any candidate's campaign, with an annual ceiling of $25,000 in gifts to all federal candidates. Under those same reform laws, the federal government, rather than the Stones and the Scaifes, would pay for presidential general elections.

With those reform laws in place, most citizens scratched their Watergate worries off their mental lists, confident that public disclosure of and ceilings on contributions would prevent renewed abuses.

But in the post-Watergate years, ingenious politicians and their lawyers sought and found ways to skirt the new restrictions. The Supreme Court opened gaping (some said limitless) loopholes with its 1976 interpretation of the new reform laws. Congress eroded those laws through "technical" amendments that turned out not to be so technical after all.

Viewing all this in 1984—a decade after Watergate—the *Wall Street Journal* reporter Brooks Jackson observed that "the 'new' system of financing congressional and presidential campaigns is starting to bear a startling resemblance to those pre-Watergate days."

The *Journal* view may be overly bleak. After all, the reform statutes outlawed huge and secret contributions by companies and the very rich. But are such gifts really barred today? The answer is no. Not only do they take place; they are entirely legal.

For example, in 1985, reporter Edward Zuckerman discovered, and revealed in his newsletter *PACs & Lobbies*, that Minneapolis department-store heir Mark Dayton had given $100,000 to the Democratic National Committee. So had California investor Stuart Moldaw; and so had Thomas J. Watson, retired IBM chairman and former U.S. ambassador to Moscow.

Another study, by the Center for Responsive Politics, disclosed that corporate raider T. Boone Pickens gave $30,000 to the Republican National Committee. Fred Hayman, a Beverly Hills perfumer, gave $45,000.

Even those sizable contributions seem tiny compared with the check the Democratic National Committee got in 1987 from Joan Kroc (widow of McDonald's Ray Kroc) for $1 *million*.

Clearly these gifts far exceeded the ceilings on the post-Watergate reform law. Yet they were perfectly legal. How come?

The answer is that these contributors took advantage of a feature of the election law, added in 1979, that created a new category of contribution known as "soft money." Gifts of this kind could go only to political parties, not to candidates. In theory, this soft money was confined to "party-building" activities, and, because it is supposedly insulated from federal *election* activity, it is exempt from both the usual ceilings and the disclosure requirements. Thus, the large Dayton and Pickens gifts were made in secret, as in pre-Watergate days.*

The rationale for opening the soft-money loophole to allow unlimited gifts to political parties by corporations, unions, and the rich was that in the late seventies, politicians discovered that the new contribution ceilings combined with the upward surge of TV costs left the parties with distressingly little money to pay for the traditional local trappings of presidential campaigns: local headquarters handing out buttons, bumper stickers, banners, and bunting. The gap was to be filled by allowing corporations, unions, and the rich to make unlimited gifts for "party-building" activities.

It all sounded innocent enough. After all, what red-white-and-blue American patriot could oppose stronger political parties?

But the exemption of soft money from contribution limits, disclosure requirements, and the long-standing prohibition against corporate and union gifts was founded on a dubious premise: namely, that all this new "party-building" money could be introduced into the political system without any impact on federal elections.

The insulation of *federal* elections is critical, for it was the corruption of those elections that led to the reform law. Moreover, those are the only class of election over which Congress has jurisdiction.

In one important respect, the soft-money provisions made the campaign-finance laws *worse* than they had been before Watergate. Here's how: The corrupt influence of corporate money in federal elections prompted Congress, in 1907, to bar contributions from corporate treasuries in federal elections. In the Taft-Hartley law of 1947, in the name of symmetry, Congress extended the ban to labor-

---

* The disclosure of the Democratic gifts came about only because a junior staff member at party headquarters unknowingly sent the soft-money report to Harrisburg, Pennsylvania, where reporter Zuckerman stumbled across them among other Democratic finance reports.

union treasuries. But the new soft-money provision once again opened the way for the millions or billions in union and corporate treasuries to be injected into the political process. Reporter Ed Zuckerman disclosed that in the first eleven months of 1984, labor unions gave the Democrats a total of $1.8 million. Corporations were using their new-found freedom to buy memberships for their lobbyists in the influential Republican National Committee's "Eagles Club"—corporations such as Atlantic Richfield, BankAmerica, Occidental Petroleum, Shearson–American Express, Equitable Life Insurance, and Archer-Daniels-Midland (whose principal stockholder, Dwayne Andreas, and his family spread generous personal contributions among many lawmakers, as we have seen).

But critics of the soft-money provision say that the insulation premise is—or can be—a sham. For example, after Mark Dayton's $100,000 contribution to the Democratic National Committee came to light during the 1984 presidential campaign, Dayton said publicly that the real purpose of his large gift was to help his Minnesota political mentor, Walter Mondale.

Occasionally, the recipients of soft money are equally candid. In 1984, for example, the executive director of the Florida GOP deliberately used a *state* charter to form VIVA '84 (a group intended to help reelect President Reagan by mobilizing Hispanic voters), because as a state-chartered group, "we can take a check for $1 million. We can take corporate checks." Likewise, the New Jersey Republican Party that year boasted an unusually high budget of $680,000, considering that, as a party leader told a reporter, no state or local candidates were on the ballot, so all the "party-building" funds could be elevated to the Reagan reelection effort.

Another suspicious "party-building" contribution was the intriguing interest in the Illinois State Republican Party displayed in 1980 by two large California farming corporations (the Sayler Land Company and the J. G. Boswell Corporation) and by the Marriott Corporation of Bethesda, Maryland. The explanation: their gifts were part of a multi-million-dollar soft-money fund called the Victory Fund '80, dispensed at the direction of Robert Perkins from an office at the Republican National Committee headquarters. Perkins told journalist Elizabeth Drew, "We picked out the states that needed the money, identified money from major contributors, and funneled it into those states."

Even in the absence of such suspect circumstances, there remains the basic truism that money is fungible (i.e., that a dollar is a dollar is a dollar). Thus, even when soft money *is* spent purely for nonfederal purposes, it frees up money for other uses that *can* affect the outcome in federal contests. As veteran Republican practitioner (and Reagan friend) Lyn Nofziger puts it, "If I give $50,000 in corporate funds in California [where corporate donations are permitted], that frees the campaign to spend $50,000 for whatever it wants."

Both political parties recognize that their soft-money practices skirt the spirit, if not the letter, of the 1974 campaign-finance reform laws and, on occasion, seem to treat those laws with unabashed disdain.

When the Center for Responsive Politics interviewed guests at the 1984 Democratic National Convention in San Francisco, one guest said a party official told him not to worry about the federal limit in the 1974 law—all he needed to do was "decide how much he wanted to give and someone would instruct him on how to make out the checks."

Republican fundraiser Paul Dietrich told of how the law can be interpreted so as to hide the source of funds for party-financed TV commercials in a closely contested House election. "It is perfectly legal," said Dietrich, "or within the *letter* of the law" (emphasis supplied). "So we have a little dance which we dance around the law in a way that never breaks the letter but breaks the spirit of the law, but we don't agree with the law anyway."

But it isn't necessary to do a "little dance around the law" in order to shake off all the legal spending limits. In 1976, the U.S. Supreme Court ruled that the First Amendment grants people or groups the right to spend unlimited amounts for or against a candidate, provided the spending is undertaken *independently*—that is, without coordination or consultation with the candidate.

To illustrate, two Democratic congressmen, Fortney H. (Pete) Stark of California and Andrew Jacobs of Indiana, drew the opposition of the American Medical Association by advocating ceilings on Medicare fees to physicians. Jacobs had the temerity to urge his House colleagues to "vote for the canes, not for the stethoscopes," and Stark infuriated the AMA leadership by referring to doctors as "greedy troglodytes."

If the AMA had chosen to be bound by the regular election law, the expression of its outrage would have been limited to contributions of $10,000 each to Stark's and Jacobs's opponents—not enough to make a decisive difference in their election outcomes, nor even enough to teach these congressional upstarts a good lesson. But instead, in the 1986 election, the AMA and its political action committee, AMPAC, drove blithely through the loophole the Supreme Court had opened. AMPAC dumped $252,000 of "independent expenditures" on behalf of Stark's opponent, and $315,000 to defeat Congressman Jacobs—enormous amounts to inject into House campaigns. Both efforts failed miserably (the two congressmen garnered, respectively, 70 percent and 58 percent of the vote). But the AMA seemed undismayed: "I hope it sends a message to everyone in Congress who won by 51 percent," said AMPAC chairman Dr. Thomas Berglund. AMPAC executive director Peter Lauer told a seminar on campaign financing that his PAC was telling Stark and Jacobs, "That is it, you have reached that level [of AMA annoyance] and you damn well better understand that we're coming after you and we're going to make life damned miserable."

More likely to impress (and frighten) other congressmen and candidates is the decisive impact the AMA's $100,000 of "independent" money is thought to have had in helping Democrat David Skaggs to a surprise 1986 win in Colorado's Second District, in the Denver-Boulder area. Two years earlier, the AMA had supported Skaggs's opponent, but it switched in 1986 because Skaggs favored the AMA position in a state legislature fight to cap malpractice awards against doctors. Skaggs certainly is impressed by his come-from-behind victory: "When you win with 51.5 percent of the vote and the AMA spent . . . $100,000 [to] my $500,000, you can draw your own conclusions, " he said. Colorado Republicans were disturbed enough by the AMA's pro-Democratic intervention that they had the state's Republican senator, William Armstrong, call the AMA to complain.

In 1976, when the Supreme Court struck down the independent-spending ceiling, there was, as yet, no experience to disprove the Court's finding that uncoordinated expenditures do "not presently appear to pose dangers of real or apparent corruption comparable with those identified with large [direct] contributions." Subsequent events have proven the Court's supposition naïve. Independent spending enjoyed its first widespread use in 1980, when the National Conservative Political Action Committee, NCPAC, launched a barrage of TV ads against liberal senators in six states, attacking them, long before their opponents had been chosen, as "too liberal" for their respective states. NCPAC's stratagem was monumentally successful. Liberals such as George McGovern in South Dakota, John Culver in Iowa, Frank Church in Idaho, and Birch Bayh in Indiana all fell. Rightly or wrongly, the NCPAC ads were credited with major roles in those contests.

In 1982, the same NCPAC tactic was portrayed as "carpetbagging," and suffered a severe backlash. But in 1984, the conventional PACs began to adopt the independent-spending device. The National Rifle Association, for example, spent $328,000 helping elect Texas Republican Senator Phil Gramm.

Two years later, the traditional PACs pulled out the stops. AMPAC tripled its independent spending; the Realtors' PAC spent $1,700,000. A new entrant, the Auto Dealers for Free Trade, representing the sellers of imported Japanese cars, became a major player. In all, independent outlays in congressional elections rose sharply, from $2.3 million in the 1980 election to nearly $8.8 million six years later.

Independent spending is open to individuals as well as groups, although only a few have the means to spend on a large scale. One such, however, is Michael Goland, a wealthy California real-estate magnate from Los Angeles and an ardently pro-Israel activist. Beginning in 1981, Goland's ire was aroused by the conduct of Illinois Republican Senator Charles Percy, at the time chairman of the Senate Foreign Relations Committee. Percy angered Goland by his key role in engineering the sale of AWACS planes to Saudi Arabia. According to Kathy Lydon, Percy's former press secretary, Goland "warned that [Percy] wouldn't know what hit him in the next election" if he failed to alter his position. True to his word, when Percy came up for reelection in 1984, Goland threw $1.1 million of his own money into seeking Percy's defeat. (Goland got his wish. Percy lost to then-Congressman Paul Simon.)

Independent spending poses many dangers for the republic, beginning with the absence of any ceiling or other government regulation. The Supreme Court's innocent picture was predicated on the assumption that the spending would *truly* be uncoordinated with any candidate, a questionable assumption in the practical world of politics. At the least, an "independent" spender can easily tap into the close-knit network of political consultants and pollsters and glean an authoritative view of the tactics a candidate and his campaign staff want to follow. At times, the coordination is straightforward and acknowledged, as in the case of Republican James Abdnor, who was persuaded to run against Senator George Mc-Govern in South Dakota in 1980 after talking with NCPACs then-chairman, Terry Dolan, and pollster Arthur Finkelstein. NCPAC ultimately spent $178,000 on Abdnor's behalf, and Terry Dolan acknowledged his effort to recruit the candidate. "I know we did it," Dolan said. "We admit it. He admits it. We just led him up to the nomination." But the burden of proving that there was coordination rests with the aggrieved party, and when McGovern's attorney brought a complaint before the Federal Election Commission, the FEC found no collusion, despite this candid statement by Dolan.

Even in the rare case where the FEC and the courts do find collaboration, as in the New York senatorial race of 1982, where NCPAC spent $75,000 trying to defeat Democrat Daniel Patrick Moynihan, the penalty—imposed long after the votes had been counted—is ridiculously painless. In the Moynihan case, the FEC recommended a $5,000 fine against NCPAC, which the court later increased to $10,000.

As it happens, Senator Moynihan won that race handily. But what if he had *lost* by a handful of votes and there was strong evidence (say, from exit polling) that the ads paid for by NCPAC's illegal spending had tipped the balance? Of what use would that paltry fine have been?

Many object to "independent" spending on the ground that it exacerbates the extent to which modern campaigns (especially Senate campaigns) are paid for by "carpetbagging" dollars. Candidate reliance on outside PACs for their campaign money is bad enough. At least conventional PACs are restricted to contributing $5,000 per candidate per election. By contrast, the "independent" money is unlimited, and its carpetbagging nature is illustrated by the plans laid by the Auto Dealers for Free Trade to launch a $400,000 TV blitz for Republican Senator Paula Hawkins in the Florida Senate race—only to discover that the dealers' state chapter had endorsed the Democratic candidate, Governor Bob Graham. The embarrassed Auto Dealers canceled the ad campaign. When Graham won, just to show there had been nothing personal, they gave him a postelection gift of $5,000.

The independent spenders not only are unregulated in the amounts they can spend, but are unaccountable in what they say. NCPAC's Terry Dolan once said, "A group like ours could lie through its teeth, and the candidate it helps stays clean." Republican strategist Lyn Nofziger has observed that, as an independent spender, he "could go on the attack in a way the [candidate's] campaign might not be comfortable doing." Washington Republican Senator Dan Evans, himself the beneficiary of questionably "independent" expenditures in his first election, has said, "I think unquestionably . . . that independent expenditures on campaigns are probably the highest sleaze factor in campaigns today."

Senator Evans's view finds support in the 1986 TV ads aired by NCPAC against what it termed the "Ortega 33"—the principal congressional opponents of continued aid to the Nicaraguan contras. One such ad, targeting Michigan Democratic Congressman Howard Wolpe, portrayed soldiers running through the jungle, while a voice with a thick Spanish accent said, "One day we're going to take five to ten million Mexicans, and they're going to have one thing on their mind—cross the border into Dallas, El Paso, Houston, New Mexico, San Diego, and each one has embedded in his mind the idea of killing ten Americans." Cut to photo of Congressman Wolpe. Another voice: "Even so, Congressman Wolpe voted against President Reagan and aid to the freedom fighters in Nicaragua. Help President Reagan defeat Congressman Wolpe." The ad failed to defeat Congressman Wolpe.

Sleaze factor or no, the independent spenders say they are going to up the ante in 1988. The Realtors' PAC has said it intends to expand its independent spending "geometrically" in 1988; by the fall of 1987, the Auto Dealers for Free Trade had already completed a poll in seventeen states and knew what races it would enter; and one labor union—the American Federation of State, County, and Municipal Employees, better known as AFSCME—said it was looking into independent spending for the first time.

Independent spending is on the rise. And the Supreme Court has decreed there is no stopping it.

Bundling, n. the custom of unmarried couples occupying the same bed without undressing, practiced chiefly in earlier days, esp. during courtship in some British and American communities.

That's the dictionary definition of bundling. But to modern American political practitioners and interest groups, bundling has a new and different meaning. To them bundling is a way of getting around the limits in the election laws—especially the $5,000-per-election ceiling on PAC contributions to congressional candidates.

PAC defenders often insist that, with congressional campaign budgets in the hundreds of thousands or millions of dollars, it's ridiculous to imagine that a paltry $5,000 PAC contribution ($10,000 if there's a primary as well) can buy a representative's or a senator's vote.

But what about a gift of $168,000? That would at least get a legislator's attention, and it would probably win a donor a *most* sympathetic hearing.

Such a prodigious, attention-getting gift—more than thirty-three times the usual legal ceiling for a PAC—was achieved by bundling, modern-style, and was presented to Oregon Republican Senator Robert Packwood, chairman of the tax-writing Senate Finance Committee, to assist his 1986 reelection bid. The $168,000 was collected by Alignpac from insurance agents around the country, who made their checks payable to the Packwood campaign. Persuading the insurance agents to pony up was presumably no great chore, because all of them needed Packwood's support in fending off a Reagan administration effort to repeal one of the long-standing tax loopholes enjoyed by the insurance industry—the one allowing the gains in the value of life-insurance policies to be untaxed to the policyholder. As one of Alignpac's donors, Denver insurance agent Lyle Blessman, put it, the repeal of that loophole "would dry up the life-insurance product."

Taken separately, the agents' contributions would have had little impact on a campaign like Packwood's, which ended up collecting $6.7 million. The trick was to have the agents send their checks to the PAC, which bundled them together and presented them, periodically, in unforgettable packages to the Packwood campaign. So much for the $5,000 ceiling on PAC contributions.

As set forth in Chapter 6, the Council for a Livable World, a major national peace organization, has long employed, and staunchly defends, bundling of a slightly different variety. John Isaacs, the Council's highly articulate Washington director, says that since 1962, the Council has been raising substantial amounts of money from its members through the mail. The Council's letters appeal for help for one or two particular congressional candidates that the Council believes need and merit help. Members mail their checks to the Council, which then forwards them to the candidate.

The total sent to a candidate usually exceeds the $5,000-per-candi-date-per-election limit on PAC contributions.

"If a company gets twenty-five or thirty executives in a room and gets them to give $1,000 each to Candidate X, that exceeds the $5,000 PAC limit, but that's considered perfectly legal," says Isaacs. "And it could be a hundred or a hundred and fifty people, and it would be legal. What's the difference between that and what we do?

"If you want to illegalize *all* group solicitation, that's all right with us," Isaacs continues. "And if you want to do away with all PACs, that's OK too. But we think it's unfair to single out our method of fundraising and do away with it, and leave the other two methods—the PACs and the groups-of-executives-in-a-room—un-touched."

EMILY's List (EMILY being an acronym for "Early Money Is Like Yeast") engages in fundraising and bundling practices almost identical to the Council for a Livable World, and contributes the proceeds to women candidates. Ellen Malcolm, who founded and manages EMILY's List, shares John Isaacs's distaste for the cur-rent campaign finance system, but until she is advised that EMILY's bundling practices are illegal, she intends to continue this effective method of fundraising to make up for the discrepancy she finds in women's ability to raise campaign funds.

The National Republican Senatorial Committee used quite an-other version of bundling to skirt the legal ceilings on the aid the NRSC could give to individual Republican senatorial candidates that year.

This is the way that particular bundling scheme worked:

In 1986, the NRSC sent out a mail appeal, mentioning, in each letter, four Republican senate candidates who particularly needed help. When donors sent their checks, payable to the NRSC, the committee exercised its own judgment about how to apportion the funds. But in its reports to the Federal Election Commission, the NRSC attributed donations to particular givers, and thus claimed the gifts were exempt from the committee's own giving ceiling.

Apparently, though, the NRSC failed to consult its donors, for an October 22, 1986, article in the *Atlanta Journal* quotes Mr. E. W. Dixon of Tulsa, Oklahoma—who the NRSC listed as giving to the campaign of Alabama Senator Mack Mattingly—as saying, "I don't know Mattingly from Adam's old fox." Mrs. Katherine Eberhard of Grand Rapids, Michigan, listed as having contributed to Louisiana senatorial candidate Henson Moore, said, "I live in Michigan. . . . No way I would have sent money to Louisiana to Senator Moore or whoever he is."

The *Wall Street Journal* reported in October 1986 that the excess gifts to GOP Senate candidates by the NRSC had already reached $6.6 million, and that the committee expected the total to reach $13 million by election day. Most of the funds were concentrated in small, tightly contested states where TV budgets were small and money exercised great leverage. For example, the NRSC gave the reelection campaign of South Dakota Senator James Abdnor some $931,554—nine times the legal ceiling for a party donation. James Santini, the Republican senatorial candidate in Nevada, received $738,504; Ken Kramer, in Colorado, $508,910.

If you are a super-rich person and want to be sure to get an important officeholder's attention with a contribution of, say, $100,000, there may be yet another way to go about it, even though a campaign contribution of that size would exceed your legal giving ceiling fifty to a hundred times over. If you are the principal stockholder in a company, and want your sure-to-be-noticed $100,000 gift to be made by your corporation, that, too, can be achieved, even though corporate contributions to federal candidates have been forbidden since 1907.

The way around all those legal obstacles is simple if the officeholder has formed a charitable foundation. In such a case, attention-getting gifts of unlimited size are not only feasible, but entirely legal. Mr. and Mrs. William M. Keck II of Los Angeles chose precisely that route to make a $100,000 contribution ($50,000 each) to a foundation established by Republican Senator Robert Dole of Kansas. Mr. Keck is president of the Coalinga Corporation, an oil and gas investing company.

The Keck mode of giving offers a significant advantage to the donor. Gifts to such charitable foundations are tax-deductible, which means that the donors shift much of the burden to the shoulders of other taxpayers. As noted earlier, AT&T made contributions totaling $100,000 to the Dole Foundation. Because that gift was tax-deductible, it saved AT&T $46,000, a burden that had to be picked up by the rest of the taxpayers.

The tax law requires charitable organizations to be strictly non-political. But sometimes, when a foundation has close connections with a political personage, the dividing line gets very thin. Take, for example, the Fund for the American Renaissance, the foundation established by New York Republican congressman and presidential candidate Jack Kemp. In March 1986, the *Wall Street Journal* reported that Kemp's foundation had recently laid out about $20,000 to finance a fact-finding trip to Europe by the congressman and a few aides; that the foundation planned to publish a book by Mr. Kemp about that trip and his foreign-policy ideas; and that the foundation's executive director, James Roberts, who formerly headed Congressman Kemp's political action committee, "also is personally producing a Kemp-narrated TV documentary promoting Rep. Kemp's pet domestic projects."

According to Douglas Turner, writing in the *Buffalo News,* not only did the Kemp foundation and Kemp's personal PAC share an office building; at one point they actually shared office space and telephone expenses. More significantly, the foundation's board of directors once consisted of Kemp and three of his key political advisors, and its staff director had been Kemp's fundraiser. After the *News*'s revelations, the board of directors was rearranged and Kemp became "honorary chairman," eventually resigning even that post in December of 1986.

Unlike Senator Dole, Congressman Kemp was persistent about guarding the secrecy of his foundation's contributor list. He repeatedly refused to give the donor list to reporter Turner and others, although in late summer 1986 he ultimately gave Turner the list. Kemp also told the *Wall Street Journal* that some of his donors didn't mind being identified. They include Chase Manhattan Bank, Dow Chemical Company, the W. R. Grace & Company, and Pepsico. Apparently, Representative Kemp did not tell the *Journal* to what financial extent those companies ingratiated themselves with him, although a spokesman said the fund had accepted gifts as large as $50,000.

Kemp and Dole are by no means the only prominent political figures to form charitable foundations. Before his withdrawal from the Democratic presidential race, former Colorado Senator Gary Hart had a foundation that sent a mail appeal to fifty thousand 1984 presidential contributors asking for donations to help Hart "set the agenda for an American renewal." Former Governor Bruce Babbitt of Arizona has both a PAC and a foundation (American Horizons). Among nonpresidential aspirants, Senator Edward M. Kennedy has established the Social Awareness Fund, which paid for a widely publicized Kennedy trip to Africa. Senator Bill Bradley of New Jersey has formed a Fair Tax Foundation.

In February 1987, the Kemp foundation ceased operating. David Hoope, a former board member, explained that this was due to the congressman's "total concentration on politics" and a desire to avoid confusing the fund's activities with Kemp's political aspirations. But the Kemp foundation illustrates the abuses to which foundations closely connected to prominent politicians are subject—as, for example, when foundation dollars pay for a politically helpful junket by the politician, or pay the salaries of former political staff aides, or foot the bill for publishing the politician's "position papers." A 1987 study by the Center for Responsive Politics, a Washington research group, found, "There has been a significant increase in the 1980s" in the number of public charities "affiliated with federal elected officials or federal aspirants."

There are clearly abuses and loopholes aplenty, enough to occupy three or four watchdog agencies, not just the one—the Federal Election Commission—established under the post-Watergate reform laws and envisaged by the Watergate investigating committee as a tough enforcer of the law "with the confidence of the public."

But as the *Wall Street Journal* headline put it in a 1987 article, the watchdog has turned into a pussy cat. *Journal* reporter Brooks Jackson found the FEC beset by a Republican distaste for government regulation, and the GOP members of the Commission have blocked probe after probe. For example, Congressman Pete Stark brought a complaint about the American Medical Association's $259,000 "independent expenditure" against him. The FEC staff felt a probe was justified. But all three Republican commissioners opposed it, and the probe ended there, since four votes are required to pursue any investigation. Stark was especially angry at the negative vote cast by Commissioner Lee Ann Elliott, who for eighteen years worked for the AMA and continues to draw an $18,831 pension. Notwithstanding Ms. Elliott's anti-enforcement penchant, the Reagan administration reappointed her to another six-year term. By contrast, the administration refused to reappoint two enforcement-minded commissioners, Democrat Thomas Harris and Republican Frank Reiche.

Likewise, the GOP members thwarted an effort to probe a suspected spending violation by the National Republican Congressional Committee. But this time the commission was slapped down by a federal judge who ruled the FEC had acted "contrary to law." The FEC, rather than acquiesce, appealed the case.

The Republican commissioners have also refused to permit a rewriting of the loophole-ridden rules on soft money, as recommended by the FEC staff. In addition, the *Wall Street Journal* reported, "the commission got rid of all its trained investigators long ago"; it "seldom uses its subpoena power and only rarely takes sworn testimony from witnesses."

All this encourages a scofflaw attitude among political practitioners and lawyers. Moreover, as already noted, the penalties for being caught are usually painless. Campaign-finance expert Herbert Alexander told the *Journal*, "The price of operatives doing what they want to do is to pay a fine. They just consider it part of campaigning. If they catch up with you, you pay a couple of thousand dollars and you go scot-free."

Journal reporter Jackson also comments that the FEC "seems more intent on pinching off disclosure of campaign-money abuses than investigating them." For example, an investigative-journalism project founded by the author of this book helped finance a newspaper's investigation of Idaho Republican Congressman George Hansen's financial activities. When Hansen complained to the FEC, the FEC responded by trying to subpoena *all* the story proposals submitted to the project. The FEC is also vigorously seeking to prosecute two organizations seeking to disseminate data drawn from FEC candidate reports.

Ronald Brownstein of the *National Journal* summed up the many ways of circumventing the post-Watergate reform law with this observation:

> Campaign-finance reforms tend to succumb to the same immutable law that keeps the Neiman-Marcus catalogue [with its chocolate Monopoly boards] flourishing: People with money always find new ways to spend it.

To which the *Wall Street Journal*'s Brooks Jackson adds:

> Post-Watergate reforms are so eroded that secret contributions from corporations and labor unions are once again flowing, and the era of $1 million fat-cat contributions has returned.

THE
SOLUTION

HOW WE CAN GET OUT OF THE MESS WE'RE IN

11

Free and untrammeled representation of the public is possible only when men and women in high office are not indebted to special interests for financial donations.
—From the first bill proposing public financing of elections, 1956

How do we get out of this mess?

The possible approaches are virtually unlimited. To choose among them requires clearly defining the goals of a reform plan. Here are my own:

We need to be as sure as possible that when senators or representatives cast their votes in Congress, they are free from worry about who is going to give or withhold a campaign contribution—free, that is, to vote on the basis of what is best for their country and their constituents.

Average citizens who can't afford large political contributions must feel they count just as much in their representative's or senator's mind as the rich contributors and the political action committees.

Officeholders must be accountable to the people who can vote for them, not to commodity traders in Chicago or bond salesmen on Wall Street or to PACs headquartered outside their state or districts.

We must have a campaign-finance system that encourages political challenge and competition, not one where money is an obstacle to candidacy and where over 98 percent of the representatives in office are reelected.

Congressional candidates and officeholders should be freed from their incessant preoccupation with raising money, so that they can pay attention to studying the issues, formulating public policy, and attending to their legislative duties. In campaign season, they must be free to stay at home meeting their constituents instead of spending time talking to and raising money from PACs and from rich folk in distant states.

Special-interest groups must no longer have the capacity, through their political action committees, to magnify their power by aggregating money and giving campaign contributions much larger than most citizens can afford.

Finally, America needs a system that shrinks the role and influence of "interested" money, given by people and groups who hope to benefit financially from their contribution. Our country needs a system where campaigns are paid for as much as possible by "disinterested" money.

In a democracy, the ultimate in disinterested money is money that comes from each citizen equally—that is, from all the taxpayers, through their government. When campaign funds come from all the citizens, candidates and officeholders cannot identify the money as coming from any special person or group.

The most essential reform, therefore, is to give House and Senate candidates an alternative to special-interest contributions by enabling them to pay for their campaigns as much as possible by money from the general public—that is, from the U.S. Treasury.

That proposal is neither radical nor new. In fact, it is the law of the land now for presidential elections, and has been since 1974. I am suggesting broadening the plan in existing law to cover congressional elections—that is, full public funding in House and Senate general elections and public matching grants in primary elections.

That plan of public financing is both court-tested (it has been specifically approved by the Supreme Court) and time-tested. It has worked at the presidential level. Since Congress enacted that plan, no presidential contest has been marred by the illegal corporate contributions and the "laundering" of money that characterized the 1972 reelection of Richard Nixon. Thus the plan offers assurance to those concerned that an untested campaign-finance reform might have unintended consequences (as did the 1974 "reform" law, which gave rise to the PACs).

America has been late getting in step with the rest of the Western world in the way of systematic public help in election campaigns. Such governmental aid as we give to candidates was, until the 1970s, piecemeal, and we still only subsidize a tiny portion of our electoral system.

Until we adopt a comprehensive plan for financing congressional elections, just as we now finance presidential campaigns, candidates for the House and Senate will be prey to the temptations of special-interest money. They will continue to be enslaved by their constant obsession with fundraising. Politicians tend to be nervous about their political futures. The only way to free them from the blandishments of PACs, lobbyists, and large "interested" givers is to give them an alternative—an *assured* source, a *floor*, of disinterested money.

That floor is an essential minimum. But the butterflies in anxious politicians' stomachs may remain as long as they fear the possibility of being grossly outspent. So the public-finance plan for Congress should guarantee a level playing field in congressional general elections. That might work this way:

As with the existing presidential system, congressional general-election candidates who accept the public funding must agree to limit their spending to the amount of the public grant. Those who decline taxpayer money will be free of that spending limit. Then how do we keep the playing field level? Let us imagine a contest for a Senate seat, where the normal public grant is $1 million to Candidate A, but the privately financed Candidate B chooses to raise and spend $1.5 million. In that case, Candidate A would get an added $500,000 from the U.S. Treasury—that is, one dollar for every dollar by which B exceeds the spending limit. To minimize the risk of a last-minute blitz by B, too late for the federal matching funds to reach A, B would be required to report his or her spending with growing frequency during the campaign. Thus B would not be able to outspend A, and would have little incentive to try.

Logically, the Republican Party, which has in the past consistently opposed government financing of elections, *should* welcome this public-financing-with-a-level-playing-field approach. The GOP has not enjoyed control of the House since the Eisenhower landslide of 1952. The Democrats have a firm grasp on the House, due in considerable part to PAC favoritism for incumbent Democrats. The number of "contested" House seats (those won or lost by less than 55 percent of the vote) has declined from 137 in 1936, to 103 in 1946, to 72 in 1986. All this led Warren Weaver, Jr., to report in the *New York Times* in June 1987 that unless steps are taken to help Republican challengers, "the current Democratic majority of about 70 seats will have to be recognized by both parties as unofficially permanent."

The second crucial reform step is to prohibit all PAC contributions to federal candidates.

I place this high on my list for two reasons. First, as we saw in Chapters 3 and 7, PACs are the instrument whereby groups like the dairy and sugar lobbies and the auto dealers have been able to magnify their power, prevail in Congress, and impose great costs on the general public, regardless of the number of people they represented (in these cases very small) or the merits of their arguments. Second, congressmen and senators are increasingly dependent on PACs outside their districts for their campaign funds. It is appalling that more than four-fifths of U.S. representatives are "hooked" on outside PAC money, in that they have come to depend on PACs for at least a third of their campaign funds, and that many get half their funds, or more, from PACs.

Some will question this across-the-board prohibition of all PAC donations, arguing that PACs are not evil *per se*, that some are in fact "good" PACs (e.g., those that press for some ideological position entailing no economic self-interest). Nonetheless, all PACs represent outside money, and all PACs distort the democratic process by placing money-power over people-power. In fact, that is their avowed purpose. To the extent that a PAC ban would pinch off the supposed increase in citizen participation the PACs are alleged to have brought about (and there is little hard proof of any such increase), it would halt only the most undemocratic citizen action, given the way PACs decide how to dispense their money (see Chapter 2). Democracy is better served by having citizens contribute directly to candidates they believe in, rather than delegating that choice to some distant PAC manager.

Others may protest that prohibiting PAC contributions in federal elections would impair the legitimate role of interest groups and do violence to citizens' right of association. I don't agree. Without PACs, citizens would still have an undiminished right to form or join groups, as well as the right to petition Congress through the group's lobbyists if they choose. Organizations would have unimpaired rights to endorse candidates and engage in other political activity. And of course the right of group members to make political contributions *as individuals* would be unaffected.

The demise of the PAC contributions would deprive groups of only one power: the power to *aggregate* money and hand it out to candidates (especially officeholders) in conspicuous and potentially influential campaign contributions. It is precisely that power that distorts representative democracy.

The argument that ending contributions by PACs tramples on some fundamental citizens' rights is unsupported by history. The law sanctioning the PACs was not handed down on a mountain top nor is it inscribed in the Constitution. Indeed, it is not yet fifteen years old. The republic survived 187 years without that law and without the PACs.

Third on my campaign-reform list would be to prohibit political contributions to congressional candidates from persons who are not entitled to cast a ballot for them—that is, a ban on out-of-district political contributions to candidates for the House and on out-of-state contributions to Senate candidates.

The notion makes common sense, startling though it may seem at first. Indeed, the alternative—under which, say, a Representative James Howard in New Jersey receives 82.5 percent of his contributions from people and groups not entitled to vote for him—appears, on reflection, increasingly indefensible.

After all, Congressman Howard should be accountable to the people of his district, not to the Washington lobbyists, nor to executives in the industries affected by the committee he chairs—and certainly not to PACs that contribute to his campaigns with little regard for the welfare of New Jersey's Third District.

To be sure, Congress is a *national* legislature, and New Jersey lawmakers cast votes affecting the people of Chicago and New York on issues such as aid to the contras, disarmament, and military budgets. But that doesn't give the people of Chicago and New York the right to *vote* for those lawmakers. Why should they be allowed to cast proxy ballots with their money? Why, especially, should the law permit them to cast a financial vote larger than all but a handful of New Jersey citizens could afford? For example, the owner of a California highway construction firm and his wife could legally give New Jersey's Congressman Howard $4,000 (since Howard customarily has a primary as well as a general-election contest). How many of Representative Howard's constituents can afford to contribute $4,000 to his campaign?

Some may say prohibitions on contributions from nonresidents is all very nice in theory; but in the real world, how would a non-incumbent from a small and impecunious state like South Dakota ever mount a successful challenge without money from Chicago, Los Angeles, and New York? Moreover, wouldn't a ban on outside money doom to perpetual defeat a challenger such as Mike Espy, the newly elected black representative from Mississippi, whose in-district supporters could not possibly amass the needed sums?

Those concerns are understandable; but they spring from thinking in terms of *today's* ground rules. Under the reform plan outlined here, a Mike Espy and a South Dakota contender would be far better off than they are today. First, they would have the advantage of public money, which would presumably assure each of them enough money to mount a respectable campaign. Public funds offer a more certain and less troublesome source of money than the outside funds candidates now scramble frenetically to raise from PACs and rich folk. Second, under the plan proposed here, the challenger would be on a financial par with the incumbent—far different from the situation today in most congressional contests. Third, incumbents could not expect any help from outside PACs, no matter how helpful they had been to a trade group or union, because all PAC gifts would be outlawed.

Last—and perhaps most important—incumbents would be subject to the same strictures as challengers against contributions from nonresidents, even in primary elections. No longer could the heads of the congressional banking committees count on help from individual banking executives around the country. Any gifts from bankers would have to come from the bankers down the street.

Banning contributions to candidates from nonresidents would be constitutionally controversial, to say the least. I recognize that such a ban runs counter to the current Supreme Court doctrine that in politics, money is speech. But a ban on nonresident political gifts might be constitutionally supportable under past court precedents.

For example, the Burger Court held that the rights of citizens under the money-is-speech doctrine are not absolute. Those rights can be limited if there is a "significant" governmental interest in doing so. One such interest is to prevent corruption, or the appearance of "improper influence of large private contributions." More than a decade has passed since the Court enunciated the money-is-speech doctrine. Influence-buying practices have sprung up that were not presented to the Court in 1976. Many of them are set forth in this book. Is it inconceivable that this added evidence could induce a new Court to change or modify its money-is-speech rule?

Second, the Court has, in times past, declared a governmental interest in the one-person–one-vote principle. Specifically, it has defended citizens against the dilution of their voting strength by politically motivated redistricting plans. In *Reynolds v. Sims*, the landmark one-person–one-vote ruling, the Court said explicitly, "the right of suffrage can be denied by a debasement or dilution of the weight of a citizen's vote just as effectively as by wholly prohibiting the free exercise of the franchise."

It could be persuasively argued that the influence of, say, a South Dakota resident's vote in choosing his or her senator is diluted when nonresidents are allowed to cast potentially far more influential proxy votes with their often-substantial contributions.

That dilution is confirmed by former Congressman Mike Barnes's statement that in choosing which of many phone calls to return, he tended to pass over constituents who were unknown to him in favor of large out-of-state contributors whose names he vividly remembered. His observation is echoed by many congressmen and senators.

South Dakotans' voices are also enfeebled when their senatorial candidates take precious time away from legislating and from campaigning among their own constituents to journey to Los Angeles, Chicago, New York, or Houston (as most Senate candidates do nowadays) soliciting and receiving contributions of a size few South Dakotans could afford.

In opposing a ban on nonresident contributions, some argue that not all political gifts from nonresidents have a corrupt motivation. Many citizens (the argument runs) give to further their ideological convictions or out of admiration for a candidate, rather than out of economic self-interest, and since there is no way to separate the corrupt from the selfless contribution, an across-the-board ban unfairly penalizes the disinterested nonresident contributor.

But only a few citizens can afford political contributions to out-of-state candidates. Moreover, the chapter about Senator Dole and Representative Howard shows that the preponderance of their gifts from nonresidents seems to have been motivated by self-interest. Most political realists would confirm that is the rule, not the exception. Detailed studies in other localities could document that proposition. If so, for Congress to let concern for the minority of disinterested gifts prevent it from banning all nonresident political contributions would surely be to let the tail wag the dog.

Political scientists generally agree that strengthening the political parties would improve the health of the republic. Some of them reason that the parties can serve as a buffer between interest groups and political candidates. Others argue that, compared to local candidates preoccupied with regional or parochial interests, national parties can be the instrument of achieving a more cohesive national policy.

Those arguments make sense—but with one major reservation. The ability of the parties to serve both those functions (the buffer and the nationalizing functions) will be critically hampered as long as the parties rely on large contributions from rich people and from interest groups, as the parties do now. As long as that is true, the parties will tend to pay disproportionate attention to business and labor interests and the moneyed few, and to give short shrift to the interests of the average citizen.

That tendency has particular impact on the policies of the Democrats. Who would have thought that in 1982, Democratic national chairman Charles Manatt, head of "the party of Jefferson, Jackson, Roosevelt, and Truman" would plead with Democrats in Congress to retain a corporate-tax loophole (the "safe harbor" leasing provision) that even Republicans agreed was based on a total sham? Or that the Democratic House Campaign Committee would entice $5,000 *annual* donations with the promise of "lunch with Chairmen of congressional committees . . . a round of golf with the Speaker" of the House and "cocktails with the Democratic members of the Ways and Means Committee," which writes the tax laws? As long as the Democratic party depends largely on gifts from business and rich people, would such a party feel free to throw its full support behind populist candidates whose stances offend those big givers?

To liberate both parties from their reliance on special-interest money, any party-strengthening steps should be financed in two ways: publicly appropriated funds from the U.S. Treasury, and public matching gifts and tax credits * for small gifts to parties from

---

* As the author of two books on tax loopholes who railed against using the tax system to achieve "social" purposes, I am conflicted in recommending tax credits for gifts to political parties. Such credits, however, do not benefit any single industry or economic group, but are really an alternative form of governmental financing to improve the electoral system.

individuals. At the same time, we must repeal the soft-money provisions of the present law, which permit unlimited (and undisclosed) gifts to parties, including contributions from corporate and union treasuries.

Few industries are more profitable than the broadcast business. Many TV stations in the larger markets have garnered returns on equity ranging from 25 to 57 percent, compared with 10 to 12 percent on manufacturing industries. That translates into sale prices in the hundreds of millions. A network-affiliated TV station in Boston sold for $450 million and an *independent* nonnetwork station in Los Angeles went for over $500 million. The physical assets of these stations are worth about $50 million at most. The rest represents the value of the piece of paper issued, at virtually no charge, by the people of the United States: a federal license to use the public's airwaves. A VHF-TV license in the top fifty markets is a license to print money.

Meanwhile, television has become *the* accepted medium for selling political candidates, and TV has become a seller's market. So although Congress has passed a law that supposedly requires stations to sell time to political candidates at a discount, in practice it frequently works out the opposite way. That's because the peak period for reaching voters is of limited duration (the last two or three weeks of the campaign being the choice time), and candidates often find themselves paying premium rates to bump commercial advertisers from the choicest evening spot-announcement times.

The net result is that political candidates have been indebting themselves to special-interest contributors in large part to add to local broadcasters' already stupendous profits. The broadcasters, of course, apoplectically oppose any laws to compel them to donate even the smallest particle of their broadcast time to political candidates. The whole spectacle is obscene.

Granted, there are myriad complexities to any proposal to provide political candidates with free or reduced-rate broadcast time. But that is not a reason for total inaction, for leaving the obscenity wholly untouched.

As a first-cut suggestion: broadcasters should be required to donate, say 10 percent of their program and spot-announcement time in each major time category free to the political parties during the last sixty days before each congressional general election. The time should be allocated among major, minor, and new parties according to a past-performance or petition formula similar to that in the present public-financing law for presidential elections. Each party would be free to apportion its free time for general party purposes or among its respective congressional candidates as it saw fit.

Such a plan would impose minimal burdens on broadcasters, obliging them to devote a mere 0.8 percent of the total time now at their disposal,★ and leaving them free to use (and profit from) the other 99.2 percent of the time granted them by their free use of the *public's* property.

In addition to the time granted free to political parties, Congress should require that TV broadcasters sell time at, say, one-eighth the usually quoted rate to *candidates* who wish to buy time for advertisements of not less than a minute's duration, which would consist solely of the candidate in a studio talking to the camera, with no use of extraneous film footage of baby-kissing, cheering crowds, "voter" endorsements, or other techniques better suited to selling soap than candidates or issues. Just the candidate talking, hopefully about the issues. That *should* elevate the level of political discourse.

As noted above, in 1976 the Supreme Court ruled no limit could constitutionally be placed on spending that is uncoordinated with the campaign of any candidate. That holding offered an escape route for PACs and potential donors frustrated by the contribution ceilings in the election law. These independent expenditures have been increasing in recent elections, and the trend could become more acute if a new reform imposed added constraints, such as the ban on all PAC giving proposed in this chapter. If such a ban were enacted, increased independent spending could create a dual campaign system: the official campaigns by the candidates, and the independent-spending campaigns, for which no vote-seeker could be held accountable. Thus, any reform agenda must address the independent-spending issue.

Of the many proposals advanced for dealing with this problem, I favor two:

★ The free-time requirement is confined to 2 months out of each 24-month period, or roughly 8 percent of the total two years. Requiring stations to donate one-tenth of their time during that period results in their giving up only 0.8 percent of the total time available to them.

First, the dismal failure of the most recent independent-spending efforts suggests that the voting public resents outside interference by independent spenders. So the independently financed political ads should be required to identify the source of the funds as prominently as possible. For example, the law should require that TV ads bought with independent money carry a disclaimer *throughout the entire commercial*, stating, "THIS AD PAID FOR BY . . . "

Second, as a means of keeping the playing field level when independent spenders do enter congressional general-election contests, candidates against whom independent-spending efforts are directed should receive one dollar of public funds for every dollar of independent spending directed against them. Experts warn of the danger that candidates will encourage bogus independent spending efforts against them, so that they will be entitled to this "level-playing-field" public money. One solution: to require all independent spenders to declare *on oath* that their aim is to defeat Candidate X or elect Candidate Y.

I also propose that members of Congress should be prohibited from accepting honoraria (just as employees of the executive branch are now), to preclude lawmakers' serving two masters. In order that they not feel pressed for money, lawmakers' salaries should be raised to, say, the $135,000 recommended in 1986 by the Commission on Executive, Legislative and Judicial salaries (the Quadrennial Commission).

Furthermore, members of Congress should no longer be permitted to build up large campaign surpluses that discourage challengers. Instead, funds remaining in their campaign coffers after each election should revert to the Treasury. And the law that now permits many senior members of Congress to transfer surpluses to their own bank accounts upon retiring should be repealed.

To recapitulate, the reforms proposed in this chapter are as follows:

- Public financing of election campaigns for the U.S. House and Senate, including a level-playing-field provision to assure maximum equality between publicly and privately financed candidates.
- A ban on all PAC contributions to federal candidates.

- A ban on all contributions to federal candidates by individuals who are not entitled to vote for them—that is, by nonresidents of the respective candidates' states or congressional districts.
- Government aid to political parties via funds appropriated from the U.S. Treasury and public matching gifts for small gifts to parties from individuals.
- A law requiring broadcasters to donate free time to parties during the last sixty days of each federal election and to sell time at, say, one-eighth the customary rate to candidates who agree to confine their message to themselves talking to a camera in a studio, with no use of extraneous film footage.
- Regulation of "independent expenditures" by requiring that independently financed ads prominently identify the source of their funds in any advertisements and by providing public funding to general-election candidates against whom independent spending efforts are directed.
- A prohibition against members of Congress accepting honoraria, plus a salary increase for senators and representatives.
- A prohibition against members of Congress building up large cash surpluses after their campaigns and repeal of the law permitting them to take their surpluses with them when they retire from Congress.

To fairly appraise any given menu of reform proposals requires recognizing that any campaign-finance reform has its risks, its disadvantages, and its potential problems. The question is not: Is a given proposal wholly risk-free? The proper questions are: How do its potential *future* risks compare with the *here-and-now* problems in the present system? That is, taking account of all the pluses and minuses—the present dangers versus the potential risks—is the reform likely to produce a better or a worse political system than we have now?

To illustrate: many worry that any public funding of elections necessarily involves the exercise of discretion by bureaucrats subject to control by the "ins" in Congress, with an inherent incentive to find ways of denying funds to congressional challengers.

That danger does exist. But it is an "iffy" future danger that should be weighed against the system *as it is today*. It is difficult to imagine a system more heavily weighted in favor of incumbents and against challengers than the present one, especially in House races.

Remember, in the 1986 House elections, the PACs gave 88 percent of their money to incumbents; incumbents outspent challengers more than three to one; and 98 percent of the incumbents who sought reelection won.

Critics also argue that public financing will encourage "frivolous" candidates to run for Congress. Once again, that is a legitimate concern. But which risk poses the greater danger to the republic—too many candidates, or too few? The existing system, with its pro-incumbent bias, errs on the side of too few. It often freezes out challengers, sheerly for want of money.

America's interests are ill served by rationing candidacies primarily because of the money a person possesses or can raise, mainly from rich people and PACs. At the beginning of the book I raised the question: Is there another Abraham Lincoln among us who is prevented or discouraged from running for office sheerly because of *money*?

What's the cost of the reform plan outlined here? Can we afford it?

The cost of a public-financing program for congressional *general* elections can be precisely calculated, for the number of candidates and the amount of the public grants to each is a known quantity. As noted earlier, the cost of companion public finance bills introduced in 1985★ was $87 million a year for the House and $49 million for the Senate. Both figures are substantially less than the $150 million the Pentagon spends every year just on military bands!

The cost of a partial public financing plan for congressional *primary* elections is much more difficult to calculate. The expense hinges on a large number of unpredictable variables, such as how many candidates will enter the primaries, and what success they will have in meeting the eligibility requirements for federal matching funds.

But again, the important question is: How would the cost of the plan proposed in this chapter compare with the cost of the existing system? Chapter 7 conservatively places at $2 billion the annual cost to American consumers and taxpayers of just four legislative

---

★ The plan provided grants of $200,000 for each major-party nominee in House races and varying grants, depending on the voting-age population of each state, ranging from $500,000 for the smallest states to $5,719,000 for California, for major-party candidates for the U.S. Senate.

measures on whose outcome campaign contributions appear to have had a demonstrable impact.

One expert has estimated that congressional public financing will cost around $500 million every two years, or $250 million a year. Even if the cost turns out to be twice that high—$500 million dollars each year—that will be just equal the added cost to the federal government of the higher dairy subsidy passed by the House after three dairy PACs had showered congressmen and senators with over $1 million in campaign contributions. And that omits the $2 billion consumers pay every year because of higher dairy prices in the supermarket. Of course, the dairy subsidy is merely one of the many expensive government programs whose passage seems to have been aided by campaign money.

So whatever the cost of the program I have outlined in this chapter, it is virtually certain to be less—probably far less—than the cost to the American public (as consumers and as taxpayers) of the present campaign-finance system.

Moreover, the existing system is a hidden price *over which the public has little or no control*. The same cannot be said of public financing of elections. At some early date after a new public funding program is in place, Congress would get an accurate accounting of the cost. If the voters decided the cost was excessive, Congress could pare the program back.

As I write, I can almost hear the voices of skeptical readers (and reviewers) reading this reform plan, smiling, figuratively patting me on the head, and saying, "All very well-meaning and idealistic, but where has this fellow Stern been? Does he really live in the United States in the 1980s? There's not a prayer of his program being enacted."

Don't worry. I *have* been living in America. I am painfully aware of the difficulty of getting Congress to agree on any political reforms. The Republicans differ with the Democrats; and the political haves clash with the have-nots, because their respective oxen are variously gored by any given reform. The difficulties are compounded by the fact that even people of *identical* political philosophies often disagree.

These reform proposals are, however, deliberately put forward without regard for the momentary conventional wisdom as to what is politically enactable. After all, Congress *did* manage to overcome all the obstacles and agree on a reform law in 1974. And the public financing of congressional elections, which most regard as an impossible dream, *did* pass the Senate twice in the early seventies, and nearly passed the House.

Who can say what will "never" be passed? What is "politically enactable" is subject to change from year to year. For example, as recently as 1985 and 1986, public funding of congressional elections was generally regarded as a hopeless cause. Even its most ardent supporters, such as Common Cause, threw their energies behind a much milder measure, calling mainly for a cap on PAC gifts to congressional candidates.

But then came the 1986 elections, bringing with them the sea change regarding public financing of Senate elections, described in Chapter 2. When a senator as conservative as Mississippi's John Stennis throws his weight behind a public-financing bill, a basic change of sentiment has most surely begun.

CONCLUSION

I end this book as I began it: with statements by two veteran politicians—about the campaign-finance crisis facing this country:

It is not "we, the people," but political action committees and moneyed interests who are setting the nation's political agenda and are influencing the position of candidates on the important issues of the day.

The flood of money now polluting our campaign system is like drug to the addicts. The longer we go without admitting we have the problem of addiction, the more ingrained the addiction becomes and the harder it will be to ever break the habit.

The first statement is by a Republican, former Arizona Senator Barry Goldwater; the second is by a Democrat, Oklahoma Senator David Boren. Clearly there is bipartisan agreement that a crisis is upon us.

From the point of view of the U.S. *Congress*, that campaign-finance crisis may be summarized in two facts:

- *Fact No. 1:* Based on the average cost of a winning campaign for the U.S. House of Representatives in 1986 ($355,000), members must, on average, raise about $15,000 *every month* during their entire two-year terms.
- *Fact No. 2:* With the average cost of a winning 1986 Senate campaign over $3 million, U.S. senators elected in 1986 will, on

average, be obliged to raise about $10,000 *every week* during their entire six-year terms.

Those two facts portray only half the campaign-finance crisis, half of the equation—the needs of the *sellers* of influence (potential and actual): the members of the U.S. Congress.

From the viewpoint of the American *public*, however, the other side of the equation is the more troubling one, the one that threatens to disenfranchise us all: the seemingly infinite capacity of the *buyers* of influence—the special-interest groups and their political action committees—to muster whatever money senators and representatives need.

The influence-buyers' money-raising capacity is no speculative matter. Here are the amounts actually raised by the leading PACs (i.e., those that raised over $100,000) in each major category in the first six months of 1987, compared with the comparable period four years earlier:

	FUNDS RAISED IN THE FIRST SIX MONTHS OF	
	1983	1987
BY LEADING *CORPORATE* PACs	$1,709,743	$ 4,968,479
BY LEADING *LABOR* PACs	$6,612,946	$13,252,333
BY LEADING *TRADE ASS'N* PACs	$3,046,586	$ 5,583,377
BY LEADING *PROFESSIONAL* PACs	$3,410,098	$ 6,115,063

From the point of view of the republic, the campaign-finance crisis can be succinctly stated: the actual and potential *sellers* of influence—U.S. senators and representatives—need ever-increasing amounts of money. And they have come not only to rely on the interest groups to furnish that money. More, they have come to *expect* them to, and to engage in high-pressure tactics, even extortion, if the interest groups do not come through. On the other side of the table, with the federal government spending more and regulating in new areas, interest groups appear willing and able to supply the money.

In the sense that the arrangement suits both sides' interests, it's a perfect fit; perfect, that is, save for one key factor: the public—as taxpayers and as consumers—gets squeezed out. And so, all too often, does the national interest.

Within the summary figures presented above lie some dramatic examples of individual PACs that are just now flexing their money-raising muscles.

PAC	FUNDS RAISED IN THE FIRST SIX MONTHS OF	
	1983	1987
UNITED PARCEL SERVICE	$ 49,142	$ 395,140
MORGAN STANLEY CO. (INVESTMENT BANKERS)	$ 29,392	$ 219,448
UNITED AUTO WORKERS	$ 192,239	$ 688,811
AMERICAN FEDERATION OF TEACHERS	$ 56,405	$ 418,926
NATIONAL ASSOCIATION OF REALTORS	$ 611,041	$1,698,204
ASSOCIATION OF TRIAL LAWYERS	$ 230,059	$ 829,879
AMERICAN MEDICAL ASSOCIATION	$1,288,332	$2,024,269
INTERNATIONAL BROTHERHOOD OF TEAMSTERS	$ 143,929	$2,001,840

The Teamsters Union example is the most dramatic, for it suggests the heights which PAC fundraising is likely to attain, and in the near future at that. In October 1987, the *Wall Street Journal* predicted that if the Teamsters' PAC continues to grow at its present rate, before the end of the 1988 election it will have taken in a total of $10 million—outstripping by several million dollars the highest amount yet raised by a PAC that makes large contributions to congressional candidates.★

Suppose the *Journal*'s $10 million prediction comes true (the Teamsters acknowledge the amount is likely to exceed $8 million), and that $3 million goes for administrative expenses. With $7 million to give to federal candidates, the Teamsters' PAC could give the maximum $10,000 gift to a major-party nominee in every House and Senate contest, and still have between $1 million and $2 million left over to make "independent expenditures" (see Chapter 10) in key congressional races. Although union officials deny any plans for independent spending, the law permits it. Any way the Teamsters choose to slice their $10 million, it will pack an unprecedented political wallop, and Teamsters' president Jackie Presser has not

---

★ A few PACs that are unaffiliated with any interest group—notably Senator Jesse Helms's National Congressional Club and the National Conservative Political Action Committee, or NCPAC—came close to or exceeded the $10 million figure in 1985–86. However, those PACs spent almost all their money on fundraising, administration, and independent expenditures. None made major contributions to the campaigns of congressional *candidates*, the way the PACs of the Teamsters and the Realtors and the American Medical Association did. Those latter two top the 1985–86 fundraising list, collecting, respectively, $5.7 and $5 million.

been shy about saying so. In the fall of 1987, after the AFL-CIO had invited the Teamsters to rejoin them, Presser pledged to a cheering AFL convention to build "the greatest political giant this country has ever seen."

The device that is driving the Treamsters' fast-growing PAC is that most efficient of all fund-collecting mechanisms: the checkoff. Under that system, the employer withholds from paychecks whatever amount individual Teamster members agree to contribute to the PAC (said to be a $1 a week donation by 500,000 Teamster members). The checkoff is essentially the same method used by the dairy co-ops in amassing multi-million-dollar political funds from a handful of dairy farmers. The Trial Lawyers Association, the growth of whose political money-raising is cited above, has a system whereby its members can authorize automatic bank-draft donations to its PAC.

As noted throughout this book, the political-money game is a political arms race, a matter of keeping up with the Joneses. With Presser promising to build "the greatest political giant" in U.S. history, who can suppose that other organizations will sit by and allow the Teamsters to pass them by? On the contrary, is it not likely the doctors and realtors and others will adopt some form of checkoff, to keep up with the Teamsters?

And so the vicious spiral, the arms race, this "perfect fit," where one side needs money and the other side is only too eager to supply it, will perpetuate itself—*unless Congress takes action to interrupt it.*

However, since the present arrangement suits the incumbent senators and representatives just fine, Congress is unlikely to take remedial action without vigorous outside prodding. So campaign-finance reform will almost surely remain a forlorn hope until a presidential candidate takes this problem seriously and a newly elected president makes campaign-finance reform a top legislative priority during those precious first hundred days.

In mid-1987, when the U.S. Senate debated a measure to provide government financing of Senate general elections, senator after senator—especially the new ones—rose to express dismay at the enormous proportion of their time they had been obliged to spend, as candidates, appealing for money. Senator Harry Reid of Nevada, who had scoffed when a friend had predicted he would spend 70 to 80 percent of his time raising money, found the prediction to be true. Senator Brock Adams of Washington said, "I do not think a candidate for the U.S. Senate should have to sit in a motel room in Goldendale, Washington, at six in the morning and spend three hours on the phone talking to political action committees [on the East Coast] . . . to the folks who make a living figuring out the odds on each race and betting the percentages. I wish I had been able to win by debating the issues with my opponent rather than debating my political prospects with political banks."

Members of Congress from both parties claim that most of their colleagues are privately disgusted with the system. But few of them will say so publicly. Nor has a majority of them been willing to vote for sweeping reforms.

In the Antwerp zoo, the birds are confined within walls of light, rather than in cages. They *could* get out, but they don't *believe* they can. So they stay in.

Have members of Congress built their own wall of light? There is no doubt that they *could*, with a new law, liberate themselves from the incessant quest for money, from the constant and demeaning need to "tin-cup" it, from their dependence on "interested" contributors.

Yet they choose to remain in their prison.

Some contend that truly meaningful campaign-finance reform is unattainable, arguing that, given the necessities of politics, the enormous role of government and the correspondingly huge stakes in governmental actions, and the ever-fretful, ever-ambitious nature of politicians, interested money will find its way into the system no matter how many prohibitions and ceilings Congress might enact.

Perhaps so. But at the least, Congress can dilute the influence of that interested money by enacting a system that makes it possible for independent-minded, public-spirited candidates to enter the political lists—*and* to retain their independence once in office.

That possibility was suggested by what Walter Mondale said about how he felt when, as his party's nominee, he received the public funds that would finance his general-election campaign: "After I was nominated for president, and received the some $40 million in direct federal support and was totally relieved from fundraising, I was finally my own man, able to concentrate solely on the issues and the campaign. I no longer had to give first priority to fundraising and I could avoid the inevitable efforts to pressure my position on the issues."

However much Mondale detractors or political cynics wish to discount that statement, imagine the effect of broadening public funding beyond presidential elections to include congressional elections, so that House and Senate candidates could experience Mondale's feeling of liberation. In every House and Senate election, major-party nominees—as many as 870 in the House and 66 or 68 in the Senate—would be *assured* of enough money to mount a respectable campaign. And under the "level-playing-field" provision proposed in Chapter 11, they would also be assured they would not be outspent. Thus they could feel what Walter Mondale said he felt: liberated, free to speak their minds without worrying who was going to give or withhold money.

I do not suggest that the House and Senate would instantly be peopled by selfless men and women. No law on earth could guarantee that. But a law could *make possible* something virtually ruled out by the present campaign-finance system: independent-minded candidates and officeholders free of the influence of interested money.

That would be a basic improvement over the current system. It is very much worth fighting for.

The present campaign-finance law was not handed down on a mountain top. It is not graven in marble. Congress made that law, and Congress can change it.

APPENDICES

THE BEST AND THE WORST: THE SENATE

This table shows election data for every senator and gives figures and rankings for three categories of financial activity: PAC receipts, leftover cash, and honoraria. Each senator is ranked against other senators elected in the same year. For each ranking, a group of senators has been divided into roughly equal quarters, so that a senator receiving four symbols (four treasure chests, four outstretched palms, etc.) is in the top quarter of his group, and a senator with one is in the bottom quarter, and so on.

- *Name and election percentage:* The first pair of columns gives the name and party of each senator, and below that the year (or years) of election and the percentage of the vote the senator received in the most recent election (or two, if the most recent was a reelection).
- *PAC receipts:* This pair of columns shows the amount of campaign funds received from political action committees in the two years preceding the election in question. For example, the PAC figures for Alabama Senator Heflin's 1984 election reflect his receipts for the years 1983 and 1984. The right-hand column gives the percent of the senator's total campaign funds that came from PACs.

The rankings are based on the most recent election of each senator. Since costs of campaigns have risen steadily over the years, each election "class" is ranked separately, as shown below:

1985–86 PAC RECEIPTS

= More than $1,000,000

= $825,001–$1,000,000

= $600,001–$825,000

= $1–$600,000

1983–84 PAC RECEIPTS

= More than $800,000

= $600,001–$800,000

= $400,001–$600,000

= $1–$400,000

1981–82 PAC RECEIPTS

= More than $600,000

= $450,001–$600,000

= $300,001–$450,000

= $1–$300,000

= Does not accept PAC money

- *Leftover cash:* This column lists the amount left over in the senator's campaign treasury at the end of the election year. Senate rules do not permit a senator to keep the leftover funds upon retirement. Nevertheless, a sizable campaign chest can at the very least discourage challengers from seeking a senator's seat.

  As with PAC receipts, the rankings on leftover cash are based on each senator's most recent election, as follows:

1986 LEFTOVER CASH

= More than $375,000

= $130,001–$375,000

= $50,001–$130,000

= $1,000–$50,000

1984 LEFTOVER CASH

= More than $300,000

= $150,001–$300,000

= $40,001–$150,000

= $1,000–$40,000

1982 LEFTOVER CASH

= More than $125,000

= $60,001–$125,000

= $10,001–$60,000

= $1,000–$10,000

= Has no campaign surplus

▪ *Honoraria or speaking fees:* Unlike campaign contributions, which are paid to the senators' campaign funds, honoraria are paid directly to the senators, and may be pocketed by them. Senators are allowed to accept such fees (up to $2,000 per speech) from any interest group, no matter how great the conflict of interest. For example, a member of the Banking Committee is free to accept an honorarium from the American Bankers Association. (Of course, many fees come from groups such as universities, where the conflict of interest is likely to be minimal.)

The symbol rankings in this section are based on senators' total honoraria receipts in 1986; the figures are given in the left-hand column. The dollar amounts for the rankings are as follows:

1986 HONORARIA

✖✖✖✖ = More than $40,000
✖✖✖ = $30,001–$40,000
✖✖ = $19,001–$30,000
✖ = $1–$19,000
◯ = Took no honoraria in 1986

Senators first elected in 1986 are not ranked; those for whom figures are given received their honoraria while still in the House.

Senators may keep honoraria only up to an equivalent of 40 percent of their salaries, which in 1986 amounted to $30,000 for senators in nonleadership positions; they are required to donate any amount over that to charity. Such donations are shown in the right-hand column.

NAME / PARTY	MONEY FROM PACs		LEFT-OVER CASH	HONORARIA (1986)	
ELECTION CYCLE / % OF VOTE	AMOUNT	% OF ALL RECEIPTS		TOTAL RECEIVED	GIVEN TO CHARITY
A L A B A M A					
Howell Heflin (D)					
1984 62%	$ 847,573	38%	$ 484,533	$ 26,000	$ 4,000
1978 94%	$ 124,400	11%	$ 47,900		
Richard C. Shelby (D)					
1986 50%	$ 856,184	36%	$ 141,319	$ 24,000	$ 2,000
A L A S K A					
Ted Stevens (R)					
1984 71%	$ 637,798	48%	$ 184,675	$ 34,800	$ 4,760
1978 76%	$ 170,724	47%	$ 87,547		

NAME / PARTY		MONEY FROM PACs		LEFT-OVER CASH	HONORARIA (1986)	
ELECTION CYCLE / % OF VOTE		AMOUNT	% OF ALL RECEIPTS		TOTAL RECEIVED	GIVEN TO CHARITY
Frank H. Murkowski (R)						
1986	54%	$ 586,256	41%	$ 53,848	$ 25,500	$ 0
1980	54%	$ 304,971	43%	$ 13,649		
A R I Z O N A						
Dennis DeConcini (D)						
1982	57%	$ 416,166	23%	$ 107,324	$ 0	$ 0
1976	54%	$ 100,433	16%	$ 2,057		
John McCain (R)						
1986	60%	$ 747,083	30%	$ 287,217	$ 13,750	$ 13,750
A R K A N S A S						
Dale Bumpers (D)						
1986	62%	$ 504,831	29%	$ 124,978	$ 28,200	$ 0
1980	59%	$ 52,325	17%	$ 79,499		
David Pryor (D)						
1984	57%	$ 711,547	37%	$ 174,188	$ 30,000	$ 0
1978	77%	$ 97,280	12%	$ 28,037		
C A L I F O R N I A						
Alan Cranston (D)						
1986	49%	$1,319,606	12%	$ 16,593	$ 18,062	$ 0
1980	57%	$ 418,316	13%	$ 320,741		
Pete Wilson (R)						
1982	52%	$1,187,832	17%	$ 108,080	$ 32,832	$ 3,600
C O L O R A D O						
William L. Armstrong (R)						
1984	64%	$ 800,256	26%	$ 175,883	$ 2,000	$ 2,000
1978	59%	$ 310,930	27%	$ 111,165		
Timothy E. Wirth (D)						
1986	50%	$ 832,288	22%	$ 32,106	$ 25,100	$ 3,000
C O N N E C T I C U T						
Lowell P. Weicker, Jr. (R)						
1982	51%	$ 447,054	19%	$ 2,273	$ 29,924	$ 0
1976	58%	$ 52,034	10%	$ 20,296		

| NAME / PARTY | | MONEY FROM PACs | | LEFT-OVER CASH | HONORARIA (1986) | |
ELECTION CYCLE / % OF VOTE		AMOUNT	% OF ALL RECEIPTS		TOTAL RECEIVED	GIVEN TO CHARITY
Christopher J. Dodd (D)						
1986	65%	$ 721,189	30%	$ 266,781	$ 34,450	$ 4,450
1980	56%	$ 268,388	19%	$ −1,149		
D E L A W A R E						
William V. Roth, Jr. (R)						
1982	55%	$ 354,744	42%	$ 48,019	$ 53,300	$23,260
1976	56%	$ 71,600	22%	$ 4,669		
Joseph R. Biden, Jr. (D)						
1984	60%	$ 404,905	28%	$ 24,489	$ 29,472	$ 0
1978	58%	$ 126,100	26%	$ 556		
F L O R I D A						
Lawton Chiles (D)						
1982	62%	$ 10,558	1%	$ 41,646	$ 0	$ 0
1976	63%	$ 0	0%	$ 242		
Bob Graham (D)						
1986	55%	$ 924,127	15%	$ 42,247		
G E O R G I A						
Sam Nunn (D)						
1984	79%	$ 381,914	30%	$ 676,199	$ 44,350	$14,675
1978	83%	$ 135,145	19%	$ 160,844		
Wyche Fowler, Jr. (D)						
1986	51%	$ 574,101	20%	$ 133,342	$ 6,000	$ 0
H A W A I I						
Daniel K. Inouye (D)						
1986	74%	$ 571,777	49%	$ 598,388	$ 28,500	$ 0
1980	78%	$ 169,872	23%	$ 281,511		
Spark M. Matsunaga (D)						
1982	80%	$ 266,650	34%	$ 338,524	$ 40,050	$10,017
1976	54%	$ 92,983	22%	$ 20,005		
I D A H O						
James A. McClure (R)						
1984	72%	$ 550,496	43%	$ 320,402	$ 29,355	$ 0
1978	68%	$ 161,873	43%	$ 26,444		

NAME / PARTY		MONEY FROM PACs		LEFT-OVER CASH	HONORARIA (1986)	
ELECTION CYCLE / % OF VOTE		AMOUNT	% OF ALL RECEIPTS		TOTAL RECEIVED	GIVEN TO CHARITY
Steve Symms (R)						
1986	52%	$1,369,168	40%	$ 188,369	$ 42,750	$ 12,710
1980	50%	$ 638,272	36%	$ 12,651		
I L L I N O I S						
Alan J. Dixon (D)						
1986	65%	$ 958,639	43%	$ 408,427	$ 32,300	$ 4,260
1980	56%	$ 287,154	12%	$ 58,109		
Paul Simon (D)						
1984	50%	$ 907,762	20%	$ 4,784	$ 35,925	$ 5,975
I N D I A N A						
Richard G. Lugar (R)						
1982	54%	$ 712,639	24%	$ 53,814	$ 62,200	$ 32,376
1976	59%	$ 145,366	19%	$ 15,210		
Dan Quayle (R)						
1986	61%	$ 850,849	37%	$ 385,126	$ 49,985	$ 19,991
1980	54%	$ 600,045	26%	$ 18,366		
I O W A						
Charles E. Grassley (R)						
1986	66%	$ 958,431	35%	$ 486,432	$ 63,325	$ 33,285
1980	53%	$ 722,211	33%	$ 34,200		
Tom Harkin (D)						
1984	55%	$ 800,827	28%	$ 5,067	$ 20,025	$ 0
K A N S A S						
Robert Dole (R)						
1986	71%	$1,022,433	39%	$ 2,166,732	$119,575	$ 87,500
1980	64%	$ 422,531	32%	$ 102,186		
Nancy Kassebaum (R)						
1984	75%	$ 234,595	41%	$ 217,804	$ 6,000	$ 2,000
1978	54%	$ 121,721	14%	$ 7,361		
K E N T U C K Y						
Wendell H. Ford (D)						
1986	74%	$ 831,368	55%	$ 360,775	$ 26,700	$ 0
1980	65%	$ 230,175	39%	$ 112,861		

| NAME / PARTY | | MONEY FROM PACs | | LEFT-OVER CASH | HONORARIA (1986) | |
ELECTION CYCLE / % OF VOTE		AMOUNT	% OF ALL RECEIPTS		TOTAL RECEIVED	GIVEN TO CHARITY
Mitch McConnell (R)						
1984	49%	$ 284,496	18%	$ 27,443	$ 46,700	$16,660
L O U I S I A N A						
J. Bennett Johnston (D)						
1984	85%	$ 553,085	37%	$ 984,831	$ 43,650	$13,610
1978	59%	$ 206,705	21%	$ 125,483		
John B. Breaux (D)						
1986	53%	$ 823,717	27%	$ 48,130	$ 24,000	$ 1,470
M A I N E						
William S. Cohen (R)						
1984	73%	$ 421,451	36%	$ 139,971	$ 29,650	$ 0
1978	57%	$ 157,551	24%	$ 9,514		
George J. Mitchell (D)						
1982	61%	$ 562,253	46%	$ 8,523	$ 35,625	$ 5,625
M A R Y L A N D						
Paul Sarbanes (D)						
1982	63%	$ 465,487	29%	$ 8,637	$ 17,800	$ 0
1976	57%	$ 142,850	16%	$ 767		
Barbara A. Mikulski (D)						
1986	61%	$ 653,563	30%	$ 103,596	$ 11,500	$ 0
M A S S A C H U S E T T S						
Edward M. Kennedy (D)						
1982	61%	$ 306,965	12%	$ 139,041	$ 600	$ 0
1976	69%	$ 104,302	10%	$ 79,515		
John Kerry (D)						
1984	55%	$ 5,170	0.2%	$ 99,770	$ 22,225	$ 0
M I C H I G A N						
Donald W. Riegle, Jr. (D)						
1982	58%	$ 602,946	35%	$ 263,075	$ 54,950	$32,900
1976	53%	$ 188,710	22%	$ 12,686		
Carl Levin (D)						
1984	52%	$ 707,766	20%	$ 55,177	$ 0	$ 0
1978	52%	$ 206,291	21%	$ 22,662		

NAME / PARTY	MONEY FROM PACs		LEFT-OVER CASH	HONORARIA (1986)	
ELECTION CYCLE / % OF VOTE	AMOUNT	% OF ALL RECEIPTS		TOTAL RECEIVED	GIVEN TO CHARITY
M I N N E S O T A					
Dave Durenberger (R)					
1982 53%	$1,030,239	26%	$ 89,846	$ 49,430	$ 19,630
1978 62% (special election)	$ 250,448	23%	$ 10,864		
Rudy Boschwitz (R)					
1984 58%	$1,005,187	17%	$ 214,480	$ 16,100	$ 16,100
1978 57%	$ 261,257	14%	$ 32,694		
M I S S I S S I P P I					
John C. Stennis (D)					
1982 64%	$ 232,300	24%	$ 5,156	$ 0	$ 0
1976 100%	$ 2,380	1%	$ 0		
Thad Cochran (R)					
1984 60%	$ 960,361	35%	$ 138,875	$ 41,600	$ 11,600
1978 45%	$ 185,230	15%	$ 148,955		
M I S S O U R I					
John C. Danforth (R)					
1982 51%	$ 572,658	32%	$ 9,069	$ 11,875	$ 0
1976 57%	$ 71,106	9%	$ 6,037		
Christopher S. Bond (R)					
1986 53%	$1,316,556	24%	$ 67,773		
M O N T A N A					
John Melcher (D)					
1982 54%	$ 435,528	56%	$ 3,059	$ 30,250	$ 0
1976 64%	$ 143,535	44%	$ 3,330		
Max Baucus (D)					
1984 56%	$ 653,749	53%	$ 46,806	$ 30,040	$ 0
1978 56%	$ 168,220	25%	$ 14,434		
N E B R A S K A					
J. James Exon (D)					
1984 51%	$ 511,613	58%	$ 51,762	$ 24,200	$ 0
1978 68%	$ 63,250	24%	$ 27,539		
David Karnes—appointed by governor in 1987					

NAME / PARTY	MONEY FROM PACs		LEFT-OVER CASH	HONORARIA (1986)	
ELECTION CYCLE / % OF VOTE	AMOUNT	% OF ALL RECEIPTS		TOTAL RECEIVED	GIVEN TO CHARITY
N E V A D A					
Chic Hecht (R)					
1982 50%	$ 250,010	18%	$ 44,648	$ 19,500	$ 0
Harry Reid (D)					
1986 52%	$ 808,272	39%	$ 33,490	$ 0	$ 0
N E W H A M P S H I R E					
Gordon J. Humphrey (R)					
1984 58%	$ 728,608	43%	$ 20,433	$ 0	$ 0
1978 51%	$ 89,126	24%	$ 9,522		
Warren B. Rudman (R)					
1986 63%	$ 15,152	2%	$ 57,085	$ 43,900	$ 13,883
1980 52%	$ 10,840	2%	$ 1,009		
N E W J E R S E Y					
Bill Bradley (D)					
1984 64%	$ 665,782	15%	$ 376,495	$ 28,575	$ 8,425
1978 55%	$ 192,896	11%	$ 1,474		
Frank Lautenberg (D)					
1982 51%	$ 155,949	2%	$ 60,343	$ 0	$ 0
N E W M E X I C O					
Pete V. Domenici (R)					
1984 71%	$ 784,295	30%	$ 36,616	$ 78,290	$ 48,250
1978 53%	$ 150,401	16%	$ 11,336		
Jeff Bingaman (D)					
1982 54%	$ 310,717	19%	$ 20,719	$ 15,997	$ 0
N E W Y O R K					
Daniel Patrick Moynihan (D)					
1982 65%	$ 366,221	15%	$ 116,647	$108,975	$ 78,935
1976 54%	$ 185,391	15%	$ 8,943		
Alfonse M. D'Amato (R)					
1986 57%	$ 858,386	13%	$ 456,293	$ 32,800	$ 2,800
1980 45%	$ 273,260	16%	$ 6,071		

NAME / PARTY		MONEY FROM PACs		LEFT-OVER CASH	HONORARIA (1986)	
ELECTION CYCLE / % OF VOTE		AMOUNT	% OF ALL RECEIPTS		TOTAL RECEIVED	GIVEN TO CHARITY
N O R T H C A R O L I N A						
Jesse Helms (R)						
1984	51%	$ 847,337	5%	$ 22,878	$ 30,000	$ 0
1978	55%	$ 271,290	4%	$ 10,840		
Terry Sanford (D)						
1986	52%	$ 628,691	15%	$ 13,190		
N O R T H D A K O T A						
Quentin N. Burdick (D)						
1982	63%	$ 489,419	54%	$ 129,142	$ 4,500	$ 0
1976	62%	$ 59,100	48%	$ 5,158		
Kent Conrad (D)						
1986	50%	$ 484,731	49%	$ 85,667		
O H I O						
John Glenn (D)						
1986	57%	$ 628,333	30%	$ 818,910	$ 0	$ 0
1980	70%	$ 194,335	20%	$ 125,550		
Howard M. Metzenbaum (D)						
1982	58%	$ 401,528	11%	$ 970,455	$ 4,125	$ 4,125
1976	50%	$ 125,448	11%	$ 5,527		
O K L A H O M A						
David L. Boren (D)						
1984	75%	$ 4,241	0.4%	$ 52,468	$ 43,375	$ 13,962
1978	65%	$ 800	0.1%	$ 28,250		
Don Nickles (R)						
1986	55%	$ 856,385	29%	$ 375,674	$ 18,250	$ 2,750
1980	53%	$ 152,587	16%	$ 96,751		
O R E G O N						
Mark O. Hatfield (R)						
1984	67%	$ 376,693	46%	$ 243,511	$ 32,830	$ 2,790
1978	62%	$ 90,633	33%	$ 53,181		
Bob Packwood (R)						
1986	64%	$ 966,759	14%	$ 692,290	$ 41,498	$ 11,683
1980	52%	$ 349,292	22%	$ 26,041		

| NAME / PARTY | MONEY FROM PACs | | LEFT-OVER CASH | HONORARIA (1986) | |
ELECTION CYCLE / % OF VOTE	AMOUNT	% OF ALL RECEIPTS		TOTAL RECEIVED	GIVEN TO CHARITY
P E N N S Y L V A N I A					
John Heinz (R)					
1982 59%	$ 588,444	20%	$ 524,957	$ 12,625	$ 12,625
1976 52%	$ 51,987	2%	$ 12,881		
Arlen Specter (R)					
1986 56%	$1,270,951	23%	$ 64,461	$ 31,650	$ 2,980
1980 50%	$ 305,426	20%	$ 23,754		
R H O D E I S L A N D					
Claiborne Pell (D)					
1984 72%	$ 210,592	28%	$ 388,004	$ 8,500	$ 8,500
1978 75%	$ 75,945	19%	$ 27,399		
John H. Chafee (R)					
1982 51%	$ 409,253	41%	$ 53,686	$ 54,250	$ 25,037
1976 58%	$ 57,984	13%	$ 17,660		
S O U T H C A R O L I N A					
Strom Thurmond (R)					
1984 66%	$ 530,973	28%	$ 364,686	$ 17,000	$ 17,000
1978 56%	$ 216,090	12%	$ 10,654		
Ernest F. Hollings (D)					
1986 63%	$ 912,917	38%	$ 197,854	$ 98,775	$ 68,735
1980 70%	$ 249,515	31%	$ 133,668		
S O U T H D A K O T A					
Larry Pressler (R)					
1984 74%	$ 522,649	42%	$ 325,441	$ 32,760	$ 2,720
1978 67%	$ 177,345	36%	$ 40,439		
Thomas A. Daschle (D)					
1986 52%	$1,203,901	34%	$ 40,245	$ 18,750	$ 0
T E N N E S S E E					
Jim Sasser (D)					
1982 62%	$ 641,970	30%	$ 65,161	$ 32,300	$ 2,300
1976 53%	$ 119,409	14%	$ 2,264		
Albert Gore, Jr. (D)					
1984 60%	$ 795,581	25%	$ −14,967	$ 31,950	$ 2,000

NAME / PARTY	MONEY FROM PACs		LEFT-OVER CASH	HONORARIA (1986)	
ELECTION CYCLE / % OF VOTE	AMOUNT	% OF ALL RECEIPTS		TOTAL RECEIVED	GIVEN TO CHARITY
T E X A S					
Lloyd Bentsen (D)					
1982 59%	$ 800,443	18%	$ 12,801	$ 0	$ 0
1976 57%	$ 237,002	18%	$ 5,269		
Phil Gramm (R)					
1984 58%	$1,479,851	15%	$ 353,926	$ 30,000	$ 0
U T A H					
Jake Garn (R)					
1986 72%	$ 593,242	58%	$ 285,275	$ 54,340	$24,300
1980 74%	$ 285,909	25%	$ 9,132		
Orrin G. Hatch (R)					
1982 58%	$ 902,002	19%	$ 95,204	$ 73,270	$43,240
1976 54%	$ 111,208	28%	$ 22,761		
V E R M O N T					
Robert T. Stafford (R)					
1982 50%	$ 295,332	75%	$ 3,887	$ 32,725	$ 2,910
1976 50%	$ 74,750	44%	$ 9,542		
Patrick J. Leahy (D)					
1986 63%	$ 826,894	43%	$ 327,768	$ 32,208	$ 2,300
1980 50%	$ 213,760	41%	$ 95,656		
V I R G I N I A					
John W. Warner (R)					
1984 70%	$ 694,588	26%	$ 44,416	$ 13,050	$ 0
1978 50%	$ 108,144	4%	$ 9,835		
Paul S. Trible, Jr. (R)					
1982 51%	$ 671,016	30%	$ 58,091	$ 29,000	$ 0
W A S H I N G T O N					
Daniel J. Evans (R)					
1983 55% (special election)	$ 490,837	25%	$ 139,801	$ 20,000	$ 0
Brock Adams (D)					
1986 51%	$ 658,396	33%	$ 86,797		

NAME / PARTY		MONEY FROM PACs		LEFT-OVER CASH	HONORARIA (1986)	
ELECTION CYCLE / % OF VOTE		AMOUNT	% OF ALL RECEIPTS		TOTAL RECEIVED	GIVEN TO CHARITY
W E S T V I R G I N I A						
Robert C. Byrd (D)						
1982	69%	$ 710,541	39%	$ 226,143	$ 19,000	$ 0
1976	100%	$ 64,240	23%	$ 160,389		
John D. Rockefeller (D)						
1984	51%	$ 533,322	4%	$ 36,508	$ 500	$ 500
W I S C O N S I N						
William Proxmire (D)						
1982	64%	$ 0	0%	$ 0	$ 17,600	$ 0
1976	72%	$ 0	0%	$ 0		
Bob Kasten (R)						
1986	51%	$1,093,147	34%	$ 125,579	$ 30,800	$ 800
1980	50%	$ 287,083	40%	$ 38,522		
W Y O M I N G						
Malcolm Wallop (R)						
1982	57%	$ 472,240	42%	$ 19,080	$ 47,850	$ 17,810
1976	55%	$ 51,560	16%	$ 3,566		
Alan K. Simpson (R)						
1984	78%	$ 407,708	45%	$ 205,615	$ 30,040	$ 0
1978	62%	$ 124,385	28%	$ 2,677		

THE BEST AND THE WORST: THE HOUSE

B

This table shows election data for all current members of Congress and gives figures and rankings for three categories of financial activity: PAC receipts, cash left over at the end of campaigns, and honoraria received. For rankings in each category, the House of Representatives has been divided into roughly equal quarters, so that a representative receiving four symbols (four rocking chairs, four outstretched palms, etc.) is in the top quarter, a representative with one symbol is in the bottom quarter, and so on.

- *Name and election percentage:* The first column gives the election district (or AL, for At Large), name, and party of each representative. Below that are given the percentage of the vote he or she received in each election since 1980 (or since first coming to the House), and the dates of the two-year election cycle ending with each election. An asterisk (*) after a single election year denotes a special election to fill a vacancy caused by the death or resignation of a representative.
- *PAC receipts:* This pair of columns shows the amount of campaign funds received in each two-year election cycle from political action committees. The right-hand column shows what percentage of the entire campaign budget was paid by PACs.

The rankings are based on the 1986 election; the dollar figures are shown below:

1985–86 PAC RECEIPTS

🐝🐝🐝🐝 = More than $225,000

🐝🐝🐝 = $150,001–$225,000

🐝🐝 = $100,001–$150,000

🐝 = $1–$100,000

◯ = Does not accept PAC money.

- *Leftover cash:* This column gives the amount left over in the representative's campaign treasury at the end of each election cycle; the rankings are based on cash on hand at the end of 1986.

   Those representatives elected before 1980 are permitted to take those campaign surpluses with them when they leave Congress. In effect, therefore, the surpluses potentially serve as retirement funds for them, and the symbol is a rocking chair.

   Members of Congress elected in 1980 or after may not transfer their campaign surpluses to their own bank accounts when they retire. Nonetheless, large surpluses can serve another purpose: they can discourage would-be opponents who despair of being able to raise a comparable amount of campaign money. For those representatives, the symbol is a treasure chest.

   The dollar figures for each ranking are as follows:

1986 LEFTOVER CASH

🪑🪑🪑🪑 or 💰💰💰💰 = More than $150,000

🪑🪑🪑 or 💰💰💰 = $75,001–$150,000

🪑🪑 or 💰💰 = $15,001–$75,000

🪑 or 💰 = $1,000–$15,000

- *Honoraria or speaking fees:* Members of the House, like senators, are permitted to accept honoraria from any interest group, no matter how serious the conflict of interest (see discussion in Appendix A). The rankings in this table are based on representatives' total honoraria receipts in 1985, which are given in the left-hand column. The figures for the rankings are as follows:

1985 HONORARIA

🍴🍴🍴🍴 = More than $20,000

🍴🍴🍴 = $7,501–$20,000

🍴🍴 = $3,001–$7,500

🍴 = $1–$3,000

◯ = Took no honoraria in 1985

Where no honoraria figures are given, the representative was not yet in office in 1985.

Members of the House may keep honoraria only up to an equivalent of 30 percent of their salaries, which in 1985 amounted to $25,880; they must donate any excess to charity. Some contribute more than the legally required amount to charity; such donations are shown in the right-hand column.

DIST. / NAME / PARTY	MONEY FROM PACs		LEFT-OVER CASH	HONORARIA (1985)	
ELECTION CYCLE / % OF VOTE	AMOUNT	% OF ALL RECEIPTS		TOTAL RECEIVED	GIVEN TO CHARITY
A L A B A M A					
1 Callahan (R)					
1985–86 100%	$114,197	39%	$ 156,236	$ 6,000	$ 0
1983–84 51%	$196,493	35%	$ 3,945		
2 Dickinson (R)					
1985–86 67%	$180,581	47%	$ 351,585	$ 26,000	$ 3,545
1983–84 60%	$214,615	50%	$ 215,773		
1981–82 50%	$129,735	43%	$ 111,788		
1979–80 61%	$ 60,979	35%	$ 98,950		
3 Nichols (D)					
1985–86 81%	$ 67,964	33%	$ 356,616	$ 1,500	$ 0
1983–84 96%	$ 73,764	46%	$ 260,940		
1981–82 96%	$ 55,590	64%	$ 135,007		
1979–80 100%	$ 40,970	54%	$ 69,271		
4 Bevill (D)					
1985–86 78%	$107,471	47%	$ 437,485	$ 9,500	$ 0
1983–84 100%	$101,868	37%	$ 358,023		
1981–82 100%	$ 59,300	36%	$ 185,865		
1979–80 98%	$ 30,470	51%	$ 86,121		
5 Flippo (D)					
1985–86 79%	$286,891	66%	$ 603,947	$ 30,000	$ 10,000
1983–84 95%	$217,531	66%	$ 338,016		
1981–82 81%	$109,870	52%	$ 139,348		
1979–80 94%	$ 57,347	34%	$ 126,279		
6 Erdreich (D)					
1985–86 73%	$214,440	63%	$ 146,955	$ 2,750	$ 2,750
1983–84 59%	$317,050	54%	$ 20,598		
1981–82 53%	$ 91,050	39%	$ 17,712		

DIST. / NAME / PARTY ELECTION CYCLE / % OF VOTE	MONEY FROM PACs AMOUNT	% OF ALL RECEIPTS	LEFT-OVER CASH	HONORARIA (1985) TOTAL RECEIVED	GIVEN TO CHARITY
7 Harris (D)					
1985–86 60%	$182,800	38%	$ 1,501		
A L A S K A					
AL Young (R)					
1985–86 57%	$250,133	51%	$ 12,010	$ 22,250	$ 0
1983–84 55%	$185,753	38%	$ 3,842		
1981–82 71%	$ 88,698	32%	$ 9,167		
1979–80 74%	$ 94,321	28%	$ 2,778		
A R I Z O N A					
1 Rhodes (R)					
1985–86 71%	$112,065	23%	$ 5,226		
2 Udall (D)					
1985–86 73%	$139,830	35%	$ 12,916	$ 12,000	$ 0
1983–84 87%	$ 77,388	27%	$ 56,472		
1981–82 71%	$113,958	14%	$ 487		
1979–80 58%	$158,052	22%	$ 46,096		
3 Stump (R)					
1985–86 100%	$ 97,050	42%	$ 107,179	$ 0	$ 0
1983–84 71%	$109,965	42%	$ 72,127		
1981–82 63%	$128,536	46%	$ 43,418		
1979–80 64%	$ 59,397	41%	$ 59,166		
4 Kyl (R)					
1985–86 65%	$239,561	24%	$ 9,054		
5 Kolbe (R)					
1985–86 65%	$183,487	29%	$ 21,725	$ 3,500	$ 0
1983–84 50%	$244,401	34%	$ 11,448		
1981–82 48%	$132,776	23%	$ 36,731		
A R K A N S A S					
1 Alexander (D)					
1985–86 64%	$303,900	48%	$ 8,540	$ 16,850	$ 0
1983–84 100%	$138,303	45%	$ 81,689		
1981–82 65%	$145,969	33%	$ 43,785		
1979–80 100%	$ 46,715	38%	$ 100,854		

DIST. / NAME / PARTY	MONEY FROM PACs		LEFT-OVER CASH	HONORARIA (1985)	
ELECTION CYCLE / % OF VOTE	AMOUNT	% OF ALL RECEIPTS		TOTAL RECEIVED	GIVEN TO CHARITY
2 Robinson (D)					
1985–86 76%	$296,867	41%	$ 49,367	$ 15,500	$ 0
1983–84 47%	$ 84,000	9%	$ 4,017		
3 Hammerschmidt (R)					
1985–86 80%	$ 83,950	53%	$ 168,435	$ 1,000	$ 0
1983–84 100%	$ 61,176	64%	$ 72,537		
1981–82 66%	$ 76,536	30%	$ 33,997		
1979–80 100%	$ 30,600	60%	$ 43,666		
4 Anthony (D)					
1985–86 78%	$276,757	71%	$ 337,764	$ 28,500	$ 7,500
1983–84 100%	$144,750	66%	$ 126,236		
1981–82 66%	$165,161	49%	$ 330		
1979–80 100%	$ 28,078	25%	$ 13,460		
C A L I F O R N I A					
1 Bosco (D)					
1985–86 68%	$ 97,923	51%	$ 653	$ 5,500	$ 0
1983–84 62%	$108,577	46%	$ 22,420		
1981–82 50%	$125,271	46%	$ 3,062		
2 Herger (R)					
1985–86 58%	$197,641	31%	$ 18,589		
3 Matsui (D)					
1985–86 76%	$300,634	46%	$ 374,464	$ 38,250	$ 15,858
1983–84 100%	$176,243	51%	$ 277,820		
1981–82 90%	$124,790	47%	$ 163,617		
1979–80 71%	$ 80,047	32%	$ 36,631		
4 Fazio (D)					
1985–86 70%	$324,157	51%	$ 285,596	$ 23,100	$ 633
1983–84 62%	$270,378	49%	$ 36,410		
1981–82 64%	$151,187	45%	$ 51,265		
1979–80 65%	$ 77,435	36%	$ 28,340		
5 Pelosi (D)					
1987 63% (runoff)	$269,515	22%	$ 27,254		

DIST. / NAME / PARTY ELECTION CYCLE / % OF VOTE	MONEY FROM PACs AMOUNT	% OF ALL RECEIPTS	LEFT-OVER CASH	HONORARIA (1985) TOTAL RECEIVED	GIVEN TO CHARITY
6 Boxer (D)					
1985–86 74%	$164,611	46%	$ 134,467	$ 4,050	$ 0
1983–84 67%	$190,890	37%	$ 56,180		
1981–82 52%	$114,033	22%	$ 2,384		
7 Miller (D)					
1985–86 67%	$152,243	39%	$ 257,437	$ 18,635	$ 400
1983–84 65%	$102,107	37%	$ 178,602		
1981–82 67%	$ 61,025	30%	$ 88,704		
1979–80 63%	$ 22,369	17%	$ 21,177		
8 Dellums (D)					
1985–86 60%	$ 93,123	7%	$ 153,259	$ 21,900	$ 0
1983–84 60%	$ 76,752	8%	$ 5,930		
1981–82 56%	$ 45,960	6%	$ 36,004		
1979–80 55%	$ 32,605	9%	$ 45,650		
9 Stark (D)					
1985–86 70%	$355,263	63%	$ 37,565	$ 47,800	$ 26,600
1983–84 69%	$199,185	35%	$ 4,136		
1981–82 61%	$122,089	36%	$ 917		
1979–80 55%	$ 24,550	60%	$ 5,206		
10 Edwards (D)					
1985–86 71%	$112,625	60%	$ 46,556	$ 1,082	$ 0
1983–84 62%	$ 88,827	58%	$ 14,802		
1981–82 63%	$ 68,314	42%	$ 3,081		
1979–80 62%	$ 8,850	30%	$ 2,899		
11 Lantos (D)					
1985–86 74%	$ 58,850	20%	$ 353,277	$ 11,650	$ 1,000
1983–84 69%	$ 92,283	14%	$ 379,480		
1981–82 57%	$200,363	16%	$ 30,701		
1979–80 46%	$ 61,550	12%	$ 2,568		
12 Konnyu (R)					
1985–86 60%	$242,626	27%	$ 4,139		
13 Mineta (D)					
1985–86 70%	$231,921	43%	$ 265,256	$ 20,300	$ 0
1983–84 65%	$165,542	33%	$ 162,868		
1981–82 66%	$118,150	32%	$ 86,046		
1979–80 59%	$ 80,040	31%	$ 62,465		

DIST. / NAME / PARTY ELECTION CYCLE / % OF VOTE	MONEY FROM PACs		LEFT-OVER CASH	HONORARIA (1985)	
	AMOUNT	% OF ALL RECEIPTS		TOTAL RECEIVED	GIVEN TO CHARITY
14 Shumway (R)					
1985–86 72%	$139,565	43%	$ 139,098	$ 5,600	$ 0
1983–84 73%	$140,451	38%	$ 72,811		
1981–82 63%	$158,963	49%	$ 1,774		
1979–80 61%	$ 93,066	43%	$ 1,157		
15 Coelho (D)					
1985–86 72%	$338,367	47%	$ 232,032	$ 60,100	$ 37,633
1983–84 65%	$286,098	45%	$ 160,941		
1981–82 64%	$308,165	41%	$ 16,987		
1979–80 72%	$ 92,062	43%	$ 40,131		
16 Panetta (D)					
1985–86 78%	$ 78,875	47%	$ 116,169	$ 18,900	$ 0
1983–84 70%	$ 87,718	39%	$ 64,824		
1981–82 84%	$ 55,439	40%	$ 117,118		
1979–80 71%	$ 38,965	38%	$ 54,992		
17 Pashayan (R)					
1985–86 60%	$105,931	35%	$ 60,440	$ 0	$ 0
1983–84 72%	$112,473	33%	$ 57,466		
1981–82 54%	$141,935	33%	$ 7,293		
1979–80 71%	$111,538	23%	$ 13,264		
18 Lehman (D)					
1985–86 71%	$ 61,770	24%	$ 7,099	$ 16,000	$ 0
1983–84 67%	$122,522	52%	$ 43,934		
1981–82 59%	$ 72,851	42%	$ 4,644		
19 Lagomarsino (R)					
1985–86 72%	$ 63,636	19%	$ 272,488	$ 0	$ 0
1983–84 67%	$ 90,078	19%	$ 264,453		
1981–82 61%	$ 54,096	23%	$ 89,799		
1979–80 78%	$ 37,696	29%	$ 86,456		
20 Thomas (R)					
1985–86 73%	$165,617	64%	$ 220,486	$ 22,300	$ 0
1983–84 70%	$148,071	50%	$ 215,057		
1981–82 68%	$ 83,250	42%	$ 94,759		
1979–80 71%	$ 69,544	28%	$ 74,306		
21 Gallegly (R)					
1985–86 68%	$143,573	23%	$ 40,407		

DIST. / NAME / PARTY	MONEY FROM PACs		LEFT-OVER CASH	HONORARIA (1985)	
ELECTION CYCLE / % OF VOTE	AMOUNT	% OF ALL RECEIPTS		TOTAL RECEIVED	GIVEN TO CHARITY
22 Moorhead (R)					
1985–86 74%	$154,766	49%	$ 460,138	$ 9,000	$ 2,000
1983–84 85%	$ 97,525	49%	$ 288,907		
1981–82 74%	$ 86,122	41%	$ 196,958		
1979–80 64%	$ 68,886	42%	$ 95,906		
23 Beilenson (D)					
1985–86 66%	$ 0	0%	$ 5,678	$ 300	$ 0
1983–84 61%	$ 4,213	2%	$ 25,588		
1981–82 60%	$ 2,092	1%	$ 5,225		
1979–80 63%	$ 2,000	3%	$ 35,389		
24 Waxman (D)					
1985–86 88%	$105,900	72%	$ 101,881	$ 41,753	$ 19,290
1983–84 63%	$141,196	81%	$ 91,942		
1981–82 65%	$ 91,670	77%	$ 34,761		
1979–80 64%	$ 19,950	61%	$ 11,134		
25 Roybal (D)					
1985–86 76%	$ 40,400	41%	$ 224,527	$ 1,650	$ 0
1983–84 71%	$ 64,971	42%	$ 189,604		
1981–82 85%	$ 48,236	44%	$ 111,490		
1979–80 66%	$ 18,210	34%	$ 41,269		
26 Berman (D)					
1985–86 65%	$118,827	43%	$ 21,273	$ 9,950	$ 0
1983–84 62%	$ 98,588	44%	$ 16,541		
1981–82 60%	$106,201	34%	$ 378		
27 Levine (D)					
1985–86 64%	$121,524	17%	$ 310,765	$ 22,005	$ 0
1983–84 54%	$ 67,083	19%	$ 98,474		
1981–82 59%	$ 45,922	10%	$ 32,259		
28 Dixon (D)					
1985–86 76%	$ 89,005	60%	$ 80,527	$ 5,250	$ 0
1983–84 75%	$ 79,553	68%	$ 35,590		
1981–82 79%	$ 37,020	64%	$ 23,723		
1979–80 79%	$ 49,270	50%	$ 19,990		

DIST. / NAME / PARTY		MONEY FROM PACs		LEFT-OVER CASH	HONORARIA (1985)	
ELECTION CYCLE / % OF VOTE		AMOUNT	% OF ALL RECEIPTS		TOTAL RECEIVED	GIVEN TO CHARITY
29 Hawkins (D)						
1985–86	85%	$ 80,338	92%	$ 111,442	$ 5,250	$ 0
1983–84	86%	$ 60,970	83%	$ 58,105		
1981–82	80%	$ 34,036	76%	$ 40,516		
1979–80	86%	$ 17,000	38%	$ 23,151		
30 Martinez (D)						
1985–86	63%	$119,525	72%	$ 42,524	$ 5,500	$ 0
1983–84	51%	$127,180	65%	$ 11,991		
1981–82	54%	$126,923	41%	$ 7,948		
1982*	51%	$ 94,533	43%	$ 22,882		
31 Dymally (D)						
1985–86	70%	$ 71,358	19%	$ 3,788	$ 23,005	$ 650
1983–84	70%	$ 88,858	26%	$ 1,360		
1981–82	72%	$ 54,936	19%	$?44		
1979–80	64%	$ 74,728	16%	$ 4,512		
32 Anderson (D)						
1985–86	69%	$218,627	48%	$ 46,556	$ 19,800	$ 19,800
1983–84	60%	$213,483	52%	$ 6,143		
1981–82	58%	$169,850	38%	$ 8,175		
1979–80	66%	$ 62,870	46%	$ 7,452		
33 Dreier (R)						
1985–86	72%	$106,800	22%	$ 949,829	$ 7,000	$ 0
1983–84	70%	$131,650	25%	$ 606,484		
1981–82	65%	$114,849	27%	$ 183,287		
1979–80	52%	$106,753	26%	$ 35,963		
34 Torres (D)						
1985–86	60%	$ 93,259	51%	$ 124,694	$ 4,500	$ 0
1983–84	59%	$120,995	54%	$ 42,876		
1981–82	57%	$111,336	40%	$ 1,004		
35 Lewis (R)						
1985–86	77%	$105,103	75%	$ 223,268	$ 21,100	$ 0
1983–84	85%	$ 85,705	44%	$ 173,482		
1981–82	68%	$ 69,752	47%	$ 138,674		
1979–80	72%	$ 56,053	42%	$ 78,179		

DIST. / NAME / PARTY ELECTION CYCLE / % OF VOTE	MONEY FROM PACs AMOUNT	% OF ALL RECEIPTS	LEFT- OVER CASH	HONORARIA (1985) TOTAL RECEIVED	GIVEN TO CHARITY
36 Brown (D)					
1985–86 57%	$227,867	42%	$ 37,388	$ 7,550	$ 0
1983–84 56%	$225,540	34%	$ 1,392		
1981–82 54%	$123,931	28%	$ 688		
1979–80 53%	$ 27,646	31%	$ 11,466		
37 McCandless (R)					
1985–86 64%	$ 65,500	43%	$ 51,783	$ 0	$ 0
1983–84 63%	$ 50,403	41%	$ 28,142		
1981–82 59%	$ 50,928	25%	$ 6,768		
38 Dornan (R)					
1985–86 55%	$163,273	14%	$ 39,508	$ 8,026	$ 0
1983–84 53%	$155,860	15%	$ 23,908		
39 Dannemeyer (R)					
1985–86 75%	$132,750	50%	$ 80,989	$ 7,950	$ 300
1983–84 76%	$131,447	44%	$ 76,961		
1981–82 72%	$ 73,710	32%	$ 98,838		
1979–80 76%	$ 54,982	30%	$ 31,787		
40 Badham (R)					
1985–86 60%	$182,692	51%	$ 1,660	$ 18,750	$ 0
1983–84 64%	$ 81,516	54%	$ 60,335		
1981–82 72%	$ 66,913	45%	$ 82,079		
1979–80 70%	$ 43,747	34%	$ 61,222		
41 Lowery (R)					
1985–86 68%	$138,149	36%	$ 71,707	$ 16,950	$ 0
1983–84 63%	$181,847	38%	$ 84,415		
1981–82 69%	$159,630	40%	$ 6,264		
1979–80 53%	$131,415	24%	$ 1,694		
42 Lungren (R)					
1985–86 73%	$ 83,275	39%	$ 101,231	$ 8,000	$ 0
1983–84 72%	$ 61,803	25%	$ 102,474		
1981–82 69%	$ 70,639	29%	$ 20,279		
1979–80 72%	$ 72,659	30%	$ 6,190		

DIST. / NAME / PARTY	MONEY FROM PACs		LEFT-OVER CASH	HONORARIA (1985)	
ELECTION CYCLE / % OF VOTE	AMOUNT	% OF ALL RECEIPTS		TOTAL RECEIVED	GIVEN TO CHARITY
43 Packard (R)					
1985–86 73%	$ 87,700	49%	$ 99,131	$ 0	$ 0
1983–84 74%	$118,775	29%	$ 52,503		
1981–82 37%	$ 40,836	11%	$ 1,802		
44 Bates (D)					
1985–86 64%	$181,291	44%	$ 337	$ 7,150	$ 0
1983–84 69%	$115,765	44%	$ 261		
1981–82 65%	$ 61,683	26%	$ 319		
45 Hunter (R)					
1985–86 77%	$136,710	34%	$ 122,032	$ 4,250	$ 0
1983–84 75%	$138,215	35%	$ 121,569		
1981–82 69%	$143,728	33%	$ 18,726		
1979–80 53%	$ 27,575	12%	$ 12,276		
C O L O R A D O					
1 Schroedor (D)					
1985–86 68%	$105,815	44%	$ 203,758	$ 26,150	$ 3,750
1983–84 61%	$ 81,797	31%	$ 116,612		
1981–82 60%	$ 86,602	35%	$ 90,407		
1979–80 60%	$ 55,650	31%	$ 53,433		
2 Skaggs (D)					
1985–86 51%	$225,257	44%	$ 3,068		
3 Campbell (D)					
1985–86 52%	$204,968	52%	$ 11,062		
4 Brown (R)					
1985–86 70%	$ 64,700	35%	$ 109,720	$ 1,735	$ 0
1983–84 71%	$ 56,671	29%	$ 171,059		
1981–82 70%	$ 52,211	27%	$ 116,214		
1979–80 68%	$105,516	38%	$ 40,345		
5 Hefley (R)					
1985–86 70%	$113,206	38%	$ 15,282		
6 Schaefer (R)					
1985–86 65%	$ 99,833	69%	$ 44,428	$ 11,797	$ 0
1983–84 89%	$ 67,873	42%	$ 25,536		
1983* 63%	$117,268	36%	$ 27,894		

DIST. / NAME / PARTY	MONEY FROM PACs		LEFT-OVER CASH	HONORARIA (1985)	
ELECTION CYCLE / % OF VOTE	AMOUNT	% OF ALL RECEIPTS		TOTAL RECEIVED	GIVEN TO CHARITY
C O N N E C T I C U T					
1 Kennelly (D)					
1985–86 74%	$254,783	56%	$ 123,599	$ 17,000	$ 3,000
1983–84 61%	$173,558	47%	$ 54,590		
1981–82 68%	$ 60,605	35%	$ 51,409		
1982* 59%	$ 55,985	26%	$ 22,882		
2 Gejdenson (D)					
1985–86 67%	$294,448	30%	$ 6,586	$ 24,400	$ 1,950
1983–84 54%	$117,304	22%	$ 17,969		
1981–82 56%	$148,652	27%	$ 5,508		
1979–80 53%	$ 45,939	20%	$ 1,524		
3 Morrison (D)					
1985–86 70%	$230,745	39%	$ 47,297	$ 5,900	$ 5,900
1983–84 52%	$357,565	38%	$ 16,185		
1981–82 50%	$ 70,254	23%	$ −1,376		
4 No incumbent					
5 Rowland (R)					
1985–86 61%	$183,299	43%	$ 3,779	$ 2,900	$ 0
1983–84 54%	$ 77,110	32%	$ 3,338		
6 Johnson (R)					
1985–86 64%	$135,074	32%	$ 28,865	$ 1,925	$ 0
1983–84 63%	$199,037	38%	$ 25,653		
1981–82 52%	$149,806	35%	$ 5,252		
D E L A W A R E					
AL Carper (D)					
1985–86 66%	$151,669	46%	$ 32,784	$ 0	$ 0
1983–84 58%	$227,805	62%	$ 13,291		
1981–82 52%	$ 82,724	56%	$ 1,887		
F L O R I D A					
1 Hutto (D)					
1985–86 64%	$ 29,545	35%	$ 53,805	$ 10,000	$ 1,000
1983–84 100%	$ 39,820	48%	$ 103,085		
1981–82 74%	$ 43,070	33%	$ 59,522		
1979–80 61%	$ 24,550	28%	$ 23,346		

DIST. / NAME / PARTY	MONEY FROM PACs		LEFT-OVER CASH	HONORARIA (1985)	
ELECTION CYCLE / % OF VOTE	AMOUNT	% OF ALL RECEIPTS		TOTAL RECEIVED	GIVEN TO CHARITY
2 Grant (D)					
1985–86 99%	$113,257	43%	$ 508		
3 Bennett (D)					
1985–86 100%	$ 76,441	62%	$ 217,345	$ 2,070	$ 2,070
1983–84 100%	$ 38,300	64%	$ 111,157		
1981–82 84%	$ 40,870	45%	$ 56,958		
1979–80 77%	$ 0	0%	$ 4,547		
4 Chappell (D)					
1985–86 100%	$171,001	61%	$ 156,899	$ 21,000	$ 1,000
1983–84 64%	$227,990	55%	$ 13,542		
1981–82 67%	$284,116	51%	$ 1,471		
1979–80 66%	$ 52,386	42%	$ 39,663		
5 McCollum (R)					
1985–86 100%	$ 79,700	48%	$ 222,029	$ 7,600	$ 0
1983–84 100%	$ 74,510	31%	$ 177,095		
1981–82 59%	$133,115	30%	$ 104,512		
1979–80 56%	$ 56,700	20%	$ 5,524		
6 MacKay (D)					
1985–86 70%	$149,290	28%	$ 101,932	$ 2,000	$ 2,000
1983–84 100%	$ 73,067	49%	$ 36,761		
1981–82 61%	$ 49,164	22%	$ 307		
7 Gibbons (D)					
1985–86 100%	$560,270	62%	$ 390,559	$ 27,650	$ 5,400
1983–84 58%	$148,775	62%	$ 50,584		
1981–82 74%	$ 66,886	57%	$ 104,176		
1979–80 72%	$ 49,059	52%	$ 79,568		
8 Young (R)					
1985–86 100%	$ 91,945	43%	$ 306,907	$ 20,000	$ 0
1983–84 80%	$ 73,650	43%	$ 188,362		
1981–82 100%	$ 34,800	27%	$ 122,374		
1979–80 100%	$ 8,050	13%	$ 10,508		
9 Bilirakis (R)					
1985–86 71%	$151,898	32%	$ 12,063	$ 3,000	$ 3,000
1983–84 78%	$123,468	35%	$ 49,771		
1981–82 51%	$ 69,143	22%	$ 9,854		

DIST. / NAME / PARTY		MONEY FROM PACs		LEFT-OVER CASH	HONORARIA (1985)	
ELECTION CYCLE / % OF VOTE		AMOUNT	% OF ALL RECEIPTS		TOTAL RECEIVED	GIVEN TO CHARITY
10 Ireland (R)						
1985–86	71%	$167,178	36%	$ 127,819	$ 3,000	$ 0
1983–84	61%	$196,592	33%	$ 59,338		
1981–82	100%	$ 74,795	38%	$ 88,136		
1979–80	69%	$ 88,894	34%	$ 53,847		
11 Nelson (D)						
1985–86	73%	$140,783	50%	$ 113,738	$ 0	$ 0
1983–84	60%	$126,262	31%	$ 69,320		
1981–82	71%	$ 74,120	34%	$ 38,498		
1979–80	70%	$ 14,881	9%	$ 75		
12 Lewis (R)						
1985–86	99%	$ 90,238	29%	$ 150,369	$ 1,000	$ 0
1983–84	100%	$ 78,044	17%	$ 126,132		
1981–82	53%	$104,445	30%	$ 1,762		
13 Mack (R)						
1985–86	75%	$120,657	26%	$ 183,351	$ 9,445	$ 0
1983–84	100%	$ 63,013	13%	$ 40,528		
1981–82	65%	$ 46,985	9%	$ 4,652		
14 Mica (D)						
1985–86	74%	$211,732	38%	$ 196,645	$ 19,648	$ 0
1983–84	55%	$143,927	33%	$ 21,130		
1981–82	73%	$ 50,200	17%	$ 22,540		
1979–80	59%	$ 37,033	16%	$ 2,650		
15 Shaw (R)						
1985–86	100%	$ 83,075	41%	$ 120,811	$ 0	$ 0
1983–84	65%	$107,320	28%	$ 19,717		
1981–82	57%	$ 77,416	26%	$ 4,367		
1979–80	55%	$127,416	30%	$ 9,530		
16 Smith (D)						
1985–86	70%	$308,283	40%	$ 57,030	$ 22,500	$ 35
1983–84	56%	$305,070	47%	$ 87,131		
1981–82	68%	$152,939	48%	$ 1,803		

DIST. / NAME / PARTY ELECTION CYCLE / % OF VOTE	MONEY FROM PACs AMOUNT	% OF ALL RECEIPTS	LEFT-OVER CASH	HONORARIA (1985) TOTAL RECEIVED	GIVEN TO CHARITY
17 Lehman (D)					
1985–86 100%	$ 97,700	45%	$ 153,854	$ 3,000	$ 2,000
1983–84 100%	$ 81,887	40%	$ 111,370		
1981–82 100%	$ 57,088	34%	$ 59,078		
1979–80 75%	$ 53,370	22%	$ 6,015		
18 Pepper (D)					
1985–86 74%	$302,166	21%	$ 52,780	$ 13,833	$ 0
1983–84 60%	$152,208	62%	$ 162		
1981–82 71%	$ 99,900	41%	$ 25,564		
1979–80 75%	$ 59,300	39%	$ 76		
19 Fascell (D)					
1985–86 69%	$144,550	31%	$ 426,393	$ 0	$ 0
1983–84 64%	$162,220	35%	$ 246,140		
1981–82 59%	$190,911	36%	$ 71,446		
1979–80 65%	$ 12,775	16%	$ 8,300		
G E O R G I A					
1 Thomas (D)					
1985–86 100%	$132,350	54%	$ 85,580	$ 7,000	$ 0
1983–84 81%	$115,227	42%	$ 42,784		
1981–82 64%	$ 39,264	11%	$ 8,849		
2 Hatcher (D)					
1985–86 100%	$ 55,950	34%	$ 29,786	$ 13,000	$ 0
1983–84 100%	$ 85,300	52%	$ 5,162		
1981–82 100%	$102,591	36%	$ 3,300		
1979–80 74%	$ 80,681	32%	$ 7,189		
3 Ray (D)					
1985–86 100%	$120,812	41%	$ 165,621	$ 7,500	$ 0
1983–84 81%	$151,739	30%	$ 24,727		
1981–82 71%	$102,262	22%	$ 22,922		
4 Swindall (R)					
1985–86 53%	$195,906	26%	$ 147,970	$ 4,475	$ 0
1983–84 53%	$103,165	18%	$ 21,735		
5 Lewis (D)					
1985–86 75%	$157,994	41%	$ 1,437		

DIST. / NAME / PARTY	MONEY FROM PACs		LEFT-OVER CASH	HONORARIA (1985)	
ELECTION CYCLE / % OF VOTE	AMOUNT	% OF ALL RECEIPTS		TOTAL RECEIVED	GIVEN TO CHARITY
6 Gingrich (R)					
1985–86 60%	$200,726	27%	$ 11,731	$ 24,200	$ 2,000
1983–84 69%	$128,744	36%	$ 20,556		
1981–82 55%	$110,179	30%	$ 1,885		
1979–80 59%	$ 3,975	1%	$ 731		
7 Darden (D)					
1985–86 66%	$252,920	48%	$ 49,834	$ 3,500	$ 0
1983–84 55%	$137,331	48%	$ 51,746		
1983* 59%	$101,300	33%	$ 45,576		
8 Rowland (D)					
1985–86 86%	$ 90,125	39%	$ 142,306	$ 6,000	$ 0
1983–84 100%	$ 67,075	35%	$ 59,178		
1981–82 100%	$ 34,138	15%	$ 3,954		
9 Jenkins (D)					
1985–86 100%	$212,473	64%	$ 416,351	$ 25,000	$ 3,000
1983–84 67%	$176,840	64%	$ 230,312		
1981–82 77%	$110,735	53%	$ 69,348		
1979–80 68%	$ 70,164	60%	$ 2,901		
10 Barnard (D)					
1985–86 67%	$183,071	53%	$ 427,257	$ 21,850	$ 0
1983–84 100%	$113,875	60%	$ 290,556		
1981–82 100%	$ 85,701	58%	$ 175,646		
1979–80 80%	$ 72,261	55%	$ 97,649		
H A W A I I					
1 Saiki (R)					
1985–86 59%	$154,550	29%	$ 7,509		
2 Akaka (D)					
1985–86 76%	$ 48,735	37%	$ 54,791	$ 500	$ 0
1983–84 82%	$ 60,694	46%	$ 33,085		
1981–82 89%	$ 38,340	44%	$ 24,423		
1979–80 90%	$ 38,925	29%	$ 47,090		

DIST. / NAME / PARTY	MONEY FROM PACs		LEFT-OVER CASH	HONORARIA (1985)	
ELECTION CYCLE / % OF VOTE	AMOUNT	% OF ALL RECEIPTS		TOTAL RECEIVED	GIVEN TO CHARITY
I D A H O					
1 Craig (R)					
1985–86 65%	$115,056	36%	$ 14,829	$ 1,000	$ 0
1983–84 68%	$106,357	39%	$ 6,873		
1981–82 54%	$146,381	40%	$ 1,020		
1979–80 54%	$109,251	35%	$ 4,315		
2 Stallings (D)					
1985–86 54%	$271,815	57%	$ 4,773	$ 1,300	$ 0
1983–84 50%	$182,429	57%	$ 393		
I L L I N O I S					
1 Hayes (D)					
1985–86 96%	$ 83,475	57%	$ 35,507	$ 1,800	$ 0
1983–84 95%	$ 62,518	83%	$ 1,686		
1983* 94%	$100,040	23%	$ 0		
2 Savage (D)					
1985–86 84%	$ 81,500	53%	$ 2,452	$ 3,250	$ 0
1983–84 82%	$ 46,058	38%	$ 90		
1981–82 87%	$ 17,900	73%	$ 0		
1979–80 88%	$ 9,650	12%	$ 938		
3 Russo (D)					
1985–86 66%	$201,755	59%	$ 2,105	$ 25,500	$ 23,500
1983–84 64%	$166,706	54%	$ 6,855		
1981–82 74%	$134,639	50%	$ 137		
1979–80 69%	$ 80,463	38%	$ 92		
4 Davis (R)					
1985–86 52%	$124,337	44%	$ 2,855		
5 Lipinski (D)					
1985–86 70%	$ 64,925	43%	$ 18,225	$ 2,000	$ 0
1983–84 63%	$ 49,075	46%	$ 20,505		
1981–82 75%	$ 24,484	24%	$ −313		
6 Hyde (R)					
1985–86 75%	$ 93,337	39%	$ 133,497	$ 21,926	$ 0
1983–84 75%	$ 88,232	37%	$ 121,438		
1981–82 68%	$ 70,116	26%	$ 110,234		
1979–80 67%	$ 57,819	28%	$ 68,468		

DIST. / NAME / PARTY	MONEY FROM PACs		LEFT-OVER CASH	HONORARIA (1985)	
ELECTION CYCLE / % OF VOTE	AMOUNT	% OF ALL RECEIPTS		TOTAL RECEIVED	GIVEN TO CHARITY
7 Collins (D)					
1985–86 80%	$230,570	76%	$ 103,880	$ 5,800	$ 0
1983–84 78%	$168,301	82%	$ 38,637		
1981–82 86%	$ 48,210	78%	$ 36,171		
1979–80 85%	$ 17,125	57%	$ 21,595		
8 Rostenkowski (D)					
1985–86 79%	$199,124	82%	$ 596,703	$137,500	$115,033
1983–84 71%	$321,231	68%	$ 592,935		
1981–82 83%	$293,175	56%	$ 494,894		
1979–80 85%	$181,975	60%	$ 224,202		
9 Yates (D)					
1985–86 72%	$ 16,401	11%	$ 110,010	$ 0	$ 0
1983–84 67%	$ 25,167	17%	$ 58,347		
1981–82 67%	$ 67,478	20%	$ 14,230		
1979–80 73%	$ 7,859	10%	$ 24,529		
10 Porter (R)					
1985–86 75%	$ 77,041	41%	$ 96,786	$ 3,300	$ 0
1983–84 72%	$ 89,467	40%	$ 84,674		
1981–82 59%	$ 92,607	31%	$ 3,313		
1979–80 61%	$117,637	42%	$ 502		
11 Annunzio (D)					
1985–86 71%	$130,832	58%	$ 147,155	$ 2,500	$ 0
1983–84 62%	$ 91,123	44%	$ 92,826		
1981–82 73%	$ 39,800	30%	$ 98,257		
1979–80 70%	$ 26,950	25%	$ 79,414		
12 Crane (R)					
1985–86 78%	$ 1,000	0%	$ 129,371	$ 37,298	$ 14,831
1983–84 77%	$ 7,967	0.2%	$ 156,251		
1981–82 66%	$ 2,438	1%	$ 201,592		
1979–80 74%	$ 3,085	1%	$ 157,021		
13 Fawell (R)					
1985–86 73%	$ 71,028	36%	$ 35,230	$ 0	$ 0
1983–84 67%	$ 67,612	32%	$ 34,226		

DIST. / NAME / PARTY	MONEY FROM PACs		LEFT-OVER CASH	HONORARIA (1985)	
ELECTION CYCLE / % OF VOTE	AMOUNT	% OF ALL RECEIPTS		TOTAL RECEIVED	GIVEN TO CHARITY
14 Hastert (R)					
1985–86 52%	$138,737	41%	$ 15,251		
15 Madigan (R)					
1985–86 100%	$194,796	58%	$ 262,375	$ 34,318	$ 12,000
1983–84 73%	$170,043	58%	$ 136,912		
1981–82 66%	$126,090	46%	$ 52,290		
1979–80 68%	$ 51,405	35%	$ 40,291		
16 Martin (R)					
1985–86 67%	$153,261	43%	$ 145,740	$ 19,700	$ 0
1983–84 58%	$118,244	38%	$ 25,147		
1981–82 57%	$ 78,040	35%	$ 41,711		
1979–80 67%	$147,720	44%	$ 14,957		
17 Evans (D)					
1985–86 56%	$334,136	53%	$ 14,307	$ 3,700	$ 0
1983–84 56%	$277,669	60%	$ 2,095		
1981–82 53%	$126,918	53%	$ 2,153		
18 Michel (R)					
1985–86 63%	$456,371	66%	$ 100,315	$ 49,735	$ 24,500
1983–84 61%	$388,896	57%	$ 50,231		
1981–82 52%	$477,037	68%	$ 76,531		
1979–80 62%	$ 98,624	58%	$ 67,327		
19 Bruce (D)					
1985–86 66%	$221,790	60%	$ 96,020	$ 5,500	$ 0
1983–84 52%	$182,316	60%	$ 2,708		
20 Durbin (D)					
1985–86 68%	$168,774	49%	$ 62,833	$ 9,750	$ 0
1983–84 61%	$232,282	48%	$ 37,513		
1981–82 50%	$205,285	26%	$ 3,007		
21 Price (D)					
1985–86 50%	$113,175	89%	$ 3,094	$ 0	$ 0
1983–84 60%	$ 71,393	79%	$ 19,062		
1981–82 64%	$ 32,575	73%	$ 22,363		
1979–80 64%	$ 16,830	60%	$ 12,428		

DIST. / NAME / PARTY ELECTION CYCLE / % OF VOTE	MONEY FROM PACs AMOUNT	% OF ALL RECEIPTS	LEFT-OVER CASH	HONORARIA (1985) TOTAL RECEIVED	GIVEN TO CHARITY
22 Gray (D)					
1985–86 53%	$152,900	49%	$ 13,393	$ 0	$ 0
1983–84 50%	$ 60,675	31%	$ 3,576		
I N D I A N A					
1 Visclosky (D)					
1985–86 73%	$ 97,067	61%	$ 14,301	$ 200	$ 0
1983–84 70%	$ 50,682	26%	$ 19,056		
2 Sharp (D)					
1985–86 62%	$264,410	66%	$ 67,639	$ 1,050	$ 1,050
1983–84 53%	$244,270	57%	$ 47,929		
1981–82 56%	$190,148	48%	$ 27,705		
1979–80 53%	$ 83,236	51%	$ 5,665		
3 Hiler (R)					
1985–86 50%	$135,101	34%	$ 115,830	$ 6,750	$ 0
1983–84 52%	$188,904	40%	$ 52,265		
1981–82 51%	$111,518	31%	$ 36,123		
1979–80 55%	$120,921	27%	$ 38,319		
4 Coats (R)					
1985–86 70%	$106,161	36%	$ 147,443	$ 8,500	$ 0
1983–84 60%	$107,839	45%	$ 80,711		
1981–82 64%	$ 82,394	42%	$ 42,768		
1979–80 61%	$ 89,191	37%	$ 16,979		
5 Jontz (D)					
1985–86 51%	$292,749	63%	$ 762		
6 Burton (R)					
1985–86 68%	$143,292	44%	$ 148,379	$ 6,800	$ 0
1983–84 72%	$100,422	39%	$ 39,506		
1981–82 65%	$127,914	30%	$ 15,938		
7 Myers (R)					
1985–86 67%	$ 79,000	44%	$ 125,521	$ 2,000	$ 0
1983–84 67%	$ 78,092	38%	$ 107,915		
1981–82 62%	$ 48,723	28%	$ 70,146		
1979–80 66%	$ 41,053	27%	$ 70,514		

DIST. / NAME / PARTY ELECTION CYCLE / % OF VOTE	MONEY FROM PACs AMOUNT	% OF ALL RECEIPTS	LEFT-OVER CASH	HONORARIA (1985) TOTAL RECEIVED	GIVEN TO CHARITY
8 McCloskey (D)					
1985–86 53%	$337,686	54%	$ 3,832	$ 3,300	$ 0
1983–84 49%	$279,653	58%	$ 2,652		
1981–82 51%	$ 68,265	43%	$ 277		
9 Hamilton (D)					
1985–86 72%	$124,400	43%	$ 15,851	$ 7,450	$ 0
1983–84 65%	$104,157	43%	$ 35,422		
1981–82 67%	$ 58,005	36%	$ 447		
1979–80 64%	$ 33,532	30%	$ 21,474		
10 Jacobs (D)					
1985–86 58%	$ 1,500	3%	$ 18,346	$ 0	$ 0
1983–84 58%	$ 82	0.2%	$ 6,920		
1981–82 67%	$ 0	0%	$ 870		
1979–80 57%	$ 0	0%	$ 3,778		
I O W A					
1 Leach (R)					
1985–86 66%	$ 0	0%	$ 31,443	$ 2,300	$ 2,300
1983–84 66%	$ 999	0.4%	$ 33,773		
1981–82 59%	$ 0	0%	$ 1,000		
1979–80 53%	$ 0	0%	$ 2,502		
2 Tauke (R)					
1985–86 61%	$181,394	46%	$ 103,575	$ 17,800	$ 17,800
1983–84 63%	$144,912	43%	$ 99,210		
1981–82 59%	$161,544	42%	$ 30,575		
1979–80 54%	$103,865	32%	$ 18,741		
3 Nagle (D)					
1985–86 55%	$171,071	59%	$ 1,618		
4 Smith (D)					
1985–86 68%	$109,400	71%	$ 143,017	$ 0	$ 0
1983–84 60%	$120,911	73%	$ 90,014		
1981–82 66%	$ 91,750	63%	$ 32,312		
1979–80 54%	$ 58,330	60%	$ 20,908		
5 Lightfoot (R)					
1985–86 59%	$207,047	45%	$ 3,467	$ 1,100	$ 0
1983–84 50%	$198,802	47%	$ 13,530		

DIST. / NAME / PARTY ELECTION CYCLE / % OF VOTE	MONEY FROM PACs AMOUNT	% OF ALL RECEIPTS	LEFT-OVER CASH	HONORARIA (1985) TOTAL RECEIVED	GIVEN TO CHARITY
6 Grandy (R)					
1985–86 51%	$231,472	34%	$ 3,109		
K A N S A S					
1 Roberts (R)					
1985–86 77%	$101,606	56%	$ 219,871	$ 14,950	$ 0
1983–84 75%	$ 65,195	42%	$ 125,309		
1981–82 68%	$ 76,086	41%	$ 64,915		
1979–80 62%	$ 69,395	27%	$ 24,000		
2 Slattery (D)					
1985–86 71%	$240,455	64%	$ 25,888	$ 8,900	$ 0
1983–84 60%	$167,674	54%	$ 6,345		
1981–82 57%	$ 79,191	29%	$ 5,986		
3 Meyers (R)					
1985–86 100%	$108,612	63%	$ 33,914	$ 1,000	$ 0
1983–84 54%	$217,139	49%	$ 848		
4 Glickman (D)					
1985–86 65%	$180,225	40%	$ 10,391	$ 8,000	$ 3,550
1983–84 74%	$ 56,339	28%	$ 77,510		
1981–82 74%	$ 38,591	25%	$ 40,962		
1979–80 69%	$ 27,520	23%	$ 38,484		
5 Whittaker (R)					
1985–86 71%	$116,795	56%	$ 341,269	$ 400	$ 0
1983–84 73%	$123,526	60%	$ 229,092		
1981–82 68%	$ 87,721	48%	$ 103,354		
1979–80 74%	$ 66,609	38%	$ 66,494		
K E N T U C K Y					
1 Hubbard (D)					
1985–86 100%	$196,775	68%	$ 251,699	$ 27,650	$ 5,183
1983–84 100%	$164,950	69%	$ 200,155		
1981–82 100%	$104,136	72%	$ 129,442		
1979–80 100%	$ 79,743	70%	$ 79,008		
2 Natcher (D)					
1985–86 100%	$ 0	0%	$ 0	$ 0	$ 0
1983–84 62%	$ 1,268	18%	$ 0		
1981–82 74%	$ 0	0%	$ 0		
1979–80 66%	$ 0	0%	$ 0		

DIST. / NAME / PARTY	MONEY FROM PACs		LEFT-OVER CASH	HONORARIA (1985)	
ELECTION CYCLE / % OF VOTE	AMOUNT	% OF ALL RECEIPTS		TOTAL RECEIVED	GIVEN TO CHARITY
3 Mazzoli (D)					
1985–86 73%	$ 79,700	54%	$ 23,680	$ 9,988	$ 0
1983–84 67%	$ 81,709	52%	$ 2,463		
1981–82 65%	$ 92,026	50%	$ 3,202		
1979–80 64%	$ 58,350	61%	$ 10,057		
4 Bunning (R)					
1985–86 55%	$250,865	28%	$ 2,937		
5 Rogers (R)					
1985–86 100%	$ 63,962	25%	$ 135,552	$ 3,994	$ 0
1983–84 75%	$ 79,292	36%	$ 79,999		
1981–82 65%	$116,206	36%	$ 45,780		
1979–80 67%	$ 91,745	29%	$ 259		
6 Hopkins (R)					
1985–86 74%	$129,428	32%	$ 547,846	$ 17,000	$ 0
1983–84 71%	$141,317	40%	$ 299,238		
1981–82 57%	$189,717	39%	$ 116,182		
1979–80 59%	$122,288	33%	$ 79,661		
7 Perkins (D)					
1985–86 80%	$144,200	66%	$ 12,226	$ 0	$ 0
1983–84 73%	$ 53,718	71%	$ 35,463		
L O U I S I A N A					
1 Livingston (R)					
1985–86 100%	$ 46,995	20%	$ 403,766	$ 22,500	$ 50
1983–84 87%	$104,883	31%	$ 368,781		
1981–82 86%	$ 40,865	17%	$ 241,537		
1979–80 88%	$ 54,375	22%	$ 137,447		
2 Boggs (D)					
1985–86 91%	$157,150	49%	$ 60,219	$ 3,000	$ 3,000
1983–84 60%	$297,584	37%	$ 3,794		
1981–82 77%	$ 63,924	13%	$ 14,331		
1979–80 61%	$ 59,775	11%	$ 2,148		
3 Tauzin (D)					
1985–86 100%	$150,975	40%	$ 421,002	$ 22,400	$ 0
1983–84 100%	$177,686	41%	$ 372,024		
1981–82 100%	$ 82,627	20%	$ 139,939		
1979–80 85%	$ 58,775	20%	$ 10,499		

DIST. / NAME / PARTY	MONEY FROM PACs		LEFT-OVER CASH	HONORARIA (1985)	
ELECTION CYCLE / % OF VOTE	AMOUNT	% OF ALL RECEIPTS		TOTAL RECEIVED	GIVEN TO CHARITY
4 Roemer (D)					
1985–86 100%	$ 0	0%	$ 54,322	$ 20,500	$ 0
1983–84 100%	$ 1,050	1%	$ 61,475		
1981–82 100%	$ 24,833	5%	$ 13,458		
1979–80 64%	$ 8,600	2%	$ 3,511		
5 Huckaby (D)					
1985–86 68%	$113,895	49%	$ 222,559	$ 12,750	$ 0
1983–84 100%	$ 77,609	37%	$ 314,483		
1981–82 84%	$ 82,071	31%	$ 217,698		
1979–80 89%	$ 60,343	52%	$ 62,172		
6 Baker (R)					
1985–86 51%	$ 85,467	20%	$ 1,008		
7 Hayes (D)					
1985–86 57%	$ 46,550	6%	$ 3,987		
8 Holloway (R)					
1985–86 51%	$133,803	30%	$ 4,157		
M A I N E					
1 Brennan (D)					
1985–86 53%	$130,410	45%	$ 124		
2 Snowe (R)					
1985–86 77%	$ 79,075	37%	$ 3,791	$ 0	$ 0
1983–84 75%	$ 85,150	36%	$ 3,050		
1981–82 67%	$ 42,612	24%	$ 2,699		
1979–80 79%	$ 53,308	28%	$ 5,705		
M A R Y L A N D					
1 Dyson (D)					
1985–86 67%	$243,049	68%	$ 6,821	$ 2,000	$ 1,000
1983–84 58%	$158,997	59%	$ 4,459		
1981–82 69%	$135,882	66%	$ 10,589		
1979–80 52%	$ 87,157	52%	$ 923		
2 Bentley (R)					
1985–86 59%	$361,985	34%	$ 13,577	$ 11,450	$ 0
1983–84 51%	$181,469	30%	$ 10,036		

DIST. / NAME / PARTY	MONEY FROM PACs		LEFT-OVER CASH	HONORARIA (1985)	
ELECTION CYCLE / % OF VOTE	AMOUNT	% OF ALL RECEIPTS		TOTAL RECEIVED	GIVEN TO CHARITY
3 Cardin (D)					
1985–86 79%	$143,977	28%	$ 30,731		
4 McMillen (D)					
1985–86 50%	$307,549	39%	$ 1,281		
5 Hoyer (D)					
1985–86 82%	$166,262	43%	$ 237,908	$ 0	$ 0
1983–84 72%	$124,788	42%	$ 153,823		
1981–82 80%	$ 94,085	46%	$ 72,062		
1981* 55%	$114,584	32%	$ 45,485		
6 Byron (D)					
1985–86 72%	$126,603	59%	$ 72,853	$ 15,500	$ 0
1983–84 65%	$107,565	52%	$ 65,815		
1981–82 74%	$ 76,450	50%	$ 48,547		
1979–80 70%	$ 69,665	41%	$ 18,377		
7 Mfume (D)					
1985–86 87%	$ 61,523	41%	$ 45,331		
8 Morella (R)					
1985–86 53%	$147,240	24%	$ 3,591		
M A S S A C H U S E T T S					
1 Conte (R)					
1985–86 78%	$130,577	51%	$ 268,326	$ 19,250	$ 7,000
1983–84 67%	$111,522	56%	$ 217,327		
1981–82 100%	$ 54,700	53%	$ 111,702		
1979–80 75%	$ 41,715	39%	$ 62,051		
2 Boland (D)					
1985–86 66%	$ 82,890	40%	$ 24,157	$ 0	$ 0
1983–84 68%	$ 71,376	75%	$ 99,579		
1981–82 73%	$ 10,500	35%	$ 55,738		
1979–80 67%	$ 33,900	40%	$ 57,530		
3 Early (D)					
1985–86 100%	$ 86,710	36%	$ 95,439	$ 7,000	$ 0
1983–84 67%	$ 38,688	19%	$ 38,724		
1981–82 100%	$ 16,350	19%	$ 7,895		
1979–80 72%	$ 12,800	17%	$ 31,983		

DIST. / NAME / PARTY	MONEY FROM PACs		LEFT-OVER CASH	HONORARIA (1985)	
ELECTION CYCLE / % OF VOTE	AMOUNT	% OF ALL RECEIPTS		TOTAL RECEIVED	GIVEN TO CHARITY
4 Frank (D)					
1985–86 89%	$ 68,975	33%	$ 37,478	$ 24,050	$ 2,000
1983–84 74%	$113,714	28%	$ 42,855		
1981–82 59%	$223,516	15%	$ 7,354		
1979–80 52%	$ 40,095	9%	$ −177		
5 Atkins (D)					
1985–86 100%	$ 5,127	1%	$ 5,359	$ 3,000	$ 0
1983–84 53%	$ 5,541	1%	$ 4,683		
6 Mavroules (D)					
1985–86 100%	$ 91,250	39%	$ 94,283	$ 10,500	$ 0
1983–84 70%	$107,568	38%	$ 43,010		
1981–82 58%	$142,425	29%	$ 3,747		
1979–80 51%	$ 83,480	24%	$ 2,969		
7 Markey (D)					
1985–86 100%	$ 10,600	3%	$ 101,126	$ 2,218	$ 0
1983–84 71%	$ 38,552	6%	$ 1,014		
1981–82 78%	$ 71,653	31%	$ 97,808		
1979–80 100%	$ 22,745	19%	$ 45,663		
8 Kennedy (D)					
1985–86 72%	$ 77,795	4%	$ 21,244		
9 Moakley (D)					
1985–86 84%	$171,485	43%	$ 178,641	$ 13,500	$ 0
1983–84 100%	$ 87,098	31%	$ 89,111		
1981–82 64%	$ 96,703	26%	$ 36,634		
1979–80 100%	$ 25,400	24%	$ 76,622		
10 Studds (D)					
1985–86 65%	$ 83,820	22%	$ 34,826	$ 2,750	$ 1,125
1983–84 55%	$156,860	27%	$ 46,396		
1981–82 69%	$ 43,301	31%	$ 25,771		
1979–80 73%	$ 14,000	21%	$ 7,757		
11 Donnelly (D)					
1985–86 100%	$138,065	54%	$ 365,379	$ 14,500	$ 0
1983–84 100%	$ 65,393	45%	$ 157,757		
1981–82 100%	$ 24,725	23%	$ 67,860		
1979–80 100%	$ 28,829	42%	$ 8,381		

DIST. / NAME / PARTY		MONEY FROM PACs		LEFT-OVER CASH	HONORARIA (1985)	
ELECTION CYCLE / % OF VOTE		AMOUNT	% OF ALL RECEIPTS		TOTAL RECEIVED	GIVEN TO CHARITY
M I C H I G A N						
1 Conyers (D)						
1985–86	89%	$ 66,845	51%	$ 8,352	$ 5,050	$ 0
1983–84	89%	$ 45,415	60%	$ 39,513		
1981–82	97%	$ 15,643	78%	$ 856		
1979–80	95%	$ 13,400	56%	$ 3,562		
2 Pursell (R)						
1985–86	59%	$ 67,445	29%	$ 155,432	$ 6,100	$ 0
1983–84	68%	$ 55,038	39%	$ 64,619		
1981–82	65%	$ 60,098	41%	$ 47,730		
1979–80	57%	$ 74,114	46%	$ 38,365		
3 Wolpe (D)						
1985–86	60%	$252,649	29%	$ 107,429	$ 8,800	$ 0
1983–84	52%	$193,403	41%	$ 81,539		
1981–82	56%	$146,500	39%	$ 3,293		
1979–80	52%	$160,064	47%	$ 550		
4 Upton (R)						
1985–86	62%	$ 42,685	11%	$ 377		
5 Henry (R)						
1985–86	71%	$102,592	30%	$ 39,583	$ 1,400	$ 0
1983–84	61%	$132,489	29%	$ 128		
6 Carr (D)						
1985–86	57%	$448,672	61%	$ 52,534	$ 10,561	$ 0
1983–84	52%	$329,666	56%	$ 10,402		
1981–82	51%	$164,874	43%	$ 1,120		
1979–80	49%	$ 59,065	40%	$ 1,546		
7 Kildee (D)						
1985–86	80%	$ 80,510	84%	$ 984	$ 0	$ 0
1983–84	93%	$ 48,467	81%	$ 6,439		
1981–82	75%	$ 47,053	73%	$ 7,237		
1979–80	93%	$ 15,685	47%	$ 3,893		

DIST. / NAME / PARTY	MONEY FROM PACs		LEFT-OVER CASH	HONORARIA (1985)	
ELECTION CYCLE / % OF VOTE	AMOUNT	% OF ALL RECEIPTS		TOTAL RECEIVED	GIVEN TO CHARITY
8 Traxler (D)					
1985–86 73%	$ 90,112	60%	$ 103,143	$ 4,600	$ 0
1983–84 64%	$ 77,408	56%	$ 79,671		
1981–82 91%	$ 46,900	54%	$ 66,849		
1979–80 61%	$ 64,995	52%	$ 64,022		
9 Vander Jagt (R)					
1985–86 64%	$217,830	51%	$ 102,356	$ 39,167	$ 16,700
1983–84 70%	$209,325	55%	$ 73,310		
1981–82 65%	$179,280	51%	$ 52,571		
1979–80 97%	$114,440	41%	$ 96,049		
10 Schuette (R)					
1985–86 51%	$346,481	39%	$ 17,657	$ 2,500	$ 0
1983–84 50%	$165,827	22%	$ 23,583		
11 Davis (R)					
1985–86 63%	$164,190	41%	$ 197,990	$ 12,249	$ 0
1983–84 58%	$ 85,805	46%	$ 8,732		
1981–82 61%	$ 54,890	54%	$ 43,074		
1979–80 66%	$ 70,668	51%	$ 22,362		
12 Bonior (D)					
1985–86 66%	$203,455	65%	$ 48,366	$ 3,383	$ 0
1983–84 58%	$ 80,270	53%	$ 16,726		
1981–82 66%	$ 91,872	52%	$ 2,255		
1979–80 55%	$ 56,268	58%	$ 4,516		
13 Crockett (D)					
1985–86 85%	$ 38,370	54%	$ 50,359	$ 1,200	$ 0
1983–84 86%	$ 28,918	43%	$ 34,849		
1981–82 88%	$ 17,747	24%	$ 22,175		
1979–80 92%	$ 15,550	26%	$ 4,022		
14 Hertel (D)					
1985–86 73%	$120,549	60%	$ 48,563	$ 7,650	$ 0
1983–84 59%	$ 85,929	54%	$ 21,433		
1981–82 95%	$ 68,607	67%	$ 23,192		
1979–80 53%	$ 74,027	46%	$ 1,751		

DIST. / NAME / PARTY	MONEY FROM PACs		LEFT-OVER CASH	HONORARIA (1985)	
ELECTION CYCLE / % OF VOTE	AMOUNT	% OF ALL RECEIPTS		TOTAL RECEIVED	GIVEN TO CHARITY
15 Ford (D)					
1985–86 75%	$220,735	67%	$ 55,943	$ 24,250	$ 2,000
1983–84 59%	$184,543	66%	$ 31,117		
1981–82 73%	$135,485	63%	$ 11,099		
1979–80 68%	$ 65,673	58%	$ 8,405		
16 Dingell (D)					
1985–86 78%	$375,177	76%	$ 100,677	$ 36,000	$ 13,600
1983–84 63%	$234,118	64%	$ 88,048		
1981–82 74%	$180,589	57%	$ 78,916		
1979–80 70%	$ 88,750	60%	$ 75,918		
17 Levin (D)					
1985–86 76%	$121,903	55%	$ 102,814	$ 1,000	$ 1,000
1983–84 100%	$ 80,295	48%	$ 15,533		
1981–82 67%	$ 57,362	27%	$ 1,490		
18 Broomfield (R)					
1985–86 74%	$ 33,520	19%	$ 430,594	$ 0	$ 0
1983–84 79%	$ 45,800	20%	$ 319,684		
1981–82 73%	$ 22,216	13%	$ 193,929		
1979–80 73%	$ 23,074	25%	$ 89,822		
M I N N E S O T A					
1 Penny (D)					
1985–86 72%	$151,491	40%	$ 104,056	$ 5,000	$ 0
1983–84 56%	$226,437	47%	$ 62,914		
1981–82 51%	$ 80,671	42%	$ 9,533		
2 Weber (R)					
1985–86 52%	$283,203	30%	$ 165,888	$ 17,200	$ 0
1983–84 63%	$135,585	30%	$ 134,260		
1981–82 54%	$186,251	32%	$ 8,251		
1979–80 53%	$185,460	39%	$ 10,423		
3 Frenzel (R)					
1985–86 70%	$280,442	57%	$ 313,940	$ 48,500	$ 26,500
1983–84 73%	$227,722	52%	$ 143,667		
1981–82 72%	$123,060	44%	$ 176,695		
1979–80 76%	$ 56,212	39%	$ 139,455		

DIST. / NAME / PARTY	MONEY FROM PACs		LEFT-OVER CASH	HONORARIA (1985)	
ELECTION CYCLE / % OF VOTE	AMOUNT	% OF ALL RECEIPTS		TOTAL RECEIVED	GIVEN TO CHARITY
4 Vento (D)					
1985–86 73%	$145,790	67%	$ 110,355	$ 10,483	$ 0
1983–84 73%	$113,071	64%	$ 89,049		
1981–82 73%	$ 98,203	64%	$ 31,856		
1979–80 59%	$ 84,976	57%	$ 4,598		
5 Sabo (D)					
1985–86 73%	$ 86,681	37%	$ 99,669	$ 12,450	$ 0
1983–84 70%	$ 88,937	52%	$ 69,944		
1981–82 66%	$ 54,180	52%	$ 29,431		
1979–80 70%	$ 43,160	44%	$ 17,672		
6 Sikorski (D)					
1985–86 66%	$310,155	61%	$ 16,421	$ 22,000	$ 0
1983–84 60%	$388,627	57%	$ 1,812		
1981–82 51%	$172,144	67%	$ 10,051		
7 Stangeland (R)					
1985–86 50%	$264,428	46%	$ 49,377	$ 16,500	$ 0
1983–84 57%	$207,821	46%	$ 18,766		
1981–82 50%	$155,009	38%	$ 4,480		
1979–80 52%	$ 94,405	33%	$ 41,849		
8 Oberstar (D)					
1985–86 73%	$211,247	72%	$ 134,706	$ 15,750	$ 0
1983–84 67%	$207,965	80%	$ 1,451		
1981–82 77%	$ 95,344	59%	$ 33,234		
1979–80 70%	$ 88,267	52%	$ 9,522		
M I S S I S S I P P I					
1 Whitten (D)					
1985–86 66%	$187,770	74%	$ 230,809	$ 7,000	$ 0
1983–84 88%	$114,800	82%	$ 147,823		
1981–82 71%	$113,289	75%	$ 53,967		
1979–80 63%	$120,403	66%	$ 66,031		
2 Espy (D)	$$$$				
1985–86 52%	$307,865	51%	$ 9,373		
3 Montgomery (D)					
1985–86 100%	$ 31,799	63%	$ 98,995	$ 500	$ 0
1983–84 100%	$ 37,700	45%	$ 118,867		
1981–82 93%	$ 41,951	46%	$ 98,526		
1979–80 100%	$ 7,568	48%	$ 68,184		

DIST. / NAME / PARTY	MONEY FROM PACs		LEFT-OVER CASH	HONORARIA (1985)	
ELECTION CYCLE / % OF VOTE	AMOUNT	% OF ALL RECEIPTS		TOTAL RECEIVED	GIVEN TO CHARITY
4 Dowdy (D)					
1985–86 72%	$278,535	68%	$ 173,731	$ 13,500	$ 0
1983–84 54%	$299,728	62%	$ 92,298		
1981–82 53%	$175,393	46%	$ 17,744		
1981* 50%	$ 44,000	16%	$ −2,304		
5 Lott (R)					
1985–86 82%	$225,465	60%	$ 441,592	$ 32,029	$ 9,562
1983–84 84%	$194,743	54%	$ 332,167		
1981–82 79%	$132,220	58%	$ 168,295		
1979–80 74%	$ 69,725	36%	$ 57,645		
M I S S O U R I					
1 Clay (D)					
1985–86 66%	$141,457	69%	$ 58,734	$ 19,000	$ 0
1983–84 68%	$140,675	78%	$ 45,417		
1981–82 66%	$149,252	49%	$ 8,582		
1979–80 70%	$ 60,400	56%	$ 17,218		
2 Buechner (R)					
1985–86 52%	$ 73,652	23%	$ 3,409		
3 Gephardt (D)					
1985–86 69%	$420,827	51%	$ 178	$ 27,050	$ 4,670
1983–84 100%	$240,685	56%	$ 50,824		
1981–82 78%	$188,014	55%	$ 900		
1979–80 78%	$ 96,615	49%	$ 3,390		
4 Skelton (D)					
1985–86 100%	$150,050	50%	$ 187,017	$ 14,752	$ 0
1983–84 66%	$149,770	54%	$ 70,973		
1981–82 55%	$183,368	41%	$ 10,726		
1979–80 68%	$ 56,215	43%	$ 26,803		
5 Wheat (D)					
1985–86 71%	$188,627	70%	$ 136,933	$ 2,000	$ 0
1983–84 66%	$285,091	60%	$ 61,761		
1981–82 58%	$117,374	37%	$ 2,056		
6 Coleman (R)					
1985–86 57%	$126,269	52%	$ 102,879	$ 13,000	$ 0
1983–84 64%	$108,259	53%	$ 112,186		
1981–82 55%	$ 80,030	34%	$ 56,335		
1979–80 71%	$ 71,943	35%	$ 47,257		

DIST. / NAME / PARTY		MONEY FROM PACs		LEFT-OVER CASH	HONORARIA (1985)	
ELECTION CYCLE / % OF VOTE		AMOUNT	% OF ALL RECEIPTS		TOTAL RECEIVED	GIVEN TO CHARITY
7 Taylor (R)						
1985–86	67%	$145,468	54%	$ 441,650	$ 8,000	$ 0
1983–84	69%	$129,331	43%	$ 284,986		
1981–82	51%	$ 60,826	27%	$ 159,294		
1979–80	68%	$ 68,370	39%	$ 187,828		
8 Emerson (R)						
1985–86	53%	$298,571	50%	$ 5,548	$ 12,000	$ 0
1983–84	65%	$203,828	42%	$ 9,726		
1981–82	53%	$186,332	40%	$ 9,915		
1979–80	55%	$ 87,078	31%	$ 1,442		
9 Volkmer (D)						
1985–86	57%	$249,736	67%	$ 462	$ 4,500	$ 0
1983–84	52%	$180,638	56%	$ 10,131		
1981–82	61%	$101,222	54%	$ 2,201		
1979–80	56%	$ 76,835	45%	$ 397		
M O N T A N A						
1 Williams (D)						
1985–86	62%	$168,055	61%	$ 75,173	$ 8,500	$ 0
1983–84	65%	$ 85,307	51%	$ 26,425		
1981–82	60%	$ 81,353	62%	$ 20,112		
1979–80	61%	$ 62,000	45%	$ 7,017		
2 Marlenee (R)						
1985–86	53%	$110,725	42%	$ 51,639	$ 5,800	$ 0
1983–84	65%	$137,272	38%	$ 36,902		
1981–82	54%	$ 96,615	28%	$ 3,647		
1979–80	59%	$ 59,982	25%	$ 26,767		
N E B R A S K A						
1 Bereuter (R)						
1985–86	64%	$101,757	51%	$ 24,091	$ 2,400	$ 0
1983–84	74%	$ 74,978	43%	$ 51,534		
1981–82	75%	$ 48,011	36%	$ 42,197		
1979–80	79%	$ 53,934	29%	$ 16,422		
2 Daub (R)						
1985–86	59%	$281,482	50%	$ 116,402	$ 30,550	$ 9,000
1983–84	64%	$175,852	37%	$ 57,249		
1981–82	57%	$122,030	54%	$ 2,445		
1979–80	53%	$135,222	41%	$ 2,230		

DIST. / NAME / PARTY	MONEY FROM PACs		LEFT-OVER CASH	HONORARIA (1985)	
ELECTION CYCLE / % OF VOTE	AMOUNT	% OF ALL RECEIPTS		TOTAL RECEIVED	GIVEN TO CHARITY
3 Smith (R)					
1985–86 70%	$ 86,475	39%	$ 11,108	$ 1,000	$ 0
1983–84 83%	$ 76,056	44%	$ 44,430		
1981–82 100%	$ 45,758	49%	$ 18,496		
1979–80 84%	$ 42,990	38%	$ 21,385		
N E V A D A					
1 Bilbray (D)					
1985–86 54%	$166,825	43%	$ 3,324		
2 Vucanovich (R)					
1985–86 58%	$126,534	39%	$ 8,158	$ 2,000	$ 0
1983–84 71%	$161,168	37%	$ 62,809		
1981–82 55%	$189,740	30%	$ 29,602		
N E W H A M P S H I R E					
1 Smith (R)					
1985–86 56%	$160,518	42%	$ 3,034	$ 0	$ 0
1983–84 58%	$139,996	47%	$ 1,985		
2 Gregg (R)					
1985–86 74%	$119,975	50%	$ 182,310	$ 16,750	$ 0
1983–84 76%	$ 40,175	28%	$ 81,690		
1981–82 71%	$ 38,150	32%	$ 25,560		
1979–80 64%	$ 45,305	23%	$ 12,684		
N E W J E R S E Y					
1 Florio (D)					
1985–86 76%	$265,860	56%	$ 156,949	$ 22,435	$ 0
1983–84 71%	$162,382	30%	$ 3,902		
1981–82 73%	$102,908	69%	$ 2,954		
1979–80 77%	$130,756	62%	$ 6		
2 Hughes (D)					
1985–86 68%	$ 98,915	40%	$ 89,313	$ 2,300	$ 0
1983–84 63%	$ 97,852	46%	$ 83,749		
1981–82 68%	$ 65,573	39%	$ 19,993		
1979–80 57%	$ 21,975	15%	$ 9,372		
3 Howard (D)					
1985–86 59%	$340,280	57%	$ 79,531	$ 28,000	$ 5,535
1983–84 53%	$315,650	58%	$ 19,301		
1981–82 62%	$318,238	50%	$ 7,698		
1979–80 50%	$112,812	49%	$ 69,088		

DIST. / NAME / PARTY	MONEY FROM PACs		LEFT-OVER CASH	HONORARIA (1985)	
ELECTION CYCLE / % OF VOTE	AMOUNT	% OF ALL RECEIPTS		TOTAL RECEIVED	GIVEN TO CHARITY
4 Smith (R)					
1985–86 61%	$ 98,850	30%	$ 628	$ 2,000	$ 0
1983–84 61%	$136,871	45%	$ 14,140		
1981–82 53%	$163,903	51%	$ 569		
1979–80 57%	$ 32,650	41%	$ 35		
5 Roukema (R)					
1985–86 75%	$156,837	44%	$ 89,326	$ 2,300	$ 0
1983–84 71%	$110,124	37%	$ 36,332		
1981–82 65%	$ 87,503	35%	$ 35,810		
1979–80 51%	$177,637	42%	$ 15,458		
6 Dwyer (D)					
1985–86 69%	$106,325	74%	$ 58,750	$ 500	$ 0
1983–84 55%	$ 92,441	72%	$ 29,381		
1981–82 68%	$ 60,250	75%	$ 15,740		
1979–80 53%	$ 52,500	34%	$ 5,852		
7 Rinaldo (R)					
1985–86 79%	$230,823	37%	$ 508,842	$ 22,250	$ 0
1983–84 74%	$223,572	36%	$ 265,467		
1981–82 56%	$156,421	26%	$ 26,959		
1979–80 77%	$ 67,727	23%	$ 155,160		
8 Roe (D)					
1985–86 63%	$204,483	56%	$ 216,339	$ 22,500	$ 33
1983–84 62%	$164,528	62%	$ 105,303		
1981–82 71%	$106,686	68%	$ 2,905		
1979–80 67%	$ 65,315	40%	$ 5,533		
9 Torricelli (D)					
1985–86 69%	$170,048	29%	$ 256,355	$ 20,950	$ 0
1983–84 62%	$230,825	38%	$ 85,446		
1981–82 53%	$ 85,156	32%	$ 150		
10 Rodino (D)					
1985–86 96%	$235,252	60%	$ 22,176	$ 2,250	$ 0
1983–84 83%	$172,039	85%	$ 34,660		
1981–82 83%	$ 83,237	67%	$ 37,240		
1979–80 85%	$ 93,200	46%	$ 5,617		

DIST. / NAME / PARTY ELECTION CYCLE / % OF VOTE	MONEY FROM PACs		LEFT-OVER CASH	HONORARIA (1985)	
	AMOUNT	% OF ALL RECEIPTS		TOTAL RECEIVED	GIVEN TO CHARITY
11 Gallo (R)					
1985–86 68%	$178,936	25%	$ 73,445	$ 0	$ 0
1983–84 55%	$202,563	27%	$ 20,231		
12 Courter (R)					
1985–86 63%	$115,888	16%	$ 123,793	$ 6,130	$ 0
1983–84 64%	$ 95,290	19%	$ 172,356		
1981–82 67%	$102,204	18%	$ 86,837		
1979–80 72%	$ 68,301	28%	$ 90,364		
13 Saxton (R)					
1985–86 65%	$154,238	39%	$ 72,292	$ 0	$ 0
1983–84 60%	$145,026	28%	$ 2,514		
14 Guarini (D)					
1985–86 71%	$293,078	78%	$ 86,627	$ 11,050	$ 0
1983–84 65%	$242,732	62%	$ 14,545		
1981–82 74%	$ 83,689	47%	$ 11,101		
1979–80 64%	$ 70,053	34%	$ 26,527		
N E W M E X I C O					
1 Lujan (R)					
1985–86 71%	$128,905	38%	$ 119,598	$ 6,050	$ 0
1983–84 64%	$197,763	38%	$ 27,250		
1981–82 52%	$137,019	18%	$ 3,397		
1979–00 51%	$ 61,150	33%	$ 9,778		
2 Skeen (R)					
1985–86 63%	$119,602	42%	$ 3,593	$ 1,000	$ 0
1983–84 74%	$ 94,076	29%	$ 9,804		
1981–82 58%	$ 71,508	22%	$ 17,067		
1979–80 38%	$ 24,075	29%	$ 2,601		
3 Richardson (D)					
1985–86 71%	$244,188	66%	$ 30,556	$ 21,300	$ 0
1983–84 60%	$257,985	59%	$ 15,075		
1981–82 64%	$124,266	25%	$ 1,264		
N E W Y O R K					
1 Hochbrueckner (D)					
1985–86 51%	$245,054	59%	$ 467		

DIST. / NAME / PARTY	MONEY FROM PACs		LEFT-OVER CASH	HONORARIA (1985)	
ELECTION CYCLE / % OF VOTE	AMOUNT	% OF ALL RECEIPTS		TOTAL RECEIVED	GIVEN TO CHARITY
2 Downey (D)					
1985–86 64%	$251,005	31%	$ 239,970	$ 27,200	$ 5,000
1983–84 54%	$174,657	32%	$ 155,758		
1981–82 64%	$148,882	38%	$ 98,577		
1979–80 56%	$ 79,127	42%	$ 5,189		
3 Mrazek (D)					
1985–86 56%	$239,608	33%	$ 123,517	$ 10,800	$ 0
1983–84 50%	$304,576	41%	$ 43,315		
1981–82 52%	$154,040	47%	$ 3,110		
4 Lent (R)					
1985–86 65%	$274,092	56%	$ 336,403	$ 18,000	$ 0
1983–84 68%	$165,849	44%	$ 181,101		
1981–82 60%	$103,896	30%	$ 66,353		
1979–80 67%	$ 59,706	31%	$ 65,622		
5 McGrath (R)					
1985–86 65%	$242,669	55%	$ 162,017	$ 10,150	$ 0
1983–84 62%	$ 79,787	33%	$ 17,092		
1981–82 58%	$ 97,895	45%	$ 1,791		
1979–80 58%	$ 80,866	30%	$ 2,381		
6 Flake (D)					
1985–86 68%	$ 23,350	6%	$ 41,879		
7 Ackerman (D)					
1985–86 77%	$ 87,417	48%	$ 114,070	$ 2,312	$ 300
1983–84 69%	$ 76,385	40%	$ 49,796		
1983* 50%	$ 54,752	27%	$ 36		
8 Scheuer (D)					
1985–86 90%	$ 45,300	56%	$ 22,526	$ 150	$ 0
1983–84 62%	$ 28,341	43%	$ 5,387		
1981–82 90%	$ 44,347	36%	$ 3,035		
1979–80 74%	$ 33,521	64%	$ 8,220		
9 Manton (D)					
1985–86 69%	$246,776	59%	$ 6,924	$ 5,750	$ 0
1983–84 52%	$137,988	52%	$ 3,740		

| DIST. / NAME / PARTY | MONEY FROM PACs | | LEFT-OVER CASH | HONORARIA (1985) | |
ELECTION CYCLE / % OF VOTE	AMOUNT	% OF ALL RECEIPTS		TOTAL RECEIVED	GIVEN TO CHARITY
10 Schumer (D)					
1985–86 93%	$ 52,025	32%	$ 503,941	$ 0	$ 0
1983–84 72%	$ 56,845	35%	$ 436,752		
1981–82 79%	$ 74,625	15%	$ 355,901		
1979–80 77%	$ 49,116	19%	$ 41,619		
11 Towns (D)					
1985–86 89%	$116,618	52%	$ 39,036	$ 4,719	$ 0
1983–84 85%	$ 99,471	48%	$ 396		
1981–82 84%	$ 18,374	12%	$ 193		
12 Owens (D)					
1985–86 92%	$ 92,500	55%	$ 1,053	$ 6,300	$ 0
1983–84 90%	$ 84,942	46%	$ 50		
1981–82 91%	$ 39,538	30%	$ 2,932		
13 Solarz (D)					
1985–86 82%	$ 40,370	7%	$ 812,706	$ 25,218	$ 2,751
1983–84 65%	$ 24,042	3%	$ 621,978		
1981–82 81%	$ 64,497	10%	$ 605,899		
1979–80 79%	$ 26,095	11%	$ 200,860		
14 Molinari (R)					
1985–86 69%	$ 58,020	29%	$ 137,333	$ 0	$ 0
1983–84 70%	$ 71,344	39%	$ 89,119		
1981–82 56%	$124,110	44%	$ 94,242		
1979–80 48%	$ 47,345	31%	$ 4,457		
15 Green (R)					
1985–86 58%	$127,630	18%	$ 9,863	$ 4,550	$ 0
1983–84 56%	$169,533	15%	$ 23,043		
1981–82 54%	$ 49,092	20%	$ 171		
1979–80 57%	$ 84,698	29%	$ 11,922		
16 Rangel (D)					
1985–86 96%	$305,749	64%	$ 259,760	$ 21,250	$ 0
1983–84 97%	$194,098	67%	$ 154,186		
1981–82 97%	$ 96,565	63%	$ 48,883		
1979–80 96%	$ 57,246	60%	$ 20,651		

DIST. / NAME / PARTY	MONEY FROM PACs		LEFT-OVER CASH	HONORARIA (1985)	
ELECTION CYCLE / % OF VOTE	AMOUNT	% OF ALL RECEIPTS		TOTAL RECEIVED	GIVEN TO CHARITY
17 Weiss (D)					
1985–86 86%	$ 95,927	35%	$ 46,952	$ 0	$ 0
1983–84 81%	$ 39,902	29%	$ 9,879		
1981–82 85%	$ 29,197	41%	$ 21,330		
1979–80 82%	$ 20,121	55%	$ 6,418		
18 Garcia (D)					
1985–86 94%	$150,900	37%	$ 146,449	$ 5,785	$ 0
1983–84 89%	$123,672	44%	$ 51,234		
1981–82 99%	$ 82,912	26%	$ 141		
1979–80 98%	$ 53,031	38%	$ 17,574		
19 Biaggi (D)					
1985–86 90%	$103,438	29%	$ 316,084	$ 5,000	$ 5,000
1983–84 94%	$ 97,267	32%	$ 212,002		
1981–82 94%	$ 92,431	30%	$ 112,455		
1979–80 94%	$ 32,936	63%	$ 48,759		
20 DioGuardi (R)					
1985–86 54%	$301,378	24%	$ 16,722	$ 2,000	$ 0
1983–84 50%	$132,438	20%	$ 835		
21 Fish (R)					
1985–86 77%	$140,224	57%	$ 88,093	$ 10,200	$ 0
1983–84 78%	$ 94,257	44%	$ 58,892		
1981–82 75%	$ 39,132	31%	$ 19,295		
1979–80 81%	$ 29,175	30%	$ 29,540		
22 Gilman (R)					
1985–86 70%	$129,771	38%	$ 103,292	$ 900	$ 0
1983–84 68%	$100,609	29%	$ 63,238		
1981–82 53%	$106,094	28%	$ 1,551		
1979–80 74%	$ 35,010	24%	$ 56,993		
23 Stratton (D)					
1985–86 96%	$ 55,029	71%	$ 117,714	$ 13,000	$ 0
1983–84 77%	$ 43,558	48%	$ 78,624		
1981–82 76%	$ 32,420	42%	$ 40,039		
1979–80 78%	$ 23,622	41%	$ 36,274		

DIST. / NAME / PARTY	MONEY FROM PACs		LEFT-OVER CASH	HONORARIA (1985)	
ELECTION CYCLE / % OF VOTE	AMOUNT	% OF ALL RECEIPTS		TOTAL RECEIVED	GIVEN TO CHARITY
24 Solomon (R)					
1985–86 70%	$ 63,780	39%	$ 54,018	$ 0	$ 0
1983–84 73%	$ 72,354	43%	$ 45,428		
1981–82 74%	$ 62,839	41%	$ 31,524		
1979–80 67%	$ 65,306	56%	$ 4,950		
25 Boehlert (R)					
1985–86 69%	$ 98,113	33%	$ 68,810	$ 550	$ 0
1983–84 72%	$ 72,135	39%	$ 43,585		
1981–82 56%	$ 58,110	31%	$ 7,788		
26 Martin (R)					
1985–86 100%	$ 73,656	60%	$ 55,729	$ 4,500	$ 0
1983–84 70%	$ 68,250	55%	$ 8,283		
1981–82 72%	$ 44,295	56%	$ 10,071		
1979–80 64%	$ 67,603	27%	$ 8,021		
27 Wortley (R)					
1985–86 50%	$306,654	43%	$ 12,653	$ 3,750	$ 0
1983–84 56%	$152,063	43%	$ 3,424		
1981–82 53%	$111,412	34%	$ 5,038		
1979–80 60%	$ 50,415	29%	$ 2,821		
28 McHugh (D)					
1985–86 68%	$ 85,414	31%	$ 6,161	$ 3,650	$ 0
1983–84 56%	$134,121	34%	$ 14,007		
1981–82 56%	$139,648	31%	$ 4,961		
1979–80 55%	$ 90,810	27%	$ 11,978		
29 Horton (R)					
1985–86 71%	$101,850	76%	$ 109,567	$ 10,525	$ 0
1983–84 69%	$ 71,726	63%	$ 71,072		
1981–82 66%	$ 30,700	65%	$ 36,278		
1979–80 73%	$ 15,300	59%	$ 27,245		
30 Slaughter (D)					
1985–86 51%	$292,984	50%	$ 28,792		

DIST. / NAME / PARTY	MONEY FROM PACs		LEFT-OVER CASH	HONORARIA (1985)	
ELECTION CYCLE / % OF VOTE	AMOUNT	% OF ALL RECEIPTS		TOTAL RECEIVED	GIVEN TO CHARITY
31 Kemp (R)					
1985–86 57%	$327,741	13%	$ 52,018	$ 54,235	$ 31,785
1983–84 74%	$123,865	22%	$ 134,639		
1981–82 75%	$125,031	27%	$ 98,348		
1979–80 82%	$ 19,935	12%	$ 37,997		
32 LaFalce (D)					
1985–86 91%	$ 79,112	52%	$ 342,253	$ 22,450	$ 0
1983–84 69%	$ 72,268	41%	$ 298,710		
1981–82 91%	$ 60,475	44%	$ 225,614		
1979–80 72%	$ 49,095	35%	$ 170,365		
33 Nowak (D)					
1985–86 85%	$ 34,050	31%	$ 152,256	$ 6,200	$ 0
1983–84 77%	$ 73,418	52%	$ 118,885		
1981–82 84%	$ 41,795	51%	$ 59,928		
1979–80 83%	$ 27,925	45%	$ 44,333		
34 Houghton (R)					
1985–86 60%	$149,388	21%	$ 1,989		
N O R T H C A R O L I N A					
1 Jones (D)					
1985–86 70%	$134,650	68%	$ 253,016	$ 9,000	$ 0
1983–84 67%	$125,964	65%	$ 143,372		
1981–82 81%	$ 48,374	60%	$ 112,770		
1979–80 100%	$ 34,000	52%	$ 76,645		
2 Valentine (D)					
1985–86 75%	$109,755	62%	$ 51,098	$ 3,100	$ 0
1983–84 67%	$165,986	43%	$ 37,463		
1981–82 54%	$103,413	28%	$ 2,885		
3 Lancaster (D)					
1985–86 64%	$140,004	32%	$ 1,702		
4 Price (D)					
1985–86 56%	$234,118	27%	$ 9,207		

DIST. / NAME / PARTY	MONEY FROM PACs		LEFT-OVER CASH	HONORARIA (1985)	
ELECTION CYCLE / % OF VOTE	AMOUNT	% OF ALL RECEIPTS		TOTAL RECEIVED	GIVEN TO CHARITY
5 Neal (D)					
1985–86 54%	$294,413	60%	$ 43,650	$ 10,700	$ 0
1983–84 50%	$178,406	59%	$ 44,182		
1981–82 60%	$140,638	41%	$ 713		
1979–80 51%	$ 60,942	34%	$ 2,227		
6 Coble (R)					
1985–86 50%	$253,161	43%	$ 18,486	$ 400	$ 400
1983–84 50%	$113,899	30%	$ 13,434		
7 Rose (D)					
1985–86 64%	$211,845	53%	$ 257,769	$ 22,000	$ 500
1983–84 59%	$154,496	51%	$ 156,616		
1981–82 71%	$ 79,943	38%	$ 57,788		
1979–80 69%	$ 45,020	49%	$ 36,898		
8 Hefner (D)					
1985–86 58%	$224,892	63%	$ 256,999	$ 22,467	$ 0
1983–84 50%	$189,668	60%	$ 58,238		
1981–82 57%	$115,133	50%	$ 7,646		
1979–80 59%	$ 63,455	57%	$ 43,257		
9 McMillan (R)					
1985–86 51%	$319,809	36%	$ 20,069	$ 1,090	$ 0
1983–84 50%	$191,587	28%	$ 10,421		
10 Ballenger (R)					
1985–86 57%	$116,416	25%	$ 5,447		
11 Clark (D)					
1985–86 51%	$125,290	29%	$ 565		
N O R T H D A K O T A					
AL Dorgan (D)					
1985–86 76%	$314,486	69%	$ 203,570	$ 23,250	$ 952
1983–84 78%	$216,615	59%	$ 136,946		
1981–82 72%	$169,784	50%	$ 49,128		
1979–80 57%	$ 70,211	35%	$ 4,903		

DIST. / NAME / PARTY	MONEY FROM PACs		LEFT-OVER CASH	HONORARIA (1985)	
ELECTION CYCLE / % OF VOTE	AMOUNT	% OF ALL RECEIPTS		TOTAL RECEIVED	GIVEN TO CHARITY
O H I O					
1 Luken (D)					
1985–86 62%	$203,261	52%	$ 135,628	$ 19,250	$ 0
1983–84 57%	$246,464	52%	$ 5,030		
1981–82 63%	$178,560	59%	$ 92,581		
1979–80 59%	$174,778	59%	$ 4,524		
2 Gradison (R)					
1985–86 71%	$ 0	0%	$ 292,762	$ 62,700	$ 62,700
1983–84 68%	$ 438	0.2%	$ 163,379		
1981–82 63%	$ 0	0%	$ 74,504		
1979–80 75%	$ 1,150	1%	$ 78,455		
3 Hall (D)					
1985–86 74%	$119,510	66%	$ 239,470	$ 1,500	$ 0
1983–84 100%	$ 83,331	62%	$ 134,380		
1981–82 88%	$ 50,183	49%	$ 64,644		
1979–80 57%	$ 78,424	46%	$ 15,134		
4 Oxley (R)					
1985–86 75%	$155,352	72%	$ 176,024	$ 16,400	$ 1,500
1983–84 77%	$143,055	61%	$ 145,126		
1981–82 65%	$ 80,010	46%	$ 17,620		
1981* 50%	$ 61,394	22%	$ 3,211		
5 Latta (R)					
1985–86 65%	$140,469	46%	$ 157,952	$ 15,000	$ 0
1983–84 62%	$112,763	53%	$ 121,178		
1981–82 55%	$ 81,735	54%	$ 97,926		
1979–80 70%	$ 43,004	46%	$ 78,451		
6 McEwen (R)					
1985–86 70%	$147,897	41%	$ 120,602	$ 17,250	$ 0
1983–84 74%	$ 72,951	59%	$ 5,727		
1981–82 59%	$ 68,725	48%	$ 1,182		
1979–80 55%	$ 89,001	49%	$ 935		
7 DeWine (R)					
1985–86 100%	$ 90,069	49%	$ 51,838	$ 7,400	$ 0
1983–84 76%	$ 80,363	43%	$ 7,884		
1981–82 56%	$100,541	46%	$ 5,349		

DIST. / NAME / PARTY	MONEY FROM PACs		LEFT-OVER CASH	HONORARIA (1985)	
ELECTION CYCLE / % OF VOTE	AMOUNT	% OF ALL RECEIPTS		TOTAL RECEIVED	GIVEN TO CHARITY
8 Lukens (R)					
1985–86　68%	$136,608	61%	$　5,272		
9 Kaptur (D)					
1985–86　78%	$185,706	65%	$　2,139	$　0	$　0
1983–84　55%	$191,381	53%	$　35,949		
1981–82　58%	$ 98,985	46%	$　5,928		
10 Miller (R)					
1985–86　70%	$ 69,349	81%	$　71,615	$　0	$　0
1983–84　73%	$ 69,080	74%	$　52,790		
1981–82　63%	$ 23,580	29%	$　29,270		
1979–80　74%	$ 24,188	59%	$　35,186		
11 Eckart (D)					
1985–86　72%	$221,653	55%	$　94,056	$ 16,085	$　0
1983–84　66%	$149,803	53%	$　39,477		
1981–82　61%	$124,237	33%	$　4,374		
1979–80　55%	$ 79,209	22%	$　1,027		
12 Kasich (R)					
1985–86　73%	$129,817	37%	$　24,835	$　3,000	$　0
1983–84　69%	$199,929	40%	$　101,513		
1981–82　51%	$169,931	45%	$　2,425		
13 Pease (D)					
1985–86　63%	$252,800	58%	$　118,167	$　5,330	$　1,250
1983–84　66%	$ 80,518	52%	$　95,378		
1981–82　61%	$ 70,791	54%	$　43,068		
1979–80　64%	$ 28,985	43%	$　26,801		
14 Sawyer (D)					
1985–86　54%	$233,445	47%	$　19,288		
15 Wylie (R)					
1985–86　64%	$185,352	61%	$　13,813	$ 23,750	$　2,120
1983–84　71%	$120,503	59%	$　46,289		
1981–82　66%	$ 66,050	48%	$　22,572		
1979–80　73%	$ 41,510	44%	$　21,304		

DIST. / NAME / PARTY	MONEY FROM PACs		LEFT-OVER CASH	HONORARIA (1985)	
ELECTION CYCLE / % OF VOTE	AMOUNT	% OF ALL RECEIPTS		TOTAL RECEIVED	GIVEN TO CHARITY
16 Regula (R)					
1985–86 76%	$ 0	0%	$ 84,348	$ 5,500	$ 5,500
1983–84 72%	$ 888	1%	$ 59,496		
1981–82 66%	$ 0	0%	$ 51,096		
1979–80 79%	$ 560	1%	$ 78,205		
17 Traficant (D)					
1985–86 72%	$ 76,780	55%	$ 51,577	$ 1,000	$ 0
1983–84 53%	$ 19,400	19%	$ 3,155		
18 Applegate (D)					
1985–86 100%	$ 57,825	55%	$ 96,185	$ 0	$ 0
1983–84 75%	$ 48,528	54%	$ 75,025		
1981–82 100%	$ 34,547	54%	$ 44,168		
1979–80 76%	$ 38,365	61%	$ 30,370		
19 Feighan (D)					
1985–86 55%	$345,029	52%	$ 33,115	$ 3,150	$ 0
1983–84 56%	$255,854	48%	$ 3,467		
1981–82 59%	$116,013	37%	$ 14,948		
20 Oakar (D)					
1985–86 85%	$231,759	57%	$ 95,567	$ 23,000	$ 0
1983–84 100%	$118,289	79%	$ 64,714		
1981–82 86%	$ 72,712	70%	$ 30,580		
1979–80 100%	$ 10,075	19%	$ 18,382		
21 Stokes (D)					
1985–86 82%	$103,440	48%	$ 122,718	$ 24,450	$ 2,000
1983–84 82%	$ 60,518	45%	$ 61,327		
1981–82 86%	$ 50,261	32%	$ 43,717		
1979–80 88%	$ 28,550	43%	$ 26,114		
OKLAHOMA					
1 Inhofe (R)					
1985–86 55%	$142,731	34%	$ 5,486		
2 Synar (D)					
1985–86 73%	$ 375	0.1%	$ 82,108	$ 20,050	$ 0
1983–84 74%	$ 22,162	7%	$ 79,618		
1981–82 73%	$ 18,525	7%	$ 10,897		
1979–80 54%	$ 13,726	5%	$ 845		

DIST. / NAME / PARTY	MONEY FROM PACs		LEFT-OVER CASH	HONORARIA (1985)	
ELECTION CYCLE / % OF VOTE	AMOUNT	% OF ALL RECEIPTS		TOTAL RECEIVED	GIVEN TO CHARITY
3 Watkins (D)					
1985–86 78%	$ 79,430	38%	$ 117,836	$ 3,300	$ 0
1983–84 77%	$ 59,300	28%	$ 119,120		
1981–82 82%	$ 60,515	23%	$ 103,936		
1979–80 100%	$ 581	0.3%	$ 82,166		
4 McCurdy (D)					
1985–86 76%	$130,725	53%	$ 75,721	$ 22,700	$ 250
1983–84 63%	$ 99,600	39%	$ 3,660		
1981–82 65%	$111,586	33%	$ 10,073		
1979–80 51%	$ 39,900	17%	$ 3,043		
5 Edwards (R)					
1985–86 71%	$ 87,195	29%	$ 39,285	$ 11,650	$ 0
1983–84 75%	$ 60,430	21%	$ 27,137		
1981–82 67%	$ 62,591	32%	$ 5,003		
1979–80 68%	$ 77,350	19%	$ 34,140		
6 English (D)					
1985–86 100%	$132,558	53%	$ 164,549	$ 14,650	$ 150
1983–84 58%	$102,900	53%	$ 66,090		
1981–82 75%	$ 94,314	44%	$ 80,939		
1979–80 65%	$ 53,260	41%	$ 72,596		
O R E G O N					
1 AuCoin (D)					
1985–86 62%	$438,377	46%	$ 25,698	$ 22,450	$ 0
1983–84 53%	$399,545	47%	$ 14,441		
1981–82 54%	$241,659	50%	$ 8,484		
1979–80 66%	$117,754	40%	$ 5,734		
2 Smith (R)					
1985–86 60%	$120,154	36%	$ 49,601	$ 2,000	$ 0
1983–84 56%	$137,210	30%	$ 38,836		
1981–82 56%	$142,229	29%	$ 2,156		
3 Wyden (D)					
1985–86 86%	$152,004	57%	$ 128,875	$ 22,450	$ 0
1983–84 72%	$169,699	50%	$ 102,124		
1981–82 78%	$ 77,636	42%	$ 68,479		
1979–80 72%	$ 72,472	31%	$ 2,535		

DIST. / NAME / PARTY	MONEY FROM PACs		LEFT-OVER CASH	HONORARIA (1985)	
ELECTION CYCLE / % OF VOTE	AMOUNT	% OF ALL RECEIPTS		TOTAL RECEIVED	GIVEN TO CHARITY
4 DeFazio (D)					
1985–86 54%	$179,857	59%	$ 7,945	$ 400	$ 0
5 Smith (R)					
1985–86 60%	$163,026	39%	$ 131,965	$ 4,475	$ 0
1983–84 54%	$251,653	40%	$ 27,792		
1981–82 51%	$160,991	33%	$ 6,044		
1979–80 49%	$154,091	23%	$ 1,719		
P E N N S Y L V A N I A					
1 Foglietta (D)					
1985–86 75%	$204,445	48%	$ 36,332	$ 0	$ 0
1983–84 74%	$206,256	45%	$ 34,819		
1981–82 72%	$141,478	35%	$ 13,165		
1979–80 38%	$ 14,450	10%	$ 2,213		
2 Gray (D)					
1985–86 98%	$460,861	69%	$ 156,747	$ 41,250	$ 18,880
1983–84 91%	$127,668	63%	$ 38,004		
1981–82 76%	$117,062	47%	$ 1,191		
1979–80 96%	$ 38,600	26%	$ 2,278		
3 Borski (D)					
1985–86 62%	$269,014	66%	$ 19,781	$ 5,750	$ 0
1983–84 63%	$187,696	62%	$ 1,959		
1981–82 50%	$ 61,992	25%	$ 9,206		
4 Kolter (D)					
1985–86 60%	$215,132	77%	$ 63,815	$ 0	$ 0
1983–84 56%	$146,632	70%	$ 37,619		
1981–82 60%	$132,688	67%	$ 5,594		
5 Schulze (R)					
1985–86 66%	$205,038	55%	$ 291,355	$ 25,500	$ 3,033
1983–84 72%	$166,449	52%	$ 235,038		
1981–82 67%	$ 96,952	41%	$ 145,470		
1979–80 75%	$ 62,350	36%	$ 118,546		
6 Yatron (D)					
1985–86 69%	$ 83,380	65%	$ 111,244	$ 2,000	$ 0
1983–84 100%	$ 57,150	51%	$ 79,962		
1981–82 72%	$ 48,970	49%	$ 35,383		
1979–80 67%	$ 45,800	56%	$ 24,163		

| DIST. / NAME / PARTY | MONEY FROM PACs | | LEFT-OVER CASH | HONORARIA (1985) | |
ELECTION CYCLE / % OF VOTE	AMOUNT	% OF ALL RECEIPTS		TOTAL RECEIVED	GIVEN TO CHARITY
7 Weldon (R)					
1985–86　61%	$172,576	27%	$　54,187		
8 Kostmayer (D)					
1985–86　55%	$338,713	51%	$　18,151	$　6,150	$　　　0
1983–84　50%	$253,549	47%	$　5,506		
1981–82　50%	$205,953	37%	$　2,829		
1979–80　49%	$ 76,725	35%	$　　579		
9 Shuster (R)					
1985–86　100%	$152,002	51%	$　44,821	$ 22,460	$　　　0
1983–84　66%	$181,034	40%	$　21,374		
1981–82　65%	$102,946	33%	$　69,480		
1979–80　100%	$ 59,650	38%	$　11,571		
10 McDade (R)					
1985–86　75%	$203,665	52%	$　313,730	$ 22,750	$　　285
1983–84　77%	$150,615	56%	$　211,347		
1981–82　68%	$ 84,970	32%	$　90,235		
1979–80　77%	$ 37,625	52%	$　18,211		
11 Kanjorski (D)					
1985–86　71%	$417,690	54%	$　72,470	$　7,050	$　　　0
1983–84　58%	$102,973	32%	$　8,072		
12 Murtha (D)					
1985–86　67%	$244,705	66%	$　206,198	$ 22,000	$　　　0
1983–84　69%	$176,568	64%	$　107,328		
1981–82　61%	$140,675	52%	$　23,652		
1979–80　59%	$ 54,350	48%	$　22,180		
13 Coughlin (R)					
1985–86　59%	$226,446	32%	$　48,228	$　8,500	$　　　0
1983–84　56%	$158,127	33%	$　45,803		
1981–82　64%	$ 45,151	29%	$　32,411		
1979–80　70%	$ 32,110	29%	$　26,010		
14 Coyne (D)					
1985–86　90%	$101,100	92%	$　103,535	$　6,000	$　5,000
1983–84　76%	$ 49,500	69%	$　53,997		
1981–82　75%	$ 46,255	53%	$　38,348		
1979–80　69%	$ 43,180	23%	$　3,232		

DIST. / NAME / PARTY	MONEY FROM PACs		LEFT-OVER CASH	HONORARIA (1985)	
ELECTION CYCLE / % OF VOTE	AMOUNT	% OF ALL RECEIPTS		TOTAL RECEIVED	GIVEN TO CHARITY
15 Ritter (R)					
1985–86 57%	$153,178*	35%	$ 35,501	$ 15,900	$ 1,100
1983–84 58%	$263,677	46%	$ 36,172		
1981–82 58%	$124,908	37%	$ 202		
1979–80 60%	$126,619	40%	$ 456		
16 Walker (R)					
1985–86 75%	$ 31,297	39%	$ 22,586	$ 3,000	$ 0
1983–84 77%	$ 32,003	47%	$ 18,618		
1981–82 71%	$ 24,917	43%	$ 5,439		
1979–80 77%	$ 4,875	12%	$ 7,946		
17 Gekas (R)					
1985–86 74%	$ 50,014	34%	$ 108,171	$ 0	$ 0
1983–84 80%	$ 61,600	35%	$ 50,049		
1981–82 58%	$ 83,289	43%	$ 14,399		
18 Walgren (D)					
1985–86 63%	$293,409	51%	$ 51,795	$ 1,750	$ 1,000
1983–84 62%	$132,691	62%	$ 31,912		
1981–82 54%	$127,235	49%	$ 10,764		
1979–80 68%	$ 37,975	37%	$ 17,685		
19 Goodling (R)					
1985–86 73%	$ 0	0%	$ 9,007	$ 7,200	$ 0
1983–84 75%	$ 0	0%	$ 6,174		
1981–82 71%	$ 1,616	4%	$ 4,864		
1979–80 76%	$ 1,565	4%	$ 3,157		
20 Gaydos (D)					
1985–86 99%	$109,175	69%	$ 42,748	$ 12,500	$ 0
1983–84 75%	$ 86,475	65%	$ 2,962		
1981–82 76%	$ 70,775	51%	$ 21,326		
1979–80 73%	$ 51,050	47%	$ 23,956		
21 Ridge (R)					
1985–86 81%	$138,235	46%	$ 84,931	$ 6,250	$ 0
1983–84 65%	$237,462	50%	$ 54,183		
1981–82 50%	$ 80,683	34%	$ 9,834		

DIST. / NAME / PARTY	MONEY FROM PACs		LEFT-OVER CASH	HONORARIA (1985)	
ELECTION CYCLE / % OF VOTE	AMOUNT	% OF ALL RECEIPTS		TOTAL RECEIVED	GIVEN TO CHARITY
22 Murphy (D)					
1985–86 100%	$ 98,586	74%	$ 103,364	$ 2,800	$ 0
1983–84 78%	$ 78,514	64%	$ 88,200		
1981–82 79%	$ 59,191	40%	$ 57,978		
1979–80 70%	$ 46,500	34%	$ 36,438		
23 Clinger (R)					
1985–86 55%	$286,361	41%	$ 9,150	$ 6,650	$ 0
1983–84 51%	$144,695	42%	$ 1,605		
1981–82 65%	$ 42,730	35%	$ 37,908		
1979–80 74%	$ 28,670	37%	$ 17,530		
R H O D E I S L A N D					
1 St Germain (D)					
1985–86 58%	$305,452	48%	$ 376,962	$ 0	$ 0
1983–84 68%	$228,800	51%	$ 492,375		
1981–82 61%	$177,276	52%	$ 242,568		
1979–80 68%	$ 70,805	48%	$ 145,194		
2 Schneider (R)					
1985–86 72%	$162,999	45%	$ 123,222	$ 10,700	$ 0
1983–84 67%	$132,135	44%	$ 82,514		
1981–82 56%	$132,241	37%	$ 16,802		
1979–80 55%	$105,118	37%	$ 5,356		
S O U T H C A R O L I N A					
1 Ravenel (R)					
1985–86 52%	$ 41,250	15%	$ 6,984		
2 Spence (R)					
1985–86 54%	$144,996	52%	$ 9,912	$ 0	$ 0
1983–84 62%	$120,291	46%	$ 27,050		
1981–82 59%	$ 74,986	39%	$ 2,994		
1979–80 56%	$110,297	40%	$ 2,450		
3 Derrick (D)					
1985–86 68%	$167,750	59%	$ 227,992	$ 27,500	$ 6,500
1983–84 58%	$151,613	60%	$ 122,857		
1981–82 90%	$ 83,078	64%	$ 55,158		
1979–80 60%	$101,167	53%	$ 20,629		

DIST. / NAME / PARTY	MONEY FROM PACs		LEFT-OVER CASH	HONORARIA (1985)	
ELECTION CYCLE / % OF VOTE	AMOUNT	% OF ALL RECEIPTS		TOTAL RECEIVED	GIVEN TO CHARITY
4 Patterson (D)					
1985–86 51%	$148,405	24%	$ 25,202		
5 Spratt (D)					
1985–86 100%	$ 67,226	43%	$ 118,089	$ 2,000	$ 1,920
1983–84 91%	$ 66,124	81%	$ 28,977		
1981–82 68%	$ 60,326	16%	$ 5,345		
6 Tallon (D)					
1985–86 76%	$126,650	37%	$ 76,934	$ 1,500	$ 0
1983–84 59%	$221,947	53%	$ 2,526		
1981–82 52%	$ 93,371	22%	$ 4,576		
SOUTH DAKOTA					
AL Johnson (D)					
1985–86 59%	$230,864	53%	$ 7,331		
TENNESSEE					
1 Quillen (R)					
1985–86 69%	$363,400	77%	$ 321,484	$ 6,000	$ 0
1983–84 100%	$226,350	76%	$ 308,341		
1981–82 74%	$132,290	68%	$ 113,105		
1979–80 86%	$ 83,600	58%	$ 15,099		
2 Duncan (R)					
1985–86 76%	$401,301	75%	$ 512,878	$ 26,800	$ 3,900
1983–84 77%	$195,000	67%	$ 127,510		
1981–82 100%	$115,770	57%	$ 172,884		
1979–80 76%	$ 84,243	43%	$ 109,865		
3 Lloyd (D)					
1985–86 54%	$323,624	51%	$ 305	$ 5,250	$ 0
1983–84 52%	$125,670	48%	$ 2,973		
1981–82 62%	$ 87,995	40%	$ 3,354		
1979–80 61%	$ 48,910	36%	$ 8,702		
4 Cooper (D)					
1985–86 100%	$ 90,754	62%	$ 20,648	$ 5,130	$ 0
1983–84 75%	$ 79,390	89%	$ 899		
1981–82 66%	$ 81,397	9%	$ 48		

DIST. / NAME / PARTY		MONEY FROM PACs		LEFT-OVER CASH	HONORARIA (1985)	
ELECTION CYCLE / % OF VOTE		AMOUNT	% OF ALL RECEIPTS		TOTAL RECEIVED	GIVEN TO CHARITY
5 Boner (D)						
1985–86	58%	$330,400	41%	$ 76,591	$ 22,500	$ 0
1983–84	100%	$114,704	28%	$ 180,840		
1981–82	80%	$107,211	33%	$ 120,733		
1979–80	65%	$ 92,890	32%	$ 45,698		
6 Gordon (D)						
1985–86	77%	$191,237	48%	$ 148,578	$ 20,750	$ 250
1983–84	62%	$189,740	29%	$ 6,606		
7 Sundquist (R)						
1985–86	72%	$139,739	34%	$ 189,861	$ 8,500	$ 1,130
1983–84	100%	$138,417	38%	$ 62,029		
1981–82	51%	$155,691	30%	$ 7,237		
8 Jones (D)						
1985–86	80%	$ 88,300	71%	$ 148,059	$ 6,300	$ 0
1983–84	100%	$103,575	75%	$ 132,677		
1981–82	75%	$119,725	50%	$ 31,355		
1979–80	77%	$ 60,899	49%	$ 56,984		
9 Ford (D)						
1985–86	83%	$225,275	69%	$ 68,059	$ 25,672	$ 3,205
1983–84	71%	$178,108	72%	$ 61,458		
1981–82	72%	$123,195	53%	$ 9,981		
1979–80	100%	$ 47,670	29%	$ 275		
TEXAS						
1 Chapman (D)						
1985–86	100%	$197,439	23%	$ 20,282	$ 1,500	$ 0
1985*	51%	$ 34,046	6%	$ 25,281		
2 Wilson (D)						
1985–86	66%	$265,206	72%	$ 48,222	$ 21,500	$ 0
1983–84	59%	$284,156	47%	$ 21,023		
1981–82	94%	$127,414	47%	$ 10,782		
1979–80	69%	$ 96,286	42%	$ 6,038		

DIST. / NAME / PARTY ELECTION CYCLE / % OF VOTE	MONEY FROM PACs AMOUNT	% OF ALL RECEIPTS	LEFT-OVER CASH	HONORARIA (1985) TOTAL RECEIVED	GIVEN TO CHARITY
3 Bartlett (R)					
1985–86 94%	$169,986	21%	$ 438,405	$ 0	$ 0
1983–84 82%	$144,436	25%	$ 220,350		
1981–82 77%	$177,163	22%	$ −138		
4 Hall (D)					
1985–86 72%	$171,616	62%	$ 128,654	$ 0	$ 0
1983–84 57%	$127,804	53%	$ 122,094		
1981–82 73%	$115,011	43%	$ 98,762		
1979–80 52%	$ 45,670	13%	$ 3,265		
5 Bryant (D)					
1985–86 59%	$365,500	36%	$ 109,738	$ 18,800	$ 4,000
1983–84 100%	$153,542	40%	$ 83,821		
1981–82 65%	$118,007	42%	$ 2,135		
6 Barton (R)					
1985–86 56%	$344,210	34%	$ 3,153	$ 2,500	$ 0
1983–84 56%	$174,147	35%	$ 21,929		
7 Archer (R)					
1985–86 87%	$ 0	0%	$ 540,472	$ 0	$ 0
1983–84 86%	$ 0	0%	$ 411,515		
1981–82 85%	$ 350	0.1%	$ 411,241		
1979–80 82%	$ 1,782	1%	$ 325,181		
8 Fields (R)					
1985–86 68%	$265,683	45%	$ 42,055	$ 6,150	$ 0
1983–84 64%	$345,216	37%	$ 26,404		
1981–82 57%	$159,996	26%	$ 16,045		
1979–80 52%	$268,932	34%	$ −587		
9 Brooks (D)					
1985–86 62%	$242,809	54%	$ 242,155	$ 7,000	$ 0
1983–84 58%	$229,926	52%	$ 195,082		
1981–82 68%	$241,055	38%	$ 5,445		
1979–80 100%	$ 46,400	36%	$ 72,117		
10 Pickle (D)					
1985–86 72%	$424,667	37%	$ 137,936	$ 6,500	$ 0
1983–84 100%	$ 45,818	18%	$ 356,574		
1981–82 90%	$ 40,073	20%	$ 262,011		
1979–80 59%	$ 96,908	26%	$ 145,169		

DIST. / NAME / PARTY ELECTION CYCLE / % OF VOTE	MONEY FROM PACs		LEFT-OVER CASH	HONORARIA (1985)	
	AMOUNT	% OF ALL RECEIPTS		TOTAL RECEIVED	GIVEN TO CHARITY
11 Leath (D)					
1985–86 100%	$ 89,035	57%	$ 397,935	$ 15,750	$ 12,000
1983–84 100%	$ 40,665	15%	$ 325,161		
1981–82 96%	$ 56,152	26%	$ 173,151		
1979–80 100%	$ 52,531	20%	$ 87,053		
12 Wright (D)					
1985–86 69%	$176,011	14%	$ 248,314	$ 26,085	$ 1,000
1983–84 100%	$179,805	46%	$ 109,174		
1981–82 69%	$255,065	46%	$ 69,152		
1979–80 60%	$345,073	29%	$ 30,542		
13 Boulter (R)					
1985–86 65%	$216,573	29%	$ 9,525	$ 2,702	$ 0
1983–84 53%	$ 75,253	18%	$ 614		
14 Sweeney (R)					
1985–86 52%	$268,431	30%	$ 12,182	$ 0	$ 0
1983–84 51%	$123,333	19%	$ 5,708		
15 de la Garza (D)					
1985–86 100%	$134,500	80%	$ 127,733	$ 35,000	$ 14,000
1983–84 100%	$ 92,710	53%	$ 100,706		
1981–82 96%	$ 59,775	54%	$ 51,171		
1979–80 70%	$ 38,871	46%	$ 41,834		
16 Coleman (D)					
1985–86 66%	$257,367	50%	$ 11,123	$ 10,000	$ 0
1983–84 57%	$200,860	47%	$ 2,996		
1981–82 54%	$136,692	36%	$ 18		
17 Stenholm (D)					
1985–86 100%	$ 91,840	41%	$ 200,152	$ 22,350	$ 0
1983–84 100%	$ 92,727	36%	$ 192,484		
1981–82 97%	$ 78,773	38%	$ 145,809		
1979–80 100%	$ 44,280	31%	$ 46,642		
18 Leland (D)					
1985–86 90%	$161,506	74%	$ 20,407	$ 17,500	$ 0
1983–84 78%	$128,328	56%	$ 14,078		
1981–82 83%	$ 94,719	48%	$ 835		
1979–80 80%	$ 61,600	44%	$ 8,639		

DIST. / NAME / PARTY	MONEY FROM PACs		LEFT-OVER CASH	HONORARIA (1985)	
ELECTION CYCLE / % OF VOTE	AMOUNT	% OF ALL RECEIPTS		TOTAL RECEIVED	GIVEN TO CHARITY
19 Combest (R)					
1985–86 62%	$139,266	44%	$ 6,409	$ 5,250	$ 0
1983–84 58%	$149,676	35%	$ 5,430		
20 Gonzalez (D)					
1985–86 100%	$ 28,750	20%	$ 11,329	$ 0	$ 0
1983–84 100%	$ 24,758	37%	$ 1,681		
1981–82 91%	$ 11,830	18%	$ 1,862		
1979–80 82%	$ 14,750	19%	$ 883		
21 Smith (R)					
1985–86 61%	$122,076	12%	$ 4,379		
22 DeLay (R)					
1985–86 72%	$157,949	50%	$ 45,652	$ 1,000	$ 0
1983–84 65%	$107,880	37%	$ 24,311		
23 Bustamante (D)					
1985–86 91%	$ 89,500	35%	$ 66,457	$ 1,550	$ 0
1983–84 100%	$118,196	21%	$ 3,548		
24 Frost (D)					
1985–86 67%	$336,099	43%	$ 81,566	$ 22,600	$ 135
1983–84 59%	$238,904	37%	$ 16,161		
1981–82 73%	$233,914	38%	$ 2,830		
1979–80 61%	$138,329	35%	$ 3,855		
25 Andrews (D)					
1985–86 100%	$134,054	45%	$ 246,561	$ 4,500	$ 0
1983–84 64%	$158,195	48%	$ 80,305		
1981–82 60%	$165,530	26%	$ 693		
26 Armey (R)					
1985–86 68%	$192,410	35%	$ 13,267	$ 2,150	$ 0
1983–84 51%	$100,810	26%	$ 48,949		
27 Ortiz (D)					
1985–86 100%	$105,296	58%	$ 94,577	$ 0	$ 0
1983–84 63%	$110,890	32%	$ 41,247		
1981–82 64%	$ 89,024	28%	$ 5,082		

DIST. / NAME / PARTY	MONEY FROM PACs		LEFT-OVER CASH	HONORARIA (1985)	
ELECTION CYCLE / % OF VOTE	AMOUNT	% OF ALL RECEIPTS		TOTAL RECEIVED	GIVEN TO CHARITY
U T A H					
1 Hansen (R)					
1985–86 52%	$214,610	53%	$ 23,561	$ 0	$ 0
1983–84 71%	$ 74,562	45%	$ 37,731		
1981–82 63%	$110,284	41%	$ 10,864		
1979–80 52%	$ 80,450	34%	$ 2,996		
2 Owens (D)					
1985–86 55%	$389,113	56%	$ 0		
3 Nielson (R)					
1985–86 67%	$ 93,990	80%	$ 30,659	$ 6,500	$ 650
1983–84 74%	$ 78,039	70%	$ 17,355		
1981–82 77%	$ 70,000	30%	$ 3,077		
V E R M O N T					
AL Jeffords (R)					
1985–86 89%	$120,250	68%	$ 212,676	$ 14,400	$ 7,397
1983–84 65%	$ 89,049	64%	$ 121,574		
1981–82 69%	$ 54,310	54%	$ 37,409		
1979–80 79%	$ 26,325	41%	$ 14,339		
V I R G I N I A					
1 Bateman (R)					
1985–86 56%	$222,709	36%	$ 31,129	$ 500	$ 0
1983–84 59%	$211,646	42%	$ 11,782		
1981–82 55%	$ 99,989	38%	$ 3,451		
2 Pickett (D)					
1985–86 49%	$163,949	27%	$ 5,125		
3 Bliley (R)					
1985–86 67%	$288,468	37%	$ 8,007	$ 10,500	$ 0
1983–84 85%	$142,587	50%	$ 44,469		
1981–82 59%	$ 96,840	33%	$ 3,074		
1979–80 52%	$ 71,763	27%	$ 3,503		
4 Sisisky (D)					
1985–86 100%	$ 90,910	55%	$ 224,269	$ 6,500	$ 0
1983–84 100%	$121,058	56%	$ 113,492		
1981–82 54%	$ 56,201	11%	$ 2,835		

DIST. / NAME / PARTY	MONEY FROM PACs		LEFT-OVER CASH	HONORARIA (1985)	
ELECTION CYCLE / % OF VOTE	AMOUNT	% OF ALL RECEIPTS		TOTAL RECEIVED	GIVEN TO CHARITY
5 Daniel (D)					
1985–86 82%	$103,515	62%	$ 144,114	$ 23,250	$ 1,000
1983–84 100%	$ 68,720	67%	$ 102,577		
1981–82 100%	$ 48,814	63%	$ 68,071		
1979–80 100%	$ 18,010	88%	$ 26,192		
6 Olin (D)					
1985–86 70%	$128,807	35%	$ 12,206	$ 0	$ 0
1983–84 53%	$197,504	43%	$ 5,459		
1981–82 50%	$ 48,950	20%	$ 4,278		
7 Slaughter (R)					
1985–86 98%	$ 78,916	32%	$ 47,844	$ 0	$ 0
1983–84 56%	$123,067	23%	$ 7,069		
8 Parris (R)					
1985–86 62%	$177,392	28%	$ 215,092	$ 1,000	$ 0
1983–84 55%	$269,083	31%	$ 15,621		
1981–82 50%	$277,383	36%	$ 27,695		
1979–80 49%	$128,626	31%	$ 1,387		
9 Boucher (D)					
1985–86 99%	$179,037	51%	$ 119,898	$ 0	$ 0
1983–84 52%	$202,710	42%	$ 34,183		
1981–82 50%	$ 63,573	26%	$ 2,739		
10 Wolf (R)					
1985–86 60%	$310,833	28%	$ 12,309	$ 7,000	$ 0
1983–84 62%	$222,529	34%	$ 39,817		
1981–82 53%	$223,515	40%	$ 6,082		
1979–80 51%	$215,645	46%	$ 11,527		
W A S H I N G T O N					
1 Miller (R)					
1985–86 51%	$156,174	26%	$ 2,800	$ 1,600	$ 0
1983–84 56%	$ 98,257	26%	$ 943		
2 Swift (D)					
1985–86 72%	$167,575	63%	$ 56,527	$ 14,000	$ 0
1983–84 58%	$204,957	62%	$ 30,826		
1981–82 60%	$113,873	60%	$ 6,141		
1979–80 64%	$ 93,512	63%	$ 4,601		

DIST. / NAME / PARTY	MONEY FROM PACs		LEFT-OVER CASH	HONORARIA (1985)	
ELECTION CYCLE / % OF VOTE	AMOUNT	% OF ALL RECEIPTS		TOTAL RECEIVED	GIVEN TO CHARITY
3 Bonker (D)					
1985–86 74%	$114,935	62%	$ 56,752	$ 24,650	$ 6,950
1983–84 71%	$125,418	65%	$ 65,037		
1981–82 60%	$114,276	46%	$ 8,347		
1979–80 63%	$ 37,220	41%	$ 8,332		
4 Morrison (R)					
1985–86 72%	$ 70,244	39%	$ 148,864	$ 4,100	$ 0
1983–84 76%	$ 76,710	46%	$ 75,093		
1981–82 70%	$ 58,279	34%	$ 1,414		
1979–80 57%	$ 51,161	13%	$ 3,926		
5 Foley (D)					
1985–86 75%	$392,701	73%	$ 272,194	$ 24,250	$ 2,000
1983–84 69%	$292,023	66%	$ 154,021		
1981–82 64%	$284,442	61%	$ 90,132		
1979–80 52%	$190,716	49%	$ 52,810		
6 Dicks (D)					
1985–86 71%	$179,660	60%	$ 198,732	$ 21,350	$ 0
1983–84 66%	$164,397	67%	$ 126,520		
1981–82 63%	$147,047	50%	$ 42,739		
1979–80 54%	$108,636	43%	$ 17,242		
7 Lowry (D)					
1985–86 73%	$104,400	52%	$ 55,376	$ 0	$ 0
1983–84 70%	$ 96,823	66%	$ 26,122		
1981–82 71%	$ 79,572	43%	$ 31,803		
1979–80 57%	$109,390	45%	$ 8,731		
8 Chandler (R)					
1985–86 65%	$120,581	47%	$ 73,256	$ 9,750	$ 0
1983–84 62%	$125,249	41%	$ 24,309		
1981–82 57%	$ 84,075	24%	$ 2,700		
W E S T V I R G I N I A					
1 Mollohan (D)					
1985–86 100%	$135,583	56%	$ 30,284	$ 2,750	$ 2,750
1983–84 54%	$243,048	67%	$ 2,840		
1981–82 53%	$ 80,169	40%	$ 309		

DIST. / NAME / PARTY ELECTION CYCLE / % OF VOTE		MONEY FROM PACs		LEFT-OVER CASH	HONORARIA (1985)	
		AMOUNT	% OF ALL RECEIPTS		TOTAL RECEIVED	GIVEN TO CHARITY
2 Staggers (D)						
1985–86	69%	$133,695	85%	$ 25,537	$ 0	$ 0
1983–84	55%	$199,788	66%	$ 5,021		
1981–82	64%	$ 92,857	58%	$ 685		
3 Wise (D)						
1985–86	65%	$ 94,421	64%	$ 41,381	$ 2,000	$ 2,000
1983–84	67%	$162,842	77%	$ 32,853		
1981–82	58%	$ 82,216	60%	$ 861		
4 Rahall (D)						
1985–86	71%	$124,079	59%	$ 214,118	$ 19,800	$ 0
1983–84	66%	$ 98,643	67%	$ 70,944		
1981–82	81%	$ 33,090	85%	$ 34,996		
1979–80	77%	$ 85,590	66%	$ 28,729		
W I S C O N S I N						
1 Aspin (D)						
1985–86	74%	$195,382	39%	$ 80,127	$ 22,350	$ 0
1983–84	56%	$200,955	54%	$ 74,362		
1981–82	61%	$ 96,483	48%	$ 4,153		
1979–80	56%	$ 59,985	40%	$ 344		
2 Kastenmeier (D)						
1985–86	56%	$106,730	31%	$ 32,234	$ 3,250	$ 0
1983–84	63%	$ 71,912	33%	$ 14,669		
1981–82	61%	$113,439	36%	$ 4,354		
1979–80	54%	$ 97,381	40%	$ 19,894		
3 Gunderson (R)						
1985–86	64%	$125,847	43%	$ 6,176	$ 11,350	$ 0
1983–84	68%	$ 98,181	37%	$ 26,875		
1981–82	57%	$107,101	33%	$ 5,407		
1979–80	51%	$ 28,987	14%	$ 14,514		
4 Kleczka (D)						
1985–86	100%	$109,983	68%	$ 111,635	$ 2,500	$ 0
1983–84	66%	$ 91,981	66%	$ 43,118		
1984*	65%	$ 13,696	5%	$ 11,570		

DIST. / NAME / PARTY	MONEY FROM PACs		LEFT-OVER CASH	HONORARIA (1985)	
ELECTION CYCLE / % OF VOTE	AMOUNT	% OF ALL RECEIPTS		TOTAL RECEIVED	GIVEN TO CHARITY
5 Moody (D)					
1985–86 99%	$155,056	56%	$ 4,551	$ 4,500	$ 0
1983–84 98%	$104,081	62%	$ 27,917		
1981–82 64%	$ 51,103	20%	$ 3,268		
6 Petri (R)					
1985–86 97%	$ 92,875	45%	$ 217,162	$ 2,000	$ 2,000
1983–84 75%	$ 90,240	42%	$ 118,818		
1981–82 65%	$ 67,619	35%	$ 42,709		
1979–80 59%	$ 74,325	32%	$ 2,349		
7 Obey (D)					
1985–86 62%	$261,906	55%	$ 102,022	$ 14,986	$ 0
1983–84 61%	$110,397	50%	$ 91,542		
1981–82 68%	$ 85,677	52%	$ 71,913		
1979–80 65%	$ 60,175	39%	$ 47,927		
8 Roth (R)					
1985–86 67%	$140,097	47%	$ 91,347	$ 14,210	$ 0
1983–84 67%	$ 84,717	33%	$ 78,229		
1981–82 57%	$ 75,644	38%	$ 43,433		
1979–80 68%	$ 64,842	43%	$ 2,184		
9 Sensenbrenner (R)					
1985–86 78%	$ 60,950	35%	$ 123,693	$ 500	$ 0
1983–84 73%	$ 90,579	30%	$ 126,404		
1981–82 100%	$ 41,370	29%	$ 75,374		
1979–80 79%	$ 56,793	33%	$ 33,491		
W Y O M I N G					
AL Cheney (R)					
1985–86 69%	$169,523	68%	$ 99,239	$ 47,950	$ 22,490
1983–84 73%	$117,468	56%	$ 11,281		
1981–82 71%	$ 69,861	63%	$ 23,882		
1979–80 69%	$ 58,020	52%	$ 24,785		

THE 100 LARGEST PACs

This table lists the 100 largest-giving PACs that distributed the most money in 1985–86, ranked in order of their total contributions to federal candidates. For clarity's sake, the name of the PAC's sponsoring organization is listed (including, where not self-evident, a thumbnail description of the nature of the sponsoring group, drawn from *The Almanac of Federal PACs*, 1986 edition). The contribution figures are from the Federal Election Commission, as compiled by *PACs & Lobbies*.

	1981–82	1983–84	1985–86
1. National Association of Realtors	$2,115,135	$2,429,552	$2,738,338
2. American Medical Association	1,737,090	1,839,464	2,107,492
3. National Education Association	1,183,213	1,374,003	2,033,133
4. United Auto Workers of America	1,623,947	1,405,107	1,621,055
5. National Association of Retired Federal Employees	562,725	1,099,243	1,491,895
6. National Association of Letter Carriers	387,915	1,234,603	1,490,875
7. International Brotherhood of Teamsters	253,178	714,090	1,457,196
8. National Association of Home Builders	1,005,628	1,625,539	1,424,240
9. Association of Trial Lawyers of America	448,930	634,650	1,404,000
10. International Association of Machinists	1,444,959	1,306,497	1,364,550
11. Seafarers International Union	821,081	1,322,410	1,187,106
12. American Federation of State, County & Municipal Employees	496,400	905,806	1,122,075
13. United Food & Commercial Workers Union	728,213	1,271,947	1,116,879
14. National Association of Life Underwriters	563,573	900,200	1,087,859
15. National Automobile Dealers Association	917,295	1,057,165	1,059,650

	1981–82	1983–84	1985–86
16. **Auto Dealers for Free Trade** (dealers of Japanese cars)	100,600	483,050	1,016,699
17. **International Brotherhood of Electrical Workers**	369,390	694,500	969,840
18. **United Brotherhood of Carpenters & Joiners**	637,479	697,024	947,836
19. **American Bankers Association**	947,460	882,850	934,440
20. **National PAC** (pro-Israel)	542,500	749,500	912,000
21. **National Rifle Association**	710,092	700,324	909,549
22. **Associated Milk Producers, Inc.**	962,450	1,087,658	887,200
23. **Air Line Pilots Association**	281,800	543,500	876,000
24. **United Transportation Union**	556,265	649,928	863,309
25. **AFL-CIO Committee on Political Education**	906,425	650,795	840,006
26. **International Union of Operating Engineers**	707,035	775,722	823,300
27. **Fund for America's Future** (V.P. George Bush)	—	—	809,917
28. **American Telephone & Telegraph Co.**	212,495	156,731	799,760
29. **Sheet Metal Workers International Association**	546,266	649,851	778,364
30. **Communications Workers of America**	642,928	694,096	766,006
31. **American Dental Association**	609,450	672,750	761,675
32. **American Federation of Teachers**	292,025	328,680	745,874
33. **National Committee to Preserve Social Security**	—	377,050	736,135
34. **American Postal Workers Union**	372,880	587,540	723,395
35. **United Steelworkers of America**	715,757	585,335	705,755
36. **National Right to Life Committee**	194,667	384,244	695,795
37. **National Committee for an Effective Congress** (supports liberal candidates)	408,929	796,522	694,782
38. **Marine Engineers Beneficial Association**	701,153	735,642	602,650
39. **Valley Education Fund** (Rep. Tony Coelho)	—	—	567,000
40. **Philip Morris, Inc.**	188,327	356,875	559,505
41. **Marine Engineers Beneficial Association District 2**	409,800	463,828	555,831
42. **Citizens for the Republic** (President Reagan)	471,367	762,320	539,748
43. **Associated General Contractors of America**	683,766	580,715	529,414
44. **National Rural Letter Carriers Association**	131,025	359,782	503,705
45. **Independent Insurance Agents of America**	398,917	349,847	487,440
46. **United Parcel Service of America, Inc.**	93,049	186,528	480,524
47. **Mid-America Dairymen, Inc.**	469,650	580,175	467,000

	1981–82	1983–84	1985–86
48. **Tenneco, Inc.** (conglomerate—oil and gas, manufacturing, life insurance)	454,150	366,700	447,250
49. **Brotherhood of Railway & Airline Clerks**	538,818	488,806	446,569
50. **International Association of Ironworkers**	121,775	195,371	434,653
51. **Lockheed Corp.**	184,880	420,441	430,858
52. **Rockwell International Corp.**	175,233	361,007	428,675
53. **U.S. League of Savings Institutions**	322,875	302,285	425,925
54. **Amalgamated Transit Union**	138,730	327,400	416,275
55. **National Rural Electric Co-operative Association**	320,894	394,672	410,770
56. **Credit Union National Association**	241,378	305,130	382,411
57. **General Dynamics Corp.**	172,440	256,031	378,908
58. **Textron, Inc.** (manufacturing, military products, financial services)	112,085	156,549	373,050
59. **Laborers International Union**	292,850	230,650	363,420
60. **National Beer Wholesalers Association**	48,250	52,750	362,350
61. **American Family Corp.** (life and health insurance)	232,775	278,350	360,825
62. **International Ladies Garment Workers Union**	621,601	575,688	358,792
63. **Service Employees International Union**	160,620	259,072	357,788
64. **American Trucking Associations**	319,295	324,700	354,685
65. **Associated Life Insurance Group** (independent insurance agents)	—	184,050	353,756
66. **Public Service Research Council** (opposes unionism among government workers)	344,627	361,635	351,273
67. **American Hospital Association**	180,925	226,691	346,305
68. **Majority Congress Committee** (Rep. Jim Wright)	88,100	223,300	341,000
69. **Amoco, Inc.**	234,300	356,275	340,900
70. **Chicago Mercantile Exchange**	319,072	285,950	323,950
71. **Northrop Corp.**	101,576	231,630	315,784
72. **Democrats for the 80s** (supports Democratic candidates)	360,983	314,000	314,250
73. **Brotherhood of Locomotive Engineers**	156,375	247,690	314,175
74. **United Association of Journeymen Plumbers**	99,000	107,900	311,125
75. **E.F. Hutton Group, Inc.**	85,300	165,900	310,125
76. **Mortgage Bankers Association of America**	195,349	250,417	309,796
77. **United Mine Workers of America**	247,208	248,166	306,599
78. **J.C. Penney Co.**	81,100	169,150	304,150
79. **Washington PAC** (pro-Israel)	89,075	191,800	293,400
80. **American Nurses Association**	181,615	295,789	292,703

	1981–82	1983–84	1985–86
81. **Citicorp**	182,257	181,757	289,484
82. **Mobil Oil Co.**	28,900	122,769	283,250
83. **Food Marketing Institute** (trade association of supermarkets)	131,477	111,850	282,195
84. **FMC Corp.** (oil, chemical, and defense products)	151,952	220,690	281,230
85. **America's Leaders' Fund** (Rep. Dan Rostenkowski)	—	—	279,871
86. **Winn-Dixie Stores, Inc.** (supermarket chain)	281,375	261,825	279,700
87. **American Federation of Government Employees**	283,154	395,085	274,985
88. **KidsPAC** (supports strong federal role in child development)	75,300	161,082	274,666
89. **Fund for a Democratic Majority** (Sen. Ted Kennedy)	176,209	201,565	273,858
90. **Allied-Signal Co.** (high-tech engineering and chemicals)	51,250	143,350	273,850
91. **Pacific Telesis Group** (telecommunications)	54,124	108,404	271,716
92. **Campaign America** (Sen. Bob Dole)	156,210	405,846	271,422
93. **Amalgamated Clothing & Textile Workers Union**	192,846	269,850	271,334
94. **National Abortion Rights Action League**	296,863	210,491	270,968
95. **American Council of Life Insurance**	73,569	201,768	269,866
96. **Republican Majority Fund** (Sen. Richard Lugar)	450,547	416,660	258,706
97. **Union Pacific Corp.**	151,250	207,115	258,325
98. **Boeing Co.**	125,400	191,312	256,975
99. **Grumman Corp.**	189,978	223,410	254,889
100. **Harris Corp.** (communications, computer equipment)	249,250	261,550	254,600

ACKNOWLEDGMENTS

Life, Jimmy Carter observed, is unfair—especially for authors who have just completed a book. Having spent months wrestling to get just the right words to couch this thought or that, they find themselves confronted with the nearly impossible task of expressing the inexpressible: the full extent of their indebtedness to the many without whose help the book would not have come into being.

Notwithstanding, I cheerfully acknowledge, albeit inadequately, my debt to the following:

First, to the ever-cheerful, ever-cooperative, ever-informative staff of the Public Records Office of the Federal Election Commission—especially Mike Dickerson and Jacqueline Doubinis. Of course, being cheerful, cooperative, and informative is made easier when you have a boss like Kent Cooper who, in my eyes, is the model civil servant: courageous, imaginative, and forever watching, not the clock, but for ways of better serving the public.

I am grateful to the staffs of the Cleveland Park and West End branches of the District of Columbia Library, to which I and my laptop word processor repaired for concentration and refuge from the temptations of telephone, refrigerator, and countless other distractions. I am especially indebted to Laird Horrell and his cheerful crew at West End, where I most often sought and found that refuge. (And while I am on the subject of welcome refuges, let me thank my friends David and Susan Pyles for sharing with me their breathtaking place on the Maryland eastern shore, where many of the words in this book were written.)

I drew often from the writings of Joseph Cantor of the Congressional Research Service at the Library of Congress—one of the paramount experts in the field of campaign finance. The Library is fortunate to have a person of Dr. Cantor's caliber and dedication.

Everyone in the campaign-finance arena owes a debt to all those persistent folks at Common Cause, especially those researchers who crank out the many useful analyses cited in the Notes and Sources. Led by the indefatigable Fred Wertheimer, they refuse to disappear, even when the prospects for reform seem nil.

In the realm of journalism, I am indebted to Allen Ehrenhalt and his staff who, every two years, turn out the immensely useful political almanac, *Politics in America,* on which I have often relied; to Elizabeth Drew, who wrote an especially incisive book on this topic; to Paul Houston of the *Los Angeles Times,* an enterprising investigator; and, leading the journalistic pack by several lengths, Brooks Jackson of the *Wall Street Journal.* As both the text and the source notes indicate, I have drawn often and with benefit from the body of Jackson's work, which I believe worthy of a Pulitzer prize (or at least a Pulitzer nomination by his newspaper). Competing editors can learn from Jackson's work the value of assigning an enterprising reporter full-time to the campaign-finance beat. And young reporters in their second or third year on the obituary page who long to make a name for themselves can use Jackson's work as a model to persuade their editors to assign them full-time to this much-neglected but fertile area.

A special word of admiration and thanks must go to the editors and writers on *Common Cause Magazine,* who have plowed the campaign-finance furrow with a courage and diligence exceptional for any magazine, especially an "in-house" journal.

Thanks must go to those who furnished special information or technical help: Stephen Gillers, William Oldaker, Edward McMahon, Ed Zuckerman, Henry Geller, Douglas Harpel, and Eric McFarland.

I feel a special debt to two public servants who have, each in his own way, provided me with models of that old-fashioned and little-used word, "rectitude." One is the late Senator Paul H. Douglas of Illinois, for whom I had the honor to work nearly forty years ago. The other is Whitney North Seymour, Jr., whose friendship has been one of the great serendipities in my recent life. Their unwavering standards of honesty and rectitude have furnished moral guidelines for this book.

I owe particular thanks to Julian Bach, the hardest-working literary agent on the face of the earth; and to three at Pantheon Books

—David Frederickson and Diane Wachtell, for patience and conscientiousness beyond any proper call; and, of course, to André Schiffrin, who first expressed confidence in the idea of this book.

My thanks to the friends who took time out from busy lives to read and comment on portions of the manuscript: Herbert Alexander; Walter Slocombe; Richard Conlon, the ever-inundated, ever-wise director of the Democratic Study Group; Michael Podhorzer; Murray Indick; Mark Green (who took precious hours out of a much-needed, sorely deserved family vacation to dissect my reform plan, expressing his friendship by sparing no sentence from his blunt comments); and, above all, my treasured friend Daniel Mayers, who subjected chapter after chapter to his fine mind and then paid me the compliment of arguing with me about every idea he found wanting. I shall not soon forget that.

Ever-present in my heart and mind has been my beloved Susan, who was unfailingly loving and supportive throughout the writing of this book. But, then, that's not surprising: with Susan, being unfailingly loving and supportive comes with the territory.

Finally, there's the Terrific Trio—Anne Plaster, Mark Zuckerman, and Maryann Blouin.

The latter two have been Vice-Presidents in Charge of Facts, Figures, and Accuracy. They were responsible for filling in blanks in my draft manuscripts and for the monumental task of tracking down the sources for every fact in this book, checking the manuscript against the source. They also prepared the voluminous Notes and Sources that follow. They performed those often-tedious tasks with resourcefulness, meticulous care, and unfailing good cheer, for which I will be forever in their debt. I naturally absolve them of responsibility for whatever errors remain in the book in spite of their (and my) efforts.

What can one say about a person like Anne Plaster, Vice-President in Charge of Everything Else, and my Good Right Arm for nearly six years now. "Mzzz. P" is is the soul of conscience and conscientiousness for whom Life and Job are blessedly (from my viewpoint) blended. There are few people in the world like her; I am blessed to have her as right arm and as friend, and I know it.

P.M.S.

Washington, D.C.
January 1988

NOTES AND SOURCES

★
ABBREVIATIONS

CBO   Congressional Budget Office.

Cong. Rec.   *Congressional Record.*

Corn   David Corn, "Bob Dole and the Tobacco Connection," *Nation*, March 28, 1987.

CQ   Congressional Quarterly, a Washington publisher of reports on government agencies and affairs, such as the *Weekly Report* and the *Almanac* (see below), and directories such as *PIA* (see below).

CQ Almanac   Annual published by CQ summarizing congressional activities for the year covered.

CQ Weekly Report   A report on the week's activities in Congress, published by CQ.

CRP   Center for Responsive Politics, a foundation-supported Washington, D.C., research group; its reports deal primarily with congressional effectiveness.

CRP Foundations Report   CRP, *Public Policy and Foundations: The Role of Politicians in Public Charities*, 1987.

CRP Soft Money Report   CRP, *Money and Politics: Soft Money—A Loophole for the '80s*, 1985.

CRS   Congressional Research Service, a department of the Library of Congress that does research and issues reports for members of Congress.

CRS 87-469   CRS Report No. 87-469, *Campaign Financing in Federal Elections: A Guide to the Law and Its Operation*, by Joseph E. Cantor, Aug. 8, 1986, rev. July 20, 1987.

CTJ Study   Robert S. McIntyre and Jeff Spinner, *130 Reasons Why We Need Tax Reform*, Citizens for Tax Justice, Washington, D.C., July 1986.

Dairy PACs: The PACs of the three largest dairy co-ops: Associated Milk Producers, Inc.; Dairymen, Inc.; and Mid-America Dairymen, Inc.

Disclosure statements   Statements that must be filed annually by U.S. senators with the Secretary of the Senate, and by representatives with the Clerk of the House, pursuant to the Ethics in Government Act of 1978. They must list all financial holdings and sources of outside income, including honoraria received. They are filed each May to cover the prior year; in these notes, the year *covered* by the report is given.

Drew   Elizabeth Drew, *Politics and Money: The New Road to Corruption* (New York: Macmillan, 1983).

FEC   Federal Election Commission.

FEC Blue Books   FEC *Reports on Financial Activity*, which provide complete campaign-finance information on federal elections for each two-year election cycle (e.g., 1981–82). All (except the one for 1977–78) are final reports. Unless otherwise specified, the Blue Books cited here are reports on (a) U.S. Senate and House campaigns. Other Blue Books, containing data on PACs and political party committees, are cited by volume number. Vol. III deals with corporate and labor PACs, and Vol. IV contains data on other categories of PACs, such as those of trade associations and cooperatives discussed in Chapter 2.

FEC Indexes   The FEC produces several listings, most available on computer printout, among them:
B Index   All PACs extant on a given date.
D Index   All contributions made to congressional candidates by a given PAC in a two-year election cycle. You can request a *Combined D Index* for a particular group of PACs.
E Index   Every PAC that contributed to a given candidate in a two-year election cycle.
G Index   Individual donors who give $500 or more in federal elections.
K Index   Summaries of financial activities of PACs.
L Index   Summaries of financial activities of candidates.

FEC press releases   The titles and the dates of most FEC press releases are given in the notes, but two frequently cited releases are cited by date only:
May 10, 1987: "1986 Congressional Spending Tops $450 Million."
May 21, 1987: "FEC Releases First Complete PAC Figures for 1985–86."

FEC reports   The reports on receipts and disbursements required by law to be filed with the FEC *by candidates* at specified intervals—more frequently as an election approaches. In general, the citations in these notes refer to the date the report was filed, although on occasion the citation is to the title of the report.

Fumento   Michael Fumento, "Some Dare Call Them Robber Barons," *National Review*, Mar. 13, 1987.

GAO   Government Accounting Office.

Graves and Norrgard   Florence Graves and Lee Norrgard, "Money to Burn—How Chicago's Commodity Traders Get Their Way on Capitol Hill," *Common Cause Magazine*, Jan./Feb. 1985.

H.R. (followed by a number)   Designates a bill introduced in the House of Representatives. **H. Res.** stands for House Resolution, which only requires approval by the House to become effective; **H. Con. Res.** stands for House Concurrent Resolution, which requires Senate concurrence but is not subject to presidential veto.

H. Rep. and H. Doc.   House committee reports and House documents.

Money Talks   *How Money Talks in Congress—A Common Cause Study of the Impact of Money on Congressional Decision Making* (Common Cause, Washington, D.C., 1979).

NADA   National Automobile Dealers Association.

OAAA   Outdoor Advertising Association of America, the main lobbying organization of the billboard industry.

Opp. Att. Gen.   Opinions of the Attorney General; 33 Opp. Att. Gen. 275 refers to Volume 33 of the Opinions of the Attorney General, p. 275.

PAC Almanac   Edward Zuckerman, *Almanac of Federal PACs* (Washington, D.C.: Amward, 1986).

PACs & Lobbies   A semi-monthly newsletter on campaign-finance issues, edited and published by Ed Zuckerman, 2000 National Press Building, Washington, D.C. 20045.

PIA   *Politics in America* (see CQ, above), a biennial almanac of biographical and statistical information about members of the current Congress (as well as governors) and about their states or districts.
   1986 PIA   *Politics in America: Members of Congress in Washington and at Home, 1986*
   1987 PIA   *Politics in America: The 100th Congress*

S.   Designates a bill introduced in the Senate. For explanations of *S. Res., S. Con. Res., S. Rep.,* and *S. Doc.,* see explanations above for *H.R., H. Rep.,* etc.

Sabato   Larry J. Sabato, *PAC Power: Inside the World of Political Action Committees* (New York: W. W. Norton, 1985).

Stat   The General Statutes of the United States.

Top Guns   Philip J. Simon, *Top Guns: A Common Cause Guide to Defense Contractor Lobbying* (Washington, D.C.: Common Cause, 1987).

USC   United States Code: the continuously updated compilation of federal laws.

USDA   United States Department of Agriculture.

Washington On-Line   A commercial data-base in Washington, D.C., which provides on-line access to computerized information drawn from FEC campaign-finance disclosure reports.

★ ━━━━━━━━━━━━━━━━━━━━━━━━━━━━━━━━
PREFACE

xi–xii *Harper's cover article:* "A Cure for Political Fund-raising," *Harper's*, May 1962, p. 59.

xii *1987 survey of legislators:* CRP study, *Congressional Operations: Congress Speaks—A Survey of the 100th Congress*, 1988.

xiii *PAC funds comprised less than 1 percent of 1984 presidential spending:* Herb Alexander and Brian A. Haggerty, *Financing the 1984 Election* (Lexington, Ky.: Lexington Books, 1987), pp. 84, 111.

xv *Eagleton statement:* Interview with author, April 21, 1987.

xv *Conrad statement:* Interview with author, April 21, 1987.

xvi *Wright statements: Columbia Law Review*, Vol. 82, No. 4, (May 1982), pp. 631, 610.

★ ━━━━━━━━━━━━━━━━━━━━━━━━━━━━━━━━
1. THE CAMPAIGN-MONEY CRISIS

3 *Byrd statement: Cong. Rec.*, Jan. 6, 1987, p. S15.

3 *Goldwater statement:* U.S. Senate Committee on Rules and Administration, "Hearings on Campaign Finance Reform Proposals of 1983," p. 403, as quoted in *Annals, American Academy of Political and Social Sciences*, July 1986, p. 94.

3 *Goldwater favored repeal of public funding law:* S. 59, 99th Cong., 1st Sess., introduced by Senator Goldwater on Jan. 3, 1985.

4 *Ceilings on PAC and individual gifts:* USC Title 2, Ch. 14, Sub. I, Sec. 441a (a), para. 3.

4 *Sixteen PACs contributed over $1 million in 1986; three gave over $2 million:* FEC press release, May 21, 1987, p. 11.

4–5 *Statistics on Rangel:* (a) *average winning percent:* 1987 *PIA*, p. 1050; (b) *increase in PAC receipts, 1980–84:* FEC Blue Books, 1979–80, p. 344, and 1983–84, p. 257; (c) *1986 PAC receipts:* 1987 *PIA*, p. 1050.

5 *Rangel can keep cash surplus on retirement:* Sec. 493a of the 1976 amendments to the Federal Election Campaign Act (FECA) of 1971 (90 Stat. 475 [1976], Public Law 93–443) states that excess campaign funds may be used (a) to defray ordinary and necessary expenses of office holding; (b) for donations to certain charitable organizations; or (c) "for any other lawful purpose." Pursuant to (c), it was deemed legally permissible for representatives to take campaign surpluses with them when they left Congress. In 1979, under Public Law 96–187 (93 Stat. 1339), the FECA was amended to bar this privilege to members of the House elected after 1980. For those representatives holding office before Jan. 8, 1980 (including Representative Rangel, who was elected in 1970), large surpluses still serve as a potential retirement fund.

5   *Eighty-eight percent of PAC funds to House incumbents in 1986:* Compiled from FEC press release, May 21, 1987. Statistic is for those races where incumbent sought reelection, and does not include "open-seat" races.

5   *Committee chairmen received 20 percent more PAC money:* Author's compilation of data from 1987 *PIA*.

6   *Rate of growth of PAC contributions:* (a) *For 1978–86:* FEC press release, May 21, 1987; (b) *For 1974–76:* CRS 87–469, p. 36.

6–7   *Bentsen and Packwood breakfasts: Washington Post*, Feb. 3, 1987, p. A1.

7   *American Trucking Association PAC statement:* Sabato, p. 136.

7   *Defense-contractor contributions and honoraria: Top Guns*, pp. 36, 41.

7   *PAC names: FEC B Index* for 1985–86.

7   *Madison on factionalism:* From *The Federalist, No. 10* (New York: Bantam, 1982), pp. 42–49, esp. p. 43.

7   *Early history of money in politics:* Sabato, pp. 3–10.

7–8   *New contribution limits:* 88 Stat. 3 1263 (1974); Public Law 93–443.

8   *Increase in spending in South Dakota Senate Races:* (a) *1978 figure:* FEC Blue Book, 1977–78, p. 298; (b) *1986 figure:* 1987 *PIA*, p. 1394.

8   *Rise in average campaign costs:* CRS 87–469, p. 53.

8   *1976 Supreme Court ruling: Buckley* v. *Valeo*, 424 U.S. 1 (1976).

8   *Number of representatives receiving half their funds from PACs:* Author's calculation based on data in 1987 *PIA*.

8   *Two representatives got more than 90 percent of campaign funds from PACs:* Author's calculation based on data in 1987 *PIA*.

9   *Banking PAC contributions to St Germain:* Author's calculation based on FEC data on banking PAC contributions to members of the House Banking Committee, Jan 1, 1979, to Dec. 31, 1986.

9   *Two hundred thousand dairy farmers: 1982 Census of Agriculture*, U.S. Census Bureau, Table 11, p. 218.

9   *Dairy vote:* 166–244, recorded vote on the Olin-Michel amendment to the 1985 farm bill. Roll call no. 319, *Cong. Rec.*, Sept. 26, 1985, p. H7857.

9   *Dairy cooperatives' collections 1979–86:* Data on three principal dairy PACs

from FEC Blue Books, Vol. IV, for 1979–84, and from *FEC K Index* for 1985–86.

9 *Dairy contributions to pro-dairy representatives:* Vote recorded in *Cong. Rec.*, Sept. 26, 1985, p. H7857. Dairy PAC contributions from *FEC Combined D Indexes*, 1979–86, for principal dairy PACs.

10 *Dole on "Poor-PAC":* *Wall Street Journal*, July 1982, from Common Cause compilation of Dole statements.

10 *One hundred thirty no-tax companies: CTJ Study*, pp. 15–16.

10 *Simon statement:* U.S. Senate Committee on Rules and Administration, hearing on S. 1787, Nov. 5, 1985.

10–11 *Tribute to Rostenkowski: New Republic*, July 15–22, 1985.

11 *Rostenkowski's 1984 campaign surplus:* FEC Blue Book, 1983–84, p. 176.

11 *Rostenkowski's and O'Neill's 1985 honoraria:* Common Cause press release, "Speakers of the House," May 23, 1987.

11 *Rules on keeping of honoraria:* Under 2 USC 31–1 (b)(1), members of Congress may accept honoraria equivalent to 40 percent of their salaries. House Rule XLVII imposes a lower limit of 30 percent on representatives.

12 *"Lobbyists say privately": Wall Street Journal*, Aug. 9, 1985.

12 *Gibbons's non-election-year PAC increase:* Common Cause press release, "PACs Give Congressional Tax Writers Three Times More Money in 1985 than in 1983," Aug. 11, 1985.

12 *AT&T taxes and rebates: CTJ Study*, p. 17.

12 *AT&T tax savings:* AT&T paid zero taxes on the $24.8 billion in profits earned 1982–85. If those profits had been subject to the corporate tax rate of 46 percent, AT&T would have paid taxes as high as $11.4 billion. In addition, AT&T received $635 million in tax rebates, bringing its overall tax savings during 1982–85 to just over $12 billion. *CTJ Study*, p. 17.

12–13 *AT&T PAC contributions:* From Jan. 1, 1979, through Dec. 31, 1986, various PACs organized by AT&T contributed $1,394,761 to federal candidates. For 1979–84, these included contributions from American Telephone & Telegraph Co. PAC (terminated in 1984), AT&T Communications Inc. PAC (terminated in early 1985), AT&T Technologies Inc. PAC (terminated at end of 1984), and American Telephone & Telegraph, Inc. PAC (formed in 1984). Data from *PAC Almanac*, p. 17. For 1985–86 contributions from American Telephone & Telegraph, Inc. PAC: FEC press release, May 21, 1987, p. 11.

12–13 *AT&T rate of return:* See preceding two notes.

13 *Sears Roebuck and General Electric rate of return:* Sears's 1979–86 PAC outlays netted the company $2.3 billion in tax savings. GE's PAC contributions in that same period saved GE $4.7 billion in taxes. Figures from FEC Blue Books and *CTJ Study*.

13 *Barnes statement:* Interview with author, Mar. 27, 1987.

13 *Senate suspends voting:* Senator Charles McC. Mathias interview with author, May 21, 1987.

14 *terHorst statement:* Interview with author, Aug. 5, 1987.

15 *$10,000 every week:* CRS 87–469, p. 56.

16 *1987 fundraising campaigns of thirteen new senators:* Common Cause press release, "Senators up for Re-Election in 1988 Raised $20 million in First Six Months of 1987, More Than Triple the Amount They Raised During the Same Period in 1981," Aug. 13, 1987.

★ ━━━

2. A PAC PRIMER

20 *Monthly milk checkoff:* Michael McMenamin and Walter McNamara, *Milking the Public: Political Scandals of the Dairy Lobby from L.B.J. to Jimmy Carter* (Chicago: Nelson-Hall, 1980), p. 45.

20 (a) *Dairy cooperative PACs' 1984 receipts:* FEC Blue Books, Vol. IV, 1983–84, pp. 410, 416. (b) *Number of contributing members:* Information provided via phone interview with representativies of the three principal dairy cooperatives.

20 *Sabato findings:* Sabato, p. 59.

20 *How PACs decide:* Sabato, p. 38.

20 *Sorauf quote:* Sorauf, "PACs in the American Political System," background paper, Twentieth Century Fund, Task Force on Political Action Committees, 1984, pp. 82–83.

20–21 *1986 Bank PAC contributions to Banking Committees: PACs & Lobbies,* Aug. 5, 1987, p. 1.

21 *PAC favoring of House incumbents:* (a) *1983:* FEC press release, "FEC Publishes Final 1981–82 PAC Study," Nov. 29, 1983. (b) *1986:* FEC press release, May 21, 1987.

21 *Incumbents outspent challengers:* FEC press release, May 10, 1987.

21 *98 percent of House incumbents won: CQ Weekly Report,* Nov. 15, 1986, p. 2891.

21 *Incumbents favored by corporate, labor, ideological PACs:* FEC press release, May 21, 1987.

21 *Eagleton on PACs as an investment:* Interview with author, April 21, 1987.

22 *Business-labor ratio:* FEC press release, May 21, 1987.

22 *Early history of PACs:* Sabato, pp. 3–10.

22 *Rostenkowski's first campaign: Wall Street Journal*, July 18, 1986.

22 *Insurance-company contribution to Roosevelt:* Robert Mutch, *Campaigns, Congress, and Courts: The Making of Federal Campaign Finance Law* (New York: Praeger, 1988), pp. 2–3.

22–23 *Hemenway and Hackler statements:* Quoted in Sabato, p. 4.

23 *1971 and 1974 reform laws:* CRS Report No. 84–107 GOV, Joseph E. Cantor, *Public Financing of Congressional Elections: Legislative Proposals and Activity in the Twentieth Century*, Aug. 15, 1984, pp. 85–124.

23 *1984 PAC administrative costs:* Herbert E. Alexander and Brian A. Haggerty, *Financing the 1984 Election* (Lexington, Ky.: Lexington Books, 1987), p. 114.

23 *1974 Amendments to FECA:* 88 Stat. 1263 (1974); Public Law 93–443.

23 *Union support of 1974 amendments:* Sabato, p. 9.

23–24 *Cohen comments:* Interview with author.

24 *Business and labor PAC giving:* CRS 87–469, p. 36.

24 *Table on number of PACs and contributions:* (a) *Number of PACs:* FEC press release, "FEC Releases New PAC Count," July 10, 1987; (b) *1974 contributions:* CRS 87–469, p. 36; (c) *1978–86 contributions:* FEC press release, May 21, 1987.

24n *Consumer price index, 1974–86:* U.S. Department of Labor, Bureau of Labor Statistics, Consumer Price Index, All Urban Consumers, U.S. City Average.

24–25 *Decline in small contributions:* Richard P. Conlon, "The Declining Role of Individual Contributions in Financing Congressional Campaigns," *Journal of Law & Politics*, Winter 1987, p. 468.

25 *House dependency on PACs:* (a) *Number who got more than one-third from PACs: 1978–84:* CRP study, *Campaign Spending Out of Control*, 1985, p. 12. *1986:* Calculated from FEC data provided in 1987 *PIA*. (b) *Number who got more than one-half:* 1978 figure provided in Common Cause press release, "Almost Half of U.S. Representatives Received 50% or More of Campaign Funds from PACs," Apr. 7, 1987; 1986 figure calculated from 1987 *PIA*. (c) *Number who got more than 60 percent:* Author's calculation based on figures in 1987 *PIA*.

25 *Average campaign cost table:* CRS 87–469, p. 53.

25 *Nearly successful public-financing bills:* CRS Report No. 84–107 GOV, Cantor, *Public Financing*, pp. 292–93.

26 *Boren bill:* Amendment 2690 to S. 655, 99th Cong., 2nd Sess., roll call no. 209, *Cong. Rec.*, Aug. 12, 1986, p. S11311.

26 *1976 Court ruling: Buckley* v. *Valeo*, 424 U.S. 1 (1976).

26—27 *Boren-Byrd proposal:* S. 2., 100th Cong., 1st Sess.

27 *S. 2 cosponsors:* Provided by Senator Boren's office, Dec. 1987.

★ ━━
3. THE BUYERS OF INFLUENCE

31 *GE PAC contributions to sure winners: FEC D Index* for GE PAC, 1985–86.

32 *GE corporate rank: Fortune,* Apr. 27, 1987, p. 364.

32 *U.S. Chamber of Commerce Ratings:* (a) *Cranston:* 1987 *PIA,* p. 95. (b) *Zschau:* 1986 *PIA,* p. 132.

32 *GE double giving: FEC D Index* for GE PAC, 1985–86. The GE PAC made two post-election gifts to candidates it had previously tried to defeat: when North Dakota Democrat Kent Conrad bested incumbent Republican Senator Mark Andrews, and in the open-seat race in North Carolina's 4th District.

32 (a) *Overall 1986 PAC contributions to unopposed House candidates and sure winners:* Author's calculation based on data from 1987 *PIA.* (b) *For previous winning percentages: PACs & Lobbies* table: "Campaign Finance in the 99th Congress," 1985.

32 *PAC double giving in 1986:* Common Cause press release, "If at First You Don't Succeed, Give, Give Again," Mar. 20, 1987.

32 *Post-election PAC switches, 1986:* Common Cause press release, "The Sure Thing," Oct. 17, 1986.

32 *PAC post-election switches in North Dakota:* Common Cause press release, Mar. 20, 1987.

33 *GE post-election switch to Conrad and GE giving to House and Senate incumbents: FEC D Index* for GE PAC, 1985–86.

33 *GE PAC pro-incumbent favoritism:* Author's analysis based on *FEC D Index,* 1985–86 for GE PAC, and 1987 *PIA.*

33 *How leading PACs favor incumbents:* Common Cause press release, "For Members Only," Sept. 4, 1987.

33—34 *Overall PAC and corporate PAC favoring of House incumbents:* Based on FEC press release, May 21, 1987.

34 *House incumbents outspent challengers:* FEC press release, May 10, 1987.

34 *Ninety-eight percent of House incumbents won: CQ Weekly Report,* Nov. 15, 1986, p. 2891.

35 *Duncan's 1984 and 1986 PAC contributions:* 1987 *PIA,* p. 1410.

35—36 *Increase in PAC favoritism of incumbents (including statistics in table):* (a) *PAC favoritism:* Compiled from FEC press releases: *1978:* June 29, 1979 (no title); *1982:* "FEC Releases Final 1981–82 PAC Study," Nov. 29, 1983; *1986:* "FEC Releases First Complete PAC Figures for 1985–86," May 21, 1987. (b) *For percentage of incumbents reelected: CQ Weekly Report*, Nov, 15, 1986, p. 2891.

36 *Statement about "Congressman-for-Life": Wall Street Journal*, Dec. 4, 1986.

36—37 *1986 pre-election cash balance:* FEC press release, "FEC Releases 18-Month Congressional Figures," Aug. 17, 1986.

37 *Goldwater statement: Washington Post*, Nov. 4, 1986.

38 *United Technologies PAC solicitation:* Findings of Fact and Constitutional Questions for Certification under 2 USC S.437(h), finding 19, p. 14, *International Association of Machinists and Aerospace Workers* v. *FEC*, Civil Action No. 80–0354.

38 *Top defense PAC contributions and honoraria to defense-related committee members: Top Guns*, pp. 36, 41.

38 *General Dynamics PAC: FEC D Index* for General Dynamics PAC, 1985–86.

38 *Defense PAC contributions to Dickinson and Chappell:* Author's calculation based on FEC data for defense-contractor PACs to members of the defense committees, Jan. 1, 1979, to Dec. 31, 1986.

39 *Wall Street PAC and individual contributions to D'Amato: Wall Street Journal*, Sept. 25, 1986.

39 *Paul Houston statement on "political milkmen": Los Angeles Times*, Aug. 7, 1984, p. 10.

39 *Dow, USX contributions to Dole:* (a) *From Dow and USX PACs:* Dole *FEC E Index*, 1985–86. (b) *From individuals connected to Dow and USX:* Author's calculation based on FEC data on individual contributions to the Dole for Senate Committee.

40 *Facts on "Gallo Amendment": Wall Street Journal*, Oct. 31, 1985, p. 81.

40 *1986 Gallo family contributions to Campaign America:* Campaign America FEC disclosure report, April, 1986.

41 *Table on law-firm PACs:* Author's calculations based on *FEC D Indexes*, 1979–80, 1985–86 for law-firm PACs.

41—42 *Akin-Gump anecdote:* Confidential interview with author.

42 *Arnold and Porter PAC:* Formed in August, 1987. Information provided by the office of John M. Quinn, member of the board, Arnold and Porter PAC.

43 (a) *Number of used-car dealers:* Motor Vehicle Manufacturers Association, *Facts & Figures '87*, 1982 data, p. 64. (b) *Number of dairy farmers:* U.S. Census Bureau, *1982 Census of Agriculture*, Table 11, p. 218.

44 *Congressional veto of FTC rules:* H.R. 2313, Public Law 96-252, passed May 21, 1980, 1980 *CQ Almanac*, p. 233.

44 *NADA PAC contributions:* (a) *For 1972 and 1976:* Common Cause, Campaign Finance Monitoring Project, "Federal Campaign Finances" for 1972 and 1976. (b) *For 1980:* 1980 FEC Blue Book, Vol. IV, p. D30.

44 *Resolution to kill used-car rule:* S. Con. Res. 60, 97th Cong., 2nd Sess., *Cong. Rec.*, May 26, 1982, p. H2882. See also H. Rep. No. 97-586.

44 *NADA contributions to Edwards:* Representative Edwards's *FEC E Indexes* for 1979–80, 1981–82.

44 *Edwards cosponsors lemon-law veto measure: Cong. Rec.*, Sept. 22, 1981, p. 21591.

44 *Edwards's vote on used-car rule: Cong. Rec.*, May 26, 1982, p. H2882.

45 *Table matching NADA money to pro-NADA votes:* Based on contributions and votes in the U.S. House. computed from vote recorded in *Cong. Rec.*, May 26, 1982, pp. H2882–83; and NADA contributions from *FEC D Indexes* for NADA PAC, 1979–80, 1981–82.

45 *Sabato on impact of NADA contributions:* Sabato, p. 134.

45 *Senate used-car vote:* On May 18, 1982; see 1982 *CQ Almanac*, p. 24-S.

45 *NADA rewarded its friends:* Sabato, p. 134.

45 *Congressman's statement on used-car vote:* Drew, p. 78.

45–46 *Dairy vote: Cong. Rec.*, Sept. 26, 1985, p. H7857.

46 *Higher cost for milk:* Letter from John W. Bode, assistant secretary for food and consumer services, USDA, to Representative E. (Kika) de la Garza, chairman, House Committee on Agriculture, Sept. 3, 1985.

46 *Higher taxes:* CBO estimate, reported in Dear Colleague letter from Representative James R. Olin (D-Va.), Sept. 18, 1985.

46 *Dairy PAC collection method:* Michael McMenamin and Walter McNamara, *Milking the Public: Political Scandals of the Dairy Lobby from L.B.J. to Jimmy Carter* (Chicago: Nelson-Hall, 1980), p. 45.

46 (a) *1984 dairy coops' kitty:* 1984 FEC Blue Books, Vol. IV, pp. 409–15. (b) *Number of recipients: FEC Combined D Index* for dairy PACs.

46 *Frost's district:* (a) *Three dairy farmers:* Furnished by Mark Orrin in Representative Frost's Grand Prairie field office; the Texas Department of Agriculture, Milk Division; and the Dairy Herd Improvement Association. (b) *527,000 people; 210,000 below poverty line:* Bureau of the Census, *Congressional District Profiles, 98th Congress*, Publication PC 80-S1-11, Table 2, p. 27.

46–47 *Dairy PAC contributions to Frost and other representatives: FEC Combined D Indexes* for three principal dairy cooperative PACs, 1979–86.

47 *Table matching dairy money to pro-dairy votes:* House vote in *Cong. Rec.*, Sept. 26, 1985, p. H7857; and dairy-cooperative contributions from *FEC Combined D Indexes* for the three principal dairy PACs, 1979–86.

47 *Number of billboard companies:* based on estimates contained in *The Bill-*

board Industry, Robert Young, Marketing Research Assistant, Barclays American/Business Credit, Inc., Nov. 1986, p. 10; and in press release, "Small Advertisers Say Senate Legislation Will Create Monopoly," Small Advertisers Council, Washington, D.C. See also *Advertising Age*, June 30, 1986.

48 *Highway Beautification Act of 1965:* Public Law 89-285.

48 *Billboards removed and erected:* GAO Report No. RCED-85-34, *The Outdoor Advertising Control Program Needs to Be Reassessed*, Jan. 3, 1985. (Data from 45 states.)

48 *Billboard income swelled: Reader's Digest*, June 1985, p. 4.

48 *Stafford statement:* See *Cong. Rec.*, Feb. 3, 1987, p. S1544.

48–49 *Background on billboard regulation:* GAO Report, Jan. 3, 1985; also GAO Report No. CED-78-38, *Obstacles to Billboard Removal*, Mar. 27, 1978. See also *Readers Digest*, June 1985; and Dept. of Transportation Report No. R4-FH-4-158, *Report on Highway Beautification Program Federal Highway Administration*, Aug. 31, 1984.

49 *Changes to Highway Beautification Act, 1978:* Incorporated in 1985 highway bill (H.R. 11733, Public Law 95-599). See also House Public Works Committee Report (H. Rep. 95-1485).

49 *Additional costs of 1978 amendment:* GAO Report, Jan. 3, 1985, p. 22.

49 *Billboard-removal expenditures, 1984:* GAO Report, Jan. 3, 1985, Appendix I.

49–50 *"Unzoned commercial zone" loophole:* Department of Transportation Report, Aug. 31, 1904, p. 6, Exhibit A.1, pp. 11, 14.

50 *Number of billboards erected:* GAO Report, Jan. 3, 1985, p. 16.

50 *Billboard vs. used-car industry sales:* (a) *For used-car sales:* $23 billion in 1986, Motor Vehicle Manufacturers Association, *Facts and Figures '87*, p. 60. (b) *For billboard industry:* $1.2 billion in 1985, *National Journal*, Aug. 9, 1986, p. 1978.

50 *Billboard and auto-dealer PAC contributions:* (a) *For billboard PACs:* FEC press release, May 21, 1987. *FEC D Indexes* for OAAA PAC, Highway Advertisers PAC, Lamar Corp. PAC, PAC-ONE (MGH Management), and Nat'l. Electric Sign Assn. PAC, 1985–86. (b) *For auto-dealer PACs:* FEC press release, May 21, 1987, p. 11.

50 *Billboard PAC contributions to Howard:* Representative Howard *FEC E Indexes* for 1978–86 for PACs listed in preceding note.

51 *Vernon and Elaine Clark contributions:* FEC data, provided by Washington On-Line.

51 *Individual billboard contributions to Howard:* Drawn from Howard's FEC reports, for the 1985–86 election cycle.

51–52 *Billboard and tobacco honoraria to Howard:* Drawn from Howard's 1985 financial disclosure statement, filed May 15, 1985.

51–52 *1985 OAAA convention: Washington Post,* Sept. 14, 1986; see also *Common Cause Magazine,* Sept./Oct. 1986.

52 *Congressional aides at OAAA convention: National Journal,* Feb. 1, 1986, p. 274.

52 *Billboard-reform vote:* Roll call vote no. 15, *Cong. Rec.,* Feb. 3, 1987, p. S1554.

52–53 *Committee's approval of "sweeping change": Washington Post,* Aug. 10, 1982. According to the *Post,* the industry's amendment would have eliminated all federal funding for billboard compensation. The states would still be required to develop plans for billboard removal, but would have had to shoulder the entire burden of compensating billboard owners for any signs removed.

52 *OAAA PAC gifts and honoraria to Public Works Committee; Howard Kurtz comment: Washington Post,* Aug. 10, 1982.

53 *Committee votes in 1986 and 1987:* S. Rep. 100-4, 100th Cong., 1st Sess., Jan. 27, 1987.

53 *Environmental groups' endorsements:* Confirmed by the Washington legislative offices of the Sierra Club and the League of Conservation Voters.

53 *Graham turnaround:* (a) *For staff reaction:* McMahon, interview with author. (b) *Floor vote: Cong. Rec.,* Feb. 3, 1987, p. S1554.

53–54 *OAAA fundraising parties:* Report of Receipts and Disbursements, OAAA PAC. (a) *For Mikulski:* Apr. 15, 1987, quarterly report. (b) *For Reid:* report filed with FEC, Oct. 23, 1986.

54 *Brock Adams turnabout: Washington Post,* Feb. 24, 1987, p. A19.

54 *Billboard contributions to Brock Adams:* Adams *FEC E Index* for 1985–86; data on individual contributions drawn from Washington On-Line.

54 *Top industries in 1985 congressional honoraria:* Common Cause press release, June 25, 1986, p. 2.

54 *Defense and tobacco industry annual sales:* (a) *Defense contractors:* "100 Companies Receiving the Largest Dollar Volume of Prime Contract Awards, FY 1986," and "500 Contractors Receiving the Largest Dollar Volume of Prime Contract Awards for Research, Development, Test, and Evaluation, FY 1986," Dept. of Defense, Washington Headquarters Services, Directorate for Information Operations and Reports. (b) *Tobacco sales:* "Tobacco Industry Profile for 1986," Tobacco Institute, Washington, D.C.

54–55 *Roadside Business Association appeal:* Roadside Business Association memo, May 3, 1979, from William V. Reynolds to all RBA members.

55–56 *McMahon comments:* Interview with author, Mar. 27, 1987.

★
4. THE SELLERS OF INFLUENCE

57 *Vacarro case:* 409 NYS 2d 1009 (1977).

58 *St Germain banking PAC and Dickinson defense PAC contributions:* Author's calculations based on FEC data.

59 *Statistics on Flippo:* (a) *PAC receipts: For 1978:* 1977–78 FEC Blue Book, p. 124. *For 1986:* 1987 *PIA*, p. 27. (b) *Leftover cash: For 1978–84:* FEC Blue Books, 1977–78, p. 122; 1979–80, p. 150; 1981–82, p. 114; 1983–84, p. 120; *For 1986:* Common Cause press release, "Almost Half of U.S. Representatives Received 50% or More of Campaign Funds from PACs," Apr. 7, 1987, appendix.

59 *Retiring representatives can keep campaign surpluses:* See note for p. 5, *Rangel can keep . . .*

60 *Representatives using campaign surpluses for retirement funds:* "You Can Take It with You," *Common Cause Magazine*, May/June 1985, p. 9.

60 *Campaign surpluses:* (a) *Total for 1986:* FEC press release, May 10, 1987, p. 9. (b) *Increase over 1984:* FEC press release, "FEC Releases Final Report on 1984 Congressional Races," Dec. 8, 1985, p. 7.

60 *Table on large campaign surpluses:* (a) *For 1976–84:* Author's calculation based on FEC Blue Books, 1976–84. (b) *For 1986:* Author's calculation based on Common Cause press release, April 7, 1987.

60n *Questionable use of campaign funds: Wall Street Journal*, Dec. 3, 1985.

61 *Statistics on Moore:* (a) *1984 surplus:* Moore FEC report, Feb. 3, 1984. (b) *Statement on 1984 surplus:* Moore's televised comments in response to a Citizens Against PACs ad published in the *Baton Rouge Times-Advocate*, May 1, 1984.

61 *1986 surplus:* FEC press release, May 10, 1987, p. 15.

61–63 *Statistics on D'Amato:* (a) *Cash surpluses:* FEC year-end reports, *for 1981–85:* D'Amato in 86, and Friends of Senator D'Amato; *for 1985:* D'Amato for Senate. (b) *History of 1980 race:* 1987 *PIA*. (c) *Holtzman declines to run: New York Times*, Nov. 16, 1985. (d) *Dyson-Green contest: New York Times*, Sept. 13, 1986. (e) *Contributions from Wall Street: Wall Street Journal*, Sept. 25, 1986.

63 *Richard Armstrong statement:* Interview on National Public Radio *Weekend Edition*, Oct. 11, 1986.

63 *Abdnor invitation: Washington Post*, Nov. 31, 1985, p. A3.

64 *Statistics on Aspin:* (a) *Statement on defense contractors: Racine Journal Times*, Jan. 27, 1986. (b) *PAC contributions: For six years prior to chairman-*

ship: FEC D Indexes for defense industry PACs, 1979–84. *For first ten months as chairman: FEC E Index,* Friends of Les Aspin, 1985–86.

64–65 *Statistics on Wright:* (a) *Cowtown Jamboree:* Letter from Representative Wright to Whitney North Seymour, Jr., co-chair, Citizens Against PACs, Mar. 11, 1986. (b) *Contributions by Wright's PAC: FEC D Index,* Majority Congress Committee, 1985–86.

65 *Waxman's PAC: PAC Almanac,* p. 363.

65–66 *Statistics on Simon:* (a) *Raised $4.6 million, including $908,000 from PACs:* 1983–84 FEC Blue Book, pp. 168–69. (b) *Statements on fundraising and on forming his PAC:* conversations with author. (c) *Introduced public-finance bill:* S. 1787, 99th Cong., 1st Sess., Oct. 24, 1985.

66–67 *Statistics on Bingaman:* (a) *Personal loan:* Bingaman FEC year-end reports for 1981 and 1982. (b) *AMA contributions: FEC D Index,* American Medical Association PAC, 1981–82. (c) *Response to citizens' group:* Telephone conversation with Whitney North Seymour, Jr., co-chair, Citizens Against PACs, Jan. 1984.

67 *1986 Senate and House loans: FEC L Indexes* of House and Senate newcomers, 1985–86.

68 *Kastenmeier anecdote:* Conversation with author.

68 *Matsui quote: CQ Weekly Report,* Sept. 14, 1985, p. 1806.

68 *Hance PAC increase: For 1980:* 1979–80 *FEC Blue Book,* p. 434. *For 1982:* 1981–82 FEC Blue Book, p. 312.

68 *Anthony PAC increase: For 1980:* 1979–80 FEC Blue Book, p. 164. *For 1982:* 1981–82 FEC Blue Book, p. 120.

68–69 *Statistics on Guarini:* (a) *1982 campaign funds:* 1981–82 FEC Blue Book, p. 246. (b) *Breakfast series: Los Angeles Times,* May 20, 1985. (c) *1984 PAC receipts:* 1984 FEC Blue Book, p. 249.

69–72 *Statistics on Flippo:* (a) *PAC contributions from interest groups:* Flippo's *FEC E Index,* 1985–86. (b) *Flippo amendment for banks: Washington Post,* Oct. 16, 1985. (c) *Two-thirds of Flippo funds from PACs:* 1987 *PIA.* (d) *Out-of-district individual contributers:* Calculation by author based on Washington On-Line data. (e) *Proportion of money from PACs:* 1987 *PIA.*

73 *Percentage of Hawkins's and Coyne's funds from PACs:* Common Cause press release, Apr. 7, 1987, Chart I.

73 *Members getting 50 percent and 60 percent or more of funds from PACs:* Author's calculation based on 1987 *PIA.*

73 *Table on winners getting 50 percent or more of funds from PACs: For 1978–84:* Common Cause press release, Apr. 7, 1987. *For 1986:* Author's calculations based on 1987 *PIA.*

73 *Forty of fifty representatives in "safe" seats:* Common Cause press release, Apr. 7, 1987, Chart I.

73 *Table on winners getting 30 percent or more of funds of PACs: For 1974–82:* CRP, *Money and Politics: Campaign Spending out of Control,* Washington, D.C., 1985, p. 12. *For 1986:* Author's calculations based on 1987 *PIA.*

74 *ABA contributions to banking committee: Los Angeles Times,* Aug. 7, 1984.

74–75 *Statistics on Morrison:* (a) *History of 1982 election:* 1986 *PIA,* pp. 268–70. (b) *Telephone bill's beneficiaries: business PAC money in 1982 and mid-1984; statement on "standard practice": Los Angeles Times,* Aug. 7, 1984. According to the *Times* article, J.C. Penney benefited from a provision in the bill approved by the Banking Committee that allowed three companies, including J.C. Penney, to continue offering banking services for an additional six months beyond the cut-off date for other nonbank banks. (c) *$21,000 by 1984 election:* Author's calculations based on FEC reports. (d) *1982 PAC contributions:* 1982 FEC Blue Book, p. 152. (e) *1984 campaign finances:* 1984 FEC Blue Book, pp. 152–153.

75 *Denardis 1984 expenditure:* 1984 FEC Blue Book, p. 152.

76–77 *Statistics on Boxer:* (a) *1984 and 1986 PAC money:* 1987 *PIA,* p. 108. (b) *Statements on war chest and defense-contractor money:* Interview with author, Nov. 4, 1987.

77 *Statistics on Schneider:* (a) *1984 and 1986 PAC money:* 1987 *PIA,* p. 1362. (b) *Seeks interest-group money:* Interview with author, Oct. 29, 1987.

77 *Dole statement on PAC expectations: Wall Street Journal,* July 1982, from Common Cause compilation of Dole statements.

77 *Dole and Cranston PAC receipts, 1972–86: New York Times,* Aug. 10, 1987.

77–78 *Dole 1986 PAC receipts and leftover cash:* FEC press release, May 10, 1987, pp. 15, 24.

78n *Dole 1986 opponent raised less than $5,000.* Dole's 1986 opponent Guy Mac-Donald did not file any reports with the FEC on his 1986 race, which he could do legally only if he raised or spent less than $5,000 (2 USC Sec. 431 [2]).

79 *Dole PAC contributions from interest groups:* Dole *FEC E Index,* 1985–86.

79 *Dole 1986 individual and PAC receipts:* FEC press release, May 10, 1987, p. 24.

79 *Campaign America fundraising history: For 1977–84:* FEC Blue Books, Vol. IV, 1977–78, p. 8; 1979–80, p. 20; 1981–82, p. 38; 1983–84, p. 32. *For 1985–86:* Campaign America FEC reports, Jan. 31, 1986, and Jan. 26, 1987.

79 *Commodity traders' contributions to Campaign America:* Graves and Norrgard, p. 25.

79–80 *Gallo contributions:* Campaign America FEC monthly report, Apr. 1986.

80 *Corporate contributions barred since 1907:* Tillman Act of 1907, 34 Stat. 864 (1907).

80 *Contributions to Dole Foundation:* Dole Foundation 1985 tax form 990 (for fiscal year July 1, 1985–June 30, 1986).

80   *Kemp foundation refuses disclosure: Buffalo News*, June 15, 1986.

80   *Jackie Strange statement:* Letter to author from Jackie A. Strange, president and chief executive officer, the Dole Foundation, Aug. 11, 1987.

80   *Kemp foundation outlays: CRP Foundations Report*, p. 24.

80–81   *Dole Foundation financial data:* Dole Foundation 1985 tax form 990.

81   *Dole is chairman of Dole Foundation:* Dole disclosure statement, 1986.

81   *RJR honorarium and jet ride for Dole:* Corn, p. 398.

81   *Top honoraria recipient: For 1981 and 1982:* Common Cause press release, "Talk Ain't Cheap," May 15, 1984, Table II. *For 1983:* Common Cause press release, "Senators receive $3 Million in 1983 Honoraria, Part II of 'Talk Ain't Cheap,' " May 18, 1984, p. 3. *For 1984:* Common Cause press release, "Senators and Representatives Received $5.2 Million in 1984 Honoraria," May 24, 1985, Chart IV. *For 1985:* Common Cause press release, "Taking It to the Limit," May 20, 1986, p. 3. *For 1986:* Common Cause press release, "Pocket Money," May 20, 1987, p. 2.

81   *Dole honoraria for 1978–86: For 1978–84: Kansas City Star*, Aug. 20, 1985. *For 1985–86:* Dole disclosure statements, 1985, 1986.

82   *Dole "Multiple Giver" table:* (a) *Dole Senate Reelection committee:* Dole *FEC E Index*, 1985–86. (b) *Campaign America: FEC G Index*, Campaign America, 1985–86. *(c) Dole Foundation:* Dole Foundation 1985 tax form 990. (d) *Honoraria:* Dole disclosure statements, 1985, 1986.

82   *Contributions from ADM:* (a) *Contributions by PAC, Andreas, and Andreas's family: Kansas City Star*, Aug. 20, 1985. (b) *Donation by foundation:* Dole Foundation 1985 tax form 990. (c) *Honoraria:* Dole disclosure reports, 1982, 1983. (d) *Corporate plane rides:* Dole disclosure report, 1983. (e) *Radio debates:* Since the cost of the show was shared equally by ADM and Mobil, each company paid $500 per broadcast, $250 each to Dole and Kennedy. Fumento calculates that through 1986 this amounted to $195,000 worth of free radio exposure for Dole. (f) *Bal Harbour apartment:* Martin Tolchin and Jeff Gerth, "The Contradictions of Bob Dole," *New York Times Magazine*, Nov. 8, 1987.

83   *Dole PAC receipts since 1972: New York Times*, Aug. 10, 1987.

83   *Individual donors:* (a) *To Dole senatorial committee:* Dole FEC reports, Jan. 31, 1986, Jan. 28, 1987. (b) *To Campaign America:* Campaign America FEC reports, Jan. 31, 1986, Jan. 26, 1987.

83   *Total Dole honoraria: For 1978–84: Kansas City Star*, Aug. 20, 1985. *For 1985–86:* Dole disclosure statements, 1985, 1986.

83   *Dole Foundation total receipts:* Dole 1985 tax form 990.

83   *Corn sweetener and flour milling profits:* Fumento, p. 33.

84   *Frenzel-Crane provision:* Sheila Kaplan, "A Sweet Deal," *Common Cause Magazine*, May/June 1986, p. 29.

84–85   *Facts on tobacco subsidy:* Corn, pp. 381–99.

85   *Tobacco contributions:* (a) *To Dole reelection campaign:* Dole *FEC E Index*, 1985–86. (b) *To Dole Foundation:* Dole Foundation 1985 tax form 990. *(c) Dole honoraria:* Dole disclosure report, 1983. (d) *U.S. Tobacco jet: Newsday*, Sept. 17, 1987.

85–86   *Commodity traders:* Graves and Norrgard, pp. 20–31.

86   *Subsidy for gasohol; Dole response to Michael Isikoff:* Fumento, pp. 32–38.

87–88   *Dole votes against PAC bill:* Roll call no. 209, *Cong. Rec.*, Aug. 12, 1986, p. S11311.

87–88   *Dole statements, filibuster votes:* Common Cause press release, "Common Cause Attacks Senate Minority Leader Robert Dole for Blocking Senate Action on Campaign Finance Reform Bill," Dec. 2, 1987.

88–89   *Specific PAC contributions to Howard:* Howard *FEC E Index*, 1985–86.

90   *Howard 1986 PAC receipts:* 1987 *PIA*, p. 946.

90   *Five out of six dollars from out of district:* Author's calculation based on Howard FEC reports for 1985 and 1986.

90–91   *Howard campaign spending: For 1979–84:* FEC Blue Books, 1979–80, p. 324; 1981–82, pp. 241–44; 1983–84, pp. 243–45. *For 1986:* 1987 *PIA*, p. 946.

91   *Howard 1986 PAC money and rank:* FEC press release, May 10, 1987, p. 19.

91   *"Interested" campaign contributions to Howard:* (a) *From PACs, by area of interest:* Author's calculation based on Howard *FEC E Index*, 1985–86. (b) *From individuals:* Author's calculations based on Howard FEC reports for 1985 and 1986.

91–92   *American Busing Association contributions to Howard:* (a) *PAC money:* Howard *FEC E Indexes*, 1981–86; (b) *Puerto Rico trips and honoraria:* Howard disclosure statements, 1981–86.

92   *Howard attendance at OAAA meeting:* Howard disclosure statement, 1985.

92   *Howard honoraria:* (a) *From billboard interests:* Howard disclosure statements, 1981–85. (b) *From tobacco interests* (footnote): Howard disclosure statements, 1984–86.

93   *Table on special interest contributions and trips: For honoraria and trips:* Howard disclosure statements, 1981–86. *For PAC contributions:* Howard *FEC E Indexes*, 1981–86.

93–94   *Lamar Corp. and Parsons Co. contributions:* Howard *FEC E Index*, 1985–86.

94   *Billboard money from individuals:* Calculations by Edward McMahon, executive director, Coalition for Scenic Beauty, based on Howard FEC reports, 1985–86.

94 *Rubin and White examples: Eric Rubin:* Howard FEC report, July 15, 1985. *Barbara White:* Howard FEC report, Dec. 4, 1986. *Dean White:* Howard FEC reports, July 15, 1985, Jan. 21, 1986, and July 7, 1986.

94—95 *Out-of-state contributions to Howard:* Calculations by author based on Howard FEC reports for 1985 and 1986.

★ ▬▬▬▬▬▬▬▬▬▬▬▬▬▬▬▬▬▬▬▬▬▬▬▬▬▬▬▬▬▬▬

5. PRESENT AND FORMER MEMBERS OF CONGRESS SPEAK

Introductions: Material for background introductions drawn largely from 1986 and 1987 *PIA.*

99—101 *Barnes comments:* Interview with author, Mar. 27. 1987.

102—4 *Moffet comments:* Interview with author, Aug. 8, 1987.

104—6 *Mathias comments:* Interview with author, May 21, 1987.

106 *Boren-Goldwater measure:* Amendment 2690 to S. 655, 99th Cong., 2nd Sess., roll call no. 209, *Cong. Rec.,* Aug. 12, 1986, p. S11311.

106—7 *Goldwater comments:* Interview with author, Sept. 23, 1987.

107—10 *Eagleton comments:* Interview with author, Apr. 21, 1987.

110—11 *Conrad comments:* Interview with author, Apr. 21, 1987.

111 *Schneider's previous campaign finances: 1978:* FEC Blue Book, 1977–78, pp. 294, 296. *1980:* FEC Blue Book, 1979–80, p. 410.

111—13 *Schneider comments:* Interview with author, Oct. 19, 1987.

113—14 *Synar comments:* Interview with author, July 1987.

115—16 *Stennis comments:* Interview with author, Aug. 10, 1987.

116 *Synar-Leach campaign reform bill:* H.R. 3799, 99th Cong., 1st Sess.

116—17 *Leach comments:* Interview with author, May 5, 1987.

118—19 *Edgar comments:* Interview with author, Apr. 6, 1987.

119—21 *Chiles comments:* Interview with author, Sept. 22, 1987.

121—22 *Railsback comments:* Interview with author, Mar. 24, 1987.

★ ▬▬▬▬▬▬▬▬▬▬▬▬▬▬▬▬▬▬▬▬▬▬▬▬▬▬▬▬▬▬▬

6. THE PAC MANAGERS SPEAK

123 *Machinists 1986 PAC contributions:* FEC press release, May 21, 1987, p. 11.

124–26 *Holayter interview:* Interview with author, July 30, 1987.

124 *Machinist PAC gifts in marginal races and to Conyers:* Calculations by author based on Machinists *FEC D Index*, 1985–86.

126–29 *Brown and terHorst interview:* Interview with author, Aug. 8, 1987.

127–28 *Facts on Ford PAC:* (a) *Ford PAC 1986 receipts:* Ford *FEC D Index*, 1985–86. (b) *Incumbent support:* Author's calculations based on Ford *FEC D Index*, 1985–86.

129–30 *Isaacs interview:* Interview with author, Aug. 12, 1987.

129 *Council for a Livable World 1986 receipts:* FEC press release, May 21, 1987. p. 9.

131–34 *Frank Vacca interview:* Interview with author, Aug. 10, 1987.

131–32 *Dairy PACs:* (a) *1986 contributions:* FEC press release, May 21, 1987, pp. 11, 26. (b) *Number of candidates helped by dairy PACs: FEC D Indexes*, 1985–86, for principal dairy PACs.

131 *Dairymen, Inc., PAC participation rate:* Provided by James H. Sumner, Director of Corporate Communications, Dairymen, Inc.

133 *Mid-America contributions to easy winners:* Calculations by author based on Mid-America *FEC D Index*, 1985–86.

★ ───
7. THE TRUE COSTS OF THE PAC SYSTEM

138 *12,000 sugar producers:* USDA, "Sugar," *Agriculture Information Bulletin*, No. 478, Sept. 1984, pp. 4, 6. See also *Economic Report of the President*, Feb. 1986, p. 138.

138 *Payment to sugar growers:* "A Sweet Deal for America's Sugar Producers," *Business and Society Review*, Winter 1983; see also Allen R. Ferguson, "The Sugar Price Support Program," prepared for the U.S. Cane Sugar Refiners' Association, June 1985; and Public Voice for Food and Health Policy Report, "How Sweet It Is: Sugar Dollars/Sugar Votes," September 1986.

138 *Comparative sugar prices:* Statement of Nicholas Kominus, U.S. Cane Sugar Refiners' Association, before the Senate Committee on Agriculture, Nutrition and Forestry, Apr. 2, 1985, citing U.S. Department of Agriculture statistics. See also Representative Gradison's statement, *Cong. Rec.*, Sept. 26, 1985, p. H7820.

138–39 *Comparative commodity profit rates:* Provided by U.S. Cane Sugar Refiners' Association; see also *Cong. Rec.*, Sept. 26, 1985, p. H7817.

139 *Number of sugar-producing states and districts:* Based on information provided by the Economic Research Service, Sugar and Sweetener Division, USDA.

139 *Cost of sugar program:* See Allen R. Ferguson, "The Sugar Price Support Program," prepared for the U.S. Cane Sugar Refiners' Association, June 1985. There are various estimates of the subsidy's cost to consumers, ranging from $2.0 billion to $4.3 billion a year. The cost of $41 per household per year is derived from Ferguson's estimate that the sugar program cost consumers $3.75 billion in 1984. Mr. Ferguson is with the Economists' Committee on Public Policy in Washington, D.C.

139 *Hawaii and Florida's sugar crop:* See Representative Gradison's statement, *Cong. Rec.*, Sept. 26, 1985, p. H7826.

139 *Fanjul brothers:* Sheila Kaplan, "A Sweet Deal," *Common Cause Magazine*, May/June 1986, p. 27.

139 *Corn-sweetener firms' 1984 total sales: PAC Almanac*, pp. 16, 35, 152.

139 *Growth of sugar PACs, contributions: Common Cause Magazine, May/June 1986, p. 28.*

140 *Candidates receiving 1984 sugar money: FEC Combined D Index*, 1983–84, for the following sugar-industry PACs: U.S. Beet Sugar Ass'n; Texas Sugar Beet Growers Ass'n; Alexander and Baldwin, Inc; Amalgamated Sugar Co.; American Crystal Sugar Co.; Sugar Cane League of the USA; AMFAC Inc; Archer-Daniels-Midland Co.; California Beet Growers Ass'n Ltd; Cargill Inc; Castle & Cooke Inc.; Florida Sugar Cane League; Hawaiian Sugar Planters' Ass'n; IU International Corp.; Rio Grande Valley Sugar Growers Inc.; So. Minnesota Sugar Beet Coop; A. E. Staley Manufacturing Co.; American Sugarbeet Growers Ass'n.

140 *1985 sugar industry contributions: Common Cause Magazine*, May/June 1986, p. 28.

140 *Coalition supporting sugar amendment:* Provided by the Coalition to Reduce Inflated Sugar Prices (CRISP), Washington, D.C.—a coalition of consumer groups, labor unions, and sugar-user industries lobbying for reform of the sugar subsidy program.

140 *Sugar subsidy vote: Cong. Rec.*, Sept. 26, 1985, p. H7829.

140 *Table matching sugar money with pro-sugar votes:* From House vote in *Cong. Rec.*, Sept. 26, 1985, p. H7829, and FEC data on sugar-industry PACs (listed above) for Jan. 1983 through Mar. 1986, provided in Public Voice Report, "How Sweet It Is," Sept. 1986.

141 *1985 dairy legislation:* Olin-Michel amendment to dairy section of 1985 Farm Bill (H.R. 2100), *Cong. Rec.*, Sept. 26, 1985, p. H7838.

141 *Dairy cost estimates:* Provided in "Dear Colleague" letter, Representative Jim Olin (D-Va.), Sept. 18, 1985. See also letter from Rudolph G. Penner, director of CBO, to Representative Robert Michel, Sept. 5, 1985; USDA, Office of Public Liaison, "USDA Backgrounders: 1985 Farm Bill," Sept. 1985;

and letter from John W. Bode, assistant secretary for food and consumer services, USDA, to Representative E. (Kika) de la Garza, Sept. 3, 1985.

141 *Dairy vote: Cong. Rec.*, Sept. 26, 1985, p. H7857.

141–42 *Hospital cost containment: Money Talks*, p. 12.; *AMA opposing argument:* 1979 *CQ Almanac*, p. 513.

142 *1986 AMA PAC contributions:* FEC press release, May 21, 1987, p. 11.

142 *House Commerce Committee vote on hospital costs:* June 18, 1978, vote, in *Money Talks*, p. 13.

142 *1979 consumer savings estimate:* Hospital-cost containment, presidential letter of transmittal, Mar. 7, 1979, H. Doc. No. 96–68, p. III.

142 *Hospital-cost containment vote:* 1979 *CQ Almanac*, p. 176-H.

142 *Table matching AMA money with pro-AMA votes:* From cost containment vote (see 1979 *CQ Almanac*, p. 176-H); and *FEC D Indexes* for AMA PAC, 1977–80.

142–143 *Background of domestic content legislation:* Democratic Study Group Fact Sheet No. 98-1, "Domestic Content," Nov. 1, 1983.

143 *CBO estimate on auto-price increase:* CBO special report, *The Fair Practices in Automotive Products Act (H.R. 5133), An Economic Assessment,* Aug. 1982, p. 33, printed in Ways and Means Committee Print, 97–33.

143 *1982 U.S. car sales:* CRS Report No. 85-34 E, "U.S. Economic Policy in an International Context," Jan. 2, 1985, p. 64.

143 (a) *UAW 1986 PAC contributions:* FEC press release, May 21, 1987. (b) *Number of recipients: FEC D Index,* UAW PAC, 1985–86.

143 *Domestic-content votes:* 1982 *CQ Almanac*, p. 128-H; 1983 *CQ Almanac,* p. 124-II.

143 *Table matching UAW money with pro-UAW votes:* From domestic-content vote (see 1982 *CQ Almanac*, p. 128-H) and *FEC D Indexes* for UAW PAC, 1979–82.

144–45 *Public financing bill:* S. 1787, 99th Cong., 1st Sess., introduced Oct. 24, 1985. Costs computed by staff of Senate Rules Committee.

★ ━━━━━━━━━━━━━━━━━━━━━━━━━━━━━━━━━━━
8. CAMPAIGN CONTRIBUTION OR BRIBE? A HAIRLINE'S DIFFERENCE

146 *Russell Long statement: Money Talks,* p. 17.

146 *Brewster case:* 506 F.2d 62 (1974).

147 *Bribery statute:* 18 U.S.C.A. 201 (b)(2).

147—48 *Dole-Rostenkowski deal:* Graves and Norrgard, pp. 20–31.

148 *Vote on Stafford amendment:* Motion to table Stafford Amendment No. 13 to Federal Aid Highway Act of 1987, roll call 15, *Cong. Rec.*, Feb. 3, 1987, p. S1554.

148—49 *Brock Adams:* (a) *Statements on billboard compensation: Washington Post*, Feb. 24, 1987, p. A-19. (b) *Billboard-industry contributions:* PAC receipts from Adams *FEC E Index*, 1985–86, and individual receipts from FEC data for 1985–86 provided by Washington On-Line.

149—50 *Facts on cost-disclosure law; defense contributions to Quayle: Wall Street Journal*, July 30, 1986, p. 48.

150 *Defense honoraria to Quayle:* Quayle disclosure statements, 1984 and 1985.

150 *Spector and Dravo Corp.:* (a) *Facts on Dravo:* "A Case of Rank vs. Privilege: How a Senator Helped a Contractor Outflank the Navy," *Time*, Sept. 14, 1987, p. 29. (b) *Dravo contributions:* Dravo-Spector *FEC Combined D Index*, 1985–86.

151 *Addabbo helps Avco:* (a) *Addabbo as prime mover; tank's gas mileage: Cong. Rec.*, July 20, 1983, p. H5300. (b) *Inadequate engines, deficiencies:* Letter to Representative Norman Dicks from James Ambrose, undersecretary of the Army, July 13, 1983. (c) *Addabbo votes for AVCO monopoly: Cong. Rec.*, July 20, 1983, p. H5308. (d) *Bid by competing firm:* Letter to Representative Addabbo from J. D. Sculley, assistant secretary of the Army for research, development, and acquisition, Aug. 10, 1983. (e) *AVCO contributions to Addabbo:* Addabbo *FEC E Index*, 1983–84. See also *Wall Street Journal*, Oct. 13, 1983, which first exposed these facts.

151—52 *Facts on Perot Amendment: Money Talks*, p. 14.

152 *Perot amendment vote: Cong. Rec.*, Dec. 4, 1975, p. 38670.

152 *Wall Street Journal exposes Perot: Wall Street Journal*, Nov. 7, 1975.

152 *Facts on Drexel Burnham and D'Amato dinner: Wall Street Journal*, Sept. 25, 1986.

153 *No-fault insurance:* (a) *1974 Senate Bill:* S. 354, passed Senate May 1, 1974. 1974 *CQ Almanac*, p. 315. (b) *Twenty-four states have no-fault:* U.S. Department of Transportation, DOT-P-30-84-20, "Compensating Auto Accident Victims: A Follow-up Report on No-Fault Auto Insurance Experiences," May 1985. (c) *1976 Senate Vote; nine vote switches: CQ Weekly Report*, Apr. 3, 1976, pp. 745–46. (d) *Vote switches by senators receiving contributions; Taft returns money: Money Talks*, p. 46.

153 *Barnes statement:* Interview with author, Mar. 27. 1987.

154 *U.S. Court of Appeals statement:* 506 F.2d 62 (1974), p. 81.

154 *New York Times statement:* Cited in Graves and Norrgard, p. 31.

★
9. HONORARIA: A LEGAL WAY OF LINING POLITICIAN'S POCKETS

155–56 *Facts re American Trucking Association breakfasts and distillers' honoraria: Wall Street Journal,* June 21, 1986.

156n *American Pork Congress: Washington Post,* May 20, 1986.

156 *Brewers' coalition honoraria: Wall Street Journal,* July 11, 1985.

156 *Banking industry honoraria: Los Angeles Times,* Aug. 7, 1984.

156 *Executive Branch employees barred from accepting honoraria:* USC, Title 18, Ch. 11, Sec. 209, forbids executive-branch employees from accepting fees or travel expenses for public appearances connected with their official duties.

156–57 *$2000 limit on congressional honoraria:* 2 USC section 441i.

157 *Attorney General Daugherty ruling:* 33 Opp. Att. Gen. 275 (1922).

157 *Defense contractor honoraria: Top Guns,* p. 42.

157 *Amount of honoraria that may be kept:* Under 2 USC 31-1 (b) (1), members of Congress may accept honoraria equivalent to 40 percent of their salaries. House Rule XLVII imposes a lower limit of 30 percent on representatives.

157 *Lawmakers keep more than 75 percent of their total honoraria.* Author's calculation based on Common Cause press releases, "Taking It to the Limit," May 20, 1986, and "Speakers of the House," May 23, 1986.

157 58 *United Coal Company story: Washington Post,* June 11, 1986.

158 *Livingston's honoraria: National Journal,* Oct. 11, 1986.

158 *Product-liability honoraria and PAC gifts:* Cited in the *Washington Post,* July 31, 1984.

158–59 *GTE breakfast and EFT honorarium to Barnard: National Journal,* Oct. 11, 1986.

159 *Barbados meeting:* Pressler, Boucher, and Borski disclosure statements, 1986.

159–60 *Williams example: National Journal,* Oct. 11, 1986.

160 *Members who took no honoraria or gave it all to charity:* Calculations by author based on Common Cause press release, "Taking It to the Limit," May 20, 1986, and unpublished Common Cause data on House honoraria for 1985.

160 *Boucher and Wyden statements: Washington Post,* June 11, 1986.

160 *Coal Industry Tax Savings: Tax Notes,* April 22, 1985, p. 402.

★
10. THE MANY WAYS OF SKIRTING THE "REFORM" LAWS

161 *Watergate scandals:* J. Anthony Lukas, *Nightmare: the Underside of the Nixon Years* (New York: Viking, 1973), pp. 111–34.

161 *Mott contribution: New York Times,* Dec. 5, 1972.

162 *1972 disclosure requirements:* FECA of 1971, 86 Stat. 3 (1971), Public Law 92-225.

162 *Reform laws:* Revenue Act of 1971 (Public Law 92-178) and Federal Election Campaign Act Amendments of 1974 (Public Law 93-443).

162 *1976 Supreme Court decision: Buckley* v. *Valeo,* 424 U.S. 1 (1976).

162 *Jackson on "startling resemblance": Wall Street Journal,* July 5, 1984.

162 *Dayton, Maldow, and Watson contributions: PACs & Lobbies,* Jan. 16, 1985, pp. 1–2.

162 *Pickens and Hayman contributions: CRP Soft Money Report,* p. 19.

162 *Kroc contribution: Wall Street Journal,* Oct. 19, 1987.

163 *Creation of "soft money":* 93 Stat. 1339 (1979), Public Law 96-187.

163n *Accidental disclosure by Democrats: PACs & Lobbies,* Feb. 6, 1985, p. 2. Also, conversation between author and Edward Zuckerman, editor of *PACs & Lobbies.*

163—64 *Ban on corporate and labor contributions:* (a) *Corporate:* Tillman Act of 1907, 34 Stat. 864 (1907). (b) *Labor:* Taft-Hartley Act of 1947, 61 Stat. 159 (1947), which made permanent the temporary restrictions on labor, enacted under the Smith-Connally Act of 1943, 57 Stat. 167 (1943).

164 *Union soft money contributions: PACs & Lobbies,* Feb. 6, 1985, pp. 1–2.

164 *"Eagles Club" memberships: PACs & Lobbies,* Jan. 16, 1985, p. 4.

164 *Dayton statement: Minneapolis Star and Tribune,* Jan. 17, 1985.

164 *Facts on VIVA '84, Victory Fund '80, and the New Jersey Republican Party: CRP Soft Money Report,* pp. 4–7.

165 *Nofziger statement:* Drew, p. 106.

165 *Statements by convention guest and Paul Dietrich: CRP Soft Money Report,* pp. 9–10, 14.

165 *Supreme Court ruling on independent expenditures: Buckley* v. *Valeo,* 424 U.S. 1 (1976), p. 79ff.

165 *Stark statement: Oakland Tribune,* Oct. 24, 1986.

165 *Jacobs statement: Wall Street Journal,* Sept. 9, 1986.

166 *AMA 1986 independent expenditures:* AMA *FEC D Index,* 1985–86.

166 *Statements by Berglund, Lauer, and Skaggs; Armstrong's complaint; Supreme Court finding:* Viveca Novak and Jean Cobb, "The Kindness of Strangers," *Common Cause Magazine,* Sept./Oct. 1987, pp. 32–37.

167 *Independent expenditures by NRA PAC, 1984: Wall Street Journal,* Sept. 9, 1986.

167 *AMA independent expenditures: For 1984:* 1983–84 *FEC Blue Book,* Vol. IV, p. 250. *For 1985–86:* AMA *FEC D Index,* 1985–86.

167 *1986 independent spending by realtors and auto dealers: FEC D Indexes,* 1985–86.

167 *1980 and 1986 independent expenditures:* CRS Report No. 87-649 GOV, *Campaign Financing in Federal Elections: A Guide to the Law and Its Operation,* Aug. 8, 1986, rev. July 20, 1987, p. 68.

167–68 *Facts on Goland, NCPAC coordinated expenditures, and auto dealers' independent expenditures: Common Cause Magazine,* Sept./Oct. 1987, pp. 35–36.

168–69 *Dolan statement:* Sabato, p. 101.

169 *Nofziger statement:* Drew, p. 138.

169 *Evans statement; "Ortega 33" ads; independent spending in 1988: Common Cause Magazine,* Sept./Oct. 1987, pp. 34–36.

170 *Bundled contributions to Packwood: Wall Street Journal,* Oct. 10, 1985.

170 *Packwood 1986 total receipts:* FEC press release, May 10, 1987, p. 27.

170–71 *John Isaacs statements:* Interview with author, Aug. 12, 1987.

171 *Ellen Malcolm statement:* Interview with author.

171–72 *NRSC bundling:* (a) *Mail appeal: Washington Post,* Oct. 20, 1986, p. A8. (b) *Statements in Atlanta Journal: Atlanta Journal-Constitution,* Oct. 22, 1986, cited in Common Cause press release, "Common Cause Files Complaint with Federal Election Commission," Oct. 28, 1986, p. 2. (c) *Funds dispensed: Wall Street Journal,* Oct. 24, 1986.

172 *Kecks's contribution:* Dole foundation 1985 tax form 990.

173 *Kemp foundation:* (a) *Outlays on Kemp; limited donor identification: Wall Street Journal,* Mar. 7, 1986. (b) *Ties to Kemp: Buffalo News,* June 15, 1986. (c) *Kemp as "honorary chairman": CRP Foundations Report,* p. 36.

173 *Gary Hart appeal: Wall Street Journal,* Mar. 7, 1986.

173–74 *Babbitt, Kennedy, and Bradley foundations: CRP Foundations Report,* pp. 52–53.

174 *Kemp foundation terminated:* Ibid., p. 36.

174 *CRP finding on increase in politicians' foundations:* Ibid., p. 3.

174   *FEC a "pussy cat":* Wall Street Journal, Oct. 19, 1987.

174   *Lee Ann Eliott's AMA pension:* Wall Street Journal, June 24, 1987.

174—175   *Inadequacy of FEC enforcement:* Wall Street Journal, Oct. 19, 1987.

175   *Ronald Brownstein's statement:* National Journal, Dec. 7, 1985, p. 2828.

175   *Jackson's statement on erosion of enforcement:* Wall Street Journal, Oct. 19, 1987.

★
11. HOW WE CAN GET OUT OF THE MESS WE'RE IN

179   *Public financing bill statement:* Sec. 1 of S. 3242, Senator Richard Neuberger, introduced Feb. 20, 1956.

180   *Presidential public financing:* The Revenue Act of 1971 (Public Law 92-178) provided for public financing of presidential general elections. The 1974 amendments to the FECA (Public Law 93-443) provided public matching grants in presidential primary elections. CRS Report No. 84-107 GOV, *Public Financing of Congressional Elections*, pp. 85–86, 114.

181—82   *Permanent Democratic House majority:* New York Times, June 15, 1987, p. 1.

184   *Free-speech rights not absolute:* Buckley v. Valeo, 424 U.S. 1 (1976) p. 25 (citing *CSC* v. *Letter Carriers*, 413 U.S. 548, 567). *"Significant" governmental interest exception: Buckley*, p. 25ff.

185   *Reynolds* v. *Sims:* 377 U.S. 533, p. 555.

186   *Manatt supported "safe harbor" leasing provision:* Letter to Democratic members of Congress from Charles T. Manatt, Chairman, Democratic Nat'l. Committee, and Byron C. Radaker, Chairman, Democratic Business Council, Apr. 29, 1982.

186   *$5,000 annual enticement:* Brochure for the Speakers Club, Democratic Congressional Campaign Committee, 1984.

187   *Comparative returns on equity:* (a) *For Broadcast industry:* New York Times, July 1, 1985. (b) *For manufacturing industry:* Economic Report of the President, transmitted to Congress Feb. 1986, Table B88, p. 355.

187   *TV station market values:* New York Times, July 1, 1985.

189   *Quadrennial Commission recommendations:* "High Quality Leadership—Our Government's Most Precious Asset," Report of the Quadrennial Commission on Executive, Legislative, and Judicial Salaries, Dec. 15, 1986.

191   *Public-financing bills:* S. 1787, 99th Cong., 1st Sess., introduced Oct. 24, 1985; H.R. 3806, 99th Cong., 1st Sess., introduced Nov. 20, 1985.

191   *Military-bands budget:* Letter from Dept. of Defense to Terry Cornwell, U.S. director of the Congressional Arts Caucus, Mar. 27, 1985.

★
CONCLUSION

194 *Goldwater statement: Wall Street Journal*, July 18, 1986, p. 85.

194 *Boren statement: Cong. Rec.*, Jan. 6, 1987, p. S109.

194 *Average cost of 1986 House and Senate campaign:* CRS 87-469, p. 56.

195 *Table on 1983 and 1987 fundraising by PAC category: PACs & Lobbies*, Sept. 2, 1987.

196 *Table on increase in fundraising by certain PACs: PACs & Lobbies*, Sept. 2, 1987.

196 *Teamsters' PAC fundraising: Wall Street Journal*, Oct. 19, 1987, p. 62.

196n *1985–86 PAC fundraising:* FEC press release, May 21, 1987.

196–97 *Jackie Presser statement; Teamster PAC check-off system: Washington Post*, Oct. 30, 1987, p. A10.

197 *Trial Lawyers check-off:* Confirmed by telephone by the American Trial Lawyers Association, Washington, D.C.

197 *1987 public-financing bill:* S. 2, 100th Cong., 1st Sess.

197–98 *Reid and Adams statements: Washington Post*, June 14, 1987.

198 *Antwerp zoo "light fence" for birds: Encyclopaedia Britannica*, Vol. 19, p. 1162 (1975).

198 *Mondale quote:* Letter to author, June 11, 1985.

★
APPENDICES

204–15 *Appendix A:* Election data for 1976–84 from FEC Blue Books. Election data for 1986 from FEC press release, May 10, 1987. Honoraria data from Common Cause press release, May 20, 1987.

217–75 *Appendix B:* Election data for 1980 and 1982 from FEC Blue Books, Final Report. Data for 1984 from FEC Interim Report, in which the figures differ only slightly from those in the Final Report. 1986 election data (except leftover cash) from *1987 PIA*. Data on 1986 leftover cash from Common Cause press release, April 7, 1987. Honoraria from unpublished data furnished by Common Cause.

277–80 *Appendix C:* Adapted from *PACs & Lobbies*, June 3, 1987. Used by permission.

INDEX

Note: For reasons of space, the word *favors* is often used in this index to include campaign contributions (through PACs or individuals), honoraria, free trips, and the like.

Abdnor, Sen. James, 63, 168, 172
access to lawmakers via contributions, 126, 128, 130, 133–34
Adams, Sen. Brock, 54, 197–98
   and billboard issue, 148–49
   loan to own campaign, 67
Addabbo, Rep. Joseph, 151
ADM. *See* Archer-Daniels-Midland
airline industry, contributions to Rep. Howard, 88, 91
Akin, Gump, Strauss, Hauer & Feld, 41–42, 71
Alexander, Herbert, 23, 175, 278
Alignpac, 170
Almanac of Federal PACs, 65, 277
American Federation of State, County, and Municipal Employees (AFSCME), 169
American Academy of Ophthalmology, 70
American Airlines, 88, 161
American Bankers Association, 32, 72, 125
   favors to banking-committee members, 74
American Busing Association PAC, favors to Rep. Howard, 89, 91–92

American Dental Association, 70
American Federation of Teachers, 196
American Horse Council, 71
American Medical Association (AMA), 4, 22, 70, 102–3, 138, 196
   congressional contributions and votes, 141–42
   independent spending by, 165–66, 174
   opposes hospital-cost curbs, 141
   postelection switch, 66
American Podiatry Association, 70
American Road and Transportation Builders, 93
American Seating Company, 88
American Trucking Association, 7
   gifts to Rep. Howard, 89, 93
   honoraria to lawmakers, 155
American Yarn Spinners Association, 71
AMPAC. *See* American Medical Association
Andreas, Dwayne, 87, 140
   and gasohol tariff, 86
   sells Dole Florida apartment, 82
   See also Archer-Daniels-Midland
Andrews, Sen. Mark, 32
Anthony, Rep. Beryl, 68

Antwerp zoo, 198
Archer-Daniels-Midland (ADM), 87,
    139–40, 164
  and Dole support of sugar subsidy,
    83–84
  and Dole support on gasohol, 86
  Dole indebtedness to, 82–83
  See also Andreas, Dwayne
Armstrong, Richard, 63
Armstrong, Sen. William, 166
Arnold & Porter, 42
Aspin, Rep. Les, 64
Associated General Contractors of
    America, 93
AT&T:
  gifts to Dole Foundation, 172
  return on PAC contributions, 12–13
Atlantic Richfield, 164
Auto Dealers for Free Trade
    independent spending, 167, 169
automobiles:
  bill for domestic content in, 142–43
  See also National Auto Dealers
    Association, used-car dealers
Avco Corporation, 151

Babbitt, former Gov. Bruce, 173
Badham, Rep. Robert, 150
Baker & Botts, 41
BankAmerica, 164
banking industry. See American
    Bankers Association
Barnard, Rep. Doug, honoraria to,
    159
Barnes, Rep. Michael, 13, 99–101,
    153, 185
Beer Wholesalers Association, 71
  PAC of (SIXPAC), 7
beermakers, honoraria to tax-law
    writers, 156
Beilenson, Rep. Anthony, 144n
Bentsen, Sen. Lloyd, and $10,000
    breakfast series, 6–7
Berglund, Dr. Thomas, 166
billboard industry, 47–56
  congressional aides at convention of,
    52
  favors to Rep. Howard, 51, 92

  and fundraisers for lawmakers, 54
  PAC gifts to Howard, 50
Bingaman, Sen. Jeff, 66–67
Blessman, Lyle, 170
Boren, Sen. David, 26, 194
Borski, Rep. Robert, 159
Boswell, J.G., Corp., 164
Boucher, Rep. Frederick, 157–58, 160
Boxer, Rep. Barbara, 76–77
Bradley, Sen. Bill, 174
Brewster, Sen. Daniel B., 146, 154
bribery statute, 147
broadcasting industry
  free political time proposed, 187–88
  profits of, 187
Brown, Bill, 126–29
Brownstein, Ronald, 175
Bumpers, Sen. Dale, 130
bundling, 169–72
Burdick, Sen. Quentin, 52
Burleson, Rep. Omar, 151–52
business PACs, 7. See also names of
    industries and organizations
Business Industry PAC (BIPAC), 22
busing industry:
  contributions to Rep. Howard,
    88–89, 191–92
  See also American Busing
    Association
Byrd, Sen. Robert C., 3, 26

Callan, James, 159
campaign contributions, evidence of
    congressional impact:
  on dairy subsidy, 47
  on domestic content bill, 143
  on hospital-cost containment, 142
  on sugar subsidy, 140
  on used-car "lemon law," 45
campaign costs. See costs of
    campaigns
Campbell, Russell, 158
Cargill, Inc., 139
Carter, Pres. Jimmy, 141
ceilings on political contributions, 7–8
Center for Responsive Politics, xii,
    165, 174
  study of "soft money," 162, 165

CH2M Company, 88
Chamber of Commerce ratings of
    lawmakers' votes, 32
Chappell, Rep. Bill, 38
Chase Manhattan Bank, 70, 173
check-off for PAC collections, 131
    by dairy co-ops, 46
    by Teamsters' Union, 197
    by Trial Lawyers Association, 197
Chemical Bank, 70
Chicago Board of Trade, 70, 157
Chicago Mercantile Exchange, 70, 157
Chiles, Sen. Lawton, 119–21
Church, Sen. Frank, 167
Citicorp, 70
Citizens Against PACs, xii, 67
Clark, Vernon and Elaine:
    gifts to lawmakers, 51
    gifts to Rep. Howard, 51
Coalinga Corporation, 172
Coelho, Rep. Tony, 40
Columbia Savings & Loan, 152
commercials, TV, special rates
    proposed, 188
commodity traders:
    contributions to Sen. Dole, 148
    tax favors for, 147–48
Common Cause, 32, 60, 193
Concerned Romanians for a Strong
    America, 7
conflict of interest:
    bank-PAC favors to banking-
        committee members, 9, 20, 58, 74
    D'Amato gifts from Wall Street
        firms, 39
    Dole actions aid contributors, 87
    Howard gifts from regulated groups,
        88–89, 91, 93
    military contractors' favors to
        defense-committee members,
        38, 58, 157
    Rostenkowski gifts from tax-
        interested groups, 12
    Schneider gifts from maritime, high-
        tech groups, 112
    standards for judges vs. legislators,
        57–58
Congress of Industrial Organizations
    (CIO), 22

Conlon, Richard P., 24
Conrad, Sen. Kent, xv, 32–33, 110–11
contributions:
    from individuals vs. PACs, 39, 79
    large, and favoritism to outsiders,
        101, 108, 109
    See also campaign contributions
Conyers, Rep. John, 125
Corn, David, 84
corn-sweetener industry, 139–40
corporate contributions:
    barred in federal elections, 163
    "soft-money" loophole, 163
corporations, 130 escape taxes, 10
costs of campaigns:
    burden on lawmakers, 194–95
    ceiling, desirability of, 109, 111
    increases, 16, 25
        in Arizona, 106
        in Missouri, 108
        in Oklahoma, 113–14
        in South Dakota, 8
    totals, xv
costs of present system, 137–45
    vs. public financing, 144
Council for a Livable World,
        129–30
    rebuts "bundling" charges,
        170–71
Cox, Archibald, 115
Crane, Rep. Philip, 84
Cranston, Sen. Alan, 32, 52, 77n
Culver, Sen. John, 167

D'Amato, Sen. Alfonse:
    $4 million war chest, 61–62
    Wall Street contributions to, xiii–
        xiv, 39, 63, 152
dairy industry:
    contributes to Rep. Moffett's Senate
        campaign, 103
    evidence of PAC gifts' influence on
        Congress, 47
    PAC fundraising and contributions,
        20, 131–34
dairy subsidy, 9, 45–47, 137–38
    cost of, 141
Dayton, Mark, 162, 164

defense industry
  favors to defense-committee
    members, 38
  increase in contributions, honoraria,
    7
Delta Airlines, 88
Democratic House Campaign
  Committee, 186
DeNardis, Rep. Lawrence, 74–75
Department of Transportation and
  billboard regulation, 50
Dickerson, Mike, 277
Dickinson, Rep. William, 38, 58
Dickstein, Shapiro & Morin, 41
Dietrich, Paul, 165
disclosure, public, difficulty of, xiii,
  93, 175
Distilled Spirits Council, 156
Dixon, E.W., 171
Dolan, Terry, 168–69
Dole, Sen. Robert, 10
  aids contributors, 84, 87
  and campaign-finance reforms,
    87–88
  and commodity traders, 85–87,
    147–48
  contributions from individuals, 39,
    79, 83
  Florida apartment purchase, 82
  and Gallo family gifts, 40, 79–80
  and gasohol tariff, 86
  obligations to PACs and interest
    groups, 77, 83
  and sugar tariffs, 84
  and tobacco industry, 84–85, 87
  tops in Senate campaign surplus, 61,
    78
  tops in Senate PAC receipts, 77
Dole Foundation, 79–82
Douglas, Sen. Paul, xi
Dow Chemical Company, 39, 173
Dow, Lohnes & Albertson, 71
Dowdy, Rep. Wayne, and trip to
  Barbados, 159
Dravo Corp., 150
Drexel Burnham Lambert, Inc.,
  152
Duncan, Rep. John J., 35
Dyson, John, 62

"Eagles Club," 164
Eagleton, Sen. Thomas, xv, 21,
  107–10
Eastern Airlines, 88
Eberhard, Mrs. Katherine, 171–72
Edgar, Rep. Bob, 118–19
Edwards, Rep. Mickey, and auto
  dealers' PAC, 44
Electronic Funds Transfer Association,
  159
Elliott, FEC Commissioner Lee Ann,
  174
EMILY's List, 171
Energy and Commerce Committee:
  defeats hospital-cost limits, 142
  members on coal-company junket,
    158
  PAC interest in, 102–3
Equitable Life, 164
Erdreich, Rep. Ben, 47
Espy, Rep. Mike, 184
Evans, Sen. Dan, 169
extortion tactics by lawmakers
  reported, 14, 63–64, 195

Fanjul brothers, 139
Federal Election Commission (FEC),
  168, 174–75
Federal Trade Commission, 43
Finklestein, Arthur, 168
Flippo, Rep. Ronnie G., 59–60
  1986 PAC donations, 69–72
  and tax break for banks, 70
Ford Motor Company, 126–29
foundations, charitable, formed by
  political figures, 172–74
France, Anatole, xvi
Frenzel, Rep. Bill, 84
Frost, Rep. Martin, 46
Fulbright & Jaworski, 41
Fumento, Michael, 83, 86
Fund for an American Renaissance
  (Rep. Kemp), 80, 173
fundraising, political, 120
  begins years before election, xvi,
    16
  burdens on lawmakers, 16, 194
  interrupts Senate's sessions, 105

prompts lawmakers to retire, 105, 108
time devoted to, 13, 16, 100, 101, 108, 114, 118, 119, 197–98
funeral industry, 100

"Gallo Amendment," 40
Gallo, Ernest and Julio, 40
General Accounting Office on billboard regulation, 50
General Electric's PAC, 125
1986 giving pattern, 31–33
return on contributions, 13
General Telephone and Electronics, 158–59
Gibbons, Rep. Sam, 12
Glenn, Sen. John, 61
Goland, Michael, independent spending against Sen. Percy, 167
Goldwater, Sen. Barry, 3, 37, 106–7, 194
Gorton, Sen. Slade, 54
Gottlieb, Kevin, 52
Grace, W.R., and Company, 173
Graham, Sen. Robert, 53, 168
Gramm, Sen. Phil, 167
Grandy, Rep. Fred, 67
Greenaway, Roy F., 52
Greyhound Bus Corp., 88
Guarini, Rep. Frank J., 68–69
Gulf Oil, 161

Hackler, Lloyd, 23
Halvorsen, Jerald, 155
Hamberger, Martin, 150
Hance, Rep. Kent, 68
Hanna, Mark, 22
Hansen, Rep. George, 175
Harpel, Douglas, 278
Harris, Tom, 174
Hart, Sen. Gary, 173
Hatfield, Sen. Mark, 130
Hawkins, Sen. Paula, 168
Hayes, Rep. James A., 67
Hayman, Fred, 162
Helms, Sen. Jesse, 84

Hemenway, Russell, 22
Highway Advertisers, American Council of, hosts lawmakers, 159
Highway Beautification Act, 48–49
Holayter, Bill, 123–26
Holland, Rep. Ken, 60
Holtzman, Rep. Elizabeth, 62
honoraria, xiv, 155–60
barred in executive branch, 156–57
from billboard industry, 54
monetary limits, 11, 157
not barred in Congress, 11, 160, 189
Rostenkowski leads House, 11
Hoope, David, 174
hospital-cost containment, 141–42. See also American Medical Association
Houston, Paul, 39, 69, 74
Howard, Rep. James, 34n, 88–95
at billboard conventions, 51
billboard-industry favors, 50–51
contributions from groups connected with public-works projects, 91
out-of-state contributions, 90, 94–95, 183
transportation-industry favors, 88–89, 91, 92
Huckaby, Rep. Jerry, 60n

incumbents:
1986 reelection success, 34
PACs' preference for, 5, 20, 33, 35
freezes out challengers, 6, 36–37
independent expenditures, 165–69
reforms proposed, 189
International Brotherhood of Teamsters, PAC, 196–97
contributions to Rep. Howard, 89
International Telephone & Telegraph Corporation (ITT), 161
Isaacs, John, 129–30, 170–71
Isikoff, Michael, 86

Jackson, Brooks, 36, 152, 162, 174, 175
Jacobs, Rep. Andrew, 165
Jenkins, Rep. Edgar, 40

Johnson, Lady Bird, 49
Johnston, Sen. Bennett, 61n
Jones, Day, Reavis & Pogue, 41, 71
Jordan, Harris, 84

Kalmbach, Herbert, 161
Kaplan, Sheila, 51, 84
Kastenmeier, Rep. Robert, 68
Keck, William M., contribution to Dole
    Foundation, 172
Kemp, Rep. Jack, 80, 173. *See also*
    Fund for an American
    Renaissance
Kennedy, Sen. Edward M., 83, 173
Kennedy, Rep. Joseph P., 67
Kerr, Sen. Robert, 23
Konnyu, Rep. Ernest, 67
Kramer, Ken, 172
Kroc, Joan, 162
Kutak, Rock & Campbell, 41

labor contributions, 163–64
labor-union PACs, 7, 22
Lamar Corporation, 88–89, 93–94
Lauer, Peter, 166
law-firm PACs, 14, 41
Leach, Rep. Jim, 116–17
League of Conservation Voters, 53
"lemon law" for used cars, 43–45
"level playing field" proposed, 181–82
Livingston, Rep. Bob, 158
loans by candidates to their own
    campaigns, 66–67
Long, Sen. Russell B., 146
Lydon, Kathy, 167

MacDonald, Guy, 78n
Machinists Union, 123–26
Madison, James, 7
Malcolm, Ellen, 171
Manatt, Charles, 186
Manatt, Phelps, Rothenberg &
    Tunney, 41
Manufacturers Hanover bank, 70
Marine Engineers Union, 32
Marriott Corporation, 164

Mathias, Sen. Charles McC., 104–6,
    144n
Matsui, Rep. Robert, 60n, 68
Mattingly, Sen. Mack, 171
McDade, Rep. Joseph, 60n
McGovern, Sen. George, 167, 168
McKinley, William, 7, 22
McMahon, Edward, 55–56
Meister, Fred, 156
Merrill Lynch, 75
Michel, Rep. Bob, 141
Mid-America Dairymen, 131–34
Mikulski, Sen. Barbara, 53–54
Milk Producers, Associated (AMPI),
    131–32
    $2 million pledge to Nixon, 103n,
        132, 161
Miller, James, 84
Mobil Oil, 83
Moffett, Rep. Toby, 102–4
Moldaw, Stewart, 162
Mondale, Vice-Pres. Walter, 198
Moore, Rep. Henson, 61, 172
Morgan, J.P., & Co., 70
Morgan Stanley Company, 196
Morrison, Rep. Bruce, 74–76
Mott, Stewart, 161
Moynihan, Sen. Daniel Patrick, 168
Mulcahy, John, 161

Naegele Outdoor Advertising Co., 55
National Association of Manufacturers'
    PAC, 22
National Association of Realtors, 196n
    independent spending, 167, 169
National Automobile Dealers
    Association (NADA), 44–45
    effect on lemon-law vote, 44–45
    future plans, 169
National Congressional Club (PAC of
    Sen. Helms), 196n
National Conservative PAC (NCPAC),
    166–69, 196n
    1980 independent spending, 166–67
    accused of illegal candidate
        consultation, 168
    claims ability to lie without dam-
        aging its candidates, 168–69

National Education Association, 4
National Rifle Association, 167
National Venture Capital Association, 69
Nixon, Pres. Richard M., 103n, 115, 161, 180
no-fault auto insurance, 153
Nofziger, Lyn, 165, 169

O'Neill, Speaker Tip, 10, 64
Occidental Petroleum, 164
Olin, Rep. Jim, 141
one person, one vote, 9, 46, 137, 185
Oral and Maxillofacial Surgeons, 7
out-of-state contributions, desirability of prohibiting, 117, 120–21, 183–86
Outdoor Advertising Association of America (OAAA), 51–52, 54, 92, 94. See also billboard industry.

PAC contributions viewed as "investments," 12–13, 21
"PAC heaven" committees and gifts to lawmakers, 68
Packwood, Sen. Robert, 170
    $5,000 breakfast series, 7
PACs, 4, 19–21, 22
    aggregation of funds to magnify power, xiv, 8, 9, 14, 125, 180, 183
    ban on contributions proposed, 182–83
    and candidates:
        gifts to both, 32
        switches after elections, 32
    corporate vs. labor, 23
    growth in, 6, 24, 195, 196
    incumbents, preference for, 5, 6, 21, 33, 35–37
    influence-buying motives of, 4, 6, 34, 71
    lawmakers' dependence on, 8, 14, 25, 71–72, 76

lawmakers' personal PACs, 12, 19n, 64, 65, 66
    as outsiders, 72
    presidential campaigns, minor role in, xiii
    undemocratic nature of, 14, 20
parties, political:
    reliance on interested givers, 186
    tax credits for gifts to, proposed, 186–87
Patterson, Rep. Elizabeth, 67
Penney, J.C., 75
Pepsico, 173
Percy, Sen. Charles, 66, 167
Perkins, Robert, 164
Perot, H. Ross, 151–52
Philip Morris, 85
Pickens, T. Boone, 162
Pillsbury, Madison & Sutro, 41
postelection switch-giving, 32
    by AMA, 66
    by General Electric, 32
    by Marine Engineers Union, 32
    by Mid-America Dairymen, 133
Presser, Jackie, 196
Pressler, Sen. Larry, to Barbados for Highway Advertisers, 159
Preyer, Rep. Richardson, 65
pro-Israel PACs, 7
product-liability coalition, honoraria paid by, 158
prohibition of out-of-state contributions proposed, 183–86
    constitutionality of, 184–86
prohibition of PAC contributions proposed, 182–83
public financing of elections:
    vs. interest-group money, 77
    Mondale on, 199
    for Senate, 25–26
    would "liberate" congressional candidates, 199

Quayle, Sen. Dan, reversal on military costs, 150

Ralph M. Parsons Company, 93–94
Rangel, Rep. Charles, 4–5
Reagan tax-reform program, 5, 158
  prompts large 1985 PAC gifts, 12
real estate. *See* National Association of
    Realtors
reforms, campaign-finance, proposals,
    189–90
  approval unlikely without prodding
      by public and president, 197
  costs, *vs.* true costs of current
      system, 191–92
  history of, 23, 25–26
  realism of, 192–93
  Republican opposition, 27, 122
  risks *vs.* demonstrated present
      dangers, 190–91
Reiche, Frank, 174
Reid, Sen. Harry, 53, 197
Reistad, Dale, 159
Republican Senatorial Committee,
    National (NRSC), and
    "bundling," 171–72
Reynolds, R.J., 85
Riegle, Sen. Donald W., 52
Roadside Business Association, 54–55.
    See also billboard industry.
Roberts, James, 173
Rodino, Rep. Peter, 47
Rogers, Will, xii
Roosevelt, Theodore, 22
Rostenkowski, Rep. Dan, 10–12
  campaign costs, 11, 22
  and commodity traders, 147
  forms personal PAC, 12
Rubin, Eric, 94

Sabato, Prof. Larry, 20, 45
safe harbor leasing, 186
Sanford, Sen. Terry, 67
Santini, Rep. James, 172
Sayler Land Company, 164
Scaife, Richard Mellon, 161
Schmitt, Sen. Harrison, 66
Schneider, Rep. Claudine, 111–13
  on conflict of interest, 76–77
Seymour, Whitney North, Jr., 278
Sears, return on PAC contributions, 13

Shearson–American Express, 164
Shelby, Sen. Richard, 67
Simon, Sen. Paul, 65–66, 144n
  on taxes paid by GE and its janitor,
    10
  on campaign-finance reform, 65–66
  forms personal PAC, 66
Skaggs, David, 166
small contributions decline, 24–25
"soft money," 162–65
Sorauf, Prof. Frank, 20
Specter, Sen. Arlen, and Dravo Corp.,
    150
spending in campaigns. *See* costs
St Germain, Rep. Fernand, 9, 58
Stafford, Sen. Robert T., 48, 53, 148
Staley Co., 139
Stark, Rep. Fortney H. (Pete), 165, 174
Stennis, Sen. John, 27, 115–16, 193
Stokes, Rep. Louis, 60n
Stone, W. Clement, 161
Strauss, David M., 52
Strauss, Robert, 41
sugar industry, 139
  contributions to Rep. Flippo, 70
  evidence that contributions affected
      Congress, 140
sugar subsidy, 138–41
Sugawara, Sandra, 158
Supreme Court:
  bans candidate-spending cap, 8, 26
  ruling on independent spending, 166
surpluses in campaign treasuries, 60
  discourage challengers, 60
  representatives may keep when they
      retire, 5, 11, 59–60
  should revert to U.S. Treasury, 189
Swift, Rep. Al, 158–59
Synar, Rep. Mike, 113–14, 116

Taft, Sen. Robert A., 153
teachers' unions. *See* American
    Federation of Teachers,
    National Education Association
terHorst, Jerald, 14, 127–29
tobacco industry and Sen. Dole, 84–85
Tobacco Institute, 92
  honoraria to lawmakers, 52

Trailways, 89
Trial Lawyers, Association of, 72, 153, 196, 197
trucking industry:
  and Rep. Howard, 89, 91, 93
  See also American Trucking Association

U.S. Tobacco flies Sen. Dole, 85
United Auto Workers Union (UAW), 142–43, 196
United Coal Company, 157
United Parcel Service, 196
United Technologies Corporation, 38
used-car dealers, 43–45
  evidence that gifts influenced Congress, 45
USX Corporation, 39

Vacca, Frank, 131–34
Vaccaro, Justice Frank, 57–58
Verner, Lipfert, Bernard, McPherson & Hand, 41

Vinson, Elkins, Searls, Connally & Smith, 41, 71
VIVA '84, 164

Waggoner, Rep. Joe, 151
Watson, Thomas J., 162
Waxman, Rep. Henry, 65
Wheat, Rep. Alan, 47
White, Barbara and Dean, 94
Williams, Rep. Pat, 159
Wine and Spirit Wholesalers, 71
Wolpe, Rep. Howard, 169
Wright, Judge J. Skelly, xvi
Wright, Rep. Jim, and "Cowtown Jamboree," 64
Wyden, Rep. Ron, 160

Yellow Freight System, 89

Zschau, Rep. Edward, 32
Zuckerman, Ed, 162, 163n, 164

ABOUT THE AUTHOR

Philip M. Stern was, successively, reporter and editorial writer for the New Orleans *Item;* legislative assistant to Congressman (later Senator) Henry M. Jackson of Washington and to Senator Paul H. Douglas of Illinois; aide to presidential candidate Adlai Stevenson; director of research for the Democratic National Committee; publisher of *The Northern Virginia Sun* in Arlington, Virginia; and Deputy Assistant Secretary of State. He has written several books: *The Great Treasury Raid,* a best-seller about tax loopholes; *The Shame of a Nation,* on American poverty (with photographs by George de Vincent); *The Oppenheimer Case: Security on Trial; The Rape of the Taxpayer; Lawyers on Trial,* on the legal profession; and *O Say Can You See* (with Helen B. Stern), contrasting the tourist's view of Washington, D.C., with the neglected aspects of the capital.

Mr. Stern has long been interested in campaign-finance reform: In 1962, he wrote a cover article for *Harper's* Magazine proposing government financing of elections. In 1973, he founded the Center for Public Financing of Elections, and in 1984, he founded Citizens Against PACs, a bipartisan citizens group.

Mr. Stern has five children and makes his home in Washington, D.C.